RISING LIKE DUST

THE STORY OF A RURAL GIRL WHO KEPT RISING AND RISING

LETHABO MALEKA

Copyright © Lethabo Maleka

First edition, first impression:

RISING LIKE DUST:
THE STORY OF A RURAL GIRL WHO KEPT RISING AND RISING

Published by Lethabo Maleka

Johannesburg, South Africa

mamodulom@gmail.com

ISBN 978-0-7961-9432-9

2 4 6 8 10 9 7 5 3 1

© All rights reserved. Apart from any fair dealing for the purpose of research, criticism or review as permitted under the Copyright Act, no part of this book may be reproduced, or No part of this publication may be reproduced, stored in a retrieval system, or transmitted in any form or my means, electronic or mechanical, including photocopying, recording without the prior written permission from the author.

Layout and cover design by Boutique Books

The title of this book is taken from one of Maya Angelou's quotes: *You may write me down in history, With your bitter, twisted lies, You may trod me in the very dirt But still, like dust, I'll rise.*

Hence, the cover of my book reflects the image of a whirlwind (*sediatsane goba setsokotsane* in North Sotho) that is rising from the ground and swirling higher and higher up. That is me.

About the Author

Lethabo Maleka (Gwangwa) grew up in rural Limpopo in South Africa, where she attended most of her schooling years: that is lower and higher primary to secondary levels. Lethabo obtained her matric from the Joint Matriculation Board through correspondence at Turret Correspondence College, funded by SACHED TRUST. She graduated with undergraduate and postgraduate degrees from Wits University and received her master's degree from the University of Johannesburg (UJ), formerly Randse Afrikaanse Universiteit (RAU).

After graduating, she started her career at Educational Opportunities Council (EOC), a non-governmental organisation (NGO) in Johannesburg. The same organisation offered her a full four-year scholarship sponsored by the British Council. She worked as a student counsellor, coordinator and administrator for a local scholarship programme. Her scope of work entailed recruitment, screening, selection interviews and student placement at relevant tertiary institutions, as well as counselling.

When donor agencies pulled out their funding after South Africa's 1994 democratic elections, she joined the public service in the Gauteng Provincial Government. Her first job was with the Department of Development Planning and Local Government, as a researcher at assistant director level. After a year she moved to the Premier's Office, promoted to deputy director. She was employed as an assistant secretary to the Gauteng Executive Council. She later moved to the Department of Finance and Economic Affairs' Gauteng Liquor Licensing Chief Directorate to Head of Gauteng Liquor Board, Secretariat Unit until she retired.

My Praise Poem (*Sereto*) is:

Ke Mamodulo, Lethabo, Pheladi, ke Mampokoro 'Ek sal jou, ek sal jou bokor, ek sal jou donor'.

Ke ngwana a Hunadi, Malesolo, Bolalane a Phaahla, morwedi a Rebone Shatadi le Kgarole Phogole Mahlase. Motsoto, Mphoto, Mmina Tau. Shatee wa sa reng Moshate o a duma. Ke tshaba baditi!

Ke letebele le konkwana la hloka kgomo le ja motho. Nde Mrwedi a Fata Gilbert mohlankana a Ngwetsana na Raesetja Gwangwa. Mrongwa, sena Mthimkhulu, Ndrrhebele wee. Ndrebele ga lefe, le sa yo khotha mante. Nrhebele lekgowa ledla lebese nge mforoko. Wa... Wa...ke!

Your name is Lethabo: remember to smile; a simple metaphor in life.

Contents

About the title of the book 9

Dedication 13

Introduction 15

Chapter One: My Life With My Maternal Family 19

Chapter Two: My Life With My Paternal Family 81

Chapter Three: My Life Past Primary Schooling
and Entering Secondary School Level 130

Chapter Four: Life After School-Going Age 156

Chapter Five: My First Time Working in Johannesburg 200

Chapter Six: In the Quest For a Better Life,
Education Is the Key 220

Chapter Seven: Married Life and Moving to Stay in Soweto .. 273

Chapter Eight: Marriage and Life In Soweto 297

Chapter Nine: University Life As a Mature Student 324

Chapter Ten: When the Unthinkable Happens 333

Chapter Eleven: Finally Entering the Work
Environment as a University Graduate 360

Chapter Twelve: Conclusion: The Person I Became 538

Bibliography 549

About the title of the book

Rising Like Dust is the story of my personal journey, which has gone a full cycle: from my early life and how I discovered my purpose in life through sheer power of determination, perseverance, hard work and endurance, to now.

I started writing my autobiography in 2011 and only finished it mid-2024. I abandoned it when I decided to write two books with different topics and titles concurrently. In 2018, after my retirement, I started writing a book about the South African political landscape. The focus and scope of the book is on the role that the previous and current presidents played from 1994 until 2019, that is twenty-five years of democracy. At that point, incidents related to gender-based violence escalated sharply, especially from 2010 to date. This turn of events captured my mind. It was only in 2019 that I decided to keep the two books on hold but not abandoning them altogether.

My mind shifted to writing about the subject of patriarchy and its devastating consequences for both women and girls. For me, it was very urgent that I open a conversation about the plight of women by documenting the awful things that happen to them. I could not stop researching and writing and, by the time my manuscript was ready for editing and proofreading, it was so huge it had to be broken down into eight volumes. The delay in completing it was exacerbated when the country reached stage six loadshedding. The plan had been to have it finished in November 2023, but it dragged on until February 2024, to be released in April 2024. It took me three years to write it.

When I started writing my autobiography in 2011, I already knew that I was gifted in writing but never thought of making it my career, probably due to lack of exposure, the know-how and absence of role models. I remember that while growing up the only means of communication was through writing letters. The first person I wrote letters to was my father, who was working in Johannesburg as a migrant labourer. Every now and again he would commend me for writing. He said that my letters were helpful to him because they were informative and factual. He always said, "My baby, you really write very well". It was just that I impressed him because I would mention the dogs' and the live stock's well-being.

Then, when I met my boyfriend, now my husband, and we started writing letters to each other, he praised my writing skills.

Although I appreciated those comments, I did not make too much of them. When I decided to enrol for my PhD, he advised me to dedicate my efforts to writing books instead, but I was not ready for that. My focus was on academic achievements. At the university, most of my studies revolved around writing essay assignments, and time and again my political studies and sociology lecturers commented on the fact that I write very well.

While I was working for EOC, the COO asked me to write an annual report for her. Upon reading it, she was so impressed that she called me to tell me that the report I wrote was very impressive, that I am gifted in writing, and that I should do something about it.

Working for the Department of Development Planning and local government gave me the opportunity to write articles that appeared in the departmental news bulletin, and my colleagues commented positively about them.

When I joined government, my job revolved around writing: minutes, proposals and reports. Those who came across my written work commended me for being such a good writer. For example, two members of the Executive on whose sub-committees I sat, were fascinated by my ability to capture minutes accurately and produced them without any correction to be made.

I was therefore puzzled when I joined the Gauteng Liquor Licensing board to find that those who hated me for being a whistleblower always spoke ill about my writing. Some of my colleagues even went to the extent of trying to influence senior managers, board chairpersons and members to believe that I am unable to write, and capitalised on the minutes I captured. They focused on finding mistakes and making a mockery of them just to frustrate me, until I realised that it was to do with my being a whistleblower. Their behaviour emanated from their hatred and all that was happening was a further victimisation. They would stop at nothing. All they wanted to do was to try to get me fired. I was so ill-treated that I did not know what to do but I never gave up on my job.

Nonetheless, the Rural Girl Who Like Dust Kept on Rising and Rising did the unthinkable, which can only be explained by this worship prayer: Lord God, I want to worship You as the Creator God; I want to see You in every aspect of nature. Lord God, I want to lay boundless trust, my deepest wonder by absolute awe and my humble reverence at Your feet when I praise and worship You for the mercy and love you have showed me. From the deepest pit of my life to the highest top of my life, I thank You.

Dedication

This autobiography is dedicated to my beloved late mother – I called her "African Woman" – and my second mother, my dearest mother-in-law. Both women of substance, they have showed great wisdom and courage. They both enriched and catapulted me to be the woman I am today.

To my darling late father and late father-in-law. Their humble lives, which were full of hardships but rich with wisdom, tenacity, courage and resilience, moulded me.

To my husband – I call him "Man of the Century and the best thing ever happened to me".

To my sister and the siblings from another mother, my in-laws.

To my daughter and my grandchildren. I pray that they become women of substance and great integrity.

Introduction

I decided to write about myself in a chronological narrative of my personal or life history that outlines my autobiographic background. It gives details of where I was born, my family background and the communities I grew up in. The focus of my autobiography is the events that influenced and shaped my life as a child and made me the person I have become, despite the pressures and temptations presented by the notion of rural vis-à-vis urban life and biases. The aim is to highlight the fact that despite the circumstances and environment in which one finds oneself in, one can still emerge and overcome many challenges. This can only happen if one has a clear vision and focus, works hard, and shows an attitude of determination, perseverance and endurance. One needs the will to carry on, and above all believe in God and have a strong faith. I must say that writing this book and reviewing my life in these terms has been a rewarding experience for me.

The second objective is to highlight the fact that to become the person I have become did not come easy: it was uphill and a roller coaster. This is, therefore, elaborated through a reflection or depiction of the hurdles I had to cross. I have as well painted a picture of how the environment can make or break a person.

The story further outlines how my mother and mother-in-law impacted my life. They have both remained my source of inspiration and pillars of hope. I held them both dear because they both suffered under one of apartheid's most humiliating systems and the wrath that is the migrant labour system. The system of apartheid encouraged the breakdown of the family unit through migrant labour. The concept of the absentee father was entrenched. It was not uncommon for men to leave their rural homes to seek work in the mines and elsewhere; most of them never went back to their families. The brutality of the system left many scarred for life, both physically and emotionally.

This is the system that separated African women from their husbands for months on end, depriving them of bringing their children together like every normal family. Both my late father and father-in-law experienced the notorious *dompas* and the humiliating migrant labour system first hand. I am grateful to them in that, despite all challenges, trials and tribulations of the Dark Days era of South African history, they stood the test of time and remained there for me and my husband respectively. They never gave up on us and did not succumb to the temptations of the notion of *mafamolelele* or *makgolwa* by hooking up with urban women, commonly known back home as the "Bakgatla women".

According to Wikipedia, the term Bakgatla describes all Kgatla groups in Botswana and South Africa. The South African Kgatla women were the first to work in the cities as domestic workers. Most men from rural areas did not have places to stay other than hostels. As a result, they had relationships with these women because they could accommodate them in their employer's work quarters. One out of five men from the so-called rural areas became what was commonly known as *makgolwa* because most of them gave in to the belief "out of sight out of mind". Hence, they would disappear and never visit the families they left behind in the rural areas. They only went back when they were of no use to their urban concubines.

Most of them would by then be old or sick and no longer employed, and literally on the brink of the grave's mouth; that is, dying. They would sheepishly return to their wives and children whom they'd left behind and whose names they no longer remembered. All that they cared for was to be given a decent funeral and for the forgotten wives to go through a gruelling one-year mourning period (*go roula*). More often than not, there would be humiliating and embarrassing incidents where the urban (those who happened to marry them in Western weddings) and rural area wives (married by customary processes) would fight for the man's remains for a burial: what is called "*Muvhango*" in the Venda language.

Thank you to my two special mothers, who kept the home fires burning, never falling prey to those men who could not stomach long months of being away from home and hard labour in the mines, factories and domestic employment (*bomahlalela*). Instead of being man enough, they opted to remain at home to keep husbandless wives company and produce illegitimate children in the process. Loneliness kills, or so they say.

The reason why I have emphasised how blessed I am is because the background that I was born and bred in could be a trap that many Africans could not get out of. The circumstances can be so dire that one must be strong willed to be able to see a way out of it. It can get very dark in a tunnel and one may never see a light at the end and so instead give up. It is an overwhelming and desperate environment and those who have got accustomed to it are still trapped in poverty, destitution and despair.

This book also tries to project how rural life can impact negatively on those living there: that is, there is glaring evidence of the suffering of people. I still witness this every time I visit my people in Limpopo and I am still shocked by the legacy that apartheid has left and the backlog that the incumbent new government has had to deal with. It is overwhelming when one tries to fathom out the possibility of the current government addressing the backlog, in terms of infrastructural development, and realising a "better life for all".

For me, it is just a pipe dream in the sense that the new democratic government does not help the situation either. Considering the level of corruption, mismanagement and maladministration, the country is in an even bigger mess than it was before.

The first chapter gives an account of where I was born and raised.

Chapter One

MY LIFE WITH MY MATERNAL FAMILY

I was born in Limpopo, in a village called ga-Masemola in the Sekhukhune District. Although it is well known that in African culture, once a woman is married she is expected to leave her parents' home (the maternal family) to go and stay with the in-laws (paternal family), this was not the case with my parents in the initial stages of their marriage. My father stayed with his wife's in-laws, for reasons that are still unclear to me. Basically, he left home due to serious family feuds while he was still a young man and he never wanted to return there, even after he married my mother, so ga-Masemola became his perfect hiding place.

Ga-Masemola village is a beautiful place with spectacular, magical views of the mountains that enclose it . We had gravel roads then. They were not tarred as you see them in the picture, so things have improved a bit. The landscape has  many rock formations. There are the biggest boulders there that I have ever seen.

 Right at the back of my grandparents' homestead on the foot of the mountain there is giant boulder . It is so huge that it is breath-taking. Underneath it there

is a cave that we used to play in when we were children. However, our parents did not approve of it as there are many crawling creatures, some of them dangerous species, around, such as snakes (*dinoga*), spiders (*digokgo*) and scorpions (*dikgome goba diphepheng*). *Kgome* is a species of *phepheng* but more poisonous than *phepheng*.

There are many rock monitors (*legogomedi*). This is a species of lizard (*mokgarutsane*), as is a crocodile (*kwena*) and alligator. Rock monitors and lizards are both harmless. In the mountains one finds much wildlife, such as baboons, and various plant life such as the morula tree, as well as bird life. In summer, the weather is very hot and dry, and at times it is very dusty, like the rest of the Sekhukhune area.

Talking about bird life, when growing up there was this myth about an owl (*leribishi*) having a bad spell (*e ya hlola*) if it comes near the homestead and starts to hoot. As a result, it was unloved and I heard older people saying that we should not go near it. An owl is always seen in the night, and it likes sitting on a branch of a tree. There was one that would come and sit on the trunk of a tall dead tree towards sunset, just below the boulders I mentioned above. The tree was right at the back of my grandparents' home. But I had this fascination with it. When I heard its sound or hoot, I would sneak out to go and check on it. I would look at it while it also looked at me with its big eyes.

Maybe I was curious about looking at its eyes because one of my cousins always teased me (*go kwera*) that I have strange, big eyes (*mahlo a magogoropo*) like those of the owl, and I would be so upset because no one ever spoke good about it. I hated my eyes. I remember how I did not like my legs because they used to tease me about them, saying that I had calves (*dipotirisi*) like that of a giant. Usually, giants were associated with men, and this imaginary giant was known for stealing from people (*lehodu*). I never saw that imaginary man, but I would get upset to the point of crying and they would all laugh.

I am mentioning this because these kinds of jokes can lead to someone developing low self-esteem or self-worth to the point of hating her or himself. I do not think that adults should poke jokes at someone's physical appearance. I was told later in life that I have beautiful eyes and legs. Fortunately, I do not keep grudges nor personalise things I do not like. I easily forget.

My mother was born to the Mahlase family. On the other hand, my father was Ndebele, born to the Gwangwas from a village called ga-Maraba, commonly known as Kalkspruit in the Capricorn District, situated on the Southeast of Polokwane (then Pietersburg). I always wondered why we were the only Gwangwa family in the entire Masemola village. The people there, being Pedi speaking (Northern Sotho), could not pronounce the surname and simply referred to us as "Kwakwa".

The fact that my father stayed with my in-laws should have been uncomfortable for both my parents. They must have got a backlash from relatives because that arrangement was unacceptable from African culture perspective. I assume that for him, despite the discomfort, the arrangement was a blessing in disguise because, amongst other reasons, there was no male or father figure in the family.

My grandfather, I am told, died when my mother and her elder sister were young women, while their youngest sister was still young, school-going age, maybe a teenager. They were raised by a single mother. I do not know much about what happened to my grandfather. Both my uncles passed on as well. So, the three sisters remained to fend for themselves. It was obviously very difficult for my grandmother to raise children on her own, especially since at that time women were not allowed to go out and look for employment. My father's presence must have made a huge difference.

My mother's family (the Mahlases) were staunch Lutheran Christian Church members; the church is called Arkona. We were brought up in that church and I was baptised there. I was confirmed at my father's church, Anglican, in later years, after moving to a village called ga-Maraba (Kalkspruit). I started schooling when I was eight years old because during the apartheid system schooling for Africans was not important and building schools close by for the African children was not a priority. As a result, very few schools were built by missionaries in those areas where they established mission churches. Black children could not, therefore, start school early because they had to travel long distances to and from, and eight years was a reasonable year for a child to travel those long distances.

During those days there were not enough classrooms, so those in Sub-A to Standard 1 were schooled under the male morula trees and used blackboards and chalk for writing. The male trees were, I guess, cleverly selected because they do not bear fruit, unlike female trees. The idea was to avoid a situation in which their fruit would be falling on children's heads in the summer season, when they are ripe.

Children used slates and chalk to write notes. I remember how I used to take pride in my slate. It was trimmed with a wooden frame. Over weekends, I would clean the wooden part with a special soil called *mogohlo*. In these modern days this is replaced by detergents such as Vim or Handy Andy. The soil was used by mothers to clean wooden calabashes, wooden spoons (*mahuduo*), *mafehlo* (made of wood and used for churning porridge, *bogobe* or pap, to avoid lumps forming before using *leho)* and wooden bowls (*megopo*).

Studying under the trees exposed some of us to delinquency because we could witness everything happening around us. We would either listen to people talking in nearby homesteads or watch animals roaming around: donkeys, cattle, pigs and goats. Goats were very problematic because they would now and again try to snatch anything attractive to them. For example, they would chew our only book – called Spell, from the word spelling, – made available to us in the Bantu Education syllabus.

Despite being taught under the tree, there was still a sense of disciple and respect between pupils and teachers. Bunking classes was never heard of and neither was late coming. Those were the days of corporal punishment. All school children used to put on well-looked-after uniforms; they varied from school to school. For Arkona, the uniform colours were that of a black gym dress, white or khaki shirts, woollen brown and gold girdle as a belt, with black shoes and brown and gold socks, as well as a brown jersey with both neck and sleeves cuffs trimmed with brown and gold.

Most of the children who attended the school there were those coming from Christian families: the so-called civilised members of society. Most of the people did not attend church and they were referred to as heathens (missionaries' indoctrination).

Their children were still going to the mountains for initiation schools and were looked down upon as being uncivilised or *baditshaba*. I never knew what it meant and somehow the term did not make sense, other than that it is derogatory. They also looked down on Christian children because they were not initiated (*mashoboro*). They were from the area called Phiring where the chieftain's kraal is situated.

These kinds of divisions did not affect us as children, but the boys from there were very unruly and used to terrorise girls from Majakaneng – that is those who went to church, Christians – every time girls were sent to the only shop, which was situated in Phiring and owned by the chief. Otherwise, children befriended each other. I even had a best friend from Ka Phiring, that is, the chief's kraal (*moshate*). Her name was Obeolekae (where were you?) Tseke.

Talking about Obeolekae reminds me of when her father died while we were in primary school. It was such a sad thing, even more scary because then sudden deaths were unheard of and her father died in a car accident. We were used to old people dying, and then only after a long time.

In some cultures, only the parents, commonly wives, would put on black mourning clothes when they lost their husbands or siblings. At ga-Masemola, it was a tradition that even children put on black mourning clothes if they happened to lose one of their parents. It was such that girls would wear a black dress and boys a black shirt for a year. She wore the attire until it changed colour and was worn out. I used to feel sorry for her and heartbroken to see her in such tattered clothes. This is because I had known her to be well looked after because her father had money, being the chief's brother and his right-hand man.

For some reason I failed Sub A (an entry standard) twice. I was told that I failed because I was too playful, not because I was slow or what is always referred to as a slow learner (d*omkop* in Afrikaans). When I failed for the second time, I was moved to a new teacher. After the first few months in her class she recommended that I be promoted to Standard 1, jumping Sub B because, according to her observation, I was not slow but very clever. I guess she managed to convince the school principal and the school governing body. As they say, every-one has an "angel".

Being promoted to Standard 1 was such an honour for me because it meant that I was to migrate from slate and chalk to pencil and a writing book. I caught up with my age group and never looked back. I even passed Standard 1 very well despite having moved there mid-year. When I passed Standard 1 to Standard 2, I started using an ink pen. I became very motivated and in every standard I held position one, or two if I performed poorly, after all the tests written mid-year and at the end of the year, something that justified the good Samaritan teacher's recommendation that I be promoted. I was (am) indeed, a very brilliant person.

The school had a government feeding scheme. A few women and men in the community were hired to cook lunch for us, which consisted of soup made using the navy beans that we used to call *phintshane*. The beans by nature have a content of soluble fibre and raffinose that form air in one's digestive system. They made us break wind or gas a lot. They were served with porridge (*pap* in South African parlance). After everyone had eaten, it sometimes happened that there were leftovers and they would allow us to take rations home in the afternoon after school.

At some point, the feeding scheme was terminated. I did not know why but I learnt later that it was Prime Minister Hendrik Verwoerd's programme, under which people were contracted to supply food to schools. Hence, after he had been assassinated by Dimitri Tsafendas, the project was terminated. I said to myself that he had a heart after all, for him to even bother to ensure that *kaffir* (African) children were fed. Now that I have been exposed to government tenders or contracts, I suspect that he had a contract from big businesses that he personally benefited from and was what is today called a tenderpreneur.

During Verwoerd's tenure, we also used to celebrate Republic of South Africa day, which was founded on the 31st of May in 1961. That day was very special, as we were made to wear scouts' uniforms with scarves wrapped around our necks, put on hats and hold the hand-held flags called stick flags. Then we would hold hands and march around in a big circle, singing *Die Stem*, the national anthem of the time. I do not remember the lyrics of the song; it was in Afrikaans. This would take most of the morning and we would be provided with food like that I referred to earlier. Neither do I remember much about the activities, not that I care.

One thing I liked most about going to school was school trip season, especially the singing competitions, when our school singing choir went to compete with other schools in a distant village. The disadvantage for me was that I am vocally crippled: I cannot sing. One time – I think I was in Standard 1 – when we were called to come and practise singing in preparation for the competition, I went. Our choir was conducted by a fat lady by the name Gertrude Mahlare. I will never forget her, she was a sister-in-law to my Sub A teacher, Anna Mahlare.

While practising singing in the afternoon, a week before the competition, the teacher told me in front of all the children that I could not be allowed to go to the competition because I sang out of tune. She explained that if I were allowed to join the choir for their final moment, I would cause them to lose the cup (meaning the winning trophy). She told me that I was excused from coming to the practice.

I could not believe my ears. I was so shattered that I cried so loudly that they stopped practising. I screamed and threw myself on the floor and started rolling around. She did not know what to do, other than to send one child to go and call my elder cousin. She tried to comfort me, but I could not be consoled. She had to carry me home on her back.

The thing is that going to these occasions was special in that the school would hire railway buses (then the bus drivers were white males) and riding in a bus was fun and a treat. What I also liked was the efforts our parents made a day before the occasion. The preparations would include our mothers slaughtering chickens and cooking pap (*bogobe*) for us to take as road provision (*padkos* in Afrikaans; *mofago* in Pedi or North Sotho). We would be given pocket money to buy nice things that we did not often eat. Our uniforms would be washed and carefully ironed for the trip.

I remember how my mother would comb my sister's hair and wrap her head with a *doek* so that in the morning it was still intact. I always looked forward to that. But when it was my turn to go, I was told I could not go because I could not sing. The following year I was allowed to go, but I was to stand at the back so that my voice could not be heard. I did not mind because all what I wanted was to take a trip, and I did.

There were times when school children would take trips to places like the Union Building in Pretoria and Lorenzo Marques, now Maputo, in Mozambique. My sister went on both the trips. I was supposed to go the following year but it was cancelled. My mother had already paid for all the trip bookings. We were not told the reason for the cancellation. I only knew later that it was because some children from Soweto were involved in a bus accident and some children died while others were injured. But the suspicion was that there had been foul play because it was the time of civil war between Mozambique Liberation Front (FRELILMO) and Renamo (from the Portugu Resistane National Mozambicana), I was disappointed, but I accepted it, as all the children did not go.

Growing up, there was this funny practice that children would have older children as their *di mama* (mama) and *di baba* (child). It was taken so seriously that parents were also involved in it. If it happened that someone said that they wanted you to be their mama or papa, you had to get permission from your parents. Due to the fact that our fathers were always away on migrant labour, our mothers were the only ones who could give us that permission.

There was this girl who approached me, and she wanted to be my mama. I went and asked for permission from my mother. Upon hearing the name of that girl, she refused outright. The thing was that I had to go back and tell her that my mother did not agree. That was a challenge as I did not want to disappoint her. The following day, when I met her she wanted an answer. I was so embarrassed to tell her that my mother had declined her request, and I did not tell her the reason for that; it would have been hurtful for her. Apparently, she was not well brought up, she had bad manners, or so my mother told me. She had been brought up by the grandmother. I did not know what had happened to the mother or father.

Still on this topic, there was this person. She was too much older than me to call her a girl. She approached my mother and told her that she wanted to be my *di mama*: that is, I was to be her *di baba*. My mother agreed.

One time, she invited me to come and visit. It was on a Sunday afternoon. After church, my mother prepared an enamel dish for me (enamel dishes are porcelain fused onto steel; they came in light blue, white and light green and were trimmed in navy blue or a black colour, very durable). She filled it with beans (*dinawa*) and covered the bowl nicely with a neat embroidered white cotton cloth and asked me to carry it carefully, as it was a gift to her. Off I went. It was the first time I'd visited her. She had prepared a nice lunch of pap and boerewors. She dished this out and gave me my share. Suddenly, her sister came in, fuming with anger. They were two sisters staying with their elderly mother. I did not know whether they had brothers and a father.

They started fighting so fiercely that I thought they were going to kill each other, because they were fighting with thick wooden sticks, the ones we collected from the mountains for making fire. They were fighting over boerewors because the one sister had not left any for the other.

Instead of running away, I just sat there and continued eating. I was not going to leave the boerewors behind when we did not have any at home. By the time I'd finished eating, they had stopped fighting. I was frightened, though, because they were both bleeding. Their mother tried to calm them down. Once finished eating, I quickly told her that I had to go, and asked for the dish that my mother had given me. She took me up to the entrance and I ran home fast. I told my mother. She was very disappointed, and I never visited again.

Talking about boerewors, that was not the first time I'd tasted boerewors. One weekend afternoon – I do not remember whether it was on a Saturday or Sunday – my sister and I visited our relative in the neighbourhood. We called her auntie (*tannie* in Afrikaans or *mane* in Pedi). Every time her husband came home from town, she called us to come and fetch sweets, because my aunt's husband worked at a sweet factory. I did not know whether the employer gave them or they stole them. What was commonly known as *borotho* (bread) in the township lingo meant that employees stole goods to pay themselves and augment their meagre salaries.

My mother would always warn us not to eat in other people's houses, even if they offered us food, but when we got there they were about to eat lunch and offered to dish up for us: pap and boerewors. While she was busy dishing out, my sister whispered in my ear that we were not going to eat. I said that I wanted to eat because they'd cooked pap and boerewors that the husband had brought from the city where he worked. My sister became furious and said that I was not going to eat, otherwise she was going to tell our mother. I did not want to hear any of it as it was to be the first time I was to taste boerewors. This happened before visiting *di mama*. Ironically they stayed in the same neighbourhood, I think with one homestead in between.

Auntie realised that there was a commotion between us, and asked whether anything was wrong. My sister told her that she should not dish out for us. I interrupted her and said I wanted to eat. My sister became embarrassed and kept quiet. We went home and my sister told our mother, I cannot remember what her reaction was, but she probably gave me a hiding.

Like in any rural community, we were all disadvantaged, although some were worse off than others. Those in the remote rural areas were perceived as the worst off because there were no schools or churches, nor any exposure to the forms of so-called civilisation. But to the contrary, they were better off as they could still plough and live a normal traditional life.

Due to the dire circumstances that we all grew up under, our parents taught us household chores or activities at an early age. For example, myself and children of my age group – about nine or ten years old – were able to fetch wood for making fire and for cooking purposes, from far away mountains some ten kilometres away or more. We would wake up very early, before sunrise, and cross rivers to and from.

Because of the distance, we would ensure that we collected as much wood as we could, tied the sticks together with ropes to form a manageable bundle, and carried them over our heads. Tying dry wood into bundles was not easy; it needed a certain skill. Hence, most of the children struggled to get it right. If not properly tightened, the bundle would start loosening up and it would be difficult for one to carry it on one's head and support it with one's two hands.

Once we had all finished tying our bundles, we kicked the road. I do not know why we had to run instead of just walking. If you were left behind with your loose bundle of firewood, you would be left alone without anyone to help you unless one of us felt pity for you and volunteered to assist. Being left alone in those huge mountains and forests with baboons roaming around was very scary, so one had to learn the tricks fast.

At times, we would go to collect wood at a place where cattle auctioning (what we knew as *fantasie*) took place. For us, going there was a form of entertainment and we went there just to witness the auction. There would be many Afrikaners (*boers*) coming to sell their cattle. At the beginning, Africans were not allowed to participate in these auctions. Only employees were allowed because their job was to assist with directing animals to where they were supposed to wait before being auctioned. It was only later that I saw a few African men who came to auction (sell) their cattle there.

There would be a stage where auctioneers would announce prices for each cow. We would stand far away because we were afraid that those white people would chase us away. It was fun witnessing what happened, although we did not actually understand it all but were amused by the way those auctioneers spoke. This happened only in the summer months.

There was always danger lurking around, though, as there were dangerous animals as well as snakes roaming around. During rainy days we had to cross rivers. Sometimes we came across sinking sand or quicksand (*sekokomohlaba*). One day, coming from the auction we were walking in the forest along a small river. As we walked along the river bank, my sister slipped and she was almost swallowed by sinking sand. Fortunately, she went first with one foot. I jumped and pulled her out, and her sandal came off her foot. It disappeared, never to be found, and so we suspected that the area had quicksand. I was so frightened when I realised that I had almost lost my sister in the split of a second and I would never have got to know her grave. She could have died a horrible death and I do not know how my parents would have lived with that.

After the auction, towards the afternoon, we would hurry home carrying bundles of firewood on our heads. Collecting firewood chores were done on weekends, that is, Saturday. On our way, we would converge at one spot under a nice tree shade to rest briefly and sit down to eat food we had carried as a provision. Due to running for a distance in a scorching sun, we would get very thirsty. To get fresh drinking water, we would dig small wells to avoid contaminated running water.

In winter or when there was drought, water was always scarce, so we were forced to walk long distances to go to fetch water. However, on rainy days we could fetch water not far from our homes because streams and wells would have plenty of water. Those who could afford water reservoirs would harvest enough rainwater to see them through the winter season. Some of us resorted to using the big paraffin tanks (we knew them as gallons) that local shops used to store paraffin in. Before this, people used big calabashes (*dinkgo*) to store water; small ones were used to store traditional beer (*moeta*). In some years, the area would experience drought and getting water became a problem as the rivers would also dry out, including one of the biggest rivers in Sekhukhuneland, called Ngwaritsi.

During that dry season people used to dig up big wells to get water. When it rained the well got filled with water, and in winter the water in the well remained stagnant. The wells would look like pools filled with green water. I remember how we children would go and swim in those pools, oblivious to the danger. When I think about it now, I realise how dangerous that was because we never knew how deep the wells were or what was in the water. We would take off our clothes and swim naked (bare-arsed). We all knew how to swim and practised different kinds of swimming strokes.

But water-fetching activities were done every day. We would go and fetch water after school daily. I still remember running about five times to and from to the river with five-litre buckets of water on my head for a stretch of about three kilometres.

Children activists would now condemn this as child abuse, but for us it was fun and a way of life. These activities kept us away from negative things and fit. I guess these are some of the things that moulded me into the person that I am today.

Then I was totally oblivious to the difficulties around me. All that mattered to me was to have something to eat, clothes and to go to school. The fact that I would see my father twice a year did not bother me because almost all male folks in rural areas were migrant labourers, who came home only on Good Friday, Christmas time or on annual leave.

I always looked forward to the day the makeshift post office opened so that I could collect the letters my father wrote to my mother. The post office was situated in the house of the Lutheran church priest, miles away from my home. The distance was never a problem but fun. I knew my father's handwriting and I treasured that because my instinct told me that he still thought of us. This was important because most of the fathers or male figures were swallowed up by urban areas (out of sight and out of mind scenario). Most of them never returned to their families down there as they established themselves in the urban areas with other women, as mentioned above. In this sense I regarded myself as very fortunate.

The most exciting time was towards the festive season, when my father and others would come home the night before Christmas. I would be among the children who would go to the bus station to meet them and carry my father's luggage. He carried big boxes, about three of them. One would have our Christmas clothes in it, the others food. He would have accumulated and stored non-perishable rations under his bed, which was elevated on paint tins. Fortunately, they had an old fridge given to them by their employer, so the meat would be stored there until he was ready to come home. There was also a suitcase for his clothes.

The atmosphere used to be very exciting. It would be a hive of activity, with everyone going about preparing for Christmas. My mother, like other women, would be cleaning and tidying the house as well beatifying the homestead with a decoration of a mixture of cow-dung and different colours of soil. The mud houses and boundary walls around the houses would have fancy decorations (called *makwala* – in modern times it would be referred to as a paint technique, and my mother used to be an expert in that).

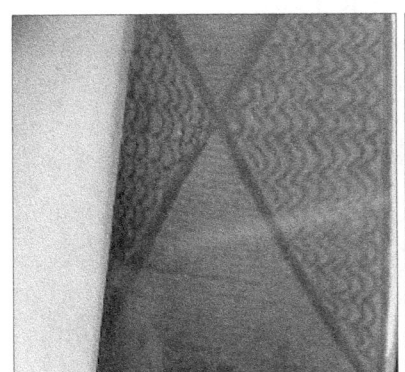 

(In the picture is my daughter and her friend and in the background is my mother's beautiful flower garden)

On Christmas Eve, young women would prepare fire made of dry cow dung to bake bread for the big day. The horizon would be covered with fire smoke everywhere. I loved the smell in the air: a mixture of cake smells and the smoke of dry cow dung (*boloko*) used for baking. There were no coal stoves then. They would dig a hole and remove the soil to make an oven. They would prepare firewood and when ready they would allow the flame to die down so that only burning charcoal remained (*magala*).

Then they would prepare a dough made of flour. Before flour was sold in the shops, people would make their own by grinding wheat seeds into a fine texture. The yeast was made from sorghum beer, called *umqomboti* in Zulu. When the beer started fermenting, there would be bubbles on the surface. They would remove the foam and dry it in the sun to make yeast. They would then mix flour and this yeast, salt, a bit of sugar for taste, and mix it with water to form a dough. The dough would be covered with a cloth and left to rise (until doubled in size).

When it was ready, the dough was rolled in the palms of their hands to form balls, in the same way as people make fat cakes (*vetkoek*) or bread rolls, and the balls were placed into a legless cast iron baking pan. To make an oven, they would arrange stones neatly and then put pieces of corrugated iron over them to support the baking pan. Once the pan was secured, they would put burning charcoal (*magala*) on top and the bread or buns would be left to bake – very delicious. Instead of wood, some would use cow dung for the baking purposes.

Like any children from Christian families (particularly in the Lutheran mission church), it was a tradition that we should go to church on Christmas Eve, and at the end of the service every family received loaves of bread. Our parents would contribute a certain amount of money during the year, and each family would get its share according to how much they had contributed. We brought along clean white cloths to wrap and carry them home in. Bread was a luxury; thus our parents could only afford to buy bread, meat and sweets for Christmas.

On the day of Christmas, we would go to church in the morning, clothed in our new attire. Some children did not have new clothes and that always hurt me.

It was a yearly tradition that after church, once we'd had lunch, all the children would travel to the chief's kraal, about five kilometres away. On our way, we would stop at the chief's shop. It was the only shop (*lebenkele*, from the Afrikaans word *winkel)* that serviced the whole village. We would form a circle, holding each other's hands, and were given sweets. We then walked to the chief's kraal and there he would be, sitting on his throne, dressed in his best suit and clothed in an animal skin made of a lion or leopard, waiting for us (*Kgosi Tseke Molomo wa Tau Masemola*). He was one of the more popular chiefs in the Sekhukhuneland then. We would sit in front of him and he would address us. I do not remember what his speech entailed. After he'd finished talking, he would personally offer us sweets.

What I do remember is that there would be entertainers: men dressed in traditional regalia, that is animal skins, while women would wear beautiful dresses called *yele* that go with traditional accessories called *ntepa* (a back apron), *le thetho* (front apron) made of animal skin, probably that of a goat. I do not have a proper English translation. The dresses were similar to the Sepedi traditional attire that I wore for my wedding. They would all start singing and dancing traditional dances while beating drums.

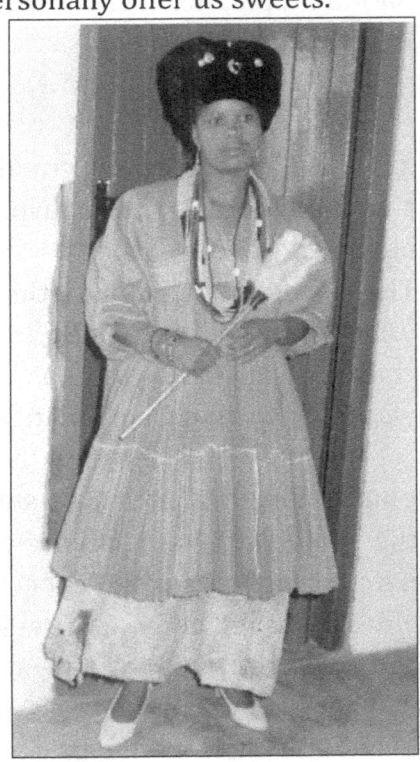

Even when someone was getting married, the couple would have to go and get their blessings from the chief. If it were a Christian wedding, they would go to church first and to the chief's kraal in the afternoon.

I really enjoyed those activities, even though I did not understand their significance. Those are some of the things that kept communities together and created some form of harmony, restoring the norms and values of societies.

Ga-Masemola was divided into two: Christians (*majakane* – translated in Afrikaans as *ja ek kan*, or in English as *yes, I can*, meaning that I can follow Jesus Christ); and non-Christians (heathens). The village that my parents stayed in was called Ga-Mmatopi. Those who were not Christian (atheists) stayed in Phiring, where the chief's kraal was.

The Lutheran church was called Arkona. The members of the community had built it with mud many years before and it looked very old. My grandparents, as well as my mother, churched there. My aunt no longer attended church because she had been ex-communicated for having children out of wedlock. The ex-communication method was (is) a way of discouraging unbecoming behaviours. So, it was only my mother who attended church as my father did not like the Christian ideal, although I was told he came from an Anglican church background.

The problem I have with ex-communication as a form of punishment is that it one sided. Ostracising women and not the men who have children out of wedlock reinforces the patriarchal horrors still experienced to date. My other aunt, the eldest, had left to go and seek employment on the farms, and she never returned to settle at ga-Masemola but only visited.

When I was nine years old, the Arkona church was re-built with mortar and bricks. The project was sponsored by

German missionaries. I thought it was the biggest and most beautiful church I had ever seen. The community threw a big feast on the day of the church opening (what is called a roof-wetting ceremony, in Western culture). A number of cows were slaughtered, and women cooked porridge in big cast iron pots. It was on a Sunday. The ceremony started with the morning church service and the theme of church service or sermon was about King Solomon. After the service, the congregation was provided with lunch.

I still vividly remember sitting next to my mother under the morula tree below the foot of the small mountain called Molelema. The mountain overlooked the church, and we were eating – actually feasting! It was a beautiful day. I am not sure where my other siblings were when my mother asked me this question: "What would you ask God for?" I responded without hesitation by saying that I would ask God to give me wisdom (*bohlale*) like Solomon. I still remembered the sermon the priest had preached earlier during the church service, and to have wisdom were the exact words the priest used as he was preaching in North Sotho or Pedi. My mother was so impressed by my response, and she encouraged me to keep on praying hard for that because that is what God would grant or bless me with. He indeed did. Hence, I have never stopped praying and until today I still pray for more wisdom.

Missionaries came to South Africa from different European countries, among them Britain, Germany, France and America, and they represented different church groups or denominations, namely Lutheran, Methodists, Roman Catholics, Anglican, and so on. Their aim was to establish themselves and their work as far as Christianity is concerned, and to convert people to Christianity. Their missionary activities were to build churches, schools and residential houses for the European priests. Although missionaries came to South Africa to spread the gospel and to teach about Christianity, they also aimed at undermining African culture to acculturate people, hoping that they would learn the way in which 'civilised' people should live. Their Christian doctrine was wrapped up in a whole set of Western attitudes and values, like the colonial governments.

Enough about missionaries and back to my life. I always liked the company of boys. I rarely played with girls and I was more interested in rough boys' games (I was a tomboy). When I was not climbing trees or jumping from one rock to another, I would make attempts at climbing humongous boulders to reach the summit.

If not out with the boys, I preferred to play alone at home. I had this boy friend. We could spend most of the day on weekends or school holidays sitting on top of one of the biggest trees called *mefaya* (wild fig tree). Its fruit is the same as that of a fig tree but very small and very delicious and healthy. Most of the destitute families would survive by eating them and many other wild fruits such as *ditlhopi*. The fruit are orange in colour and sweet, we used to pick them up and put them in a container, mash them until they form a beautiful paste like a smoothie, and we ate them – quite delicious.

I happened to know that in a year that we had plenty of them we were going to experience drought (*komelelo*) and famine, and so starvation (*tlala*). Hence they called it *tlala ya mohlopi*. But they were very delicious tiny orange-coloured fruits. I was told that during famine, the white stem of *mohlopi* were dug out (*epa*), dried (*omisa*), ground up (*bupi*) and boiled (*bidisa*) into porridge (*bogobe*).

The fig tree referred to above overlooked every house in the neighbourhood, and what was more interesting to us was that it was next to the only footpath leading to the mountain next to our houses. The path ended at the foot the mountain, forming a cul-de-sac, or a T-junction. There were almost no pit latrines, let alone proper toilets, then, so almost everyone used the mountain to relieve themselves (traditional toilets), because there were rocks and shrubs that one could hide behind comfortably and not be seen by passers-by.

As to who would clean them, that is where pigs and dung beetles (*kgokoloshane*) came in to serve the purpose of flushing them clean. The role of dung beetles is to turn any dung – animal or human – into dung balls and roll them away, either to be used by females as cocoons to lay eggs in or as food for adults. This shows how important the ecosystem is.

Talking about pit latrines, I loathed them because of one horrible incident that once happened. There was this family that was well off because the male figure in the house happened to be a principal of one of the schools there. Their standard of living was better than most people's. He was a half-brother to my uncle; they shared a father. So, they could afford a house roofed with corrugated iron and a pit latrine. They had one daughter who got married from another village, and she was blessed with a daughter. She left her daughter with her mother and hired a helper to assist the old woman. One day – I do not know exactly what happened – the helper took the child to the toilet. I think she was about two years old. I do not know whether the helper deliberately threw the child in or if it was just a freak accident. Whatever the case, the child fell into the pit latrine and she apparently drowned in the faeces and urine. It was a harrowing incident. I was more horrified and saddened because I knew the child and the rest of the family. The mother could not take it and she later died of a broken heart.

Back to my delinquency. The *mefaya* tree that my friend and I would climb on was so huge that once on top of it those beneath it could not see us. The branches were very strong and spread nicely for sitting. So, we were not visible. We preferred climbing the tree during summer, because in winter the leaves got dry and withered away, falling off and leaving the trees bare, so anyone could see us. During summertime, when the *mefaya* fruit were still raw and hard, we would watch everyone passing by, but there was this elderly woman who always walked very slowly, with her arms resting on her backside. She seemed to go to the toilet at the same time every day. We would wait for her to go past the tree a little bit and would then aim at her in such a way that we could not miss. Then we would throw the little fruits at her, and every time they hit her she would look around and we would sit there giggling. For us children it was fun, although now as a grown up I regret it because it was cruel and disrespectful.

The old lady was my friend's grandmother and was bringing him up. I never knew his biological father, of course, but I knew his mother. I learnt that she worked as a domestic worker in one of the big cities. We thought the elderly woman could not figure out where the fig fruit came from. She must have told the woman staying in the house next to the tree because one day we went and played around and once tired we decided to climb the tree. The owner of the house must have been watching us. The elderly woman came and we started with our silly game. The woman came around and ordered us to come down and gave us a hiding. We never did it again. In those days, any adult could discipline any child without their parents taking any offence.

One day, some other children and I decided to go and play on the mountain. While playing there, we uncovered lots of coins showing and shining on the surface, under the rocks. Those coins that came to the surface must have unearthed by rainwater over time. We started digging and more coins were found: there were a lot of them. We gathered them and we each went home with our share. I called my mother and showed her what I had brought along. She asked where I got them. I told her. Her face changed and she asked me to take them back to where I'd found them. I was puzzled and disappointed.

I found out later that the son to a family in the neighbourhood was a thug (*tsotsi*). I was told that he stayed in Alexandra, and he was a member of gang that robbed banks. The money belonged to him, and it had been hidden there from the police. I remember how the police used to come to the house looking for him. He had one child of my age (Fanyane Tsetsewa), and he was brought up by his grandparents. The son rarely came home. I never knew Fanyane's real mother. Fanyane's father was eventually shot and killed while involved in a robbery.

In my mother's household I stayed with my aunt's children. Their mother was not married, and my father used to provide for all of us. My mother did not have brothers. I am told that my other uncle died while still a young boy. His name was Cain and my other uncle died while working in one of the Rand Gold mines. His name was Abel and they were each named after Eve and Adam's children in the Old Testament. They did not have parents either.

My maternal grandfather died young, I do not know from what, and my grandmother died when there was an outbreak of a disease called "*drie dae*" (three days). I am told it was some sort of stomach bug outbreak and lots of people died. None of the infected people survived more than three days, I am told. They all died like flies, a very painful death as there were no hospitals, clinics or any medical facilities close by. My father told me of the story and it really hurt me a lot; the same pain I felt when I was told of the circumstances in which my uncle died. What was more devastating was the fact that the family only knew of his death after many months, when one of his co-workers from the same village went home after many months of cheap labour – probably after twelve months. Then there was no means of communication and mining magnates would not even bother to make any effort to inform the families in the rural areas, let alone compensate them. He was buried there in the mine dumps, as there were no mortuaries to keep his body and means of transportation were very poor then.

As already mentioned, my parents did not have anyone to look after them because during those days it was common that only men should be allowed to go and seek employment while women remained at home as housewives. However, my mother decided to go and look for employment as a domestic worker after her brother died. It was not easy for her because she was ridiculed and endured a backlash from the neighbours, but she had to do something to help her family.

She told me that she worked mostly in the northern suburbs of Johannesburg from an early age: that is, after completing what used to be referred to as Standard 6. It carried the same status as Matric because then it was the highest standard. She obtained first class in her end-of-the-year examinations, something that tells me that she was quite brilliant. What I know very well about her is that she was wise. I really admired her wisdom to a point that she became my pillar of hope and my confidant. She inspired me greatly.

My mother told me that she really wished she could have received a better education to have been able to do something such as teaching. She tried her luck with nursing because, unlike other professions, nurses were trained at the hospital, at the same time working and earning some money.

While training at Jane Furse Hospital, she told me that she had a very horrifying experience. She was sent with other nurses to take someone who had passed on to where the dead bodies were kept. There were no proper mortuaries then; they were stored in a thatched rondavel house because thatch makes the temperature stay cool. The bodies were kept there for a short period, one day at the most.

When they got there, they found a few bodies lying on the floor, waiting for relatives to come to collect them. She told me that she got scared and decided to leave then and there because she could not stand the sight of dead people. This is how her dream of becoming a professional nurse was dashed. She decided instead to go to Johannesburg and look for a job as a domestic worker.

People then lived communally, so not having parents did not leave much of a void. There would always be uncles and aunts who would be there to assist. For example, despite my mother and aunt not having a male figure to take care of them, my grandfather's brother was experienced in roof thatching. People hired him to roof their houses, so he did that for a living. Time and again he would come home to assist with maintaining my grandmother's thatch roofs when they needed it.

My mother and her sister siblings were also lucky that they had a very caring uncle; he was a relative to my grandmother. We did not know while growing up that he was not their blood father and not our blood grandfather. He loved the family as if it were his. He came from the Bapela family clan that stayed in a neighbouring chieftainship called ga-Marishane. I am told that both Masemola and Marishane were brothers but split up due to family feuds many years ago.

I loved my grandfather very much; he was a very kind and loving man. My mother told me that he made it a point to throw her a big white wedding when she married my father. My grandfather was still working then, and he stayed for many years at a place called Lady Selbourne in Pretoria, before the Nationalist Party implemented the forced removals policy and moved people to areas such as Atteridgeville and Saulsville. When he was pensioned, he came back home and built a retail shop business between two villages: ga-Marishane and ga-Phahla. He was an Apostolic Faith Mission (AFM) church priest. Known as the Pentecostal Christian denomination, we simply referred to them as *Mapostola*. This is one of those African Faith Mission Churches in which its members wear the blue and white uniform.

He had one of the biggest trucks I ever saw. He used it for transporting stock for his shop. Then, there were no wholesale shops nearby where people could buy and stock things in bulk. The nearest town was Steelpoort, many kilometres away. He would come to ga-Masemola every Sunday afternoon for a family church service. I would spot his big truck in the distance and would start running home very excited. It would not matter where I was, I would run home.

He would start singing even before he entered our homestead. He had such a powerful voice. I loved that and I would immediately get hold of his blue dust coat that church members wore. Men congregants of the church called the Apostolic Faith Mission (Protestant or Pentecostal) still wear blue dust coats, and the women wear long dresses and they also put a white or blue girdle around their waist.

We would all join him and form a circle as we danced, and I would be holding his coat and dancing along with him as he went around until I went into a trance. People would gather there, and it used to be an interesting entertainment for the community. One of his favourite Hymn songs was "*Ga le lakatsa go tseba ka mo ke pholositsweng, mmamelang ga ke le bjetsa ke le supetsa tsela...*" in direct translation, it means that if you'd like to know how I was saved, you should listen to me when I tell you that Jesus is my Saviour... I still love it as before, and even now still go into a trance when I play the song. It is one of my prayer songs and I have a CD of the song; it is special to me.

He would later start preaching. He was a very good orator and most charismatic. I did not quite like the preaching part, but my mother forced us to sit down and listen to the sermons.

During the school holidays he would come to fetch us for a visit. I liked visiting him. He was a good cook. He would cook us nice food, such as dumpling and meat. His wife loved baking, so we were given a treat

There was another relative that I liked going to visit. Sometimes I would stay with them for an extended period. He was my distant uncle, but, working as a soldier, always away. I would stay with the wife, and her daughter and son. They were both much older than me. The rest of the siblings were either married or working in town. Two of his sons joined him in the military: that is, they became soldiers under the South African Defence Force (SADF) during the old government.

I liked staying there because as the youngest I would receive much attention, unlike at home where I had siblings and cousins of almost the same age. What I liked most was that they had lots of pigs that they slaughtered now and again. I enjoyed pork meat a lot, especially when they made crackling (*dikgadika*). Besides, when we did not have anything in the form of relish to eat our *pap* with (*seshebo*), there was always dried pig's fat (*tsholo*). *Pap* was our only staple food. After cooking *pap*, we would use the same fire to warm fat seasoned with salt for taste, and while hot we would dip the *pap* in the fat and eat. It was very nice, better than dried *morogo* (*monawa*) from fresh bean leaves which was just like spinach.

I was close to my boy cousin. He was a very kind person, just like his father. He was one of sons who joined the military later. I'd already left ga-Masemola when he did. Sometimes he would go fishing and bring home some fish called barbel – we simply called it *babra* because of mispronunciation – and would fry them for me, and we would eat it with *pap*. It was such a treat.

I remember one day he asked me to iron his school trousers. I did not know how to iron clothes. I took the trousers. The iron was already on the fire – we did not have electricity then – and he showed me how to iron but did not show me how to fold. I just ironed it like I would do with a skirt. He was upset because he only realised that in the morning, when he had to put them on for school. I told him that I'd never ironed before.

My aunt and her daughter would leave me alone. Sometimes my boy cousin would also be away, playing with other boys, but otherwise he was always at home. He did not want to go out after sunset, especially when there is no moonlight, because it got pitch dark. I was told that he was afraid of walking alone in the dark. I still recall how he would ensure that every time he had to go and fetch water at the back of the house where the water was stored in very big pottery pots, he would ask me to accompany him. Going there, he would ask me to go before him. When coming back he would ask me to come after him. This made it clear that he feared the darkness at the back of the house. It was very dark because of the sisal that was planted around the house and that served as a boundary wall.

During the drought season, the water would get very scarce because the rivers and wells would dry out. But there was this big donga formed by soil erosion over the years, that could be mistaken for a river. During rainy days, it always had running water. However, the water was not preferred because it was salty. But, when there was no rain, there was very clean water coming from one spot on its bank, so people would queue there for water. They would wait for their turn until late in the night. My aunt and her daughter would go to queue for the water, and they would anticipate that they might come late in the night.

One day, when my aunt and her daughter left me in the night and my boy cousin was not there, they asked me to go and wait for them in a neighbour's house. I knew the girl in the house as we schooled together. They had only one thatched *rondavel* house and they used it as kitchen and bedroom: that is, everything. They were a family of five.

After eating supper, my aunt and her daughter left, and I waited for them there until late. Then came the time that the household were to go to sleep. They asked me to join them but, looking at their worn-out blankets and tattered traditional reed mats that they were to sleep on – all of them together – I refused and assured them that I would sit on a small wooden stool or bench and wait for my aunt. While they were sleeping, I heard a funny scratchy noise: something was chewing. It was termites (*mohlwa*). They woke up because these creatures were eating their mats and walking all over them. The fire had not died down altogether, so they tried to shake the mats into the fire to remove them (*hlohlorela*). The smell of burning insects filled the house.

At midnight, my relatives came to fetch me. I was not impressed. The following day I decided to go back home – it was not far – and I never went back.

The area my aunt lived in was called ga-Makobe; my place was called ga-Mmatopi. It was a very small area, but there were a number of mysterious things happening there. For example, the child I mentioned earlier fell into the pit latrine or toilet stayed there. The first albino person I ever saw stayed in the area. He was in the same class as me from Sub A, what is now called Grade 1. My uncle's brother, who also stayed in the area, was the only blind person I knew. My *di mama* who'd invited me for lunch and had fought with her sister for boerewors was from the same area.

There was this girl who also stayed in the neighbourhood. She suffered from a belly button (navel) infection (*mokhubu*) called omphalitis. Maybe it was caused by the yeast or fungal infection called candidiasis. If not treated, it could spread to involve the entire abdominal wall. It was the first time that I witnessed someone having that kind a disease. It would become so painful that she got used to walking bent over and holding her tummy. Sometimes it got very septic because of lack of treatment. I felt sorry for her. Because there were no health facilities close by, she never received proper medical care, let alone a proper diagnosis and cure. As a result, she died.

In the very same area, there was this boy with a big head but the smallest eyes and mouth. He had a condition called macrocephaly. His head was so abnormally huge that we made fun of him. He too died at a very early age, I did not know from what.

This is the same area where I first saw a coloured child. His mother had an extramarital affair with one of the white Afrikaner railway bus drivers I mentioned earlier. I only happened to know the story later in life, but for us it was just a child who looked like a white with curly hair.

There was a family adjacent to my grandparents' homestead. I was told that my grandfather was a brother to the husband of the woman in question – that is my mother's aunt, as she was married to her father's brother – so they were close relatives. There was so much animosity between my family and the relative's family that one could have mistaken them to be strangers. They never visited each other.

The homesteads were designed in such a way that closely related families, such as uncles and aunts from the same clan, could stay adjacent to one another. They would normally share the same surname. Their homestead would often be divided by long walls and houses were built of mud and roofed with thatch.

My mother's aunt hated my mother's family to the point that she would make it a habit, even a sort of a hobby, to stand next to the wall adjacent to our household and would start insulting and swearing at my mother and her sister every Sunday evening when my grandfather left. I would watch them crying every time this happened. I realised that she would in fact target my mother. It affected me so much that I no longer wanted to go and play with my peers. All that I wanted was to guard my mother and aunt.

This weekly occurrence disheartened me to the point of feeling sick and tired of it. One late afternoon, when she started I climbed on top of the wall and started shouting and swearing back at her; I mean really swearing. It was a taboo for a young child to answer back or swear at an adult and this was precisely the reason why my mother and my aunt would cry rather than insult her back: she was old enough to be their mother as she was married to the brother of my mother's father. By the way, she was the mother to a son whose wife had had a child with a white man.

Although I knew the consequences, I was so angry that I just wanted to give it back at her. I had to pluck up the courage, no matter the consequences. My mother was so embarrassed that she just watched me and instructed me to get off the wall, but she could not shut me up. Although I could no longer see her, I just kept screaming until she left. From then on she would stand far away from the wall and murmur whatever, and my parents would just ignore her until she got tired, and it was the end of her wrath. She even influenced her sons and her daughter.

Her elder son was one of the kindest persons on earth. He got along with my mother's family. Ironically, he and other cousins befriended my father whilst working in Johannesburg. My sister told me that our father was telling him one day how he happened to meet our mother. The son of this evil woman – we referred to him as uncle – and his other cousins invited my father to visit them; there was a wedding of one of their siblings or cousins.

My grandmother was at the wedding. After they greeted everyone, my grandmother asked my father whether his friends had introduced him to her daughter who was also working in Johannesburg and told him her name. I do not think my grandmother was seeing him for the first time. My father must have frequented ga-Masemola with his friends. While in Johannesburg, my father asked my uncle to arrange that he meet my mother. My father told me that at that time there were entertainment places for blacks in town, places such as clubs

and ballroom dance halls. My parents both knew how to dance, and they always dressed very well. I am told it was in those places that they learnt how to dance. They invited my mother to join them. I am not sure I know exactly where it was, but my father was there. He told my sister that it was love at first sight and everything else was history. They became my parents. I was lucky.

As already mentioned, the evil relative of ours influenced her two children negatively and they too were hostile towards my mother and aunt. One day I went home for the lunch break as usual. I found my mother and my aunt crying, and I became very concerned. I asked my mother what the matter was. She refused to tell me and insisted that I finish eating and go back to school. I told her that I was not going back to school until she told me why they were crying, but she promised to tell me after school.

After school I hurried home because I had to find out why my mother had been crying; I could not get that out of my mind. It really bothered me. My mother must have seen me running from a distance and knew why I was in such a hurry. I went straight into the house and took off my school clothes and put away my books. I walked over to her and reminded her that she had promised to tell me why she and my aunt had been crying.

She sat me down and said that I must have realised that Monsa and Molly, our dogs, were not there. I had not noticed. Now that I know what pit bulls look like I know that our dogs were those kinds of dogs: very big. I then looked around, and indeed they were not at home. She said they'd had to take them into hiding as someone wanted to harm them. They had taken them to Ga-Makobe, the place I told you about earlier. I asked could I go and see them, and she said yes. I ran to my uncle's place and found them there. I guess that after that I went to play and forgot about the whole thing.

Later in life she told me the whole story. When Uncle Jan – we called him Papago Ngwato, (Ngwato's father) because that was the name of his first-born son – got retrenched from his job, he had taken his lump sum money and had built his shop; I know where it was. Apparently, he wanted my father to give him the dogs to guard his shop, especially at night. My father refused because he loved them; my father was a dog lover. The dogs were very domesticated and tamed and they guarded us when adults were not at home. No one would enter the homestead with them there.

He got very angry and went to the chieftain and reported that my father's dogs had killed his goats. Of course he lied, just to spite him. Unfortunately, initially, they seemed to have bought his story. But even in the traditional set up there are courts where cases are discussed and dispensed with. So, while they discussed my father's dogs and some suggested that they should be put down (euthanised), other men defended them, saying that the dogs hardly went anywhere and it was strange that they had ventured out in the night to go and kill goats. They told him to bring evidence, but he did not have any, so the case was thrown out and my father's dogs were saved.

My parents decided to go and hide them because they knew he might want revenge and could harm them. My mother told me that she'd cried because he had come boasting to them that the dogs would be put down before the matter was even discussed. He was disappointed that he lost the case.

My mother revisited the story because of the accident she witnessed.

After we left ga-Masemola to ga-Maraba (Kalkspruit), my mother decided to visit the sister she'd left behind. She took a bus from Polokwane via ga-Masemola; the bus depot was in a place called Apel in Sekhukhune. While on the way, they came across a car accident and their bus stopped to go and see what was happening. Already, there were ambulances and police cars at the scene. Some people got out to see what had happened and, as she was about to get out, someone told her that the car that had been involved in the accident belonged to the owner of the shop – he mentioned its name – and the person had died. She immediately knew who he was and climbed back into the bus.

Knowing the family and their hostile relationship, she did not want to be a witness to their accident, especially since they believed very much in superstition and witchcraft. She was afraid that she would be blamed for his death because of the coincidence that she happened to be there on that day. My mother told me that she could have rejoiced at that after the dog story and the ill-treatment by her mother, but she said that she would not wish that on her worst enemy and that she was saddened by his untimely death. She believed in the Christian principle of "turning the other cheek". I honestly doubt if I could do that.

Car accidents were rarely heard of then, so it was very shocking, especially since he left young children.

What I am trying to articulate above is what the majority of people in society are familiar with: family feuds that were never contained in their initial stage and over the years are allowed to escalate from generation to generation – what I refer to as generational rivalry. In most cases they become distorted and often do not make sense. Hatred, jealousy and gossip are often to blame for these kinds of toxic relationships. I personally believe that if people could communicate better, these types of behaviours could be avoided and that it is possible for all of us to live in peace and care for each other.

Besides adult problems, there were good stories to tell. I have already mentioned that the rural areas were not developed when I was growing up, and as a result there were no formal places where children could go to play (no amenities). As children, we improvised in that we had our own indigenous games we played such as *kgwele* (what is called hockey in English), *mpa* (jumping the rope), and *moraba raba* (something like chess). I also loved a stone throwing game (*diketo*). This is a game played with pebbles: one stone is thrown into the air and as soon as the stone is in the air, the other hand scoops pebbles out of the hole. Juggling balls (*totompetsa*) is another traditional game we used to play. In our time we used small stones or pebbles and not balls because they were not available. My father bought us hula hoops; not so traditional. Some of the games were seasonal.

The area we used to live in was very mountainous and we would spend most of our times climbing over trees and rocks (boulders) and running around, either just playing or picking wild fruits, which were also seasonal. We were mountain climbers, rock and even tree climbers, and swimmers before these were fashionable pursuits. Climbing mountains or tall rocks required lots of effort and creativity, so it was not for everyone. One had to endure pain until one reached the top – what is today called a summit (*senthloreng*). We were so innovative that we had our own self-made wooden swings (*meswinki*) tied to tree branches.

Growing up in a rural area, I witnessed how our parents mastered the task of preparing soil for ploughing (*go lema*), weeding (*go hlagola*), harvesting (*go buna*) and storing (*go lota*) food. These processes formed what is known today as a household's food security. It refers to how communities can produce, preserve and store food for the future in case of drought.

Women and men performed different tasks: that is, the tasks were done through a division of labour. For example, women performed the roles of weeding, harvesting, threshing, winnowing and grading (*go fola*). Meanwhile, men performed the roles of clearing, ploughing and sowing. When about to harvest crops, they'd start preparing a dry platform that was made of soil mixed with cow dung called *seboya* or *sebowa*. After harvesting beans, sorghum (*mabele*) and millet (*leotsa*), these were spread nicely in this platform for them to dry.

In the rural areas we had in abundance indigenous wild fruits, such as *ditshidi* (*ximenia caffra*). *Ditshidi* nuts were used by men for tanning hides to make attire accessories such as *ntepa le theto*. *Mahlatswa* (stem fruit in English and in Afrikaans *stamvrug* – its scientific name is *Englerophytum magalismontanum*), *mabupudi* (*mimusops zeyheri*), marula (*sclerocarya*) and *ditoro* (cactus or prickly pear). *Mabilo* (wild medlar or *vagneria infausta*) taste like prunes. Marula (*sclerocarya caffra*) fruits were used to make beer. I used to enjoy marula nuts. Once dried, we children would crack them and eat them as snacks. My aunt used to grind them and put them in *lerotse,* soft porridge: very delicious.

In this season, everything was in abundance and the fruits really assisted our bodies with the vitamins, fibre and proteins needed by the body. We did not eat these things because we were poor, but for our sustenance. During that time there was no starvation, even during a drought year. Even if people could not harvest much, they would survive by eating edible wild fruits, vegetables or dried seeds and *morogo* harvested in summer, dried and stored during a good rainy season.

The families that would be hard hit were those without someone who was working in the family to send them some money for ploughing and to buy seeds for planting. At that time, most of us knew how to grind grains into a fine meal so that we could cook porridge, either from grains such as *mabele thoro* (red sorghum seeds) or *leotsa* (jowar or great millet seeds).

Maize was not planted at ga-Masemola, only at Kalkspruit, probably because its seeds are hard to grind and one needs a special grinding machine to turn it into mielie meal. At

Kalkspruit, after harvesting they would take their grain to a place called the Cooperative where there was a mill (*tshilong*). People would exchange their sacks or bags of grain for those of a mielie meal (*bupi*). Of course, the type of soil at a specific area plays a big part; hence, some seeds will only thrive in a certain environment.

We had *dikgobe* made of sorghum grain, *dinawa* (sugar beans), Bambara nuts (*ditloo*), *dithlodi*, and *dithotse* from *lerotse* (dried beans and a sort of pumpkin seed). *Dithlodi* are called green mung beans in English. It is a plant species in the legume family, such as cowpeas (*monawa*), beans, peas and lentils.

During harvest time, depending on the rain, there would be plenty to harvest from the fields: watermelons, traditional sugar cane, beans and so on. For relish, we would go and catch edible insects such as locusts (*mammati*), grasshoppers (*makgenthwane*), caterpillars (*dikodi*), all delicious and nutritious; very healthy.

Alternatively, we would go and pick (*go kga*) wild plants for relish (*morogo*) such as *leroto* (*gyrandropsis pentaphylla*), *theepe* (*amaranthus thunbergii*) and pigweed (*serepelele*), which were stewed and eaten with porridge (*pap*) as vegetables. Other wild spinach (*morogo*) is *letlowane* or sugar bean leaves (*morogo was monawa*), and even fried *lerotso* seeds (*dithotse*). Gourds such as citron (*lerotse*), watermelon (*legapu*), calabash (*leraka*) and pumpkin (*lefodi*) were used to make food utensils (*digo, mokgopu, magapa*) as were sweet reeds. *Lerotse* is a plant species in the watermelon family (*legapu*) but it is not sweet. We also used it to make porridge, which I loved very much, and it was also very delicious and healthy.

During the harvest seasons, creepers such as *monawa* and *leroto* give green *morogo* that can be cooked and dried (*mokhusa*), that is, processed so that they are preserved for winter when there is no rain or for a drought season (*go khusa*). I still received dried *morogo* that my mother-in-law and later my sister-in- law kept for us. My husband and I enjoyed that.

Sadly, because of climate change and other negative factors, those who still want to plough are unable to do so. This is exacerbated by acculturation; people are no longer eating those delicacies because they find them outdated. They prefer Western food, and it is such a pity. It was very rare that people then would easily get sick because of the healthy, fresh food we ate.

Domesticated animals provided people with much needed protein, for example animal products such as milk, meat and eggs. Those who had herds of cattle and goats would have plenty of milk that they turned into sour milk such as *Inkomazi* or *Maswi* that people could still eat their porridge with. Some had plenty of raw fresh milk that they would drink. Though traditional, they were not so ignorant and they understood hygiene in that they would boil the milk before drinking it. Children were taught to wash their hands before eating and so forth. The goat milk was quite delicious but very scarce.

Food preservation was very important because then people did not have fridges, so the sun played a vital part. Other than pasteurising milk or drying green *morogo*, in the instances when there was plenty of fresh meat, it was dried out into biltong (*megwapa*). We would put salt and ground pepper on it, cut it into sizeable strips and hang it on a rope outside to dry. During harvesting, the wind also played an important part because it helped in removing the chaff from the grain. These were very important life skills that I learnt growing up.

Over and above gathering (*go sela*) edible wild fruits, plants and insects, people hunted (*go tsoma*) edible wild animals such as buck (*phala*), duiker (*phuti*) and hares (*mebutla*) to complement their diet.

While growing up there was this woman in the neighbourhood who had lots of goats. She shepherded them every day. I think she was the only woman who had livestock because this role was deemed to be the preserve of men only. We used to accompany her to a grazing area in the veld. She always carried enamel dishes with her, and towards lunch she would milk the goats (*maswi a pudi*) and mix it with this edible fruit that looks like a tomato, but they are wild, green and bitter in taste (*dithola*). The milk would immediately turn sour and thicken. She would pour the milk in a dish and mix it with sorghum pap left over from the previous night (*molatsa*). She would then share this with us. It was very delicious and we loved it; hence, we did not mind assisting her in looking after her goats. I realise that goats' milk nowadays is preserved in the form of powder and sold in supermarkets, but it is very expensive.

Apart from these foraging activities, I enjoyed playing, especially with boys. I liked climbing trees and I could go for the tallest tree and come down without a scratch. Children of my age group used to get hurt from falling and some would land up in hospital. I so much liked playing that when my peers came calling for me, I ran crazy.

There was this incident that bore testimony to that. I went to church with my parents, and immediately I got home, before I could change my church clothes into playing clothes, my friends came calling for me. I would normally play barefoot. Although I always had running shoes (sneakers), other children did not have shoes, so I would take mine off. I was, however, still wearing my church shoes then. I did not want them to leave me behind and I realised that if I had to take my shoes off and put them in the house I would waste time. So, I threw them through the window of a thatch rondavel house we used for cooking; that is, as a kitchen.

We used wood to make fire for cooking on the floor and used three-legged foot cast iron pots (*drievoet* in Afrikaans). After cooking, the wood would burn into ash with no discernible flame until it died out. At the time I that I threw my shoes through the window, the fire was still smouldering and one of my shoes got burnt very badly. I did not notice as I had already flown away to join my friends. The shoe was discovered in the evening when preparing fire for supper. I got a real hiding from my mother.

Since there was no infrastructures such as running water, sewage or electricity, or tarred roads, the nearby rocks and trees served as toilets and, as already said, water was fetched from rivers and wells. Of course, we were all used to darkness, the only source of light being that of moonlight. When there was enough light from a full moon, we would play outside until late in the night, especially during the summer holidays and on weekends when we were not going to school. There were games for that period like *di-thai*, *dinonwane* (folklore or story telling), *bolopi* (hide and seek) etcetera. When it was raining quietly (*modupi*) – that is, it was not stormy – children would play in the rain naked (*matlampulele*). I was fond of that.

Then we did not have crime like we have now, so playing alone outside never posed any danger. Sekhukhune is very hot in the summer season and most people would sleep outside without fear of being attacked. The only things they feared were snakes (*dinoga*) and scorpions (*phepheng* and *kgome*), which are very dangerous if they happen to bite you. I was never stung. I want to believe people in that environment were immune to their bites. Nonetheless, people knew how to treat bites and how to immunise one another.

I remember very well when my mother and aunt used to sleep outside with all the children, usually when there was moonlight. I did not quite like it. I was afraid of the moon, especially since I was told that images reflected in the moon are those of Ananias and Sapphira. We simply called her Saraphina (their story is found in the bible, Acts 5:1 to 11). I also used to be afraid of moving clouds and a rainbow.

I liked sitting alone sometimes, when everyone was away, especially on a Sunday. I would sit on the corner alone and watch clouds moving, and I used to see them forming images such as of a lion, horse, anything. Then I would get scared and walk away. The same happened when watching a rainbow. After rain, it would descend across the horizon and I would spend much time staring at it, wondering how it formed. Ultimately, I would start to be afraid and would stop looking at it. For some reason, God's natural, mysterious things used to scare me.

I was also afraid of stormy weather. As soon as I saw dark rain clouds gathering, I knew that the storm was coming and would run if I was somewhere a bit far from home. Once it started raining, I would go straight into the house, reach for a blanket and cover myself to sleep. In most cases, I would not even eat supper. The rain would normally come in the afternoon. Ga-Masemola was prone to (*ledimo*) a very strong, scary wind that raised red dust: something like a hurricane or tornado.

I liked playing, but in some instances I was not good company to other children as I liked fighting too. I was good at it, to the point that almost every child became scared of me. As a result, I became a bully, as I liked provoking the other children, especially boys, without any reason but just to make excuses for beating them up if they resisted. My mother used to be so frustrated with my behaviour, but giving me a hiding did not help. Each day, a mother would bring a crying child to my mother, to report that I'd beaten them up: boys or girls, it was the same. Sometimes I would even provoke people older than me. There were those who would beat me, though, but I would get revenge whenever I get the opportunity to.

Beating other children's faces, especially boys, became my hobby, and I just enjoyed it, not realising how traumatised they would become, or that bullying other children was not so cool because I just alienated myself.

I remember very well one fateful afternoon. It was during winter, and I went to fetch water from the river. During dry seasons such as winter, we would dig up wells because there was not much running water; besides, wells provided us with clean fresh water unlike the running one as mentioned above. There were these two sissy-like boys. They stayed with their grandmother; I do not know what had happened to their parents. They did not have a sister and their grandmother was too old to go to fetch water that far away, so they would come to fetch water. Somehow, they just became my daily soft targets. I would beat them every day, and they would not even try to fight back. It happened so often that their grandmother got tired of reporting me to my mother and I suspect that she must have tipped them to fight me back and teach me a lesson.

One day after school, I went to fetch water. I found them at the river, next to a well, and I provoked them as usual. They ganged up against me and beat the hell out of me. They were so angry that they even tried to drown me in the well and they almost killed me by choking. Fortunately, I managed to get loose. The other children must have been fed up with me too, as they just watched. I learnt a lesson and stopped my silly bullying tendency for good.

I am reminded of one incident. There was a girl of my age in the neighbourhood who played the game that I loved with me. It was called *diketo*. We would dig out a small hole in the ground and put in it several well selected small stones (pebbles), mostly the ones that looked like a granite (*magakabje*). One can only be declared a winner of this game if one manages to pick all the stones out of the hole. One scrabbles these out the hole after throwing another stone into the air, the objective being to get as many stones out before catching the thrown stone.

If I lost, a fight would ensue and I would beat her for beating me in the game. In most cases, she would cry and run home. Her mother always asked her to stop playing with me, but she kept on coming to play with me. One day, she decided to fight back. I guess that she was just tired of the beatings. When she realised that she could not overpower me, she sank her teeth between my breasts and bit me so hard that blood came out. It was very painful and took a long time to heal. My mother reprimanded me and told me that I should stop fighting other children. Even today, the scar is still visible.

Talking about bullying, which is a big problem nowadays in schools, it is such a horrible thing because it hurts both the bully and the bullied. I remember how I used to cry every time my victims started crying, but I would not stop because it became a habit, or let's say an addiction, for me. I never actually enjoyed it. It becomes a state of mind, and it needs to be addressed immediately because if the child does not outgrow it, she or he will become abusive growing up (it is an impulse disorder). I am a testimony to that.

Although I liked playing, there were times when I would opt to be alone and do my own things. More than anything, I enjoyed my solitude, and I still do today. One of my hobbies was sewing and knitting. I mastered that at a very early age. Since we did not have sewing machines and needles were very scarce, I would improvise by using my own self-invented needles made from the thorns of a tree called *Acacia polyacantha* (*moshwana*). I would open a hole at the end that was not sharp, steal my mother's cottons and get pieces of cloth that were not used to make small dresses for dolls. Fortunately, my father used to buy us toys and the children in the neighbourhood would come to play with us, very envious.

In the event that I did not have old cloth, I would undo one of my dresses and try to start it from scratch. Sometimes, when I had a chance, I would steal real needles but, being a child, I would lose them and I would get a hiding from my mother. I became so good with my hands that I used to assist my aunt's daughters, who were much older than me, with their craft homework and they would get good marks.

My mother told me that I always had this urge to cry for no apparent reason. She said that the tendency used to bother her until she got used to it. I would come over to her to ask for permission to go and cry. Once permission was granted, I would sit there in the corner and cry for real, and when I was done I would go back to her or my aunt to report that I was finished. They would just say okay, and off I would go to play. Until today, I still have that crying urge and I still cry. Afterwards, I feel satisfied. The thing with me is that I can cry and laugh at the same time.

I also find it difficult to hold grudges. Even when I am angry and crying, and someone makes a joke, I just laugh between tears. I do not know whether it is normal, or if it is a disorder of some kind. I would be interested to know what psychologists would say.

It was only when I went to Standard 2 that I graduated from learning under the tree. I was taught in a proper classroom (mud-built school). For me, it was a form of achievement, and I really took pride in that. In every class I had been, the teachers always liked me. It was a form of status to be sent around by a teacher to do some errands for them.

Every Wednesday was a gardening day. We used to have a vegetable garden patch in the school yard. Boys were responsible for tending the garden, while girls would go to fetch water from the river and water the vegetables. But, once the produce was ready to be harvested, the teachers would share it among themselves, and we got nothing.

One afternoon, my teacher called me and asked me to carry her share/ration of vegetables to her house. It was beetroot and other things. Beetroot happened to be the only vegetable I'd never tasted before. Not aware that the teacher had counted them, while at a distance from the school I was tempted to eat one raw beetroot. I sat down behind a grey succulent plant called sisal – there were plenty of them around the school yard – trying, of course, to hide myself from passers-by, and I started eating it. One could imagine what my mouth and gums, even my teeth, looked like: I was red all over, including my hands. To my disappointment, it was not even nice to eat raw. I then took the rest to her cottage.

My teacher was not from ga-Masemola and she was boarding in one of the houses close to the school. I put the vegetables where I had been instructed to, locked the door and put the keys safely where I had been told to hide them. I went straight home.

The teacher discovered that I had taken one of the beetroots. She reported me to my mother, who reprimanded and lectured me about the importance of being honest. She reminded me about the Ten Commandments. Then I knew them by heart; I'd memorised them. I was so embarrassed that I went and apologised to the teacher. I told her the truth that I had never eaten a beetroot before and I'd just wanted to taste it. She forgave me and continued liking me anyway.

When the homeland system came into being, the homeland administrators tried to improve the situation in our communities. Ga-Masemola was one of the areas in which a magisterial office was built, next to the chieftain's homestead. I was completing my Standard 2 classes when the building was completed. Due to the shortage of classrooms, the Standards 3 and 4 children were moved from Arkona Primary School to go and attend schooling in one of the empty offices. I happened to be among those Standard 3 pupils because I'd passed my Standard 2.

I have already mentioned that the Chief's homestead was about ten kilometres from Arkona, where the real school was. So, I travelled that distance twice every day. It was never so much of an issue for me. The only problem was that I could not go home during school lunch break, to go and eat left over food of sorghum porridge, *morogo* or porridge made of beans (*dinawa*) called *semotwane* from the previous night (supper). Tea and bread were luxuries and we only had them during Christmas or when my father came home for his annual leave. On most days, other children like me would go without food for the whole day because they did not have relatives or friends close by.

I was lucky because next to the school there were relatives of my mother. She arranged with them that I could eat there during break time: the same porridge with *morogo*. I went there for a couple months, but as time went by I realised that things had changed and they were no longer happy with the arrangement. I did not know why, but as I happened to be observant I sensed discomfort and some vibes around me whenever I was there, so I stopped going and told my mother.

As mentioned earlier, I had a friend by the name Obeolekae (meaning, where were you all this time?). Perhaps her parents struggled to have children, for she was an only child. Obeolekae's home was adjacent to the chief's kraal, as her father was brother to the chief and he was one of his right-hand men. I did not like going there every day, since I never wanted to be a burden to other people. I learnt to live with what I had and to be content at a very early age, and this included enduring hunger. She would invite me to come along with her to go and eat lunch. I did not like the arrangement. I felt that it was not fair for her to have to share with me, so I started giving excuses every time she invited me until she gave up.

One day when we went on break, a distant relative of mine asked me to come along to his house. He wanted to introduce me to his parents because he had told them about me, and his parents knew my parents very well. He is a midget, dwarf, or little person (his name is Mookwane Tsetsewa) and so was his father and five of his siblings. I had never seen a midget before, but I was beginning to get used to him as we had been in the same class together since Sub A. The only thing that shocked me was when I visited his home: seeing so many midgets mingling around was so scary that I almost cried. His two sisters were tiny but not deformed, and they were very, very pretty, amazingly beautiful. His other brother was also a midget but not deformed. But Mookwane and his other siblings were deformed, with bowing of tibia, trident hands, and wide feet, as well as big heads and short stature with big bumps as well as deep voices. The father was well built too, though a midget. Their mother was very tall and normal, as was his younger sister. Ironically, he went to the same teachers' college as my husband.

I performed well in all the standards. There were only two children who would sometimes beat me to position two: my friend Lina Ramushu and Mookwane Tsetsewa. They were a real threat to me. Mookwane liked me so much that he would protect me from bullying boys. Not that I would not have confronted the bully boys and fought back, but I appreciated his protection. I am still very stubborn, but with age I can control myself: something called maturity.

While still young, I could not control my stubbornness nor my rage. One day after school, there was an older boy who owned a bicycle. He would ride it back home after school and every time he would expect us to move off the road for him to pass as he came flying by on his bicycle. I grew tired of being pushed off the road and getting pierced by thorns, so I refused to move. He just rode over me. I fell and sustained scratches from the rough gravel road. He too lost control of his bike and fell so badly, and he accused me of being responsible. He wanted to beat me, but I was ready to fight back, so he took his bicycle and left. I also believe that I suffered from short person syndrome: my peers would tease me about my height. I took after my father. He was very short and equally stubborn.

Apart from Mookwane's constant invite to his house during lunch break, I also got an invite from my other distant relative who stayed not far from school. His name was Elliot Matsemela (I am using the past tense because he died by suicide: he burnt himself to death although he was already grown up then.) Somehow, I became comfortable with the arrangements.

I remember that other children in my class gave me a nickname "Matonse". I had a very thin waistline, and every time I wrapped my school girdle around my gym dress it became so thin that I was associated with a monkey called Matonse. I never knew what it meant; I guess it was just a name. The monkey in the prescribed book was domesticated and the owner tied it on a pole at its waist. The story was in the only prescribed book that I had: that was Bantu education. The other children would tease me every time we read about it. At the beginning, I felt very offended and upset, at times angry, until I got used to it. Mookwane – although very short in physique and looked fragile, he had a very big thick voice – would stand up and reprimanded those who made a joke about my waist.

I was taught by a lady teacher who liked me very much. Every Wednesday we had a craft work session. We were taught how to knit children's jerseys, socks and hoods. She also taught other subjects, though. She liked me so much that she would ask me to help carry the steel trunk or kist (it was called a *trommel*, maybe in Afrikaans) for storing our craft work until the next class. It was like the one boarding school students used to carry to school for storing their clothes and all necessities in.

We were not allowed to take our crafts home with us. I do not know why they were not left at school, but I guess there was not enough storage space in the class, or perhaps it was for security purposes. Anyway, it was such an honour for me to

The Story of a Rural Girl Who Kept Rising and Rising

carry it, but imagine carrying it on my head for stretch of about ten kilometres.

I had this thing of wanting to outshine other classmates in everything I did. Whenever we were given a task, I would ensure that I was the one to finish first. I remember one afternoon when we were taught to knit woollen hoods. I immediately started knitting very fast; the idea was to finish before everyone else, but I made a lot of mistakes in the process. The teacher would ask us to knit one portion and submit it to her for inspection and correction. I finished first and submitted to her. As she was inspecting my work for corrections, she picked up mistakes and she pointed out to me that I had jumped three stitches, which left holes, and I must undo and rectify that.

I saw red. I was furious with rage. I do not know what got into me but I lost it. In other words, I wondered who she was to correct me. I started throwing such a tantrum that I grabbed the knitting from her hands and started tearing at it with my teeth. She went for a cane that she used to punish us with: corporal punishment was allowed then. She gave me the worst hiding anyone had ever given me. She was so angry that she stopped the class before time and instructed me to carry the steel trunk to her house. She was very disappointed in me.

On my way to her house, I tried to figure out how to rectify the whole mess. I decided to steal the knitting, and took it home and started working on it so that I could still finish before everyone else. She must have suspected that I would do exactly that. She went and checked in the trunk: my knitting was missing.

During that time, most people could not afford to buy maize meal from the shops. Instead, households would have stone millets used for grinding *mabele* seeds (sorghum seeds), for *pap*. In addition, there was a communal millet grinding stone (*malwala*) engraved on a gigantic boulder (outcrop) that planted itself on the ground and spread over a large area. It was called *dinalaleng*. There were so many of them that every family would have individual *lwala*. I think there were more than twenty holes for millet on that flat surface of huge rock. I am told they were there for many generations. It was used by young girls and boys (I mentioned earlier that at ga-Masemola, where Christians resided, girls and boys performed the same house chores and there were no gendered roles). Meanwhile, adults would prefer those that were found in the homesteads.

I went with other children to such a place. While busy grinding seeds, my younger sister was sent for me. I was called to come home immediately as my mother wanted to talk to me. I left everything and went, but something started nagging at me and I suspected that it was about my behaviour at school. My instinct was correct. Upon entering a one-roomed thatched mud-walled rondavel, my teacher was sitting with my mother around the small table.

In one corner, my parents' bed could be seen elevated on tins. The space underneath it doubled as storage for shoes and other things. There was no wall dividing the hut into a bedroom; instead they used a cloth for privacy. My siblings and I slept on a reed mat on the floor. In another corner could be seen a very strong, large chest or kist (*poporomente*, probably Afrikaans). It was used to store blankets, sheets and our clothes. Near the head of the bed, on the wall, hung my father's suits and coats. Next to this was a wooden unit or cupboard (*raka*) for storing enamel plates and mugs, as well as a bit of crockery. In the middle was a small wooden table with four chairs. On the wall overlooking the table were my parents' wedding photos, their individual studio photos shown before, and the one of us children shown below. Towards the entrance were three pictures: that of Mary, Jesus' mother; Jesus and His disciples sitting around the table (the last supper, I suppose); and that scary picture of hairy Nebuchadnezzar turned into an animal. Almost every Christian household had similar pictures.

Seeing my teacher, I just knew immediately that I was in trouble. Without wasting time, before I could even sit down, my mother wanted to know why I had stolen my knitting work. She was very angry with me and demanded that I brought it to them. I did and she gave it to the teacher, who gave me a strong warning, and my mother promised my teacher that she would teach me a lesson. I truly had disappointed her and had betrayed the trust she had in me.

My mother did not give me a hiding, but I was so ashamed that I could not look either woman in the face. I tried to behave well for a long time at school, especially in the presence of the teacher in question, to avoid upsetting her. In fact, I learnt not to do things quickly so that I could outshine everyone, but to do everything well: that is, right the first time. Until today I am still a good knitter, I make beautiful winter jerseys for myself with two needles or a crochet needle, exactly as I was taught then.

When I think of these things, I wonder what was going on in her head. I pitied her with so many regrets, but she engraved in me a life and precious lesson that, in everything one does, one must do it right the first time. I was amazed when I studied for my diploma in Total Quality Management (TQM) many years after that its motto was "Do it right the first time".

Besides my obsession with playing, I also liked learning some house chores, and I would observe and try to imitate the things that adults would do, such as making fire and preparing meals. One afternoon, it was around December month, a week before

Christmas, my mother and my aunt were busy preparing for Christmas when I requested that I help them with the cooking. I made fire for the first time, filled the self-made kettle made of galvanised zinc and placed it on a *drievoet* (three legged pot) that was also placed on top of the wood fire.

I became aware that my mother was watching me as I was working, so I started chatting to her. I forgot to tell you that I spoke a lot, including talking back whenever I was reprimanded, despite the fact that I would get a hiding. This is something I am not proud of, but something that tells me that I was a rebellious child.

This reminds me of one incident. My aunt, who loved me a lot, tried to give me a hiding one day. I do not remember what it was that I did to her but it must have been bad because she really spoiled me and never reprimanded me like she would to other children, including hers.

My aunt had beautiful hair and she looked after it. I remember how I was the only one who used to accompany her to a traditional salon to shampoo her hair. There was a spot next to a riverbank where a groundcover plant with beautiful pink colours called devil's claw (*Harpagophytum*) used to grow. It had a lot of foam when put on the hair and she used that to wash her hair.

Like a spoiled brat, I could not understand why that particular day she wanted to punish me. I jumped and got hold of her shirt and ripped all the buttons open: that was rage. She was very tall, the same as my mother and my elder aunt. My mother was there. She could have beaten me, but that day she froze. She was really dumbfounded. I felt so sorry for my aunt and I apologised and never did it again. But these kind of behaviours from children should be corrected while they are still small and should not be entertained at all.

I have spoken a lot about my mother beating me as a way of punishing me for misbehaving. Although I do not subscribe to beating as a way of punishing children, I cannot associate it with unreasonable violence because she never had to punish me without any reason. She would point to the reason why she had to beat me and therefore it was not abuse. For her, it was necessary instrument in disciplining me. I am not trying to justify physical violence *vis-a-vis* disciplining children, nor intending to express gratitude to my mother for beating me. I know of children with whom I grew up who were not beaten despite their behaviour and who still turned out to be aggressive and violent individuals, very unruly and ill-disciplined.

Those who argue that their parents' punishment by beating shaped them into disciplined individuals say it how they see it. I beg to argue that God created people in different ways for whatever reason. If you are born delinquent or ill-disciplined and rebellious, no amount of beating or lack thereof could change you into a different individual to how God designed you to be. I, therefore, find it difficult to link the type of violence we experience in this country to how children are disciplined at home. There are children who at some stage became rebellious, which goes together with violence, and outgrew it; some do not grow out of it even in adulthood.

When I grew up, I heard people saying this is a family of stubborn people who like fighting and violence. Other families were not or were a mixture. It depends on where the child's genes are stronger: mother or father. Abolishing corporal punishment in schools on the basis that it promotes violence is neither here nor there. For me, crime and violence that has engulfed South Africa could be attributed to lawlessness, eroded morals, norms and values – and as for gender-based violence, that is a result of patriarchy, period. It results from how as a society we bring up and socialise our boy children.

But back to my cooking experiment. The water in the kettle started boiling. I had already washed the three-legged cast-iron pot and prepared for cooking porridge. I removed the kettle from the fire and put it aside, brought the pot closer so that I could fill it with boiling water, not aware that the pot was too close to my right foot, just above the heel. I started pouring and talking to my mother at the same time. I was pouring boiling water inside my running shoe (sneaker) instead. My mother was watching and no longer talking because she realised what was happening. She just froze. I was cooking myself, apparently.

I could not feel anything in the beginning because the water poured over my shoe first. Perhaps afraid of screaming at me in case I threw away the kettle and burned myself or someone else, she said to me, "You are burning yourself". I started feeling the heat penetrating my flesh and began screaming. I was badly burnt. As there were no clinics nearby, they only used traditional remedies for the wound.

When my father came home a day before Christmas and found me burnt, he was shocked. I saw tears running down his cheeks quietly. I could not wear my new shoes for Christmas but, being myself, I insisted on putting them on. It was very painful and impossible to walk. My leg was heavily bandaged.

I was, however, not prepared to miss an opportunity to show off my Vaseline shoes. The type of shoes my father would buy for us from Woolworths were shiny and looked as if they were smeared with Vaseline, hence Vaseline shoes. I decided to at least put one shoe on and to walk to church and then to the chief's Kraal. I would not miss that for anything. I was in so much pain when I came back that I could not sleep. I got better before the schools re-opened but was still limping. The scar is still there. I suspect that it was a third-degree burn.

It was not the first time that I got burnt, I was told that I got burnt on a fire brazier (*mpaola*) in Alexandra, where my father used to stay. My mother and my elder sister regularly went there for a visit, although, I was too young to remember the incident. My younger sister was not yet born then. I am told that my parents were in the house. I was playing with other children outside, and decided to go back home. Apparently, the fire brazier was put on a *stoep* (veranda), to stop us falling on it. I decided to take a short cut to the house by climbing onto the stoep and was forced to move along the wall that the stoep was running along. I got too close to the brazier and it burnt me. I still have the scar running across my left thigh.

photo of my parents, myself on the left and my elder sister

Before my parents, siblings and I left ga-Masemola, there was a big dam built on Ngwaritsi River called Piet Gous Dam. During the period that the dam was constructed, we stopped going to fetch water from the river or near its vicinity, so I never knew what was happening behind the mountains. One day, we children decided to go to the top of the mountain. Our parents' houses were built below it. We stood there and looked down and I got the shock of my life. The dam was completed and filled with water. I had never seen so much water, not even when it rained and the rivers were overflowing. Looking from that spot I would normally have seen fields stretching up to the riverbank, but seeing water covering all the fields made me frightened. I want to believe that that was the reason I developed the fear of water and heights I still have today. The good thing is that people were supplied with water from the dam and the villagers' lives were improved. Now they have taps at the corner of the streets or in their yards.

The downside is that most of the people lost their fields as a result, gave up on the subsistence form of farming and that way of life, and became impoverished and destitute. My parents and others were not affected, so they kept their parents' field and they ploughed every year. Children would assist in the field with tasks such as howing and harvesting because we survived by being fed from those crops once harvested.

Before tractors, people used donkeys and a hoe (*mogoma*) for ploughing and carried the harvested crops using donkey carts. Those who did not have the means to hire donkey carts would fill bags and carry them on their heads. Only the lazy would go hungry because those without fields to plough could still work for their neighbours, family or friends and get their share.

Of significance or importance is that ga-Masemola is a place where my whole placenta was buried because my mother gave birth at home. My mother told me that she cut my umbilical cord herself after birth, because there was no one to help her. I came earlier than she expected and took everyone off guard. She told me that it had some symbolic meaning for her, and it was joyous to have had the opportunity to be the one cutting the link between us. I was the only one born at home because both my sisters were born in hospital. In the past, most people gave birth at home because of the lack of health facilities and they buried the placentas in the yard, not discarding it as is the case in hospitals, where they are regarded as medical waste.

In many traditional communities burying a placenta has some significance and hence they honour it. Although I know that in my community the placenta was honoured, I do not know the significance. Even if a child was born in hospital, the midwife would cut the baby's cord from the placenta and tie the remaining stump to pinch it off. Once the umbilical cord (*kalana*) dried out after a couple of days, it was allowed to fall off on its own before the thin cotton that tied it was removed. Once fallen off, the stump was buried in the same way as the placenta and was given the same significance. The same rituals were performed when our milk teeth came out. I remember how we used to bury our milk teeth in a hole and begged our fairy godmothers to restore them to us, more splendid than before.

Chapter Two

MY LIFE WITH MY PATERNAL FAMILY

I was thirteen years old when my parents decided to relocate to my father's birthplace, the other side of Lepelle River (*noka*) (Olifants River). My parents and two of my siblings left ga-Masemola for good to go to ga-Maraba. It was the most painful day for me. I was my aunt's favourite child, and I loved her children. Leaving them behind was the most hurtful thing for me. I remember how we all cried when a truck came to fetch us; it still feels like yesterday.

The day did not end up without a drama for me. One of the most popular kinds of work in rural areas then was people moving around, selling soft goods. One of the men who moved around selling came to our house. I had decided to play alone that mid-morning, and I went and played next to the salesperson's car. As I was playing and inspecting the car, I noticed that towards the rear of the car, next to the passenger seat, there was an opening with a lid. I had never seen it on my father's car (I later discovered that it was the petrol cap). I opened the lid, took it and moved on to play somewhere else alone. They started calling me to come home because we were about to leave. I ran home. In the meantime, the owner of the car was also leaving.

He tried to start the car but it would not start. He discovered that the lid was missing, and I was told that the car would not start. They looked everywhere, and I could not remember where I had left it. I felt so much pity for the man, but I was afraid to tell them that I had taken it. I was so afraid that they would soon discover or suspect me that I really wanted to get into the car so that we could drive off. But my mother would not leave without saying a prayer. The man was very angry and frantic, but he was not sure whether it might have fallen off on the way on the bumpy gravel road.

We finally left and I never told anyone of my part in the drama. My mother would be so angry with me, and I could not risk that.

Even though we lived apart for almost a bigger part of our lives due to the migrant labour system, I can gladly describe my father as someone who gave me a normal and therefore wonderful childhood in abnormal circumstances. He was a wonderful husband to my mother. Of course, he was not infallible – he was just human with his own weaknesses – but like any child I still loved him. I loved both my parents dearly. I truly chastised him for some of his flaws, especially when my mother was affected.

My father always protected us, something that made me grateful for the times we had together and feel lucky when I saw people whose fathers were alive but might as well be dead. So, when both my parents died within a year of each other, I found solace and closure in the knowledge that they were good parents. My life came full circle, though I was shocked.

Although my father did not want to settle with his own people, he made it a point that every time he was on leave he would take us there to meet his sisters and relatives. His parents died before I was born. His father died, of old age I am told – that is, natural causes – and his mother died while giving birth to his younger brother. My father was himself

still young then, and his elder sister and father brought him up. I think that the decision to move back home was initiated by his elder sister because she used to come to ga-Masemola to visit us, and she kept on telling us that we did not belong there. My father loved her more than all his siblings, maybe because she played the role of mother to him after her mother's death. My father had a one-room rondavel built in his brother's yard; I am told the stand belonged to their parents.

Going to ga-Maraba, we passed Pietersburg, now Polokwane town. I would always be so fascinated when we stopped at the fish and chips shop owned by a Portuguese/Greek national. My father bought each of us a packet of chips and slices of white bread; probably cold drink as well, I do not remember. I had never eaten chips before, although of course I used to eat fish that my cousin used to catch from one of the rivers in ga-Masemola.

The other interesting thing was to see a railway for the first time. There is a train rail at a level crossing immediately one leaves Polokwane town, in the direction of ga-Maraba. When driving towards the railway line I saw a passenger and goods trains passing by. I had never seen a train before and I was stunned.

My father owned a second-hand Volkswagen. Before that he had one called a Leyland, and he was perceived by everyone in the community as a rich man. We drove to Polokwane in my father's car, followed by the truck carrying our belongings. The distance from ga-Masemola to ga-Maraba is about 117 kilometres. Although I had been to visit my father's relatives many times, I was always excited when we passed Polokwane town. The buildings were so beautiful: in fact, everything was just amazing. Tarred roads, clean streets, lights and civilisation all about. I had never seen so many cars and people moving around in that fashion, especially so many whites. The only time I saw white people were those railway bus drivers who used to transport my father from Johannesburg Park Station to home during Christmas time, or doctors at one of the hospitals.

The Kalkspruit landscape was very different from ga-Masemola in that it was not mountainous but has lots of hills and valleys that create slopes that make the landscape uneven. The weather is also very different. Masemola's is very hot and humid, while Kalkspruit's is very cold, especially in winter, and often misty. The fog gets very thick and it can be difficult to see anything in the distance. Even in summer, it sometimes gets chilly. It is unique and different from most of the areas in Limpopo. It has granite stones called *magakabje* that makes it look dry and barren.

People there used dried cow dung for cooking because the place was so barren. Although there are forests with big trees, they are far away. In our area, there are only shrubs that bear fruits such as *dithetlwa* (African raisins), *dikgoto* and *mabilo*, all very delicious and nutritious. The only people who would travel miles and miles away looking for firewood were those who did not have heads of cattle.

Everything was totally different. The houses were arranged in a very systemic manner in that they had streets and stand numbers. They looked organised and clean when compared to ga-Masemola. I was told that initially people had built their houses the same way as ga-Masemola and other areas. But in 1936 the government introduced the Native Trust and Land Act, as amended (1913 Land Act). Communities were moved around and forced to stay in those areas that were allocated to them, even if they did not want to. Hence these were referred to as forced removals.

The same as ga-Masemola, there were no pit latrines when we got there. Shrub bushes were used as toilets. The area had very huge ant hills I had never seen before and they were also used for the purpose. Because people did not have toilet paper, they used small stones to clean themselves. But there was something I observed that I had never witnessed before: small children were taught to clean themselves by rubbing their bums on the ground so that the soil cleaned them, rather than them trying to use stones. It was only later that people started erecting latrine toilets for themselves.

Drinking water was collected from a windmill or boreholes using pumps to extract water out from the ground, simply known as *pompi*. The portion of land allocated for cattle grazing was cordoned off by razor wire to separate it from residential areas. Animals were not allowed to roam around the residential area; they were only brought back in the afternoon because every household with livestock had a kraal for both cows and sheep in their yard. Goats were not preferred because there were no mountains or rocks. Their fields were small and had numbers, just like their house stands. Otherwise, everything was almost the same.

Towards the winter season, there was this practice of burning the grass (veld fire). I had never seen such raging wildfires before. The vast livestock camp would be engulfed by flames and I used to be so scared. It was only set alight in the evening, once all the animals had returned home. Although the fire would have died down by the following day, the animals were not allowed to graze at a place that had been burnt to avoid injuries from smouldering ash. The camp was burnt in sections so that some areas would still be safe for grazing. The camp burning was only allowed in autumn. The reason for that, I am told, was to burn the old grass so that once the rainy season came it could grow afresh. In other words, the wildfire helped new vegetation to grow. After the fire died down and we went to fetch wood, we could see that most of the small animals had died from the fire. I thought it was very cruel.

The place had lots of jackals (*diphukubje*) and they would make a lot of noise in the night; it was my first encounter with them and that was very scary, but I eventually got used to them.

There was lots of wild fruit, though what was also different from ga-Masemola was that many households had orchards of peach trees and prickly pears, as well as fig trees.

Kalkspruit was not different from any other traditional setting. Women were and are still not valued, although things have changed to some extent. But, because patriarchy is still practised, it plays an important role in controlling people's lives. Then, for example, unmarried women were not allowed to have their own properties, even if they had children, nor fields to plough. This was some form of punishment for those who had children out of wedlock (*mafetwa*); again the idea of been childless and husbandless was also stigmatised, something that pushed many women into polygamous relationships or into a system whereby a woman was married for the family (*go nyalela lapa*).

This happened in a situation where a woman was married into a particular family for various reasons, such as when parents passed on and there was no one to take over the household. In most cases, she would be from a very poor family and she was married off so that she could take over the surname of that family and bear children to ensure that surname did not die. If she did not have children of her own and she was still young, she would be forced to cohabit with one of the male relatives, even if they had their own families, for the purpose of bearing children for that family. This is the extent to which the so-called culture and tradition could go in oppressing women.

Fortunately, in Kalkspruit, a female chief was coronated after her husband died. She was educated, a teacher by profession, and very progressive. One of the most positive things she did for women who were not married was to do away with a system that prevented or restricted them from owning houses or land. This was on the basis that they did not have husbands but they wanted to move out of their parents' homestead and build their own houses. So, empty land was made available and demarcated into new stands. Part of this land was taken from the land reserved for animal grazing. There were also plenty of infill stands, and they were allocated and filled. The other factor was a population explosion. Younger men who'd started establishing their families also wanted to move out of the homesteads and build their own houses. They were also allocated stands and the grazing land became smaller and smaller.

There were people who went to look for employment on the surrounding white farms and settled there for years as they started their families. I do not know the reasons why most of them left the farms and started to look for settlement areas in the nearby villages such as ga-Maraba (Kalkspruit), but the chieftainess allocated stands to them. As people moved into the grazing lands, the ecosystem was disturbed. For instance, there are no longer jackals in the area. The shrubs that used to bear fruits were cut down to clear land for building houses. People also started chopping trees and dried them at home for making fire and cooking.

Lately, the chiefs are allocating the land that was used as fields to people for settlement, because most of the community members no longer plough or till the land due to the scarce rainfall, as well as climate issues exacerbated by climate change. Hence, one come across glaring poverty and destitution. Lack of employment also adds to the ravaging poverty in the rural areas.

Reverting back to my school years, we relocated to ga-Maraba or Kalkspruit in December month, after the closing of schools for the festive season. The following year, I went to school there. I attended my higher primary at John Nrimbha High Primary. I did my Standards 4, 5 and 6 there. The school is named after the Ndebele Chief, John Nrimbha Maraba, Nrimbha is an Ndebele word meaning *Thipa* in North Sotho (a knife).

Ndebele from that part of Limpopo is not written nor read. Instead, the vernacular language taught is Northern Sotho, spoken by Sekhukhuneland people. The way we spoke, our accent was unfamiliar to people in Kalkspruit, so other children used to mock how we spoke. The Sepedi language, also-called Northern Sotho, has lots of waves when compared to Northern Sotho spoken by people from ga-Matlala and Moletjie. Northern Sotho has various dialects and creoles.

The school uniform colours were a black tunic with a white or khaki shirt. The girdle had black and white trimmings, and so did the jersey. It was trimmed with black and white colours on the neck, sleeve cuffs and bottom. The only thing I took time to get used to was the cold. The winter there is very cold.

The place also had a Christian and non-Christian area, but the emphasis on the differences was not as great as at ga-Masemola. Both my aunts, my father's sisters, still wore their traditional Ndebele attire with beautiful beads. I liked that. I found them very amazing. In other words, they were considered uncivilised because they did not wear Western clothes. Missionaries indoctrinated people to believe that what was not Western but traditional was of an inferior standard and was to be looked down upon. Little did I know that I loved beadwork, and bead making is still my hobby. I love beads; they are like gold to me.

I found the place more progressive than ga-Masemola in terms of school buildings and maintenance. There were no children who were taught under the trees. They had proper classrooms for both primary and high school learners. The schools were built by the community, though, not government. Their classrooms were well painted with cream and brown colours and were looked after. Everything was clean and tidy. The whole yard had a beautiful garden and peach tree orchards. It is a pity that they are no longer there. I do not know why, but maybe it is due to climate change and lack of rain.

The school was very close to home and it became very convenient for me to rush home and eat a lunch of porridge and *morogo*. My parents could not afford to buy bread for breakfast; it was a luxury. I breakfasted and lunched on yesterday's leftovers. I remember eating the same menu for breakfast, lunch and supper, yet I was never sick from nutritional deficiency related illnesses. I was always healthy.

My first and second years were not so pleasant. Most of the boys were bullies and every time my sister and I, before she went to boarding school the following year, went to fetch water they would bully us around and a fight would ensue. At the beginning, one of my cousins who was older than us would come to our rescue, but he'd already finished his Standard 6, so he went and joined the police force in Johannesburg. My sister and I were left with no one to defend us.

I still followed the same routines I'd performed for the rest of my pre- and teenage life. For example, after coming back from collecting wood, I would eat and run to go to fetch water, at the most five trips carrying a water bucket of about five litres on my head. Unlike ga-Masemola, in Kalkspruit there were no rivers, so we fetched water from the nearest windmill. We used the water to do the washing as well.

I've always wondered why we never had health challenges such as cholera and stomach aches related to water-borne diseases, as seems to be common nowadays, because the water we used for drinking and everything else was filthy. The water from the river was cleaner because it runs, and even that from the wells was better because as you scooped up the available water and new water came up from beneath. But that from the windmill just remained stagnant, and it was never emptied nor cleaned, let alone purified, especially in winter.

The windmill pumped water with the aid of the blowing wind, but in winter there was not much wind and the water would turn really green and filthy. Sometimes, naughty boys would throw all kinds of things inside the cement water tank. During summer it was much better, as the rainwater would help fill the windmill's water tank and in this way it would get cleaned when it started overflowing. The old water would flow out and the tank would be filled with fresh water.

On summer days, when it rained it was good for those who had corrugated iron roofs and water downpipes or gutters. We would put tanks used normally by nearby stores to store paraffin under the gutters. We used to buy them empty, clean them thoroughly and place them under downpipes and the rain would fill them with water. But in rural areas the rain is very scarce when compared to before, for reasons not known to us although we suspect that climate change is the culprit.

Towards midday, I would quickly gather the dirty clothes for the whole family and hurry to the place where we used to do the washing and hang the garments over every tree, preferably umbrellas thorn tree or acacia (*meshwana*) because they had thorns so clothes were not easily blown away by the slightest wind. They were allowed to dry there. Once dried, I would fold them nicely and put them in a big dish that we called *pafo,* I guess from the English word bath. Once done, I would carry it on my head and head for home.

All the girl children of my age were doing the same chores. At ga-Masemola, girls and boys performed the same house chores. This is the opportunity missed by societies in general, to correct gendered roles nonsense and sexism. I believe that all the children, irrespective of gender, should be taught house chores because they are a form of life skill one needs to know in life.

By the time I came back from doing the laundry it would already be late in the afternoon, nearing time to make fire and prepare for supper. The routine went on and on with no ending, but I do not remember complaining because that was our way of life. We did not know of any other life.

It was compulsory that I go to church on Sunday mornings: that was my mother's instruction. After church, I would prepare lunch and, in the afternoon, do the ironing as well as preparing for my school uniform so it was ready for school on Monday. I was also responsible for that of my sibling. Once finished, I would start doing my homework if there was any, or just do routine studying.

Going from how boys in Kalkspruit used to bully us, I remember that one Saturday afternoon we went to fetch water and the boys saw us. Time after time, they would leave us until we came back with buckets full of water, carried on our heads as usual. They would then start provoking and beating us while we were carrying our buckets of water and sometimes the bucket would slip from our heads and fall to the ground, spilling the water. There were always long queues at the windmill where we fetched water, and it meant that we had to go back and stand in the queue, but it would happen over and over. They had a ringleader who would lead them.

One fateful day I decided to fight back. While they were approaching us but were still at a distance, I told my sister that we were going to fight back. Once they started on us, we should lift the buckets of water off our heads and put them down at the side of the road.

They started. I put my bucket on the ground and I challenged the ringleader. He got very furious. Unfortunately, as I grabbed him I realised that he was very light. I started hitting back and the rest just stood there. My sister joined in. I asked her to take off her running shoes (sneakers, commonly known as takkies) so that I could beat him with them. He started crying and ran away, and then they all did. It was the end of our misery.

Fast forward. While in Form 1, I happened to be in the same class with him. One day, our geography teacher asked the girls in the class who had ever fought with a boy and overpowered him? We were asked to raise our hands. Although I did not understand the relevance of that to my subject, geography, I raised my hand. I wanted to deliberately embarrass him. He was so frustrated that I was going to expose him to those who did not know about the incident that he started pleading with me. He used to call me "Joy", which is a direct translation of both my names (my Christian name is Glory and my Sotho name is Lethabo; I am commonly known by that name). I felt pity for him, and I quickly sat down before the teacher noticed or recognised me.

As for fighting bullying boys, I was coached by my father on how to learn to fight them back, especially since I did not have a brother. He even advised me to protect my siblings, who were not the fighting types. Both my parents armed me with what is called martial arts so that I could defend myself against bullies, especially boys. For example, my father showed me how to fight with a stick. My mother too showed me how to head butt someone, below the chin, so that he would bite his tongue and bleed profusely and would retreat. My mother told me to fight only when I was provoked or in self-defence.

One of my cousins (one of my aunt's children) who was close to me mastered the heading technique so well that I envied her. She was taller than me.

Above all, both my parents taught me to believe in myself. I so wish that all families would do the same so that girls are able to defend themselves, especially during this time in which women are attacked, maimed, raped and killed senselessly.

My parents were not so learned but they were both very intelligent and I considered my mother a very wise person.

I must say that I attribute my success to my parents, and later in life to my husband. I also want to believe that I got all my good qualities from my parents. For example, my mother possessed a rare personality in the generation she grew up in. She was a strong woman, who was very passionate and highly independently minded. I witnessed her tilling the fields and rearing chicken and livestock such as sheep and cows. She would ensure that the chickens had a clean coop to stay in, and that the kraal was looked after, work that in my community was usually done by men. She did not wait for my father to give her permission to build additional rooms onto the house. She knew how to make mud bricks and built a room from scratch.

I would describe my father as someone who was very liberal and progressive, in the sense that he did not subscribe to patriarchal stereotypes emanating from socialisation, although sometimes he would succumb to societal pressures. He taught me how to cook porridge (*pap*) properly, and he would do it practically. He liked drinking tea, and he would make it for all of us. At that time we used primus stoves – there was no electricity – and the coal stove was used for cooking supper after we graduated from wood (*sebesho*).

I remember one time he watched me putting red polish on the veranda or stoep floor and he took the cloth and floor brush and knelt to demonstrate to me how it was done. He said to me that the floor must shine to the point of resembling a mirror: that is, I must be able to see myself in it. It was the same with cleaning the house and ironing. My mother was very particular and meticulous but my father told us that he could outshine her. He told us that he'd always helped her with house chores when they stayed together in town, including washing and hanging nappies. He had even bathed us, as well as changing our nappies.

My father later revealed to us that, when he came to Johannesburg, his first job was that of flat boy. He was a cleaner in one of the flats in Hillbrow and that is where he learnt most of the house chores. He told us that because then they did not know anything about sugar where he grew up, he only tasted sugar when he started working in town. One day, his madam boss went to the toilet, and he decided to steal her sugar and put it in the pockets of his set of trousers. Their uniform was short linen trousers and shirts (like those that were worn by Sdumo [Joe Mafela] in Sgudi's nice sitcom play).

While kneeling and shining the floors, the sugar poured on the floor from his pocket and his boss was there, watching him. Fortunately, she was not such a horrible white person and she just laughed and said, "In future you must ask". If it had been someone different, he would have been sent to jail for stealing from his white boss.

He just loved sugar and tried to encourage us to consume a lot of it because us folk from the rural areas went to Johannesburg for those kinds of luxuries. Even when sugar was accessible, to the extent that we made traditional beer with it, people then were not used to putting brown sugar in their tea, only white sugar, and he would still tell us about consuming sugar. Nowadays, drinking tea with brown sugar is fashionable for health reasons.

He was so resourceful that he would also assist us when hoeing the fields or harvesting if he happened to be at home. Apart from that he liked taking his dogs to go hunting (*go tsoma*) as well as checking on livestock. He just loved animals, especially dogs. He also loved children; he enjoyed being surrounded by kids.

My father used to assign to me the tasks known to be for boys. One day his friend at a faraway place called Uitkyk, commonly known as Bochum, in the ga-Matlala area, gave him a sheep, and he was to go to fetch it. He requested that I accompany him. I agreed, and we left. We spent most of the day there and returned in the afternoon. He wanted me to accompany him because he anticipated that the sheep might give him problems as it was not used to a car.

My father with one of his dogs that had just given birth, surrounded by my cousins' children. The one holding his shoulder is my daughter.

Coming back, he got stuck in a sand because the area is semi-desert with a sea of sand on the road. If one is not used to driving there, it is difficult, especially since private cars are low. He asked me to push the car while driving it, trying to get it out. I did so until we were out of the sand. When back at home he boasted that I had done a good job, like a typical boy, and I was proud.

One day, I was listening to his conversation with a friend, and heard him telling him, "You see this one," pointing at me, "she is my son. When you hit her make sure that you hit her hard, even if she faints, otherwise she will surprise you." I was taken aback, but just kept quiet. I was busy in the kitchen. This was unusual, especially in a society where at a young age children are socialised into gendered roles. Young boy children today still adopt patronising and patriarchal behaviours, because this is what they see in society and what they learn from their parents. In all societies, sexism is still the problem it was many years ago.

Thinking back now on what he allowed me to do, I was raised to believe that there was absolutely nothing that a boy could do that I could not. He equally instilled in me the notion that I must be independent and self-reliant. I am very fortunate because he inculcated in me self-belief. In other words, my parents taught me as well as helped me to smash glass ceilings ever since. I explored the freedom to try everything and anything to be able to reach the highs that I have now reached.

I remember how my father used to introduce me to people as his son. I did not see anything wrong with it, and I believe that he must have meant well. But, looking at it from a patriarchal perspective, maybe by singling me out because of my personality, he was trying to fill the void of not having a boy child. When I thought of it later in life, I felt saddened because referring to me as his boy would mean that I could only be strong, courageous and brave – that is, amount to anything according to societal prescript – if I were a boy and not a girl.

Now that I understand the toxic role patriarchy played in, for instance, societal stereotypes, it saddens me to realise that indoctrination is an evil thing as it clouds people's ability to reason independently from societal influence or pressure. On the other hand, I often asked myself how they must have felt about not having a son to take the family surname. It is sad to realise how Moses in the Old Testament misquoted and de-contextualised the story of Eve, Adam and the rib to justify patriarchy so that violence against women is used as a means to bring them into submission to men. Men are socialised into believing that they are superior to women, and they have internalised this idea over many years to the point that women themselves have accepted that their romantic partners have the right, even the responsibility, to use physical violence as a means of instilling discipline. Many women justify this as an expression of love.

Language also plays a critical role in fuelling patriarchal ideologies. This comes in the form of idiotic idioms and proverbs. For example, utterances such as "behind every successful man, there is a woman". I hear women saying with pride that their husbands are successful because they made them to be. What about your own success?

This type of utterances sounds inoffensive but, when one thinks about it, what it implies is that the lives of wives are lived in the shadows of their husbands. Hence, in communities or society women are obscured and invisible. Women are oblivious to the fact that they are putting themselves in danger by accepting this imposed position at their expenses, be it consciously or unconsciously. What is important is for women to start correcting this acceptance that they belong under a man. This would in turn change the societal norm that this is where women belong, irrespective of the socio-economic status and context in which women find themselves.

As I have already alluded, my parents had only three girls and it should have been hard for them to fit into a society that was so obsessed with the notion of surnames. Culturally, the issue of siring an heir to continue the family name is very important. For example, in African communities a surname is passed down the generations by sons. Hence, women in the communities are put under pressure to produce an heir to take over the family name. The youngest boy child is the one who takes the family house. I, of course, did not experience a situation where my brother was to be valued more than me because I never had one; otherwise, it would have been a problem for me.

I grew up with this thing that no one is better than me. Then life was not as easy as it is today. There was no electricity or running water, and no luxuries such as disposable napkins or prams. Nowadays, babies are dressed nicely and are carried in beautiful baby blankets. Then we used to carry our babies on our backs using check-patterned shawls that came in brown, blue and navy blue. There were no prams. I only saw whites pushing their children in them when I went to town.

Maybe it was a blessing in disguise for my mother not to have a son because in a traditional setting such as the one I grew up under, having a son meant that a mother would technically be under him. If it happened that my father died young, his son would be the head of the household, something I would have had a problem with because us girls would have been under him and I would not have accepted being under my sibling or allowed my mother to be bossed around by someone she'd birthed and whose napkins she had changed.

The reality is that our patriarchal society is not ready for what it perceives as a wayward woman. In the traditional setup from which I came, this type of woman was humiliated and punished. This was intended to make other women in the community fear losing their cultural identity by not acting according to the patriarchal standards of what constitutes a proper woman. Even in urban areas, where we expect women to be independent, women who have sexual autonomy and their economic independence are construed as "disloyal, disobedient, a betrayal of what is 'proper' in a woman and therefore of the nation" (Lewis, 2008:7). For Lewis, this is not isolated, as in the bible we have stories of women such as Vashti, a queen of Persia, and Esther in the Book of Esther. Vashti was punished for standing up against patriarchy, and Esther was embraced for meeting the criteria of a perfect woman. According to Snyman (2021:675), the Vashti narrative permeates the lives of women who take a stand against patriarchy in one way or the other. This defiance has the footprint of women who marched to Pretoria in 1956 and the Charlotte Mannya Maxeke of yesteryears, who went against the grain of what was required from them.

Reverting to the narrative about my childhood, while in Standard 4, a year after we left ga-Masemola, my aunt passed away, leaving behind four school-going children. She was not married. The fifth child, their elder sister, was already married.

This happened two months before I wrote my final examinations. I was devastated, but I managed to write my examinations and passed well. She was my mother's younger sister. All in all, she had five children, including a set of twins. I am told that a sixth one had died while still a toddler. As she was not married, and there was no one to take care of the children except my parents, my parents fostered the four of them. I had two sisters, so we were seven children in total.

My mother had known about her sister's illness but had kept it a secret. She must have hoped that she would recover, as she was relatively young, in her early forties.

Due to the lack of communication infrastructure in rural areas, emergency messages such as death were conveyed to people through telegrams. Unfortunately, the post was only collected once a week and if the telegram arrived after the post had been collected, one would only receive it the following week: not helpful at all. This was exactly what happened. Meanwhile, my father heard of her death from one of the relatives working not far from him. Knowing very well about our relationship, he decided to write to console me. He thought that by the time I received his letter I would know.

The telegram arrived on the same day as his letter, on the afternoon of a Friday before her burial on Saturday. On the same day that my aunt died, my cousin, that is my father's sister's son, was killed in a car accident, so they were to be buried on the same Saturday. My mother had gone to her sister-in-law's place for the whole week, so, when the telegram arrived, she was not at home.

I had gone to the post office to collect the post. I brought it home, but I could not open anything as post was only opened by adults. In those days, we knew that a telegram carried only sad news, so I took the telegram to one of my closest relatives and left. I was in a hurry to go and open my letter from my father. I opened it and started reading, I could not believe my eyes.

I started crying uncontrollably and screaming around the house. My younger sister came – she seemed not to understand – and my relative, having opened the letter and read the telegram, went to another relative, who was very close to my mother, to convey the bad news. They came hurrying home and found me crying. They could not understand because I had not read the telegram, so I showed them my father's letter. They sent for someone to come and sleep with us. I cried the whole night without sleeping. I just sat in my parents' bedroom, staring at one of her photos in disbelief.

One of the women who came to see us decided to walk to where my aunts' house was in the middle of the night because there was no transport then. It was quite a distance, and one had to go through thick bushes and tall blue gum or eucalyptus trees, and cross a river: very scary. She went and told my mother. They immediately came back so that my mother could catch the 8 o'clock bus going to Pietersburg and connect to the 2PM bus going to ga-Masemola.

She found me still sitting there. I could see that she was shattered, but not crying. She tried to console me. After seeing my mother, I felt a little better but could not believe that my aunt had died. I thought it was a mistake. I asked my mother if I could accompany her, but she refused. Children were not allowed to go to funerals, but I just wanted to be with my aunt's children. She told me that I could not miss school and besides, she did not have enough money for three people. The relative who had gone to inform her was to accompany her.

There was a Friday programme on Lebowa Radio station where they announced bereavements. Those who had radios would listen to that but we did not have one. I even went to my neighbour's house because I knew that they had a radio, in the hope of hearing my aunt's death announced. By the time I got there, the programme already finished. When I asked them whether they'd heard such and such name announced, they told me that indeed her name had been announced, and she would be buried the following day. I thanked them and told them it was my aunt, my mother's youngest sister.

I still hoped for a miracle because I refused to believe that she had died, she was still very young, in her early forties, and her youngest daughter was only seven years old and her eldest child twenty-one. I still remember everything because it was only a year after we had left them. She had written me a letter a year before, asking me to come back once I'd finished my Standard 6 so that I could go to school there. They'd built the first secondary school in ga-Masemola. I'd replied and said yes, I would, but my father would not allow me to go.

My mother took the bus and the relative accompanied her. Unfortunately, the next bus to ga-Masemola was only at 2 o'clock from Polokwane. When she got there, her sister had already been buried. I felt pity for her. She remained behind when this

relative of ours came back on the Monday; there was no transport on Sundays. I went to school on Monday, although I still cried every time I thought of her. The relative came to fetch us and we stayed with her family for a week. They had a big house with a beautiful garden. I took my photo at their house.

The Story of a Rural Girl Who Kept Rising and Rising

Next to me is my younger sister. I missed my parents' home and I hated staying in other people's houses.

The weekend before the following week, I convinced my sister that we must go back home. Although I did not want to be indifferent and ungrateful, I politely asked our relative to allow me and my younger sister to return home. She did not object, so we left, and I felt so happy to be at home because I'd truly longed for that. The fact that I made a point of passing home every time I came back from school, just to check whether everything was okay, did not bring me any consolation.

I'd already responded to my father's letter. He would insert a stamp so that I did not have any excuses for not responding and because stamps were not easily accessible and I was not working. I asked him to go and fetch my aunt's children, saying that otherwise I would go and stay with them, with or without his permission. Those that were there when he read the letter told my mother that he cried. My letter had been very touching and moving as well. He wrote back and agreed that he would go and fetch them. Besides, they were like his children. Their mother had never married and he had taken good care of them whilst still staying together before we moved to Kalkspruit.

I do not, in fact, condone what my aunt did. It was irresponsible of her to have so many children. We had to share everything with them. They indeed deprived me of many things in life. My mother told me that my aunt had never wanted to work. Every time my mother and my father found her domestic work in Johannesburg, she would fall pregnant. My mother told me that she was so lazy that she would wear her clothes and just put them back dirty in the kist where she'd found them clean and neat. Very upsetting.

I hope that women will learn that having many children is a drawback since, according to my observation, many children goes hand in hand with poverty. Having five children with different men is a shame, because all those men move on with their lives. Having children is not an achievement, but a cherry on the top for married couples. Having children you cannot afford to look after is sheer evil and wrong, especially for those who are left to take care of them.

My mother came back after two weeks, wearing mourning clothes. I spotted her at a distance. She had been dropped off by the 4 o'clock bus from Pietersburg (now Polokwane). I started running to her, crying. I just knew that with that black dress she was wearing, it was true. She was surprised that we'd returned home, and I told her that we'd had to come back. I pleaded with her not to send us to stay in other people's houses nor ask relatives to come over to guard us when visiting her home for couple of days. I told her that we are big girls so we could take care of ourselves. She agreed.

But towards the December school holidays she went back again because my father had arranged that my mother should go and fetch them before the schools re-opened the following year. I remember that seeing them was very sad, knowing that they no longer had a mother. But, what made it sadder was seeing them looking so destitute, wearing tattered clothes. The boy's trousers had so many patches that it was a bad sight to witness. Until today I do not seem to know how remove that picture from my head. One of them had an onset of protein malnutrition, which causes kwashiorkor, and pellagra caused by a lack of vitamins. Her hands and mouth had started peeling and she had swollen legs.

The following year I was to go to the secondary school. With the three of us, plus the additional four, must have been difficult for my father, being the only bread winner. He did a good job, though, and I will forever honour him for that. It was never easy. He made no distinction between us and them; he really took good care of them. I want to be frank and honest, though: I regretted having made my father feel guilty and coercing him into taking care of them. We are now all grown up, but none of them never expressed their gratitude to my parents, even by deeds, let alone saying it. They all felt entitled and very ungrateful. It really hurts when one think of the sacrifices my parents and we sisters made. I must say, without generalising, that orphans are difficult people to please.

In all this, what gave me pleasure was my ability to thank the distant relative who stood by my mother and risked her life by walking such a dangerous route to my aunt's place so that she could convey the message to my mother. Meanwhile, my closest relatives did not bother to do anything. My aunt who received and opened the telegram did nothing, except to take it to this other relative. It is true that everyone has got an angel.

I personally managed to let her know how grateful I was, 36 years after my aunt died. It was at the funeral of my cousin-sister I spoke about earlier. She was shocked and touched by the fact that I still remembered after so long, especially since I was very young then. I always wanted to thank her, but never had an opportunity to do so, and I was glad that I did. She thought I was much too young to have seen any significance in what she had done.

Growing up in a humble community, it was not always smooth sailing as temptations were always lurking around. When I was in Standard 5, there was this boy who always wrote me letters saying he loved me. Some of the girls of my age had boyfriends already. I was not interested, but this person pursued me. I never responded to the letters. He started waiting for me after school, demanding an answer. I did not actually understand what he wanted from me. One day I asked him what he wanted, and he explained to me. I asked him what would happen when already in love, and he explained.

I just felt that what he was asking from me was wrong and told him that I did not want to do that. I said to him in an angry voice, "What would people say of me, and what about my mother? If she happened to find out she would punish me." He responded by saying that I must be stupid because most of the girls in the neighbourhood were doing it. I refused and asked him to leave me alone, but he would not until I completed Standard 6.

He must have gone to tell other boys and girls that I was stupid. Three girls in my neighbourhood started befriending me. By nature, I am anti-social and not so good at making friends, so I would stay home, even on Sunday afternoons while children of my age dressed nicely and strolled in the streets. We became friends and they came to call me every Sunday. They started telling me about their boyfriends and how stupid I was for not wanting to be involved with this boy. They also told me that I was missing out on a wonderful thing called sex, but I could not be convinced. I was just not ready. Now and again their boyfriends would approach from nowhere and join us with this very boy who wanted me. I would leave them and walk back home, and he would follow me and only depart when approaching my homestead. He started calling me "*Batho ba tla reng*" – what would people say? The last time I met him he still called me that.

The Story of a Rural Girl Who Kept Rising and Rising

We were both adults already and he asked me whether I was still stupid.

The most important rule that my mother laid down was that no one came home after six or sunset, and when it was your turn to cook you had to come home earlier to make the coal fire.

As already mentioned, most of the children of my age, both girls and boys, were already mature and some were sexually active. They did not understand why I would not do what they were doing. One of the girls – who I thought was my friend and understood that I was not interested in boys – started gossiping about me and spreading lies that I was in love with the boy in question. The news spread so fast that it ultimately reached my ears. I ignored it for quite some time, but what made me very angry was when one afternoon I went to fetch water after school. She was sitting with a group of girls in the neighbourhood, and when I passed she made funny remarks, and they all started laughing. I walked over to them and demanded an explanation for their silly behaviour.

One of them started talking in a rude manner, telling me that I thought I was better than them when meanwhile I engaged myself with boys. I asked her where that had come from and she told me that the girl in question had told them. I left them and stood in the queue and waited for my turn to fill my bucket.

They moved away and started playing. When my turn came, I filled my bucket, carried it away to a safer place under the tree and went to them. I started with the girl I'd thought was my friend and demanded an explanation for why she'd spread lies about me. She became adamant that I was wrong. I got hold of her and gave her a beating she would remember to the grave. One by one, I beat the hell out of all the six of them until they all cried. I was not going to leave them until they cried. They never thought of ganging up against me: they all just stood there, frightened. I went and put my bucket on my head and left for home.

The girl's brother was sitting with other boys on the other side from where the girls were, and one of them was one I'd once fought with and beaten up. He witnessed everything. As I passed by, he picked up dried and hardened soil (*lekoloboto*) and hit me with it very hard, right on my back, between my shoulder blades. In the area in which the windmill is, the soil is clay like (*seloko*). On rainy days, the soil becomes muddy but once the rain stops the mud forms into a hardened clay and cracks. Hence, it was easy for this girl's brother to remove a lump of hardened soil. One could mistake the hardened soil for a stone. I turned and he looked very angry. I kept on walking. When I got home, my mother asked me why I had taken so much longer than usual. I lied to her and told her that the queue was too long. I did not tell her about what really happened.

Late in the evening, the mother of the girl sent for my mother and she went to their house. I thought it was rude. She was the one who'd wanted to see my mother; she should have come over. I did not try to discourage my mother, because if I had she would have suspected that I was hiding something. I did not tell her of what had happened. I already knew why the other woman wanted to see my mother.

The other mother told mine that she was angry with me because I'd hurt her daughter. My mother called for me and I told her for the first time what had really transpired. My mother apologised on my behalf, and we thought the matter was resolved. I was surprised when I went to school the following day and I saw the girl's mother sitting in the principal's office. It was much too early for a parent to be there already. Apparently she had not slept from anger. I sensed a problem, and indeed, she'd come to report the matter. The principal did not buy their story because he knew the type of a person I am as compared to the likes of the girl in question. After she left, he called me into his office and advised me not to fight people and advised me to try to resolve issues without violence, but he could not believe their story.

I realised that the girl was not a good friend and I never wanted to hear anything more about her. At this stage I hated provoking other children and I did not want to be provoked because, if I were, I became tempted to fight. I did not want to be bullied either.

I tried to refrain from fighting with other children after my mother praised me for having grown up and become such a responsible, sensible and caring person. All I wanted was to dedicate myself to my school work, and assist my mother with house chores after school and during weekends. After being a bully at a certain age, repenting was such a wonderful feeling.

I guess that bullying other children was a cry in the wilderness. I needed attention. My elder and younger sisters always got attention from my mother, and every time she would try to protect them but I was always told to fight back and defend myself and not to come home reporting and crying when other children beat me.

I believe that I developed what is called middle-child syndrome. This phenomenon of the first born and last born being favoured by parents – I see it mostly with mothers – is very common in society. In many families it causes sibling rivalry that extends through many generations. Although I knew I was not my mother's favourite, I never wanted that to dictate my life nor my future. I practised self-discipline, self-worth and self-love, and that helped me to love my mother, as well as my siblings, in the most special way.

My mother tried not to show me that she was practising favouritism, but I just picked the vibe up anyway, though it was very subtle. I used to blame myself because of my bad behaviour of been a bully. I thought my mother treated me that way because I was always in her bad books. But that was for a certain stage. Once I reached the pre-teenage stage, I changed to be a responsible and loving child but nothing changed as far as the discrimination my mother had towards me went. I accepted that. The rejection did not really bother me to the point resenting my sisters. There was never any form of rivalry between us because I opted to treat the whole situation with so much maturity. I managed to ignore it and lived my life.

As if what had already happened were not enough, the very same girl did something very terrible to me and I was shocked. One afternoon I was at home, preparing a coal stove fire for cooking, and there at the gate stood someone I did not know. I was told that he was looking for me. I went to him and asked who he was. He was drunk and told me to go along with him. He had been sent by the same girl to come and make advances to me. I refused and he tried to cause trouble by forcing himself through the gate. I called my mother, and everyone at home came to my rescue and he left. I was told later that he was from Seshego township, the only township in Limpopo then. It was about a 30-minute drive from my village. I had been told that boys from the township were dangerous thugs. I did not know how true that was, because it sounded like a generalisation.

Fast forward. After my nursing profession attempt failed, I decided to further my studies and write my matric through correspondence. When the June holidays came, I heard of winter school classes being held at one of the teacher training colleges in Seshego. They were meant for full time Matric pupils from various high schools, while I was doing adult education with the aim of obtaining my matric (senior certificate, as it was commonly known under Bantu Education).

I tried my luck and attended. The person responsible for the programme allowed me to attend and the lessons were free. My mother gave me money for transport. I travelled by bus to and from Seshego for the entire June school holidays. There was this girl: she was the daughter of our principal at the higher primary I'd attended. She was doing Matric full time at one of the neighbouring high schools and she also attended the winter school at the same place, so we commuted together and at least I had a company.

One afternoon, when we came back from school, we went to wait for the bus going home at the bus rank. We realised that it was still too early for the bus to arrive and decided to go and sit in a nearby café run by a Portuguese. We bought some soft drinks and sat down at one of the tables. To my shock, I saw the guy I mentioned above from Seshego approaching the door. I did not expect him to recognise me because he had seen me only once very briefly and he had been drunk, but someone must have alerted him of my whereabouts.

He walked straight to the table we sat at. He immediately started insulting me and making a lot of noise, saying he was going to teach me a lesson. It was such a terrifying scene. He started breaking an empty bottle, threatening to stab me with it and kill me because he had been told that I thought I was smarter than all the girls from my village. The shop owner apprehended him and threw him out.

I was very frightened and hurting, so we decided to leave the place and headed straight to the bus rank to catch the bus, which was about to arrive. We literally ran: we were both virtually traumatised and scared. I thought that he might be waiting for me somewhere because he knew where I lived and that I would be catching the bus.

It arrived and everyone boarded, and I was relieved when it pulled out of the rank, heading to my place. I vowed to myself that I was not going to go for my lessons anymore, I was so terrified. But, when my mother insisted that I go because I should not allow people to hold my life to ransom and steal my dreams, because they themselves were losers, I agreed with her. She strongly reminded me of the power of prayer and advised me to pray around it and have faith. I went to the school and never saw him again.

I was a very motivated person and passionate about education from a very early age. I loved my schooling and studying. As already mentioned, I was always at the top of the class in every examination not only because I was intelligent, but I was also hard working. Unfortunately, our teachers did not have the skill to help us to understand things. Maybe it was how Bantu Education was designed, considering Verwoerd's speech about black children. One teacher would teach all the subjects, and we were taught to memorise things rather than understand them. We did everything in North Sotho except English and Afrikaans.

I knew the whole Bible by heart, starting from Genesis (*Dikutullo*) to Revelations (*Ditiro*). I also knew *Graded English* and *Praktiese Taal* by heart. They were the only two prescribed books I had until I completed Standard 6. For other subjects, such as geography, (*Tsa Tikologo*), science (*Tsa Mahlale*), arithmetic (*Dipalo*), etcetera, we relied entirely on the notes that the teacher (Jack of all trades), wrote for us on the black board. We had to copy them into our exercise books. The books were to be covered neatly with khaki paper and plastic to protect them from tearing or getting wet when it rained.

Talking about Standard 6, I started seeing my menstruation (period) when I was in Standard 6. I was shocked the first day I saw blood; no one had ever told me about that. I remember how traumatised I was. We did not have flushing toilets in the rural areas, only pit latrines. The first time I realised that I was on my period, I was out in the veld collecting firewood. I went to relieve myself behind a bush and when I was finished I used a piece of stone to wipe myself. I then saw blood on my fingers and when I checked the blood was on my poo too. I did not know what to think nor do. Talking about menstruation and sex was taboo then; even my elder sister never mentioned it to me.

The same day that I started with my periods, I was feeling awkward. I felt very tired, sleepy and stressed out. I went home, and never said anything to my mother. But I remember checking the blood now and again and it kept on coming out. A day passed, then three days, and the blood was still flowing out. In our pit latrine we kept newspapers and telephone directories that my father brought home with him when he came for his annual leave or during festive seasons. Old newspapers or any paper was used as toilet paper. So, I decided to use that as my sanitary pad until I finished. I was shocked to find that my people back home are still using them instead of toilet paper. They still have pit latrines though, and they cannot afford toilet paper.

The next month, it happened again. I still did not tell anyone; I was just improvising in silence. When it happened for the third time it was December month, towards the festive season.

Everyone came home, and my cousin-sister who I said was already married when my aunt died came home too. I do not know how she happened to see my underwear. At that time there were no panties and we wore what were called Vasco da Gama (bloomers) because of their shape, as they resembled the pants worn by earlier Portuguese explorers such as Vasco da Gama and Bartholomew Diaz. They were made from a heavy textile material (like that they make T-shirts with, but heavier). They often came in black, navy blue and pink. It was not easy for me to wash them properly, so the blood stains would remain, and she saw that.

I found her showing them to my elder sister and they were laughing. I was so embarrassed, but at least they later told me why I was bleeding and that it was something normal. They could have told me earlier to raise awareness. They later told my mother. To my surprise, my mother was angry. She wanted to know whether I ever slept with boys. I did not know what she was talking about. Before I could respond, she interrupted me and said to me that if I ever slept with boys I would have a child with a goat's head. That was how far the education would go. She wanted to know what I was using for pads and I said paper from the toilet, and I told her that since I'd used it for about three months, my inner thighs were peeling from the friction and it hurt.

She brought to me a roll of material called mutton cloth or muslin cloth, the term used by furniture upholsters. I understand that it is called mutton cloth because originally it was used in New Zealand to wrap lamb to protect the meat from unwanted pests. I think my father brought it from town as well. I saw him washing his boss' car with some, one day when I went to visit him.

My mother cut it into sizeable pieces for me to use every time I went on my period. Although the cloth did not hurt my inner thighs, neither the newspaper nor the cloth were user-friendly because they did not have any adhesive to stick to one's underwear so that it would not move when one moved around.

It was only when I went for training as a nurse that I was exposed to proper pads. They still did not have adhesive but strings on both sides. I cannot remember how I used to tie them so that they did not move. These methods were not reliable. Unlike normal sanitary pads, with adhesive that sticks on the underwear, they would often move up one's spine, and in the case where there was no place to hide and fix it, it would keep on moving, leaving one unprotected. It was very embarrassing.

Still talking about pit toilets or latrines, I mentioned earlier that I hated them for the reasons given. Little did I know that I would find some solitude in them one day. I always liked reading so, when I needed somewhere quiet so that I could read my schoolbooks and study in peace, the toilet became the only place I could hide myself. The toilet was far from the homestead but in the yard. It was situated at the far corner, to avoid a smell coming to the house, I guess. In there, it would be myself, worms, flies, and the smell of faeces and urine. I was not bothered that much. After all, our toilet did not smell so bad because my father bought chemicals to treat it: some chemicals that were poured inside to kill worms and some for cleaning it so that it did not smell very bad and chased away flies. Our toilet also became handy when I wanted my solitude, especially during festive holidays when everyone was at home. Because I am anti-social by nature, I often felt crowded and then I would go and sit there for a while.

My mother's question agonised me. I tried to remember whether I had indeed ever slept with a boy, maybe by mistake. Then I kept on asking myself that maybe sleeping with your brother in one room or bed might make one see blood, but I did not have a brother. My mind ran wild; it was shocking. But the idea of sleeping with boys haunted me, especially since I did not know what it meant other than taking it literally.

Something struck my mind. I recalled that one day the boy I was at school with while I was still in primary cornered me in a spot where no one could see us. Then we did not stand with boys openly. It was regarded as disrespectful, and by doing that one would be inviting problems as any adult who saw us would not hesitate to rebuke us. I remembered that he'd touched my hand. I started thinking whether that could be the cause of my period. For the whole day, I tried to figure out what could have happened.

I was relieved when both my cousin and sister explained the whole thing to me later in the week. I made it a point that I had conversations with my daughter when she reached the pre-teen stage about the facts of life on a regular basis. This made life easy because when she started seeing her periods I was at the university, and she simply asked her father to buy sanitary pads for her. She already knew about what to do when the time came.

Still on this, I want to dispute the notion that children from disadvantaged families who cannot afford sanitary towels miss schooling during that period. Women from these communities always improvise and I am a classical example of that long before it became fashionable. I cannot recall any time when girls bunked school because of menstruation. I believe that there is a misconception here and this notion also undermines the reasoning capacity of poor people. This would mean that when women are in their period they would suspend their daily chores, such as cooking, fetching wood and water, and tilling fields.

I do agree, though, that every child deserves user friendly and hygienic sanitary pads, and government must assist in this regard. I am also saddened by the fact that I read about prominent women championing the cause of providing needy children with sanitary towels. I find it to be an insult to women leaders because it is how this hypocritical patriarchal society measures women leaders of institutions: by the provision of sanitary pads. Indeed, this is patronising as it is tantamount to patriarchal trivialisation of women leadership.

Related to the sanitary pad issue, I am again puzzled by how as a society we have the tendency to justify the unjustifiable. I often hear that girls and young women engage with so-called sugar daddies because of poverty. When growing up in a rural area and coming to the township, women were always the face of poverty and destitution. But there were never these immoral practices, where young girls would engage with older men sexually in exchange for money.

Nowadays, people have lost their morals, values and norms that guided people in the past. This is a laissez-faire time of behaviour, but we should not scape-goat poverty. Communities do not see the sugar-daddy phenomenon as abuse but as civilisation (*se bjale bjale*). Many of us grew up in abject poverty but never stooped that low. It is only recently, post 1993, when people have electricity in their houses and water nearby, that some of back-breaking chores women performed have been alleviated. So, citing poverty as the reason that girls behave in a disgraceful manner is not true. In the same breath, I do not condone the fact that people should not have access to necessities that are beneficial to them because it is inhumane.

Seeing my menstruation was not the first thing that traumatised me. I remember how I was terrified the first time I realised that I was growing hair around my genitals. I did not know to whom to talk. I was afraid of telling my mother because I'd never heard of anyone growing hair anywhere on the body except the head, and men on their faces. I was petrified to the point that I one day peeped through the window while my mother was bathing, hoping to see whether she had similar hair to mine. I did not want her to catch me because I knew that would mean a hiding. In those days, parents would not walk naked in front of their children, let alone bathe in their presence.

Out of inquisitiveness, I still wanted to find out whether I was the only one with hair on this unusual part of the body. My aunt came to visit us. We were sleeping on a mat made of reeds on the floor. My mother was sleeping alongside my aunt on one mat, and I was sleeping with my younger sister on another mat, just below their feet. It was before my cousins came to stay with us. I could not sleep as the hair issue haunted me.

I thought both my mother and my aunt were fast asleep when I stretched my arm out and tried to reach my aunt's body to touch the area where I had the hair. She woke up and kicked my hand so hard that I retracted it. I tried my luck with my mother who too woke up and wanted to know what I was doing. I just kept quiet. Everyone went to sleep and I ultimately fell asleep too.

My mother was still angry with me the following day and told me that she was going to tell my father about my silliness. I could not get to tell them about my frightening discovery. I did not know what my aunt thought of me because she never said anything about it, although, I was so embarrassed I could not look at her in the eyes until she left. I regret that I did not tell them about the incident before they both died.

It was only when my sister came back from boarding school that I made it a point that I went to sit with her while she was bathing. Then I realised that she had similar hair. I was relieved but said nothing about my fears. Naturally, I do not have much hair under my armpits so that was not noticeable. Even growing breasts was never alarming to me because I saw many women with breasts because they are visible. The thing is that I always wanted to have a conversation about the physical changes I observed. But growing up, anything to do with female sexual reproduction was always shrouded in secrecy, a taboo.

Going back to the theme of this chapter, however, while I was in Standard 6, I was taught by two teachers. The one was very kind and the other very cruel. The kind one would make sure that we sang hymns in the morning. He had a mother who was mentally ill, so she was just wandering around in the bushes wearing a blanket, whether summer or winter. I was told that the teacher was the only child. More than often, the mother would not come home for days, and the teacher would start looking for her. Some days, he would come to class very distressed and would ask us to sing and pray with him, particularly for the mother, because he did not know where she was, whether she was still alive or dead and, if alive, where she was sleeping and what she was eating. Sometimes, when we went to fetch water far away, we would see her just wandering among the bushes and in the valleys. Every time our teacher talked about his mother, he would cry so much that I remember crying too. He was a very good teacher and he would rarely punish us by lashing or shout at us.

These teachers were both *Ledwabas*. The kind one we called "Teacher Across the Desert". This was his football nickname. I was told that he was a good football player and very good at conducting the school music choir as well. In the rural areas or within black communities even in the urban areas, people who were ill mentally were not looked after. This situation was worsened by the fact that facilities to care for them were scarce. I only knew of one facility that cared for mentally challenged adults near Lebowakgomo, which was many miles away from where I resided.

For example, there was this woman in my neighbourhood. She was sick mentally. What hurt me most was that she would wake up in the morning and sit outside, whether cold or hot. In a sweltering summer sun, she would be sitting there, clapping her head throughout the day and talking alone very loudly, even though I could not hear what it was that she was talking about. She stayed in a house diagonally opposite our kitchen. I would stand there and watch her through the window, always feeling pity for her. The worst thing was that she had a little boy child, and she would sit with him there all the time.

My question was always about how she happened to have a child when she was this sick. When I came to understand women abuse, especially the issue of rape, I became convinced that someone had raped her, and that would be someone close to her. The reason for this assumption was that she never left her house. If the boy had been older, I would have thought that she might have had him before taking ill.

While she sat there in the sun, the family just ignored her. Perhaps they did not know what to do. Her situation was worsened by the fact that the family was very destitute: they only had one rondavel house. I remember how they happened to frequent my home with either a small enamel dish, asking for maize or corn meal (*mielie meel* in Afrikaans), or an enamel cup, asking for sugar. I would see them at a distance and alert my mother. She would sometimes ask me to tell them that we did not have enough, but I would convince her to share with them the little we had. I felt pity for them. I watched her son growing up, and he did not appear to be healthy. Maybe he was malnourished. He did not look like a normal child, perhaps affected by his upbringing. In addition, the stigmatisation was also a problem.

Again, in our street there was this man who was also mentally ill, but he was lucky that the family sent him to the mental hospital I mentioned above. I grew up not knowing him, because when we moved to Kalkspruit he was already in the hospital. He was later discharged. I was in the same class with one of his children: he had two girls. I am told that the wife left him when he started taking ill, and looked for employment in town to raise her children.

One morning I boarded a bus to my aunt's place in a village distant from mine. I found him sitting on the front seat. I did not know where he was going. I sat in the third row. I heard people screaming that he was infested with lice. The driver stopped the bus and reached for a disinfectant commonly known as Doom. He started spraying him. People were laughing. I was frustrated because, as an asthmatic person, the smell of doom could suffocate me. I opened the windows next to me and I was just saying, what if he is asthmatic or had some sort of allergy. I was very upset, but kept quiet until I got off. To me, that was inconsiderate, cruel and insensitive.

The shrewd and strict teacher would ask us to come to school at 6 o'clock and started reciting our lessons. Whoever came late was bitterly punished: that is, lashed with a cane. The same punishment was given to those who found it difficult to memorise all the books and verses in the bible or sections of the *Graded English* or *Praktiese Taal*. I made a point to know everything and was very punctual. Realising that I was ever punctual, he gave me the responsibility of keeping the keys to our class, so that I opened for everyone in the morning. It was such an honour for me, and I made sure that I did not disappoint him. After we wrote either the April or June tests, our results would be announced at the morning prayer session so that everyone would hear who'd obtained first position or last. I was very proud to obtain position one always.

However, I did not like the idea of seeing other children punished by lashing. One day, during break time, I organised a meeting with other pupils. I called a meeting and suggested to my classmates that we indeed must protest. I became their ringleader. There were learners who were much older than me, but they agreed. I had this long tailor's ruler or architectural ruler. My father had given it to me. It was longer than my height, but I carried it to school; how stupid. I just liked the idea that it looked unique. I told them I would lead them wielding my ruler and we would attack him and teach him a good lesson.

Unfortunately, one of the learners leaked the information by telling her mother about our secret plan. She must have got cold feet. She even mentioned that I was the organiser. Her mother went and told my aunt. Both my aunt, her mother and my mother were members of the primary school governing body. All hell broke loose. My mother must have thought of my bullying tactics while I was still very young and she panicked. Then I was such a changed, responsible individual, very composed but still stubborn. My aunt came home in the evening and they sat there with my mother, talking. I could see from their facial expressions that something was wrong, but I could not hear what they were saying. My aunt looked very angry. I even sensed her anger from her tone when she greeted me. They later called me and asked me about our scheming. I confessed and I was warned that if I went ahead with my plans I would be severely punished.

When I went to school the following day, I told my classmates to give up the idea because we had been sold out. Our betrayer was there when I announced this, looking sheepish. I made a point that I did that in the morning, before any teacher came in.

Some of those who were victims of being lashed for not been so brilliant were angry and disappointed. I had been about to save them from their misery, but I was not prepared to risk being given a hiding. Knowing the type of person my mother was, she would have beat the hell out of me.

I did not know whether the very same teacher ever knew about our plans, because he did not strip me of what is today referred to as a prefect status: that is, taking responsibility for ensuring that books that remained at school were packed nicely after school and that our class was opened on time every morning.

The schools were closed for the festive season period. I had just completed my Standard 6 examinations and received my results before Christmas. Then Standard 6 was certificated. I passed very well and I was looking forward to starting at the new school for my Form 1. My sisters also did well and to reward us my mother slaughtered a chicken to cook for us and we had a wonderful meal. I loved that.

It was a common tradition and a practice that every year towards Christmas, in November and few weeks before Christmas Day, we would practise what we called a sketch, that is a drama in proper English, about the birth of Jesus Christ and some Christmas carols (*Mahlasetsana*). It happened in the night from 18h00 to 20h00. It was still very safe in the rural areas, in that no one would attack you walking in the night, and after all, all the children from Christian families would attend. For example, children belonging to the Lutheran church denomination would have theirs, and those belonging to Anglican church, like myself, would have ours. I was a Sunday school teacher, so I had to make sure that before I left everything was in order. Other children and the teacher who helped us with the Christmas carol play helped me. Our parents had no problem with that.

One night, I found this boy I spoke about earlier waiting for me outside the church. He requested that he walked me home. I did not see any problem with that. I was not afraid of him and he was not going to force me to do whatever I did not want to do. We walked and he continued with his same story. As we approached home, next to the big blue-gum trees, a certain guy approached from who knows where. Something horrible was about to happen. This one incident almost shattered my dreams and my life in general.

I knew him, but had never spoken to him. I'd just heard that he was very troublesome and notorious. He was known for terrorising girls. He was much older than both of us, even older than my elder sister, and already working. He grabbed the boy I was walking with by his clothes and threatened to beat him and ordered him to leave me. I did not understand what was happening. Once the boy had turned away, the man started been aggressive towards me, telling me that he was going to teach me a lesson. He told me that he had heard about me; that I was a proud person and I thought that I was better than others because I was pretty. So, he was going to put a stop to that.

He grabbed me violently and tried to kiss me. I refused. He tried to throw me to the ground. I fought back viciously; I never knew I had that amount of strength. I still believe that it was God who helped me, and I am forever thankful. The man was older and stronger, and he knew what he was doing. I should have panicked or succumbed, especially since I did not know why he was doing this nor what he wanted from me. I never knew about rape at that point. Every time he threw me to the ground, I would stand up, literally bouncing back, and try to free myself from him. When I touched the ground, I would bounce back like a tennis ball.

I would not have been able to do that if God were not with me. He gave me so much strength and a zest to fight. I still regard that as a miracle. Even more than forty years since the incident happened, it is still vivid in my mind. I still recall the smell of his body odour as he pressed himself against me and every time I recall it, it comes as a shock. He pressed me against his body, trying to kiss me. It was so annoying. It was only a few months since I'd started seeing my periods and I had just completed my higher primary school level. I certainly did not understand relationships with the opposite sex. I was not scared, though, or screaming or anything else. All that I had in mind was to fight and get loose. Although I did not understand what he was trying to do, my gut feelings told me that it was something bad.

I managed to free myself and ran very fast and he ran after me. I was approaching home and he could not catch up with me. I still ran very fast and he picked up a big stone and threw it at me and missed my back by an inch. I heard it as it dropped next to my feet behind me. I ran and he was chasing after me. I managed to escape.

I never told anyone, including my mother. I did not want to put my mother in danger and my father was not there. The man involved came from a feared family. His father was feared especially because he was a traditional doctor/healer. So, I kept quiet. In the rural areas these people are feared because people believe that they possess certain supernatural powers, such as being able to strike one with an evil spell or kill one. Hence, they are referred to as witch doctors: they are known for bewitching their enemies.

After that, the boy who'd been walking me home never continued with his advances. I suspected that the incident must have been the source of his retreating. Even though we went to the same secondary school together, we never brought it up.

The following day, I saw the guy who'd attacked me walking past our house. He made it a point that I saw him. As soon as he realised that I'd seen him, he started laughing very loudly. I was so angry that I ran away. I just hated him. I suspected that he must have threatened the boy who'd walked me home because he never spoke about it nor mentioned it to me, other than just greeting me whenever he saw me, almost avoiding me.

I only realised once I'd grown up and started to hear about people being raped that he'd wanted to rape me so that I would be taught a lesson. The whole idea tormented me and my hatred towards him grew by age. The last time I saw him, he was already married to a certain wonderful girl I had gone to school with in higher primary. I was already married and living with my husband in Soweto.

One day, I was waiting for a train at Braamfontein train station, and he was riding in a train going to Randfontein. The train stopped and he was in a coach that stopped just next to me. I heard someone calling my name and I looked up. He was standing at the door and started talking. He asked me whether I still hated him. He sounded very apologetic and tried to be nice. I responded without hesitation that I would hate him until death. I knew deep down in my heart that I had forgiven him as I am one person who cannot hold grudges. I'd almost forgotten about it except that it would reflect in my mind when I happened to hear about something similar. I would start thinking about how he had almost ruined my life in a very violent manner: that is, robbing me of my teenage life and my virginity.

My late cousin-sister who stayed at home and married there, would call me every time someone I knew passed on. She did the same when this guy died. She called me to inform me of his death. I said to her that as far as I was concerned he'd died a long time ago. She was shocked and obviously puzzled by my reaction. She asked me how come I made such a horrible remark about someone who'd just passed on.

I'd never told anyone about the incident including her, and I was closer to her than all my siblings and cousins. Now, I told her of what happened for the first time, that the guy had almost made me part of the statistics; he'd almost raped me. She got so angry with me that I'd kept quiet for so long. Upon hearing what I'd told her, she could not talk out of shock. She just became tongue tied. Being the type of a person she was, very stubborn, if she had known earlier, she would have confronted him, and that was what I was trying to avoid.

My cousin passed on in 2007, after suffering from heart-related illness for all her life. The doctor said she had a rare disease called atrial septal defect (someone born with a hole in the heart). Ever since her death, I no longer have anyone updating me about the things happening in my rural village. She deemed it important that I was kept abreast. She would not telephone me, though, but sent me "please call me" SMSes. I tried to discourage her from doing that. I hated it. My take is, if you want to talk to me, call me. Do not expect me to call you so that you can talk to me. I found that manipulative. But, with this one I succumbed because I was afraid to ignore her. What if she was to report something important? Besides, she was very cheeky.

While still growing up we fought a lot, but were inseparable. I can still recall the games we used to play together. If she happened to call me after realising that I was attempting to ignore her calls, she would rebuke me for not checking in on her.

The following year, after completing my primary schooling, I went to secondary school. I was very excited.

Chapter Three

MY LIFE PAST PRIMARY SCHOOLING AND ENTERING SECONDARY SCHOOL LEVEL

After completing my higher primary schooling, I went to secondary school at ga-Mashashane. Both Mashashane and Maraba chiefs are named after one person, probably their great-grandfather called Sibasa. Mashashane is also predominately Ndebele speaking people.

Initially, there were no secondary schools in the entire Limpopo region. Almost all the children in the surrounding areas attended boarding schools after Standard 6. There were lots of progressive boarding schools in Limpopo. The most popular ones were Roman Catholic Church schools, Pax for boys and Our Ladies for girls. Setotolwane, Bopedi Bapedi and Hwiti were combined high schools. Setotolwane was one of the best and most popular high schools in Limpopo. I was also admitted to Setotolwane, but unfortunately they did away with Form 1 a year before I went.

I received a communiqué at the end of November informing me that my admission was withdrawn as the school no longer accepted Form 1s. I was very devastated and cried so much that my mother had to do something. I was not going to miss a year of schooling. She suggested that we go and do self-application at one of the day schools in ga-Mashashane. Magandangele Secondary school was the only secondary school in existence and closest to my area. It only took day scholars; there were no boarding facilities.

It was the first week of January before the opening of the schools when my mother decided to approach the principal of Magandangele Secondary School. I insisted that I accompany her, just to make sure that he would take me. He lived next to Pax High School. It was raining very heavily that day and there was no transport to that area, so we had to walk. When we got there, we were told that he had left in the morning to ga-Mashashane, where the secondary school was, quite a distance away.

The rain was pouring, but my mother looked at me and said that we must walk there. I said it was okay and we started walking. When we got there, he had already gone back home. He had a car, and we did not even know him nor his car, so he must have passed us along the way as we had taken the main road and not a foot path. I was so frustrated that I did not know what to do. The schools were to open the following week.

We found his assistant, and related our story to him. He was so impressed by my mother's efforts. He thought that she was an exceptional parent and he kept on complimenting her.

The school was already full and was no longer admitting additional children. However, he decided to register me provisionally until he could speak to the principal. He asked me to come to school on the first day of its opening. I went and he'd already told the principal about me. The principal was very grateful for my mother's initiatives. Although the school was already full and no longer accepting additional pupils, he could not dismiss the temptation of wanting to squeeze me in under the circumstances. I guess it was a conscience thing, as he was not going to let my mother down. Besides, he was also very impressed by my Standard 6 results, and he saw potential. So, I was admitted. He advised me to work hard so that I should never disappoint my mother and myself. I was registered officially. I was grateful and very excited.

The same week, before the school re-opened, my mother went and bought me my school uniform, schoolbooks and all that was needed .

Ga-Mashashane and ga-Maraba are far apart, about four hours and 19 minutes walking distance, and 35 minutes by car. For a few months after I started schooling there, there was no transport to the school and I therefore had to walk by foot to and fro. Although I was walking with other children from my village and the neighbouring villages, it was very strenuous. The school knocked off at 4 o'clock and I would reach home at 7 o'clock. I used to get to school very tired, as well as back home. Luckily, we were still very young and energetic, otherwise it would have been impossible to walk such a long distance.

One of the shop owners at ga-Mashashane heard of our plight and arranged for scholar transport. He made one of his trucks available, so that we could commute for a small monthly fee. It was much better than walking, as the truck fetched us at 6 o'clock and we would arrive home at 7 o'clock in the evening. It took longer than normal driving distance of 35 minutes because it transported other children from neighbouring villages.

It was such a relief, although I had another setback as I am asthmatic. The dust affected my health and my lungs were always wheezing. I had to improvise. I did not have a protective mask, but my mother gave me one of her scarves to put around my nose. It was better than walking on foot, though.

Mid my second year at the school, the shop owner decided to purchase a scholar transport bus. That was a luxury. Our parents paid a transport fee every month and our lives became much better.

However, the only thing that almost spoiled my excitement of going to secondary school was this common practice that the older students would ill-treat the first years, calling them *mafreshers* (I guess it meant those who were fresh from high primary). We knew it as "treatment", although in fact the correct term is bullying. There was this girl who was much older than most of the pupils at the school. During break times she would approach us and start making fun of us.

I have ginger hair by nature and while I was growing up the ginger colour was very visible. She noticed my hair and would start poking fun at my hair and saying it looked like Cobra floor polish and she would laugh endlessly. I would often be so terrified because I feared her. Almost all of us were afraid of her. I cried most of the time. She started bullying me around, in such a way that it affected my self-esteem. My hair became a factor so that while at home I tried to figure out how to change the colour of my hair so that the girl would stop making fun of me.

I decided to use shoe polish to dye my hair, but the polish would not last because I washed my hair every day, meaning that I had to put polish on it every day. I would have to do it the night before going to school because in the morning I did not have enough time. Luckily, I was waking up very early and coming back home late so my mother did not notice. When going to sleep, I had to cover my hair so that it did not dirty my pillowcases. I was the one who did the washing, so I would wash the cloth I'd used to cover the pillowcases before my mother discovered. I think my plan did the trick, because the girl bully stopped provoking me.

Waking up early and catching a 6 o'clock bus was not a big deal for me. The fact that I came back home after 6 o'clock in the evening never bothered me either. After preparing supper and eating, I would stay behind while everyone went to sleep to do my homework with a paraffin or kerosene lamp for the table, and a hurricane lamp, we called it *lantere* (lantern in English), which was used to walk about the homestead when it was dark outside because of its glass shade's ability to protect the flames from sudden draft. Later we used candles as well.

There were times when I would study until midnight, especially during exams. Studying until late was not a problem since I'd started doing this while still at primary school. I always wanted to perform the best, and the principal and his assistant's words were engraved in my mind: I could not let my mother down. My hard work paid off, as I always held position one, two or three, if I performed poorly, until I completed my Form 3.

The worst thing was that I got badly injured a few weeks before sitting for my final year examinations. I went home for a weekend. My father was on leave. He was trying to fit doors to the newly-built house that was just being completed, and I was cleaning the floor next to the doors. One of the doors was not properly balanced and it fell on my left foot and left a big wound. The doctor who attended me said I was lucky that the injuries missed my ligaments and tendons by inches, otherwise it would have had to be amputated. Even though I was taken to the doctor late, my wound was not yet very bad, although canker was starting to set in because it was becoming sceptic, with blisters that oozed water forming around it.

The members of the family I was staying with were very kind to me. My aunt from a distant relative was married to Ledwabas with her being a Gwangwa. I am forever grateful to their daughter-in-law, who stayed with her parents-in-law who were my relatives. The husband was a last-born child, so according to culture he had to remain at home. The daughter-in-law's name is Maud Ledwaba, but I referred to her as Sis Maud. She was a teacher at one of the primary schools nearby. If she had not taken me to the doctor in time my leg would have been amputated. The thought of that still brings tears to my eyes, especially that she used her own money for transport and doctor fees. I made a point of telling her how blessed I was to have had her during my difficult times and that I am very grateful that she took good care of me as well as providing a shelter and food. She was touched. It was only by God's grace that she was there, and I was healed, and my leg was saved.

Coming back from school, I still went and fetched water from the well a distance from the house. I did not want to appear as if I were a spoiled child. Those who came across me made remarks about how bad my wound was, and I would be scared. My lower limb was painful in such a way that I could feel it straining as I walked. This was worsened by the fact that there was no transport from where I was staying with my relatives to school. The place is very mountainous, so I had to climb rocks and walk on an uneven foot path to school with a severe pain on my foot. I did not want to miss my examinations nor classes, so I just kept on limping to school. Studying very late into the night was not easy as my foot would get swollen

and very painful. All these mishaps affected my performance badly, but I still obtained a good pass. I passed with a second class, missing first class by few marks, I was told. I was very disappointed but grateful at the same time as my leg was gradually showing some improvement. One thing I know is that I could have obtained first class like I did with my Standard 6 certificate.

My injury also affected me because I loved sport, and I could not play any sport. My favourite sport was netball. I was very good at that. Not that I could not have played any sport including football, but because of sexism that was reserved for boys. The school and my team relied on me for scoring the ball. As a short person it was amazing that I could aim with ease, very accurate. Every time we went to compete with other schools we always performed the best. My netball name was "Open the Gate of Jerusalem". I do not know where or who gave me the name. It was so long but they cheered me shouting, "Open..." then a pause. As soon as I scored they would shout "...the gate of Jerusalem!" It was so funny.

Besides sport, I also liked other extramural activities such as performing (sketches), what is known as drama for entertainment, what is today referred to as soapies. I could have been an actor because I could laugh and cry easily and I am not shy. There were occasions when during entertainments they would ask those who were good at singing to come and render items.

One day, I decided to go on stage, although I knew that I could not sing. I wanted to sing, vocally wounded or not. There was a song I loved, that is mimicking or imitating a song by Frank Blackfield. "I Bless the day I found you, I want to stay around you, and so I beg you, let it be me..." The worst thing was that I forgot some of the lyrics. The school hall was full to capacity with students, parents and teachers. It burst into laughter. People laughed so much, and I could not have cared less. I believed I could sing. I still wish I could sing. I really love singing.

I am reminded of my first year at Magandangele. After school, when all the children who stayed a walking distance from school left and we remained behind because we had to wait for our scholar transport that would only arrive at 6 o'clock, after studying we would go outside to play. There was a giant boulder overlooking the school. We climbed to the top of it and started singing at the top of our voices, singing our lungs out until there were echoes vibrating in the air. I would be one of those who sang the loudest, as though I am gifted in singing. We loved the song by Harry Belafonte, "Amen".

I had a good time schooling at Magandangele.

As time went on, especially in Form 2, some children went adventuring. After school, they walked to the owner of the scholar bus transport's depot, so that they could board it to Lanseklip train station. The bus was not only used to pick up students but it was used by everyone, especially those who worked in the cities and were visiting their families. It was much easier to get off at Lanseklip train station than to go to Pietersburg and wait for the 2PM bus home. At Lanseklip, the bus waited for them at around 4AM and they arrived home early. Although Lanseklip did not have a proper platform to get off at, it was still a better option for most people. So, before coming to pick up students to school it would start at Lanseklip, and the same would happen in the afternoon.

On Fridays, the school came out earlier than on other days. To while away time, some students found it fun to wait for it at the depot and ride in it to Lanseklip and back to Magandangele to pick up other students.

Some of us were not interested, and we would remain behind. One afternoon, this boy who had befriended me came to see me after school. He was also a student at the same school, but his family stayed not far away. He went home and came back. He asked me why I was not accompanying the other children to the depot because in that way I would be able to see other places in ga-Mashashane. The only place I knew was around the school. He insisted that we walk to the depot and join the other children. I agreed, and we walked there. It was quite a distance and it was the first time that I saw how big the area was.

In the far distance from the school to the depot, we had to cross a donga. While in the middle of it he suggested that we rest under a tree because we still had enough time. The bus was leaving from the depot to the station at around 3PM. We sat there and just chatted, he started telling me how he loved me and wanted me to be his boyfriend. I told him that we were already friends. He then said, meaning that I loved him. I said if I did not love him, we would not be friends. Then he moved too close to me and asked me to show him how much I loved him. I became uncomfortable, especially since I did not understand what he really wanted from me. He insisted on kissing me, but I refused.

He asked me to take off my underwear and lie down. I became irritable and asked him why I had to take off my clothes. My impression had been that he was taking me to go and see where the depot was. Now I had to undress and lie down. I stood up but I did not know where I was. I wanted to go back to school. He told me that I was playing stupid, while meanwhile I knew what he was talking about. He mentioned that I did not love him if I could not show it to him. I immediately responded that if it was about me taking my clothes off, I did not want his friendship. He then said, let us walk to the depot. We walked without talking at all.

By the time we got at the depot, people were getting into the bus. He accompanied me to the bus, and I was the last to go in. He greeted the bus driver; they must have known each other. The driver of the bus was already seated behind the steering wheel. He asked me to stand next to him. He closed the door and before driving off he asked me who I was. I told him. He said I was so pretty that I reminded him of his girlfriend of yesteryear. I went in and sat down. As they say, curiosity killed the cat, and my decision to go to the depot was a wrong one. I did not understand why I reminded him of his girlfriend and I was puzzled by his insinuations.

We drove to Lanseklip and came back, and the bus was parked at the depot. Maybe it was still too early to go and pick up students. While sitting in the bus, he was outside with his colleagues (other drivers and mechanics) and they were sitting in the workshop opposite the window I was sitting next to. The driver called me. I went over and he instructed me to lie down on the cardboard box that was spread on the floor. They used it to lie down on when fixing vehicles in the workshop, and it had lots of oil and grease on it. I asked him what for? He said, "Do not come and make yourself smart here". He said I knew what he was talking about. I said I did not know, and I could not just lie down. He became angry and started threatening me. I snapped at him and walked back to the bus and sat down. He kept on yelling at me and calling me to come back, but I said never.

Other children were very scared and insisted that I go back and do as per his instructions, otherwise he was going to beat me. As for beating me, I witnessed that later when he stopped the bus at a village after mine. He had issues with older girls of which I was told one was his girlfriend. He asked us to go outside and they remained behind. He took his shoe off and started beating them, one by one. We were terrified by their screams. After about twenty minutes he called us in and drove off. We were very late at school; the principal was very angry because we were never that late.

I said to those who insisted that I go back that I would rather he beat me. I pretended to be brave, but I was shaking with fear. I was told later that he used to terrorise girls and he impregnated lots of them in the communities and no one could do anything about it. He was notorious and he was feared by everyone because if he wanted your daughter he would come and demand her and there was nothing the parents could do. He always carried two guns and he would wear only soldier clothes. I was told that he was a gangster from Alexandra.

Nonetheless, on this day he came back to the bus without saying anything and drove the bus via Magandangele Secondary school to home. His brother taught me biology and arithmetic (*rekenkunde*) and he was a very kind person. I studied with his two siblings and his father was very kind too, as he used to transport us. He was also respected as he also owned a retail shop next to the bus depot. I learnt many years after I'd left school that he was murdered (shot dead) by one of the siblings I was at school with.

One day my father came home by train. I did not know what had happened to his car. I boarded the bus in the afternoon next to the school and found him sitting on the front seat. I sat next to him, and I was so happy to see him. We chatted, and it was so pleasant. When we got home, I helped him carry his luggage. My father spoke to the driver as we got out of the bus and told him to send his regards to his father. I did not ask him where he knew him from. I was tempted to tell him of what he'd once tried to do to me but, opted to keep quiet.

The following morning when he came to pick us up, he stopped me as I was about to pass the driver's seat. He politely asked me to sit on the small seat next to his. I did so without feeling scared of him. He asked me whether the man I was with the day before was my father. I said yes, and he said he knew him from Alexandra, way back. He told me that my father was his father's friend, because the owner of the scholar bus service was his father. He apologised for what had happened the other day and said that I should not tell my father as he was very afraid of him. He said my father was a no-nonsense person and he respected him.

I told him that he had really humiliated me and what he tried to do to me was abhorrent and filthy. I wondered if he did not rape other children and they just kept quiet, considering how they were so terrified on my behalf. The experience reminded me of what happened to me before I went to the secondary school when I was almost raped. I decided to stay at the school because that was safe for me until I completed my Form 3. I realised later that the reason why most of the children I studied and travelled with had love affairs with bus drivers was that they were enticing them with money.

The incident above reminded me of a situation while I was at ga-Masemola that made me wonder why there was always a notorious rebel in almost every community. There was this guy who was Chief (*Kgoshi*) Tseke's nephew. His name was Hodu, and he used to terrorise the community, especially young girls. He was very feared by everyone. I recall how we used to be terrified when school mates and I saw him sitting on the veranda of his uncle's shop *Kgoshi Tseke* after school. His face, especially the eyes, were very scary. He provoked people so that he could beat them. He always fought with a small axe that he carried around; he was famously known for carrying *thamaoka*. I want to believe that it referred to an axe called a tomahawk.

One fateful day, I was coming from the school in the afternoon. I saw people gathered under a morula tree next to Chief Tseke's shop in a circle. Out of curiosity, myself and other children I was walking with stopped; we wanted to see what was happening. It was Hodu fighting with another man. What I'd observed about him was that he always walked without clothes on his upper body and, as I remember him, he had what is today called biceps and a six pack (I do not think it was from gym; maybe just natural). He was, in fact, well built, tall and dark in complexion.

As the fight ensued, he hit this man with his axe on the side of the head and blood oozed out. The sight of it was terrifying. Mysteriously, this man did not fall from his injuries; maybe he was not so badly hurt. He fought back, overpowered Hodu, and hit him with a fist so hard that he fell. He grabbed Hodu's axe. Hodu stood up and tried to fight back, but the man landed the axe on his head with so much force that his brain scattered everywhere. He died on the spot. People around ululated with joy and a sense relief; a psychopath had been murdered and people would live in peace!

For quite a while I reflected on the two incidents mentioned above and the one I mentioned earlier, that is, the one in which I was almost raped. I kept on asking myself what it is that gave men the audacity to have asked me to take my clothes off and lie down, although then I did not know what it meant. As a grown up and understanding the patriarchal ripple effects as far as gendered, or rather patriarchal, hierarchy is concerned, I concluded that societies have socialised men to believe that women's bodies are theirs to take, conquer and discard. The same hypocritical society has socialised girls into the skills of becoming wife material and perfecting backbreaking household chores, including taking care of their boy brothers and later in life their husbands and children. In the same breath, boys were encouraged to loiter on the street corners and shops, learning how to conquer girls.

Today, South Africa is reaping the fruit of patriarchy, socialisation and culture that promoted the notion of superiority and inferiority complexes between women and men. This is witnessed in the ravaging gender-based violence, especially in the form of femicide and rape, and violence in general. But still, the very same society does not understand, or pretends not to, that GBV is a consequence of patriarchy because of the dividends it afforded men.

I, therefore, concur with authors who elaborate on the notion of conquering women's bodies. According to Kaminer and Dixon (1995), the notion of conquest needs to be understood in relation to patriarchy, particularly masculinity, because masculinity is not a property of men but an everyday code of practice that regulates behaviour between women and men at sites of violation. Various masculine activities fuel the spread of these. This includes the concept of an insatiable male sex drive, the notion of conquest, masculinity as penetration, males as risk takers and the notion of the idealised male body.

The discourse of the insatiable male sex drive holds that men are driven by an uncontrollable sex drive that is biologically rooted. In the face of this insatiable drive, women simply must submit to provide men with the desired relief and satisfaction, regardless of whether this constitutes harassment and abuse. The wide acceptance of this notion results in the perpetuation of risky sexual behaviour, leading to GBV. I am going to refer to this as Male Violence Against Women (MVW) to be specific, because the term GBV is very broad.

Nauright and Chandler (1996) hold another belief that masculinity is linked to penetration. To be male is to penetrate, and penetration serves to reinforce and stabilise a man's sense of masculinity. In brief, masculinity relates to penetration, regardless of whom, how or what it is that one is penetrating. In this light, the condom is regarded as an impediment to the capacity for or intensity of penetration, especially if considered in conjunction with raw, unhindered conquest, therefore reducing one's sense of masculinity. This explain why South Africa still has the highest HIV and AIDS infection, which is prevalent in African communities because it is where the notions of masculinity and manhood are mainly practised.

Talking about masculinity and manhood reminds me of one horrific incident that happened while growing up. A young man who was old enough to marry introduced several girls to his parents who at every attempt rejected the girls of his choice. He became frustrated by his parents who refused to accept any girl that he chose to marry. Thus, he decided to remove his private parts in protest. His parents' constant refusal to allow him to marry a girl of his choice was an indication that he was not a man enough. In other words, like many young men of his age, a description of being man enough lay in his ability to use his penis, apparently for the purpose of conquering and reproducing offspring.

Out of despair and anger, he took a knife and went into the veld quite far away, amongst the bushes, and took off his pants and sat down on a flat rock. He used the knife to slice off his genitals. After he finished, he left everything on the rock and went home. He was bleeding profusely, I am told. Perhaps he did that to spite the parents. I was told he died a few minutes after reaching home from having bled a lot. The parents, especially the father who was a local priest, were shocked when they realised what had happened. They must have understood the reason behind the tragedy. This man was uncle to the boy I mentioned earlier, who used to write love letters to me. This is how men value the notion of masculinity and manhood, especially the idea that penetrative sexual intercourse makes a real masculine man.

Furthermore, any forms of sexual expression that do not involve penetrative sexual intercourse are inconsistent with the definition of oneself as masculine. Petersen (1998) argues that masculinity assumes the materiality of the male body as opposed to the female body. McGinity on the other hand argues that "society defines masculinity along lines that lift men up according to how big and strong they are and how many sexual conquests they have". "It replicates this idea that men have some inalienable right to touch women at their whim." The same goes for sexist and patriarchal clumsy language that fosters prejudice against women. Patriarchy is an elephant in the room that must be dismantled if this country is serious about ridding itself of the scourge of GBV.

Susan Brownmiller articulates, "Closely related to conquest is the notion of males as risk takers. Embarking on conquests through hunting or war, men defined their sense of self as risk takers. This behaviour has been extended into various aspects of typically masculine behaviour such as substance abuse, reckless driving or participating in dangerous sports. The ideal male body is conceptualised as heterosexual and driven by a biologically determined sex drive. Heterosexual men have been established as the standard for measuring and evaluating other bodies. The ideal masculinity among the men has been used to emphasise the power that men should have over women, where men are like bulls that should conquer as many cows as possible in their kraal. The term 'conquest' in this case refers to the expression of power, bravery, and the amount of risk-taking associated with men, especially how to expose oneself to pain in pursuit of dominance in society. Now lately, men no longer refer to women as things to be conquered but smashed." This explains the escalating incidents related to horrendous way women are murdered in South Africa.

For her, similarly, "Rape is not a crime of irrational, impulsive, uncontrollable lust, but is a deliberate, hostile, violent act of degradation and possession on the part of would-be conquerors". "As we examine these cases, we must be mindful of where power lies, how it is used and abused and the victims it leaves in its wake. A reality is that violence against women is not a new phenomenon, it is a microcosm of our hetero-normative society. The society that is rooted in the structural nature of patriarchal violence. In this country, ravaging violence against women experienced daily has a direct link to the extent to which the notion of men having power over women is normalised."

Talking about the normalisation of conquering a woman in relation to rape, I am reminded of an article I once read: "... But the most widespread concerns were about Mogoeng's judgments in rape and gender-violence cases. The Nobel Women's Initiative accused Mogoeng of invoking dangerous myths about rape and of victim-blaming. Of the many judgments cited by critics in which Mogoeng had been lenient on rapists and domestic assailants, three were emphasised. In *State v Sebaeng*, Mogoeng reduced the sentence of a child rapist on the basis that he had been non-violent and indeed 'tender' in raping the victim. The 2005 case of *State v Moipolai* involved the rape of a pregnant woman by her long-term boyfriend. Despite several aggravating factors, Mogoeng reduced the man's sentence from ten years' imprisonment to five because the rape was, he said, not as serious as if a stranger had committed it.

"Finally, in *State v Mathebe*, Mogoeng reduced the sentence, from two years' imprisonment to a fine of R4 000, of a man who had tied his girlfriend to his car and dragged her 50 metres along a dirt road. Mogoeng's explanation was that the man had been 'provoked' by the victim. When these three judgments were raised in a BBC interview, Mogoeng compared his judgments in sexual assault cases to a game of football, saying it would be wrong to call Manchester United a bad team because it loses three matches in a season. Legal academic Pierre de Vos said Mogoeng was clearly the most conservative member of the Constitutional Court. He pointed to Mogoeng's ambivalence over gay rights. In *Le Roux v Dey*, Mogoeng dissented, without giving reasons, from paragraphs which said it was not defamatory to call someone gay..."

Coming from a person of Mogoeng Mogoeng's stature in society, a lawyer who is supposed to defend the rights that are trampled upon, this is paralysing. Unfortunately, Mogoeng, the same as Kemp, who was also a lawyer, represents the attitude of many men in South Africa. One thing I know is that people will always defend the things they like whether wrong or right. So, the question is, are these kinds of men not themselves women violators or children abusers? Similarly, the likes of Mogoeng and Kemp are ignorant of the fact that sexism born from patriarchal mentality is like racism born from apartheid. The comparison is justifiable insofar as they are both a crime against the people. What makes sexism so difficult to comprehend, and the perpetrators equally vile, is that the primary perpetrators claim that it is natural to act like that because the bible, culture and tradition say so, oblivious to the fact that sexism is stealing women's very existence.

The incidents I mentioned above brought shock, dismay and anger to me when I realised that if they had happened in the present times, where the culture of GBV is normalised and exacerbated by deterioration in our social norms and values, I could have died at the hands of either one of these two men. The irony was that these were men with a big age difference in that the bus driver was a mature man and the other a young man in his teenage years, who was still of school-going age. They both reacted in the same way to my resistance because they did not expect a female to resist a man's advances, an attitude that society through patriarchy had created. I was supposed to have been submissive and to do as I was commanded.

It is my belief that the ravaging GBV in this country is fuelled by emphasis on democracy, where equality between women and men is preached. The challenge, though, is that this is not aligned with what society practises in terms of gender relations. Hence, men regard equal right as a challenge to their manhood, which is afforded to them by the patriarchal system in the first place. By implication, women do not deserve these rights because the system has denied it to them from time immemorial.

I was fortunate enough to have believed at a very early age that boys were not better than me, and resisted being bullied. I knew deep down my heart that there was absolutely nothing that a boy could do that I could not. Had this not been so then, like many girls, I would have fallen victim to this conquering mentality. I resisted being humiliated by these men, but this could have put my life in danger, because in many cases of femicide, rape, sexual abuse as well as domestic violence, women were maimed and murdered because they resisted being treated as patriarchy expected them to be.

The more women fight back, the more men retaliate by hurting them because they are still socialised to think that they are superior to inferior women and therefore they can do as they wish with them: so many contradictions. It is also compounded by the extent to which patriarchal dividends afford men with too many privileges and a sense of entitlement to women's bodies. South Africa as a society should prioritise correcting what it has created as far as bringing up the male gender goes, otherwise we are to live with this kind of violence that is bedevilling the country unabated. But I am hopeful that women will one day rise and dismantle patriarchy and its tentacles, such as socialisation and culture.

Reverting to the theme of this chapter, not being admitted to a boarding school and becoming a day scholar was such a blessing in disguise for me. I really enjoyed seeing my mother daily and helping her with house chores, especially over the weekends. That gave me satisfaction. But satisfaction in that I was helping my mother, not that I loved house chores *per se*; that is the difference.

I woke up in the wee hours of the morning on Saturdays to go and chop firewood. I would make sure that I gathered enough wood in a neatly tied bundle so that it would last us at least a week. I had done the chores from when I was at primary school. I remember how my mother used to admire that. She kept on praising me by saying *ke a leboga Pheladi* (thank you, Pheladi); this is what we called *sereto*. In Pedi, every child is given a praise name (*sereto*). My elder sister is Mahlako and my younger one is Pebetse and my husband is Hlabirwa, and so forth. My father's side, that is Ndebeles, do not have such individual praise names and we are all referred to by a collective *sereto*, which is Morongwa, or Barongwa when you are many.

The chore that I ceased doing when I went to secondary school was fetching water from the windmill because my cousins and my sister were there to collect water after school. They would go and fetch wood on Saturdays. Sometimes during school holidays, I would help my mother in the fields.

While I was in Standard 6, my sister would come home with all her belongings earlier than their school holiday break. She would tell me that they were sent home because there was student revolt at Turfloop University. Turfloop was the only tertiary institution (university) in the province. It was meant to cater for North Sotho speaking, Tsonga and Venda students, according to the Separate Development Policy of the apartheid system. Thus, it was called SOVENGA. I could not understand a thing, but I could see from my mother's face that it was something very serious.

When I went to secondary school at Magandagele, schooling was interrupted again. My sister came back home, this time for a very long time. We were told of this student by the name of Onkgopotse Tiro, who organised the student revolt. I was in Form 1. Onkgopotse Tiro, a past-president of the Black Consciousness Movement (BCM) Student Representative Council (SRC) in Turfloop made a speech at the student assembly. In his speech he criticised discrimination in education, and the entire apartheid system. He was later expelled, a boycott of lectures took place, and Turfloop was closed. The boycott spread to other black campuses and soon all universities were boycotting, as well as other colleges of education and boarding high schools. Many of the students were arrested and expelled from the university.

One day, in the morning prayer assembly, our principal came to address us with a very sad face. I could see that he had been crying. He told us that the student leader in Turfloop, Onkgopotse Tiro, had been assassinated (murdered) by the South African Police force in Botswana using a petrol bomb. His son was also arrested the same time with Tiro and others. He told us about how evil the apartheid system was, but not in real detail, so I could not understand what he was talking about. At the same time, I could sense that something was not right in this country. The thing is that where I came from was a very remote rural area and there were no newspapers nor radios to listen to news. Even later, when we could afford radios, issues related to the liberation struggle, including black political leaders and their organisations, were banned. I could not make sense out of what the principal told us until I came to Johannesburg and was exposed to information.

Talking about prayer assembly, towards the end of the year examinations, the local priest would be invited to come and pray that we performed well, and passed our examinations. There were a number of different church denominations around the school, so the priest was alternated over the years. A local priest who shared the same surname as mine, Gwangwa, came to pray for us when we wrote our final examinations. He started by preaching before making a prayer. It was the first time I'd heard him talking. He preached in North Sotho, although the school was mainly for Ndebele children, but there were other children and teachers who were not Ndebeles. The theme was from the bible, *Botate ba lle matata meno gwa shia a bana* (translated as: sins of the fathers will be passed along generations; Exodus 20:5 is specific that this is to third and fourth generations.

His voice was so funny and squeaky. I'd never heard anyone talking like that and I could not contain myself, although I tried. I burst into laughter. I could not stop. Our principal and the rest of the teachers standing in front of us on the veranda stared at me in embarrassment. I could not stop. I laughed until my tummy started to hurt and other children were also giggling. He just continued preaching and praying. The more he raised his voice, the more it became scratchy and vibrating.

After he'd finished, the announcements were made, and we were dismissed to classes. The principal called me to his office. I had never been to his office before, unlike naughty children who were often called to his office. When he called one, most often it was about one's unbecoming behaviour. He stood there and called my name and said, "You of all the children!" I apologised and promised that it would never happen again. I told him that

I did not know what had come over me. He let me go without punishing me or informing my mother, otherwise I would have been in real trouble.

The incident in Turfloop was followed by the 1976 riots. Schooling and learning in Lebowa schools was already interrupted and politicised and no longer running smoothly, and the 1976 riots just finished what was already started. When I was at secondary school, we used to do most of the subjects in Afrikaans. For example, mathematics (*rekunkunde*), homecraft (*huisvluit*) and science (*wiskunde*), and Afrikaans as a vernacular. I never questioned anything because we had done all the subjects in Northern Sotho, except English, at primary school. In my mind it was how it should have been.

The story of June 1976 is well known, and it was triggered by an instruction in 1975 by the Minister of Bantu Education that half the subjects in Standard 5 and Form 1 must be taught in Afrikaans. There was widespread opposition to the regulation. Some people opposed it for educational reasons, saying that children would suffer.

Protests against using Afrikaans as a medium of instruction in black schools spread from school to school in Soweto and other townships such as Mamelodi in Pretoria and Sebokeng in the Vaal Triangle. The police used dogs, guns, tear gas, armoured cars (hippos) and helicopters. I happened to witness the 1976 riots first hand because when the riots spread from Soweto to other townships I was in Mamelodi East, visiting my cousin. I saw pupils mowed down by machine guns like flies. The gunshots and screams never stopped. Day and night were the same. The air was filled with tear gas. It was real mayhem and scary.

Radios were buzzing with news of many school children dying daily, with parents burying their children like never before.

The atmosphere was very volatile with children scattered everywhere, throwing stones at police vans. It was mayhem. The police in retaliation killed them like flies, and one would witness a police van collecting corpses. I am told most of them were not dead but unconscious when they were thrown into the vans. They apparently died of suffocation as they were packed in like sardines.

I remember one afternoon, we were just sitting in the house when tear gas was thrown into my sister's yard, close to their bedroom. The smoke entered through a window and the baby was sleeping there. We were all coughing and blinded by the smoke. That was horrible.

Large numbers of people were arrested and among them was Steve Biko, the Black Consciousness Movement (BCM) leader, whose death in detention in 1977 shocked the world. Then, I could not grasp everything other than that students were protesting the use of Afrikaans as a medium of instruction.

As I later started to be exposed to books and newspapers and read widely, I saw 1976 as part of the wider context. For example, the atmosphere of nationwide revolts in the 1970s like the trade union protest. There were the liberation struggles in Mozambique, Angola, Zimbabwe and Namibia. The economy of the country was in recession and lots of blacks were laid off. Due to the apartheid system and its policies, townships such as Soweto were overcrowded and there were inadequate facilities like transport and housing. There were problems like the pass laws, influx control and compulsory homeland citizenship. All these contributed to the background of the uprisings.

After completing my Form 3, I could not go for Forms 4 and 5; that is to matric level. I instead opted to go for nursing. Back then, people still qualified to enrol for courses such as Junior Teacher Certificate JSC, elementary nursing called Auxiliary Nursing Certificate or the police force with a Form 3 certificate.

Not being able to further my studies did not discourage me from continuing to dream high. Although some people thought we were poor, my father assured us that we were not because we had a house, food and clothes. He hammered that into our heads. I did not ask him why until I came across a song by Gloria and Gail Gaither: *Thank you Lord for Your Blessings.* It goes like this: "As the world looks upon me, as I struggle along, they say I have nothing, but they are so wrong. In my heart I am rejoicing, how I wish they could see. For there is a roof up above me, I have a good place to sleep, there is a food on my table, and shoes on my feet. You gave me Your love Lord and a fine family and to me that is all matters. Hence until today I am still saying: Thank you Lord for Your Blessing on me."

Chapter Four

LIFE AFTER SCHOOL-GOING AGE

While I was very young, I promised my mother that I would one day become the first woman priest, and my mother, being a staunch Christian, marvelled at the idea. But when I went to secondary school the idea gradually faded away. I wanted to become a nurse. Form 3 was still recognised as a higher standard of education and few children were motivated to proceed to matric then.

I applied to various hospitals for training as a nurse while still at school. Most of the children that I was with at school had already been admitted to hospitals of their choice but I had not. I was desperate because I knew that I had performed better than most of them. My mother encouraged me to stay hopeful, patient and to never stop praying, which I did.

While still waiting for admission to any of the hospitals that I'd applied to, the principal of John Nrhimba, the local primary school that I'd attended, asked my mother to allow me to come and teach as a private teacher for Standard 4 pupils. In January, when the schools re-opened, they were short of teachers, so I accepted the offer, although I was never keen on teaching. I could have been a good teacher though, because the principal of the school was satisfied with my work. I only left teaching when I received a letter of acceptance for training as a nurse.

Siloam Hospital in Venda responded to my application by sending me forms to complete. I did and sent them back. After a month, I received an acknowledgement letter and a few weeks later I was called to come and finalise the application process, with an oral interview. I had never been to Venda before. I left alone to take my journey. Then there were no taxis ferrying people from my village to town, where the railway station was, so I had to go earlier and wait for lifts to town.

It was about 4PM when the lift came. A van picked me up so that I could wait for the 2 o'clock train at Pietersburg Park Station. I boarded the train coming from from Johannesburg Park Station via Polokwane: then it was called Pietersburg to Louis Trichardt in Venda. The train arrived at exactly 2 o'clock in the morning and arrived in Louis Trichardt at 8 o'clock the same morning. I had to wait for the afternoon bus to Ntshelele village, where the hospital is situated. The bus arrived at 2 o'clock in the afternoon. I only arrived at the hospital at around 4 o'clock the same afternoon.

I stayed at the hospital for one week, doing an oral interview that was followed by some sort of orientation test and it was the outcome of that which would determine whether I was a suitable candidate or not. I went back home and waited for almost a month for a response, and finally they called me to start training as an auxiliary nurse. I was over the moon. I considered myself a professional nurse because I could not see how I could fail.

I truly enjoyed been a nurse trainee and I took my training very seriously. I envisaged myself becoming a professional nurse and going up the ladder. This was the reason why, a few months after being at the hospital, I asked those who had come before me about an adult education centre where I could further my studies and obtain a matric certificate. I did not want to be content with an auxiliary nurse position.

However, the nursing environment then was like in the military. They were very strict, starting with how you projected yourself in terms of grooming and dressing, as well as how we should walk. The dress code was emphasised. For example, we were forced to wear stockings.

The treatment was very cruel. I remember the first week I started with my job; it was in the casualty ward and I was working day shift. The nurses I worked with, including the sister nurse, did not make me aware that I had to go for dinner between 6PM and 7PM. It was only when the night shift nurses reported to work fifteen minutes before 7PM that they asked me whether I'd had supper. I told them that I did not know what time I should go. I looked through the window, as the dining hall was opposite my ward, and I could see my colleagues sitting there and eating. They told me to rush because they were about to close. When I got there, everyone just laughed at me. Even those who came back to hand over to the night nurses said nothing to me. I could have slept hungry that night because there were no shops close by and we were not allowed to keep food in our rooms.

All the newly recruited trainee nurses were inducted the same way. Our training job started in a sluice room. This is the place where soiled sheets and blankets were stored. Before they were sent to the laundry, we were to clean them: hence, sluice. There was a long pipe that was used to clean them. It was attached to a wall and had a tap to open and close it, like the ones used by Muslims in their toilets.

The first week I started there, I considered leaving and going back home because of the smell and dirt. Even when you were wearing a mask, the smell just penetrated it and latex gloves could not help because you still felt like you were dirty. Those who are very sick, sometimes mess their bed. The bedridden ones were taken care of twenty-four seven, so they would not be so messy. Some would be vomiting, relieving themselves, all that you could think of. But I looked around at my colleagues and said, "I am not alone here; what about the rest. I must be strong." I eventually got used to it.

The other function for us was to go and fetch clothes for those who were discharged. Patients were not allowed to bring their night clothes, like they do today. There were hospital clothes that they would wear. All personal clothes and other items were placed in a plastic bag, marked and stored in a room meant for that until the patient was discharged. One day, I was asked to go and get the clothes of a man who was there for a long time. I found them and, as I looked at the transparent plastic bag, I realised that there were things moving inside. There were so many that they filled the big bag and covered the clothes.

I threw it on the floor and went out running. I reported to the senior ward nurse of my encounter. She must have suspected what those things were, for she just shook her head and smiled. She asked another nurse to accompany me. I pointed to the bag, and she picked it up. She said to me, "These are lice. We must get rid of them." That meant they were to be sprayed with chemicals so that they all died. Then the clothes could be removed from the plastic bag and handed to the owner. I was so petrified; it was like there was trauma after trauma.

After the induction came to an end, I graduated to going to work in the other wards. The first ward I worked on was a female ward, a general ward. I worked there for about a month. Then later the ward sister asked me to work in intensive care. There I was not allowed to give medicines to patients; only senior nurses did that. As part of the training, my job was to change linen, make beds, take their temperature and blood pressure and ensure that I recorded them accurately in their bed record. Daily reports of the patient status were recorded in the file, and it had to hang at the foot of bed all the time. Hence they were called bed records.

We were also taught how to dress wounds. I remember how Matron would drill the words into our heads: "Do not injure the patient; do not contaminate the wound". In the intensive care unit allocated to me there was a woman who was admitted there, very gravely ill. She had cervical cancer at stage four and was bleeding throughout. My responsibility was to care for her in terms of bathing, changing linen and just making her comfortable. I had to change her nappies all the time as she was bed ridden. I felt pity for her. She eventually died one afternoon, and the sister called me to come to assist in preparing her for the mortuary, once she'd been certified dead after two hours. This was also part of my training.

She was to be bathed after closing every hole on her to avoid the spreading of diseases, and wrapped in a shroud, a plastic-like material meant to cover the bodies of dead people. But I was the only one to transport her to the mortuary by trolley. Siloam hospital did not have porters, so if someone died in your care it was your responsibility to transport her or him to the mortuary. There were trolleys that were used for the purpose. I went and fetched it and they assisted me in lifting her onto the trolley.

I had to take her to the mortuary, which was secluded from the hospital but in the same yard. It was getting dark and I was so scared to be with a corpse alone. One nurse volunteered to accompany me so that she could help me push the trolley, as dead people are often extra heavy. However, the woman in question was not heavy as she was so emaciated. She was so thin that she looked like a skeleton. Cancer is a very merciless disease. She helped me to push the trolley. One person would be at the back, and the other in front to give it balance. We went and stored her on a mortuary shelf and closed it. It was the first time I had ever been in there. The only person working there was a security person. Next to the mortuary was a small building where they burnt still-born babies. Everything was just so scary for me, but I eventually got used to the fact that the furnace (fire made of coal) was always on, although the area was cordoned off.

After some time I was transferred to the male's ward, also doing day shift. It was supposed to be like that because as a trainee nurse you need to be familiar with your environment, so rotating you was part of giving you an opportunity to learn from different scenarios. I was assigned to one row of the ward to take care of those patients. There was this one patient who just loved me, and we often talked. He was working in Johannesburg and staying in Alexandra. He was impressed by the fact that I knew Johannesburg, including Alexandra, from way back when my father had had a house there. The patient had a heart problem but looked fine. I remember that his surname was Mulaudzi but have forgotten his first name.

One afternoon at around 3PM he started gasping, having difficulties in breathing. He called my name so loudly that the whole ward vibrated. I was busy with another patient, but I rushed to him. I did not know what to do because he had thrown himself on the floor. He was a very big, heavy man. I called a senior ward nurse, and his bed was cordoned off. I was with her there as an assistant. He started bleeding through the mouth and nose, so much blood that he had to use the bucket to vomit blood into. Other nurses came to help us lift him onto the bed but he died.

I do not know what came over me, but I ran out of the ward. Before I could exit, the senior sister called me back. She said nothing other than I must watch her preparing him for the mortuary. She must have known that as a new nurse one might react like that. But, before we did anything, he was to be left there for about two hours before being certified dead. People who die from a heart attack take a long time to turn cold.

It was routine or standard policy that before the patient was sent to the mortuary, her or his eyes would be properly closed, as well as every hole in the body plugged with cotton wool and a shroud wrapped around the body. Once finished with wrapping her or him, we had to make sure that she or he was laid on their back so that the brain could not leak through ears and nostrils. That was another reason why the nose, ears and mouth should be plugged with the cotton wool.

This patient was so heavy that I felt sorry for those who were to carry him to the mortuary and lift him onto the shelf. By the time I finished, it was about time for me to knock off. I went and scrubbed my hands with a nail brush and soap for a long time, particularly my nails, although we were not allowed to grow our nails to avoid germs and bacteria building in them. There was a particular way for washing our hands, it was also part of training. Fortunately, the night nurses were the ones to carry him to the mortuary.

The sister in question stayed in the same block as mine at the residential area. She later asked me to come to her room and warned me about my behaviour earlier. She told me that this was what I would witness on a daily basis and I therefore needed to be strong. What I had to do in the morning was to take his bed outside for it to be cleaned and aired. It was a normal routine that, once a person died, their bed must be fumigated, especially the mattress, and the linen sent for laundry.

At that time there were no telephones available in communities, so the family was not informed. They only learned of his passing when they came to visit during visiting times the following day. I knew the wife already because she had visited several times. I had seen her and members of the family from a distance when they'd come visiting him. I decided to hide myself from her. Immediately, they realised that his bed had been removed from the ward he had been admitted to, and they started crying because they knew what that meant. The senior sister called them to her office to announce the sad news to them. I could hear the screams and yelling from her office. I felt sorry for them because he was apparently a bread winner.

It was after some time that I was transferred to a children's ward. During the time that I was there, there was a horrible outbreak of measles. Many children died. In fact, they were dying like flies because most of the time they were brought to hospital when it was too late. At that time, measles outbreaks were very common, and families used their own traditional remedies. Somehow, they worked because very few children would die. It was common that when one of the family's children had measles, they would put a piece of wood in front of the entrance, as a sign that people should not enter the house to avoid infecting other children or spreading the disease.

There was one time when I went to the linen room and there was a small body covered in a cloth lying there. I went closer and checked him. I could see that he was dead. I got scared and covered him quickly. The night nurses gave us their report. So many children had died that night. The one I'd found in the linen room had died earlier, but the two hours had not passed and he was still to be certified. Unfortunately, he was not in the ward section allocated to me, so I was not to do anything.

While still in children's ward, still doing night shift, I had a child that I just loved so much. Her name was Takalani Mashudu. She had been in the hospital for a long time. She had not come there because of measles but because she had a rare disease. One of the evenings when I came to work after my one day off, I went to the bathroom. I was looking for something and right there I saw the small body of a child, lying on a plank placed across the bath and covered in a white cloth. I looked closer and I could not believe my eyes. Takalani had died. I was shocked. I still remember how I felt a lump in my throat. It choked me. For seconds I could not breathe. All I could do was to scream. Nurses came running. I could not talk; I simply pointed at her. They consoled me and explained to me that she complicated late in the afternoon and there was nothing they could do for her. It was not so long after she'd died that I clocked in.

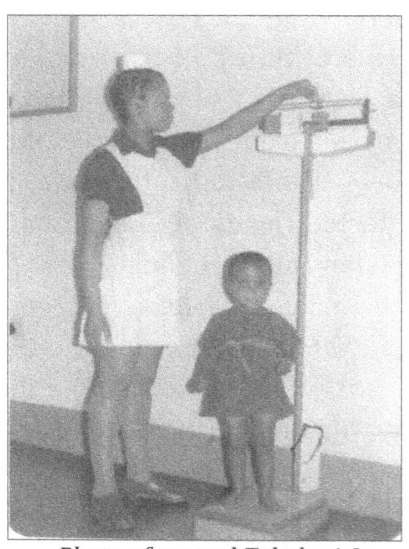

Photo of me and Takalani. I was weighing her on a scale

I was consoled by the fact that I had not seen her dying, otherwise I would have been more traumatised by not being able to save her. Saving people's lives in hospitals then was done with dedication, hard work and pride; hence, it was something taken very seriously. Above all, it was such an honour because we were encouraged to live up to the oath we took and signed for when we accepted the job offer. Unlike nowadays, nurses were paid a stipend while training. I was paid R45 then. For me it was a lot of money, especially since all that I did with the money was to send it home and buy clothes and other necessities. Food and uniform were provided by the hospital.

Takalani was one of the patients assigned to me. So, it was my duty to prepare her for the mortuary after being certified. I did all the necessary procedures, and I was to carry her there, somehow. I wanted to take her on my own as a way of finding closure.

The children who died did not have their own trolleys: those were only for adults. We had to carry them in our arms. I carried her to the mortuary and selected an empty shelf suitable for the child. Gently, and with utmost respect, I placed her on a cold corrugated shelf and said goodbye and walked away without looking back. It was indeed a sombre moment. The frustrating part was when the family came to collect her body. I still remember when the mother and other relatives came to fetch her. I was the one to take them there, and we walked without talking I did not know what to say to them.

They had not brought a coffin. They just covered her body with a blanket and put her on the back seat of the car and left. Maybe back at home they were still busy carving her small coffin, as there were no funeral parlours then. When a person died, men would make coffins for them; I witnessed that too often. There were no private mortuaries either, so from the public mortuary straight to the cemetery for those who died in hospital. But those who died at home were buried on the same day, mostly in the evening. Most people died at home, just as they were birthed at home by traditional midwives, who were commonly elderly women. Growing up, we were told that people died only in the night. In those days, only men attended the funeral; women did not. I cannot remember whether there was any cooking done, but I do not think so.

Every time we saw men converging under a tree and starting to carve a coffin, we would know that someone had died (*o hlokafetse* in Sepedi or *o hlongaphele* in Ndebele). Adults did not talk to children about this; it was shrouded in secrecy. We were not allowed to witness the funeral at all. We had to stay at home until they came back. Death and birth were sacred; thus, they were respected.

The first time I went to a funeral, I was in Standard 5 and my school classmate died. She had a rare disease. She always fainted in class from what we referred to as fits. The correct medical term is epilepsy, and this happened especially during hot summer days. As classmates, we were asked to come to her funeral. It was during the week, so we put on our uniform. I still remember how we gathered around the graveside under a tree. I was so shocked that I kept on asking myself what it must be like to die. My mind ran wild at that moment, but after a while those memories just faded away.

This practice of just putting a dead person in the back of a car covered only with a blanket was very common. Although, we were not allowed to be in the vicinity of a house where someone died then, it happened that in the neighbourhood the brother to the lady whom we always accompanied with her goats for grazing (*madishong*) died. I also used to hear that the man was the father to Lina Ramushu. I mentioned earlier that he was not living with them; they lived apart, and I never understood why. I only knew later in life that her parents were not married, and her father never got married as his funeral took place at the parents' homestead. Her father died in a hospital called Jane Furse. The arrival of the hearse took our parents off guard. They did not have time to chase us away to shield us from witnessing as people rushed there to receive the corpse. I remember seeing mothers in the neighbourhood, including my mother and aunt, rushing to the house. We were playing under a very big *mohlopi* (*Bascia albitruncia*) tree.

Nonetheless, our mothers cautioned us, literally instructing us not to move from where we were playing. We were to sit still and quiet, while off they went. Maybe things changed then because I saw women and men – *bomahlalela*: able bodied men who were too lazy to go and work faraway places like the other men in the communities; only those who were somehow disabled should have remained at home, as well as maybe professionals such as teachers and priests, otherwise the migrant labour system swallowed all of them. They were all standing next to the hearse together.

Being children and always curious, we decided to climb to the top of the tree so that we could peep. We quickly ascended to the branches with a good view of the house. We saw the lifeless body of Lina's father off loaded from the hearse. His legs were protruding from whatever he was covered with. Maybe he was very tall and there was no shroud to fit him properly. As far as I knew, shrouds were made in different sizes and designed in such a way that there was a portion for hands, the body, legs, even the head. What was left exposed was the face, I think to make it easier to identify a person. For me, curiosity did not pay off as the image of his legs protruding stayed with me for a while. I regretted not having listened to our parents, but this too faded away with time.

After some time of being at Siloam Hospital, I got used to seeing corpses to the point that sometimes some of us during our days off would decide to visit the mortuary in the afternoon.

As trainees, we were all the same age: teenagers with some in their early twenties; very young and ignorant. Visiting the mortuary was for us an entertainment, perhaps out of boredom because there was not much else to do, and we were not allowed to go and loiter in the nearby villages. So, visiting the mortuary just to go and view corpses one by one was another way of whiling away time.

The guard would open for us. He knew all of us as it was a very small hospital then. We would open the shelves, looking for those in which bodies were stored. We were not only opening the shelves, but we would also pull out the trays for a better view of them. Some would even poke fun at them, but for me corpses always carried this frightening mystery, so there was never a good side. Only the new trainees would be interested in going there and I do not think it was allowed.

There was a section of the mortuary reserved for those who had not died in hospital. One day we decided to go and check if there were corpses there. Some nurses knew the reason why some of us never had to open shelves in that section and the guard always directed us where to store those who died in hospital. I just thought maybe it was used when the other section was full.

We opened the shelves and I got the shock of my life. Some of the corpses had their teeth exposed because their lips had been cut off. Others had had their eyes gouged out, and some had had their limbs and intestines removed (disembowelled) and so forth. Literally mutilated, some were not recognisable because of the stage of decomposition. They had been discovered by police in the veld and brought there. Some were dressed and some were naked.

I did not even eat supper that day. I felt so sick. Those pictures of them kept on playing in my head. It was like a horror movie, and I vowed never to go back there. I asked what had happened to them, and it was explained that they had been killed for *muthi*, what is commonly known as *muthi* killings. In Venda, the practice of *muthi* killings for body parts was very common and rife. It was called *ko biya* in Venda or *go buwa* in Sepedi. All those dead bodies were victims of gruesome death. Mostly, they were grown up men, young men and boys, but rarely females.

I am shocked that the practice spread to almost every part and corner of this country unabated, and the majority of those that bear the brand of this barbaric act are now women and children, as well as albinos, as people believing in this nonsense became desperate. The government is losing the battle against eradicating this kind of social ill, the same as it is unable to address witchcraft killings, GBV and hate killings and murder in general.

After I was almost six months at the hospital, I was due for six days leave. One could only take annual leave of two weeks after a year. One's leave days were staggered: that is, one day, three days, six days and two weeks leave. It was too far for me to go home during the short days off, because it took me a day to reach Polokwane by train. Six days was reasonable, so I decided to visit home. It was so wonderful as I carried for them a basket full of bananas, and a box full of mangos and avocados. My mother and everyone else were happy to see me.

On the day that I was preparing myself to go back, one of the women in the neighbourhood came to see my mother. Perhaps she'd heard that I was home. I went and greeted her in a hurry, as I was to go and catch a train. The train only arrived at 2AM from Johannesburg to Beitbridge via Louis Trichardt, but I was to leave home at around 4PM because I relied on lifts to Polokwane, there being no afternoon bus going there, nor taxis.

When I left her alone with my mother, she told my mother that she suspected that I was pregnant. My mother had not noticed during all the days I was at home, and neither was I aware of this. My mother never knew that I had a boyfriend.

After she left, my mother called me and asked that I follow her to the bedroom and she asked me to lift my clothes to expose my stomach. I was wondering why, but I just did. She said to me, "The woman who was here," she called her by the daughter's name, that is Johanna's mother, with whom I'd studied, "was right when she said that you are pregnant".

I said, "What? It cannot be." I only started falling in love and I was just a teenager.

She said, "You are," and insisted that I should not go back.

I refused because I did not believe that it was true, and I wanted to complete my training, although I could not understand why my clothes did not fit me anymore. I had thought I was just getting fat. I'd never thought I could just fall pregnant: not me. I asked her who would then bring the rest of my clothes and inform the hospital that I was terminating my training. I said it was my responsibility to do that. She understood, but I could see that she was upset and disappointed, and as confused as I was.

I went back.

A few days after I came back from home, my friend Lizzy, who was already graduated, asked me to come and see her in her room. She no longer stayed in a sharing apartment, as I did. I went to see her after work and she told me that she was suspicious that I was pregnant, and that most of the nurses were gossiping about it. I kept quiet. She asked me when last I'd seen my period. I said about six and a half months ago. She said, "Meaning that you came here already pregnant".

I said it could not be and that missing periods for me was like normal; it had happened to me many times. I used to miss my periods for almost five to six months. I only discovered later in life when I struggled to conceive that I had only one fallopian tube as the other one was deformed, and that the situation was exacerbated by the fact that I had a disease called endometriosis. This is a condition resulting from the appearance of endometrial tissue outside the uterus and causes pelvic pain, especially associated with menstruation. It is the major cause of infertility in women.

She volunteered to take me to the general practitioner in town. He was her doctor. We arranged that we go as soon as possible, the following week when I was off. I do not know why she did not recommend that I see the hospital doctors. We went to Louis Trichardt (Makhado) town, commonly known as *tshitantane* in Venda. The doctor examined me and told me that I was seven months pregnant, so it was confirmed. I felt numb but somehow accepted it.

Before we left for town, Lizzy asked me to take enough cash. I thought it was for the doctor's fee. After seeing the doctor, she recommended that I go to the shops – I think it was a Foschini clothing shop – and there I bought maternity clothes. We took the bus back to hospital.

Coming back from seeing the doctor, we went to Lizzy's room and lay on her bed, talking. She narrated a story of how one of the nurses had died from an illegal abortion in her room. Upon discovering that she was pregnant, she'd decided to commit abortion illegally. Perhaps she was afraid of being expelled from the hospital, or maybe it was to avoid the stigma and embarrassment that comes with unwanted pregnancy. The botched process went horribly wrong. She bled profusely. Someone who found her had told Lizzy that the blood was everywhere. The nurse was just swimming in it as she was writhing on the floor in pain.

She was rushed to the hospital and the matron was informed. I was told that the matron could not be bothered. She simply instructed them not to assist her, nor call the doctor. She died from bleeding out. That was cruelty at its worst. Abortion then was not encouraged. It was not legalised in South Africa: hence, those who had money, that is the whites, would go to overseas for a legal abortion.

The news, or rumours, in hospital corridors about me being pregnant and that I was expelled spread like wildfire. One afternoon, coming back from my day duty, a nurse approached me. I knew her, as she called me *mokhaya*, meaning my neighbour in isiZulu. She was from Seshego, the township neighbouring Pietersburg (now Polokwane) in Limpopo, not far from my village. She told me that she was sorry about what had happened to me, but quickly offered to help me to abort. She gave me the name of the pills they used for that, and she further told me that they were sold over the counter. I just thanked her and left.

The only person I trusted was Lizzy. She could have advised me in that regard, but she must have known that it was dangerous to abort at such an advanced stage of pregnancy. Maybe that was the reason she even told me about the illegal abortion, to make me aware of the danger in case I thought about aborting. She knew how much I wanted to become a nurse. Besides, what came to mind was how would aborting help me because I was expelled for having a child out of wedlock. Having an unwanted pregnancy was against the policy of the hospital. Therefore, whether I miscarried tomorrow, aborted or had a stillborn baby was not going to help me. The bottom line was that I could come back if and only if someone married me.

While in my room, sitting alone, I recalled how the nurses stared at me. I saw some giggling. I recalled that every time I went to eat breakfast, lunch or dinner at the dining room, nurses would walk away from the table I sat at. It was only Lizzy who would come and sit with me. I had not made anything of it then. I'd thought that was how they treated new trainees.

There was this lady who came from the village adjacent to mine. She was the only person I knew, and she was one of the senior sisters. She took care of me initially, and then suddenly she stopped coming to see or talking to me. She totally avoided me, and I did not know why. I only became aware of why I was treated in that manner when Lizzy told me about nurses gossiping about me being pregnant.

When I left the hospital, we lost contact. I was shocked when I learnt few years after I'd left the hospital that Lizzy had died. She'd committed suicide by pouring petrol over her body and setting herself alight, in an outside toilet at their Diepkloof home in Soweto. She was indeed my guardian angel.

I also realised how ignorant I was because the signs were there and I'd ignored them. For example, I remembered that at the initial stage I became nauseous at the smell of certain food. I also had a problem with a smell of the hair cream I used, that is Brylcreem. The day that I was to go and start with my training, I slept at the train station and could not hear the train arriving. It had left me while I was still sleeping. When I woke up it was 3h45, one hour after it had left. I had to board the 4AM train to Tzaneen and get off in Duiwelskloof, from where I took transport to Louis Trichardt. I had to be there because I was to start with my training the following day.

At Duiwelskloof train station there was no proper platform at the station – the same as at Lansklip – so I had to jump down from the train stairs. I remember losing my balance and rolling down a slope. The train had already left. Luckily, I was wearing jeans. I was already pregnant, remember, and fortunately I was not hurt.

I asked people nearby where I could find transport to Louis Trichardt. Fortunately it was not far. I had never been to that part of South Africa before, and I did not know how to speak Venda or Tsonga, but I managed to communicate. With Tsonga I could understand a bit as I had gone to primary school with Tsonga-speaking children from a place called ga-Magongwa (Tsamahantse in Tsonga). I arrived in time to take a 2PM bus to the hospital.

At the hospital I always craved the fine ice that builds up on the roof of a freezer. I would collect it so often that one of nurses said to me one day that there must be a reason for it. I said to her it was probably because of the heat. I was not accustomed to the severe heat found in Venda and Musina. She just laughed and left.

Things were still to get worse for me. One afternoon, just after I had been transferred to the female ward, and a month after seeing the doctor in town, Matron Holmes, accompanied by the senior ward nurse, came to the ward. She always came for a routine check-up on us. I was in one section of the ward; I saw them looking and pointing at me. The matron came to me and asked me to come to her office. I followed her. She never said a word, but when we reached her office she was visibly angry and I was afraid. She told me that there was a suspicion that I was pregnant and asked me how I could, of all the students. She loved me because I was one of the brightest students in her class. She was the only one who did the training. She said to me, "You have such great potential, and you just ruin your life like this". As she was talking, she kept on banging her desk in frustration. I thought she was going to wallop me. I stared at her, terrified, and kept on saying I was sorry.

The matron then ordered me to follow her without telling me that we were going to see the doctor to confirm it, and especially the stage of my pregnancy. It was confirmed, and she asked me to follow her to her office again, still shouting at me. While still in her office, she told me that unless I got married as soon as possible, I was fired.

I just kept quiet. How would that be possible?

She then ordered me bring my ID book at the end of the month: that was October. The nursing profession had very stringent policies, and one of them was that if you fell pregnant unmarried, you were immediately expelled. Although I was one of the more promising students, that did not count on my favour as rules are rules. I always scored high marks and performed excellently in all the tests I wrote, especially biology, as I had while still at primary and secondary school. I had become very fond of anatomy and physiology. As a nurse, one must master those subjects because that is what medical practitioners deal with: it is their specialisation.

I attended my lessons the following day and she was to mark our test scripts. When it was my turn to hand over mine, she pushed it away in full view of other trainees. Usually, she would look forward to marking my scripts as I always obtained high marks. Days after, in fact for the whole month, she refused to mark my script or recognise me when I raised my hand to ask a question. I was hurt and embarrassed. I'd always participated in a class. Indeed, I'd disappointed her: myself and more so my parents and the community I came from. I only managed to train for ten months, two months short of completing my auxiliary course and becoming a qualified nurse, because I became pregnant. I'd truly let myself down.

I must say, I was the apple of the hospital matron's eye: she loved me dearly. To her, I was the brightest of all the new entry student nurses. Unfortunately, when I had accepted their offer, I was already pregnant although I was unaware of this. I was a victim of teenage pregnancy. It was not that I was naughty, but I just happened to be in the wrong place at the wrong time. It was my first relationship at 19 years of age.

My relationship with Matron Holmes changed when she discovered that I was pregnant. She became so furious with me that she instructed me to demand from my boyfriend that he married me so that I could continue with nursing. She could not believe it. She must have thought that I was the stupidest girl ever. That is what I thought of myself. There was nothing she could do. The hospital policy throughout the country was that any person who fell pregnant out of wedlock should be expelled, so I was expelled. The reason could be that many of these hospitals were run by missionaries.

All that I wanted then, was to give birth and re-organise my life.

The sad part was that during those days, contraceptives were unheard of, and our parents would not talk to us about the reality of life in any way. The subject was top secret. Of course, this cannot be an excuse because one could abstain. Teenage pregnancies then were such a taboo and I paid a great deal for it, something I will always regret for as long as I live. This is the reason I am saddened by the extent to which Africans have normalised teenage pregnancies. Until today, I still hate the idea of teenage pregnancies. I have never experienced anything in my life that threatened my future and destabilised my life as much as this incident because my dreams were almost shattered. It robbed me of my youth, and it is something teenagers and young women should stay away from as much as possible. Having a child at that age was a taboo and, besides, it added more burden to your parents, and it tore the family apart, especially parents.

At the end of the month, I went to Matron's office with my ID, as instructed. It was to be stamped, for what I did not know. Then, the following day, at the beginning of November, I boarded the bus. Lizzy accompanied me to assist me in carrying my luggage. I went to wait for a train at Louis Trichardt train station. I had to leave early because there was only one bus going there in the morning and coming back in afternoon. It took more than one hour to get there. The train came from Beitbridge to Johannesburg and stopped at all the stations.

I arrived at the Pietersburg train station at about 8AM. I waited at the station for a while, because I knew that the bus I was to board to home would only come at 2PM. At around 10h00 I headed to the bus stop. To my surprise, my mother was sitting there and waiting for me. Of course, I had written a letter to her informing her as to when I would be coming home. Most of the people who knew me did not even notice that I was pregnant at eight months; I was not showing much at all. She looked happy to see me. We waited there, and towards 12PM I went and bought food for us: fish, chips and bread. The bus arrived and I headed for home, arriving there at 4PM, after a full day of being on the road.

I must mention that I loved Venda, though. The only problem was the ever-sweltering heat. I do not know how it looks presently, but then it had this dense vegetation that looked like a rain forest. For me, it is one of the most beautiful places in South Africa because of mountainous landscape. They had plenty of rain and a lot of the fruit came from there. What I liked to eat was mopani worms (*mashonja*). I still do.

A month before I left the hospital, we went out to pose for pictures with some of my colleagues who were also on their day off. I decided to send some to my father and my sister in Johannesburg. Then, they were staying with one of my cousins' husbands. He was very ill; maybe he had gone there for treatment. My sister told me that he was the one who recognised that I was pregnant. I was wearing my private clothes when taking pictures. He told my father, who immediately asked my sister to write to me and verify the truth of it.

My sister told me that my father was upset with her. He accused her of not making me aware of the danger of a boyfriend. As an older sister, she was responsible for teaching me about the facts of life, so in my father's eyes she was an irresponsible sister.

However, it was not only my sister who was blamed. He blamed my mother too, for failing to look after me. For him, as adults you could not talk to your children about issues of menstruation, let alone sex. I received the letter and by then it was already confirmed by doctors, so I was certain of the fact. I responded to my sister to confirm, but also inserted another letter addressed to my father. The idea was to apologise to him. I cannot count how many times I apologised in the letter because I was genuinely very remorseful.

My father came home for the festive season (Christmas). I remember the day he came home; he could not hide his disappointment. I had just given birth five days earlier, and I was sleeping with my mother in their bedroom. He entered the room. I was holding my child and he stared at me, and I looked at him too. The only thing he said was, "Thabo," (shortening my name, Lethabo) "you of all the children". I just said, "Papa, I am so sorry." He wept and I cried too. His facial expression stayed with me for a long time; it haunted me.

He never wanted to touch the child in the days he was at home until he went back. Maybe it was because our culture that dictated that men should not hold a new-born baby to avoid bad spirits, or something like that. But, in my mind I still believed that he felt ashamed of me.

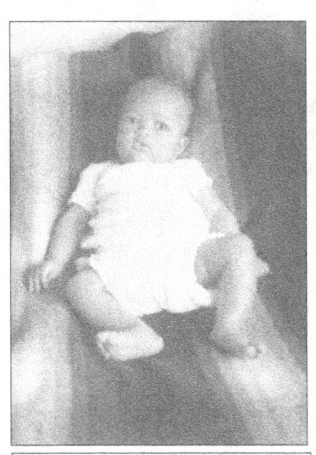
Photo of my baby daughter

Where I came from, it was commonly believed that when a girl fell pregnant before she was married, she brought shame to the family because as a girl you were considered damaged goods (*o senyegile*). This type of idiotic language became a concern to me because it only referred to women. I believed that my father was so angry with me because, in a traditional setting like the one I came from, an unmarried daughter who fell pregnant would incur shame not only on the family but on the male father figure and head of the household.

What perturbed me more is that in most cases it is women who use the type of language openly to torment another woman. In some communities they even form negative songs about a girl to spite the mother. Nothing whatsoever is said about the boy. They are glorified. Instead of women questioning the legitimacy of the structures that keep women subjugated, and developing strategies to address them, they do the opposite. Hence, I always say women are the main protectors of patriarchy. Consciously or unconsciously, it is us women who are damaged by patriarchy.

However, the ubuntu spirit was still there. I remember some of my neighbours going to fetch water for me so that I was able to wash the baby clothes, especially the napkins. Some would bring firewood. The idea was to support my mother in trying to alleviate the extra workload.

The most striking thing for me was when one of our neighbours (Jackson Dolo), who was disabled and had a condition called *sialorrhoea*, commonly known as drooling (a chronic neurological condition) made it a point that he bought me a box of matches every day, and sometimes a candle. He would explain to me why I had to have some light in the night when the child woke up for whatever reason. I thought it was so thoughtful of him, considering his health condition.

My neighbours would only stop bringing water and firewood after three months, because at that point a nursing

Photo of Jackson taken at my wedding, he is wearing a cream white trouser, faded black jacket and a brown beanie. Across him is my mother, wearing a black beanie.

mother (*motswetsi*) has recuperated and is strong enough to do things on her own. I was so happy to see Jackson at my wedding. I watched him as he walked in front of the people. Despite his movement difficulties, as he had to pull his deformed leg and arm, he had to be there for me. Back then, most disabled people like him were not looked after, and he was wearing a torn jacket while everyone else had tried to wear neat, proper clothes for the occasion.

Reverting back to my father's issue with me. When he came back for his annual leave in February the following year, I could sense that he was still upset. I tried to do everything possible to please him so that I did not make him angry, but it did not work. He was so angry with me that he never bought my child anything, including nappies or clothes. I understood. He had many mouths to feed, including mine. My sister assisted me, especially when I had to take my baby off the breast feeding and she needed powdered baby milk and all the necessities. I am always grateful for that.

One evening, my father came home a bit intoxicated; he would rarely drink liquor. He came home and I had just finished washing lantern glasses and was about to light the lamps as it was getting dark. I knew that if he came back home and the house was not lit, he would be upset because he had a phobia called nyctophobia: an extreme fear of dark. We were never without torches at home, and they always had batteries. He would not venture into darkness without a torch. My aunt, his elder sister, told me that while he was young he would not go out alone, unless there was moonlight.

Earlier that day, his friend had come looking for him, but he was not at home. When he came back in the evening, I immediately told him that *Ntate* (Mr) Bambo had been there, looking for him. He did not respond but I could read anger on his face. One thing I also knew about him was that he was very vindictive. He commanded me to follow him to his bedroom. I did, and he locked the door. He started accusing me of being disrespectful. I was puzzled. Before I could say anything, he smacked me so hard with the back of his hand right across my face that I saw stars. I was consumed with rage, but I knew I could not hit back: never to my parents, even my elder sister or any grown up person. That is how we were brought up. Besides, I would only make things worse than they already were.

While in the room I heard my mother praying outside the locked door. I do not know what came over me. I walked towards the window and smashed the glass with my fist and the glass cut my arm. I opened the window, jumped over his bed and went through it. He just stood there. When I jumped out of the window, my siblings and cousins came running. I remember seeing my younger sister holding my daughter. I was confused and angry.

The Bambo friend of my father was one of the men I referred to above as *Makgolwa* (those who left their families in the rural areas to come and work in the cities and along the way decided to abandon their families). I knew his family, that is his wife and children, but I did not know him because ever since we'd relocated to Kalkspruit he'd never come back home. I was already at secondary school when he came back after he was retrenched. Some of his children left school and went to seek employment.

I'd heard that he came back because the woman he was cohabiting with had chased him away because he was no longer working, and he was old too (of no use). When he came back to his wife and children, they were also very angry with him because he'd left them destitute. They had only a one-room rondavel house and a small hut used as kitchen. They were a family of six sleeping in one-room house, yet he expected them to welcome him back. The wife and children did not allow him to sleep with them in the main house: that is, the one room. He was relegated to sleeping in the house that was used as a kitchen, without blankets. They too did not have a bed. They even refused to dish up for him. So, he survived by eating at other people's houses.

When my father was on his annual leave, Mr Bambo would come to visit him daily so that he ate breakfast, lunch and supper with us. You can imagine how we felt about this. My father could not hide his frustration every time he saw him approaching.

I always wondered which father was the better between the ones who'd abandoned their family to fend for themselves, and the ones who would come home when other fathers came home, but with nothing. There was this father who would come home on the same transport our father used. Every time, while other men carried big cardboard boxes of clothes and food, he would be carrying only a briefcase. The worst thing was that he would be so drunk that he could not walk. When we ran to our fathers to carry their luggage, his children never bothered to run for him because he might not even recognise them. I did not know whether he had money for his family. Indeed, these are families I could count amongst those families that represented the face of poverty.

Back to my father's boxing ring. He unlocked the bedroom door and came out and sat down on his chair, saying nothing. As vindictive as him, I went into the house and sat down. He did not know that I was also harbouring his secrets that my mother did not know about. I cannot mention them in this book because

I would like to respect him, as well as my mother. When I told him, he froze and said nothing, just sat paralysed. I guess I was tired of apologising. To be honest, that is one part I did not apologise for because I hated someone who was not loyal and honest. One thing I vouched to myself was that I would always protect my mother from any form of abuse, especially when it was inflicted by men, my father included. In qualifying this, my father was not abusive in that sense, but if he had been I would not have protected him.

The following day, he tried to be nice to me without mentioning that he was sorry. The best side of me is that I never bear grudges, so I forgave him. I realised that from that time he feared me, and believe you me, I took advantage of it. Maybe he did not fear me *per se,* but respected me for whatever reason. After the incident, he would make it a point that whenever there was something he wanted to do and he had to involve us, the children, he would touch base with me first after, of course, discussing it with our mother. If I agreed with whatever it was, he would then inform everyone. If I disagreed, it would be the end of the conversation.

For example, he called me and told me that he wanted to check something with me first before talking to my siblings. He asked me whether I would be okay with him marrying another wife one day. Without hesitation I said no and never. I gave him my reasons and told him that it was not an option. I already knew that it was not his idea but there were some relatives who were putting the ideas in his head. I told him that we would take care of him and he did not need baggage at his age. He never pursued the conversation; it was me who told my siblings and they all felt the same way.

What I am trying to illustrate here regarding unwanted pregnancies is that children must know that teenage pregnancies are not only hard on them but on those who are close to them, and they can have devastating consequences. I knew of many of my peers who went through the ordeal and never picked themselves up again. To be able to dust yourself off and do something about it, one needs to be principled, visionary, have faith and be strong willed to get out of it and turn the situation positively. Unfortunately, it is something you cannot blame anyone for, other than yourself.

I understood my parents' anger, especially my father, and I am grateful that they could not hide it and made me aware of that. I owned up to that and tried to bring my daughter up with love and dedication. It was not her fault, so I managed to separate my anger resulting from my foolishness in having her under those circumstances.

It never bothered me whether my child's father was going to marry me one day or not. After all, we were still very young. I had big dreams for the two of us and all I wanted to do was to live for those dreams. But, above all, for me education was the only key to our better life. I immediately decided that I was going to enrol for matric and study part time. I knew I was brilliant and, if I put all my mind to it, I would certainly achieve it. I was very determined. I envisioned that after matric I would proceed to tertiary education, and I was certain that I would realise my dream.

I would like to register the fact that having a child at that age is not something to be downplayed; it almost crushed my life. At the beginning, I could not figure out how I was to reclaim my life: I just saw a bleak feature before me. I regretted that so much that one evening, while sitting in the kitchen with my younger sister and cousins, I decided to have a talk with them about how I felt, and I guess it was another way of trying to raise awareness about unwanted pregnancies. It was also important to talk about it so that I could heal. As I was talking, my mother came in, but I did not keep quiet and continued talking. I addressed them with authority and passion. I pleaded with them that they should not allow themselves to go through what I was going through. I advised them to stay focused and never engage with boys intimately, because they would rob them of their bright future. I also told them to focus on their studies. But that fell in deaf ears, as one after another did the same thing, and unlike me they were never able to pick up the pieces. None of them had matric, even though they had the chance to get one, unlike me. One of them fell pregnant while at boarding school doing Standard 9, which is today Grade 11. The other one fell pregnant while at boarding school doing commercial subjects, also at Grade 11. I was shattered and disheartened.

One day, I was going through an old magazine that my elder sister had brought from boarding school some time back. As I browsed through it, I came across an article written about Diana Ross, who had just had a child, and they were showing her mansion and the life that the rich and famous live. I made a promise to myself and told my baby daughter that I was going to work so hard that she and I would one day live a very fulfilling life, like that of Diana Ross and her child. There was no marriage mentioned, or the father of the child, so I just assumed that she was single. I did not really think about getting married one day. I thought about how I was going to uplift myself, that is all. Marriage was furthest from my mind.

While I am still on teenage or youth pregnancies, called unwanted pregnancies, I would like to mention that this is one of the social ills that societies ignored for so long that it became a way of life. The problem became evident post that 1976 riots, since schools throughout the country were closed and the majority or children were idling. Because of the lack of supervision, as many parents were working, children started engaging in unwanted activities or behaviours. As a result, many children had children in unplanned pregnancies. Instead of capping it while still early, adults turned a blind eye.

Then it overlapped into the 1980s, due to riots in the black townships that interrupted schools and learning until it became some sort of a norm, or rather a culture. It is no longer a shame to see young children carrying children on their backs in the townships. Today, South Africa is sitting with this epidemic, and it is compounded by the outbreak of HIV infections.

While still on the subject, I would like to register a tendency that is a concern to me. HIV became a pandemic as many people became infected with the disease and millions died. Until today we still have new HIV infections because of resistance to using condoms. This is also worsened by widespread collapsed morals, values and norms in black communities. How does one explain the fact that more than 7.5 million people were living with HIV in 2022? The majority are female teenagers and youth because of practices such a blessers, sugar daddies and slay queens and above all the ever-escalating rape incidents. In addition, the tendency of people to sleep around without using protection and girls having children that they intend to use to hook men into marriage is not helping either. It is these social ills that have infested our societies that make South Africa a very sick country.

There are so many bad things happening in black communities that needed to be corrected. Things such as GBV.

This takes me back to something I witnessed many years ago. Three months after having the baby, I was at home minding my own business. I had just put my baby to sleep – it was about 11AM – when I heard screams outside. It was three women being beaten by members of the community, alleging that they were practising witchcraft. The death of a woman in the community who was struck by lightning had sparked the community anger.

I see it necessary to talk about this incident because it is becoming an epidemic in the rural areas, especially Limpopo, for elderly women to lose their lives to mob justice. Like Malaika Mahlatsi and many in African communities, I too, buried this incident deep in the gallery of my mind until I came across the story of a 59-year-old woman, Jostina Sangweni, who was brutally beaten and then set alight in Mapetla, Soweto. I was shocked that the mob justified the violence as normal.

Women abuse is a big problem in South Africa. Most people who lose their lives and properties through witch hunts are women. The reason for this is that in society women are looked upon as inferior and hence it is easy for them to become targets. Also, this is worsened by patriarchal practices such a socialisation and culture.

Those women were touted like criminals, beaten with everything the mob came across, as the whole village converged there. It was so scary and I never believed it was actually happening. They were beaten so severely that their faces were disfigured. I saw this boy who I was with at primary school with bashing one woman's face with something, and her teeth came flying out of her mouth. Then as they were pulling them on the ground to their houses, to go and point out the woman who'd died, as they believed that they'd turned her into a zombie (*setloutlwane*), I watched in horror. The air was electrical and there was tension around. When they could not find the zombie, they frog marched the women to the chief's kraal.

One elderly woman was already unconscious, so they just pulled her on the gravel road like a dog. I did not follow them there as my daughter woke up and I had to prepare her lunch. Besides, I was not going to leave her alone, and my mother was not at home and my younger sister was still at school. I was told that when they reached the chieftain's house they were instructed to sit on the floor in the blistering sun, it was very hot, because it was summer. People surrounded them, with some mocking them, traumatising and humiliating them further. I was told that the one who fainted had already died and the green flies surrounded her. With mob mentality, no one cared.

From that day, there was a hype of activities where *sangomas* and traditional healers were called to point out the culprits accused of bewitching the woman or possibly find the zombie. Meetings were called by the chieftainess for many weeks or months. The suspects were released for lack of evidence, so the search went on.

When such meetings were called, everyone in the village had to attend, especially those called by the chieftainess. People were compelled to come because, if one did not, one would be suspected of being afraid of being pointed out by those expert witch hunters. I was afraid for my mother, because anyone could have been pointed at, especially if they were married into the community and seen as an outsider. It was so scary that we would lock everywhere at dawn, even shed houses, afraid that whoever had a zombie with them should not dump it in our yard.

Such practices are still common in rural areas, and it is shocking that even in urban areas they do happen. It is mostly women who suffer the fate. It proves that government is unable to curb GBV, and thus it is now a pandemic with femicide and domestic violence spreading like a raging wildfire in this country, be it in the rural or urban areas. But what makes it sadder is that it happens in black townships, mainly Africans, followed by coloureds.

Going back to my near crumbled life, as someone once said: "One cannot go back and make a brand-new start, but anyone can start from now and make a brand-new end". I also drew from that Sanskrit Salutation that says, "Look to this Day! For it is life, the very Life of Life." After giving birth and when strong enough to go to work, I started applying again for nursing but with no luck. I thought that it was not easy for me to find a job in this profession because of my disclosure and, besides, my identity document had been stamped with the date I had been registered and the date of discharge. So, I had to explain why I did not complete and it was a turn off, I guess.

In the meantime, the principal of a primary school called Ngwana Mphahlele from the neighbouring villages asked me to come and teach as a private primary teacher for Standards 3 and 4 on a six-month contract. I did not know who recommended me. What I remember is that one of the agriculture officials (*molemi*) and a relative to my mother came to tell my mother about the post. When my mother told me, I agreed immediately, although it was a long walking distance.

I went to see the principal of the school and he offered me the job and told me to start when the schools re-opened. I really worked very hard and tried to learn as fast as I could. After all, it was not the first time that I'd taught as a private teacher. I walked to and from school every day. It was about 45 minutes or so. There was no transport to the school, and it was not safe to walk in the fields, valleys and the forest alone. I followed a foot path that was a short cut, rather than taking a main route used by cars and buses. It was long and winding, and not so safe either.

My mother tried to negotiate with my aunt's daughter, who was married and living in one of the neighbouring villages called Christiana, which was not so far from school, that I could stay with her during the week and come home over the weekends. The conditions were not so conducive, as they had only two thatched rondavel huts, one serving as a kitchen and the other as a bedroom for the whole family. The husband worked as a migrant labourer in Johannesburg, so it was okay to sleep in one hut with them, but the problem was when he came home over weekends to see the family. It did not work, so I opted to travel by foot to school and home.

As they say, everyone has an angel, and the very same agriculturist I spoke about earlier offered me accommodation. The government used to build houses for agriculturists because they were often deployed to a place far away from their homes. For example, the one I referred to above came from Sekhukuneland, approximately 140 kilometres away from ga-Maraba. The house was very big, and he shared it with another agriculturist, also from Sekhukhuneland. Many of the children from Sekhukhune went for the profession because the only college, called then Arabie College of Agriculture and now Tompi Seleka, was in that region.

They treated me very well. I did not have to pay rent nor buy food and I tried my level best not to disappoint him nor my mother. I did their washing and cleaned the house with love and dedication because I appreciated their gesture. They never asked me nor expected me to do house chores just because I happened to be a woman. I found them doing everything for themselves. His name is Lucas Nchabeleng and his colleague was Solly Mahlare, in the past tense because he since died in a car crash. They were such a blessing to me that I still count it whenever I thank God. I kept contact with Lucas for a long time, until he retired.

At the school I was employed at, the principal and circuit school inspector were very impressed with my work and encouraged me to go for teachers' training. I was tempted to, but I did not have money. There was no way that I could approach my father since he was still angry with me for falling pregnant. My last resort was to follow nursing.

After my contract was over, I used a bit from my savings to look for nursing employment. I went to almost all the hospitals, doing self-applications because I thought that applying by post might not be effective. My mother was very supportive. She would give me her last cent, or borrow money from people so that I could travel to far away hospitals to seek employment while remaining behind with my child.

After my six- month contract ended, I still had no promise of employment in the nursing profession. My cousin who'd got married stayed in Mamelodi East, Pretoria. She requested that I come and stay with her. She had just given birth and was in need of assistance. She was hoping that while in Pretoria I might be able to secure a job in one of the hospitals called Kalafong. She had a friend who was a nursing sister there, but I was not fortunate. I stayed with her for about a year and went back home to spend the festive season with my family.

My father came home for his February annual leave. He was still determined that I find employment and take care of my child. I understood, as he had six mouths to feed, including me and my child. My elder sister was already working and living with him in Johannesburg. He'd prepared me already that, when he came back home for annual leave in two months' time, that is February, I would have to go back with him. I'd really disappointed them because the whole community had looked up to me as a respectful, obedient, loving and responsible child. All those who loved me were hurt and disappointed. I had to re-organise my life and take responsibilities at a very tender age.

At the end of his leave, I left with him. I remember that day like it was yesterday, as I was very sad to leave my daughter behind with my mother. I do not think my mother had a say in that. I truly felt guilty that I would burden my mother with a baby, though I knew my sister and cousins would assist her. But they were all still at school, and she had to stay with her during the day.

My father and other men working in Johannesburg would arrange common transport home and back. The transport (a Volkswagen Combi) came to collect us. It was supposed to go and collect someone near the Roman Catholic Mission (Romeng) in a place called ga-Mapankula. Along the way, travelling on gravel roads, not far from our destination the car broke down due to a technical problem. They had to push it up to the house where they were to pick up another passenger. We had to sleep there overnight and catch the bus in the morning to Lanseklip Railway Station. There were not enough sleeping places, so they all sat in one place around the fire the whole night, and I was sitting there amongst them for the whole night.

I thought it was a bad omen, because when I'd left home my daughter had just become ill and she was bad. Remember, at that time, there were no phones, let alone mobile phones. In the morning, we walked about 30 minutes to a bus stop. As soon as the bus approached, I started crying but not loudly. Tears were just rolling down my cheeks as I was looking in the direction of my village. My father saw me and immediately he knew what I was thinking about and tried to comfort me. Fortunately, my daughter had been rushed to hospital, and she survived. The rest is history. We arrived in Johannesburg the same day, but late at night.

The first time that I ever visited Johannesburg was when my elder sister and I came to visit our father at his workplace during the June holidays. I was still at high primary. I still remember the fascination with lights, high rise buildings and concrete everywhere. My father's employer stayed in a mansion in Upper Houghton Estate. The houses there are built on top of a mountain, overlooking the city up to Sandton and part of the central business district (CBD) and surrounding areas.

Photo: taken in the garden overlooking the areas mentioned above.

We arrived there late in the night. As we were travelling in my father's friend's bakkie which had a canopy, and we sat at the back with other passengers, all that we could see were street lights along the freeway. We could not see much else. It was only when we arrived in Houghton that I could not believe my eyes: a sea of lights everywhere. I stood outside for a while with a wow sort of sigh. It was already late, so we went to sleep. The following day my father took us to the nearest shopping centre, which was Yeoville. Yeoville and Berea on the other side of Houghton are divided by Louis Botha Avenue. This is the route going to Alexandra from Johannesburg CBD.

That was the best trip I ever took. My father really spoiled us. He bought us wrist watches, twin jerseys, wool hats or beanies with matching scarves and other nice things. He even bought us facial creams; they smelled so nice. I'd always put Vaseline Blue Seal on my face and body and nothing else, so having something with such a wonderful smell was such a treat. I was the envy of my school mates when I returned home. Then, I was only delighted by coming to Johannesburg during the holidays. It was a form of status amongst most school-going children to have an opportunity to visit somewhere during school vacations.

This reminds me how many people used skin fade creams such as Ambi to lighten their skins. They wanted to look like white people because black people were brainwashed to believe that whites are beautiful because they are light skinned, unlike those with dark or black skins. I was shocked when the issue of white skin associated with beauty came up now in the 2000s. I realised how most women pride themselves on being referred to by men as light-skinned (yellow bones). For me, to believe in that way is a sign of low self-esteem.

Anyway, I came to Johannesburg to find employment for the reasons given above. This time was very different. I was to be independent in a foreign land. The lights were no longer amusing but scary, as were the temptations. I must have felt like Dolly Parton when she went to Hollywood for the first time. She narrated her fears in one of her records, *The Best of Dolly Parton*, saying: "The bright lights of the city are a pretty sight to see, perhaps they are extra pretty for a country girl like me, temptations wave at every turn and won't let me. So, Mama says a special prayer for me"... I believed that my mother, being a spiritual person with a strong faith, must have prayed for me. I was fortunate to have a mother and to know very well that she would pray for me. This is a blessing worth counting. I needed that prayer desperately for survival.

Meanwhile, I stayed with my father and sister for a while. My father had already arranged with other people in the urban area of Johannesburg (Northern Suburbs) to find me a job as a domestic worker. My father worked as a chauffeur for a very rich man for many years. He was classified as a domestic worker

and he therefore qualified for worker's quarters and a monthly ration. My father lived with my elder sister, who was working in a bureau of a private organisation that dealt with parole for offenders or prisoners. The Ministry of Prisons, now called the Ministry of Justice and Correctional Services, being a government department, used to outsource the parole functions to private companies.

Her employer was called Mrs Piggs. My sister was their bookkeeper. However, she told me that, being a black person, she was abused in that they would make her make them tea and make their beds in the morning: that is, for the lady and her daughter. A pig indeed.

She later found a job in Braamfontein with a company called Tape Aids for the Blind and worked there for many years. She worked as a bookkeeper and performed other functions related to her profession in commercial fields.

My father and sister occupied one of the domestic quarters. The room was about 2.5 x 2.5 metres in size. The three of us stayed in that small room. We slept on his tiny bed, supported by paint tins, while he slept on the floor. I do not really know how we survived there. It could not fit a double bed, but only a single bed.

The groceries that the employers would buy monthly for their domestic workers as a ration were stored under the bed: that is, the non-perishables. His ration consisted of a bag of mielie meal, bread and red meat, the meat that they would normally buy for their dogs, tins of the cheapest mixed jam, the same flavour forever, and a bag of white sugar. Coming from the rural areas where one did not even have access to a shop to buy bread, these things were luxuries.

While there, my sister suggested that we go and look for a church, and there was only one church close by in Yeoville. One Sunday morning we went to the Anglican Church and sat down. The congregation was made up of only whites. No one wanted to sit next to us, and one could read from their facial expressions that we were not welcome. The priest walked towards us and requested that we go and sit on a bench at the back of the church. After church he told us that black people were not allowed there as it was whites-only church. We were so disappointed. We could not find any church nearby, except in Alexandra, as it was the only township near Houghton. We gave up on the idea of going to church.

Staying with our father was not all smooth sailing. I remember one day when my sister went away instead of helping me with the sale of liquor and only came back on the Sunday morning. My father was so furious that he reached for his stick, the one he made me carry to protect her from the bully boys. He tried to hit her with it. I felt pity for her. I do not know where I got courage from but, as I was standing behind him, while the stick was still in the air I managed to grab it before it hit her. He did not know what to do. He just sat down and said to her, "Themba" – he called her that though her name is Stompie – "I do not like you roaming around and sleeping out".

My father's boss was very rich, but my father told me that one day he lost a cent or penny and he asked everyone to come and look for it until they found it. He had only one child, a daughter who was married. He was a medical doctor (Dr Schniydman) and his practice was in the CBD of Johannesburg in a building situated on Bree Street. My father was his only driver or chauffeur. Beside driving him to work, he also drove him when he went to play bowls or was going out for dinner or lunch with friends until Saturday afternoon. He only went off on Sundays.

I was told that in actual fact the business side belonged to the wife, who came from a very rich Jewish family. He was a German Jew from a poor family, and he initially sold boiled eggs in the street before graduating as a doctor. You tell me, how do employees happen to know about that? He tricked the wife and took all her businesses. He abused and ill-treated her and she died at a young age from a broken heart. Something offended their daughter and they never saw eye to eye.

He owned lots of businesses, such as a carpet factory and a marble lime factory. Then, the lime was mixed with cement when building houses to give mortar and bricks strength to limit cracks, but lime no longer exists. He also owned most of the farms in Fourways. In fact, they were all his. My father would tell me, pointing at them with pride every time we passed Fourways going to Limpopo. He was like a broken record.

We always had carpets at home because he was given off cuts from his boss' factory. I remember seeing my mother selling some to people in the community.

Chapter Five

MY FIRST TIME WORKING IN JOHANNESBURG

The first job I got was that of an assistant nurse in Greenside, one of the Northern suburbs. It was known to be an upmarket area, where only the rich Jewish people stayed. I was fortunate to be offered a job as an assistant nurse because I had a bit of experience in nursing, although I was treated like a domestic worker. My father found the job for me, I guess through one of the domestic workers in the neighbourhood. I was only in my early twenties when I was hired to look after an elderly woman suffering from a stroke. I worked the night duty or shift. There was a professional nurse who worked during the day and took care of her medically. The son to the woman was very rich. He owned the shopping complex called Pan Africa in Alexandra. It was a Jewish family. The elderly woman stayed with her younger sister who was not married.

I was given one of the back yard rooms meant for domestic servant quarters. The room had one bed that we shared, no built-in wardrobes, no electric plugs. It had only a ceiling light. I used a primus stove for cooking and a dish for bathing. There was no carpet on the floor, just cement. I shared it with the day-time nurse. She was a qualified auxiliary nurse. She occupied it during the night and me during the day. I took my weekend off once a month on Thursdays, coinciding with "Sheila's Day". This was the day that domestic workers took their afternoon's off. I visited my father in Houghton during these days, returning to work on Mondays to relieve the day nurse.

Going to see my father and sister I had to walk to Houghton from Greenside because there was no transport going there other than a municipal bus to be boarded on Barry Hertzog Road. I found it a long drive and expensive, as I had to use double transport. So, walking, although far, was much cheaper. I used to walk past Emmarentia, Parkview and Parkhurst on my left, and went through Saxonwold.

While passing there I one day saw a handwritten poster that said, "jumble sale for old clothes". I realised that it was there on Thursdays and was probably meant for domestic workers. One day I decided to go in, and I was met by a domestic worker who introduced me to her madam. I said I was interested in the jumble sale. I had some money with me, so I bought a few items. They were very beautiful, as she was a very rich lady. The clothes she sold were still in good condition and beautiful.

From that time onwards, I started shopping there for my clothes every time I got paid. She was the same size as me, including the shoes size. I became friends with a domestic worker who always tipped me to come and select clothes before anyone else came. Her madam got used to me and often gave me the underwear that she no longer wanted. It was very beautiful. She apparently shopped from exclusive shops called boutiques.

I had never seen such beautiful clothes before. I used to accompany my sister to shop at Killarney Mall. She had an account at Woolworths, where she would buy both of us underwear, so I observed the difference between what we bought at Woolworths and that which I bought from the lady for almost nothing. The lady who worked there as a domestic worker told me that the family was very rich and that her madam shopped at boutique shops only. I did not know what she was talking about as I'd never heard of such shops. I tried to encourage my sister to buy jumble from the lady, as we were the same clothes size, but she was not interested. I was not happy with that because the jumble sale clothes were cheaper than those we bought from other shops, but I respected her decision. After all, it was her money and she was working hard for it. I was always keen on saving money, though she was also good at that.

From there I would continue with my trip until I reached Westcliff and passed the Johannesburg Zoo, into Foresthill, Killarney, and would take the pedestrian bridge passing over the N1 Freeway into Lower Houghton. Most white people staying there were rich and of Jewish descent: that is, the likes of Helen Suzman and the Oppenheimers. There I would pause to watch people playing golf and elderly people playing a bowling game, though I did not know what that was until later in life. In every suburb I passed I saw whites playing golf and young black boys would be following them, carrying their golf bags. They are called caddies.

When passing the Oppenheimers' place, I used to see people playing tennis. I loved the sport and wished I could have someone to teach me and somewhere to practice it.

I would then join Munro Drive, which starts at Louis Botha Avenue ending at the then Harrow Road that joins the freeway at Killarney Mall. It is a very steep and winding road that leads to Upper Houghton Estate and into the first street called Rose Road. The first mansion house on the corner of Munro and Rose Road streets was owned by the leader of the Progressive Federal Party (PFP), before it became Democratic Party (DP) and now Democratic Alliance (DA), Frederik van Zyl Slabbert.

Walking down on the same street to where my father was working, I had to go up a long and steep driveway. It was wound up the hill going up the mountain overlooking a park called The Wilds. When on top there, I could see the whole of Johannesburg up to Sandton to the north, Hillbrow to the south, and the rest of the suburbs to the west.

The elderly woman I worked for just happened to love me. She would look at me now and again and remind me that I have a very pretty face and a good heart. Although I was never fond of being told that I was pretty, especially by boys, I felt flattered, and honoured, loved and blessed at the same time. She loved and trusted me, despite her perceptions about black people. During those times, during the darkest days of apartheid, a black person was likened to a dog or worse than a dog.

She allowed me to sleep with her in the same porch bedroom, on her comfortable bed and using her sheets and blankets. She could no longer use a normal bed because of her condition, so she had a special bed like those found in hospital, with supporting steel frames on the sides so that she could not fall out during the night. The whole right-hand side of her body was paralysed due to a stroke, so she had to be aided all the time. This included bathing her, assisting her to the toilet, dressing her: that is, almost everything. I would accompany her to the hairdresser and when she had to go and eat out in the evening. When the day nurse was off, I used to work double shifts, that is daytime and night duty, and the other nurse would do the same when I was off.

Her sister did not have a problem that I slept with her in the same bedroom, but they kept it secret from her son. He was very racist. According to her son, I was not even allowed to sit on their couches or chairs, since a black person was not supposed to touch their madam or master's things. She allowed me to also use a telephone to phone my father. So, it was our secret arrangement. I only watched television and sat on their sofas when he was not there.

I had never watched TV before. It was a black and white screen and the only movies I remember watching with her were Dallas and Columbo, a detective story. I was fascinated. I could only see late movies once her son, who visited her every day, had left and her sister had gone to bed after supper.

Otherwise, I was given similar treatment to their domestic workers. I earned R95 a month and worked there for two years. Out of the salary they paid me, I had to send money home for my daughter and buy her clothes, as well as buy food for myself. The ration food parcels provided to us were very little, far less than what my father received. I think it was only bags of maize meal and sugar.

My father knew that I liked doing things with my hands. I was industrious and handy. He happened to know that a lady working next to him as a domestic worker had a hand sewing machine that she was not using, so he asked her to lend the machine to me. It became very handy as I would buy pieces of fabric and make clothes for myself, or buy wool to knit jerseys.

Johannesburg then was very cold. I remember one winter when I went to fetch water outside, as there was no running water in the rooms. I opened the tap but the water could not come out because it had frozen.

Anyway, this was how I kept myself very busy during the day when I was not working. Besides the machine, the elderly lady I worked for had a very old radio, which she lent to me. It only played one station: Radio Highveld. I happened to listen to Leo Sayer songs. My favourite was, "When I need you". I loved it. I marvelled that I'd never owned a radio before; nor had anyone in my family.

I was never exposed to the townships. I got accustomed to the white suburbs and did not know what was going on around me.

One of the things my father lent to me was a primus stove for cooking. As already mentioned, domestic workers' quarters did not have plugs, so using electricity for cooking was not possible. One day, when visiting my father, we did not agree on something, so he was angry with me. I was the only person at home who had the courage to tell him he was wrong if he did or said something wrong. If I failed to get through to him, I resorted to writing him letters and in most cases he would see it, and acknowledge or apologise. This time he took none of it. Instead, he accused me of behaving as if I were his sister. Why sister and not mother? He was not raised by his mother as she had died while he was still a toddler (giving birth to his younger brother, who later died, as already mentioned), so his closest mother figure was his elder sister.

I left for work not in talking terms. Like myself, he was vindictive. He came to my workplace in the evening. I was doing a double shift. Through the window, I saw him parking his car on the pavement. He went straight to my room; the day nurse was not there. The door was not locked. He never bothered to ask for me so that he could make me aware that he had come to take the primus stove he'd lent me. When I went out to check on him, he had already left. Upon discovering that my only means of cooking was gone, I swallowed my pride and telephoned him to apologise. He was happy and brought it back the following day, so we kissed and made up.

When the time came that I was due my annual leave, I would visit home to go and see my mother and my daughter. I always looked forward to that as I missed them very much. Waking up and seeing them every day for that short period was priceless as I could not see them for over a year. I travelled by train home on a journey that took almost the whole day. I would board a train at Johannesburg Park Station at 8PM and arrive in Pietersburg the next day at around 6AM. I would wait for the bus to home from that time to 2PM and would arrive home at 4PM.

I could have embarked the train at Lanseklip Station, as I mentioned earlier, but it was no longer safe, as hooligans had started waiting for people coming from the cities to visit their families and would rob them of their belongings. I know of incidents where people were murdered because they tried to resist. The station was very secluded as there were no houses around. It was located on a farm called Percy Five, the place where my father had been born and where his mother was buried.

The only thing that bothered me was that every time I took a train trip home I would catch flu because of my sinuses. The smell of grinding train wheels on the train track caused that. This was worsened by the draft coming from opened windows, as the train used to get very full and some people would open the windows. Stealing from Barbara Masekela, the train journey was not so pleasant because there would be testosterone-charged young men on the rampage in the train corridors, and their advances made me very uncomfortable. I heard of stories of some of them throwing people out of the moving train windows just for fun. It was scary, because as the train offloaded people at Naboomspruit (Mookgophong), Nylstroom (Modimolle) and Potgietsrust (Mokopane) stations, the train got empty, and most of the people would have fallen asleep on their seats. So, this was when the lustful conduct of these young men took place as soon as one was alone with them. Most of them would be vendors, selling all sorts of goods in the train.

Nothing frustrated me like seeing these young men turn beastly about sex, disregarding a person's dignity. It always reminded me of the sexual terrorism I had experienced in the streets of Johannesburg as a very young woman. Men always treated women as their sex objects. Men's propensity to treat women as their children is also something I experienced growing up. These are some of the societal ills that affect women and society turns a blind eye instead of correcting them. Men must understand that women too deserve respect.

The first Christmas after I lost my job in Greenside, where I used to work as an assistant nurse, I went back to stay with my father and sister in Upper Houghton. Most employees were to take their festive season holidays to go and celebrate with their families. Only a skeleton staff remained, especially those who worked in the house. His employer was looking for someone to come and assist the remaining skeleton staff with the cleaning of the house. My father told him that he knew someone, and that someone was me. He did not check with me whether I wanted to go home; he just told me to remain behind so that I could earn some money since I was not working, meaning to get money for my child, or that is what I thought.

Although I was keen to go to see my mother and my daughter, I agreed to that. My daughter was turning three years old. She had been born in December, so her birthday coincided with Christmas. I missed that. I bought the cake for her from a Malawian person who was working nearby. My sister knew him and told me that he was good at baking cakes and she took it home for her. I remained behind and worked in the house as a cleaning domestic employee assisting full time employees for the rest of the holidays.

Photo: of my parents, siblings and cousins eating Christmas lunch.

Photo: of my daughter sitting on my mother's lap and birthday cake in front of them in the background are my elder cousin's children cheering

One of the things I observed while working there was that their employer did not engage with staff, so he never bothered to know who I was. He only spoke to them when giving them instructions. I was surprised that they had to wear gloves when serving him food because he did not want black people to touch his crockery with bare hands. Even if he had asked who I was, I was not going to tell him the truth about who I was because he was not to know that another Gilbert Gwangwa daughter was staying in his room illegally.

The only time he knew about me was when he saw myself and my friend Caroline walking on his driveway pavement to her car, which she had left in the street. Caroline was a friend of mine. We met at my friend's wedding in a village called ga-Mothapo in Limpopo. She and her fellow Wits students were involved in community work project funded by Wits Programme called South African Voluntary Services (SAVS). My friend's uncle was also a student at Wits but staying in an adjacent village called ga-Molepo, where the project was based. He'd invited them to the wedding.

My father's employer asked my father about the white girl he had seen walking with a black girl in his yard. My father told him the truth; he did not chase me away. But what attracted him was the black and white girl walking together and chatting.

Talking about Gilbert Gwangwa, my father once told me that his employer had time share at one of the resorts in Swaziland. They visited the place once a year. While at the border gate, officials asked for his passport. They asked him about his driver's names and he said Gilbert. They wanted to know his surname, but he did not know it, so my father responded to say Gwangwa. They said, "Mr Gwangwa". They said to his boss, "So you do not refer to him as Mr Gwangwa, just Gilbert?" My father told me that he was very embarrassed.

While still staying with my father after I lost my job as an assistant nurse, I helped him with his secret illegal business. He was selling traditional beer called *umqomboti* in Zulu to augment his meagre salary. It was illegal because his employer did not know and then black people were not allowed to sell liquor. If they caught you, they would arrest you.

I had just started working at St Johns College full time, though I was not registered. Every Thursday after work, my father would go to the shop to buy the ingredients used to make the beer. There was a Checkers in Yeoville from where we used to purchase groceries; things were much cheaper there. The ingredients used to distil beer are King-Korn sorghum meal, specially meant for that (not the stuff they use for fermenting sour porridge or pap (*ting*) or ordinary soft porridge), brown sugar, yeast and brown bread to add to that which he got as a ration. They received two loaves weak.

He also taught me how brew it. It fermented very quickly. We would start distilling it on a Thursday evening and by Friday afternoon it was ready, depending on the temperature. One could see that the mixture was fermenting when bubbles appeared on the surface. First thing early Saturday morning, my father would strain the mixture by squeezing it inside the palms of his hand. This is called *go hlotla*. He did not have a traditional

Photos: taken during our youthful times

sieve nor any other. The idea was to separate the liquid from the chaff(called *moroko*). At home we used a traditional sieve made of woven reeds called *mohlotlo*, but some would use kitchen sieve.

He performed this task on his own as he never wanted to wake us up early in the morning because we were not going to work; even when we were still little, he'd hated us being woken up. Growing up, my mother liked to wake us very early to go and collect wood or fetch water, but my father did not condone that at all. Unfortunately, he was always home for a short period due to migrant labouring.

Nonetheless, the beer would be ready, and his clients would start trickling in during the afternoon. We always made enough for Saturday and Sunday. The task of selling was left with me as both my father and sister went their separate ways, visiting friends. I was never a friend person; my only friend then was my boyfriend. I used a medium-sized jam tin as a measure, called a scale. It cost 50 cents. The drunkards would be knocking at the door all the time, ordering scale (*skal*). Those who had money would buy several scales at one go and fill a big container that they would bring with them. Most of the men who came to drink there were from Lebowa, now Limpopo, mostly from a village called ga-Molepo.

Beside those who worked in the neighbourhood as gardeners, most were working at St Johns and St Andrews Colleges. I only knew of two women who often came to drink with their boyfriends. Few women drank liquor then. The other woman who frequented my place was a hobo living on the Yeoville streets. She was in bad shape from overindulgence in alcohol. She ultimately knew me and every time she met me in the street she would call me sweetie and insist on kissing me.

The Story of a Rural Girl Who Kept Rising and Rising

The challenge was that when drunk the drinkers would become aggressive and uncontrollable. They would be such a nuisance, as they would start fighting one another. However, they would not provoke me. They all knew my father. They respected him and feared him at the same time. He was a no-nonsense person. In the meantime, I would get on with my studies. I never compromised that. The liquor would normally get finished on Sunday afternoon. I would then count the proceeds, only coins, record the money and put it safely in a container, waiting for my father to come back. I would then get my share. He paid me well, and sometimes he would pay my sister despite the fact she had not assisted in selling liquor. My father was not aware that she would leave immediately after he left, and I never told him. I always protected her.

Maybe one might wonder why it was easy for my father to sell liquor there without his boss noticing. I was told that their boss was happy to have them around as his extra security, even though he had a security guard. All in all, he had eight employees, including my father and a white woman who was a landscaper: three gardeners, so-called garden boys; two women cooks and one lady who was a cleaner (they were referred to as girls), one body guard and a chauffeur. The landscaper worked in the garden as well but was treated differently. She did not live

One of the pictures in his garden

there, though. He owned an eleven-room house and stayed alone: stinking rich.

I always envied his garden with beautiful flowers and lush green trees. My sister and I loved taking photos in the garden when he was not there. It was because of his wealth that he was feared so much that even the police respected him. He stopped them from raiding the servant quarters, although it was the government of the day's policy. The policy was meant to control the influx of people from the Bantustans. If found trespassing, you were arrested and deported back to the rural areas. There were resources in the form of police vehicles that were meant to escort people back to the rural areas. They would not mind taking one, even if was just one person. It was a blessing in disguise that he did not allow raiding to take place on his property because my sister and I would have been arrested as we stayed on his premises illegally. Staying in backyard rooms when not working there was regarded as trespassing, a criminal offence.

Reverting to what I mentioned about the social ills societies ignored until they became a big problem. Coming from rural Limpopo, I abhorred the idea of men being in charge, of men casually treating women as children they could rebuke and even punish and control. "Although it was a common occurrence in society, I just hated it long before I understood patriarchal practices," writes Masekela.

This reminds me of Virginia Woolf's article (1977:48) that looking at England's history gives a glimpse of a tradition that gave men the rights not only to beat their wives but also their daughters. "...the daughter who refused to marry the gentleman of her parents' choice was liable to be locked up, beaten, and flung about the room, without any shock inflicted on public opinion". This, therefore, explains the reason why violence in the form rape and abuse no longer shocks people. The violation of women is taken lightly by the justice system, police, government and society at large; hence, such horrendous acts still happen in democratic South Africa. This patriarchal ideological shadow within which women find themselves has come in the forms of religion, patriarchy, colonialism, capitalism and globalism.

This notion of men in control reminds me of how patriarchy was entrenched in the rural areas. I witnessed many times men abusing women because they owned them in that they had paid *lobola* (bride price) for them. These behaviours were rarely punished because they were regarded as family matters that should be resolved by families.

My opposite neighbour used to abuse his wife so much that I felt annoyed. Every time he came home for annual leave or the festive season, he would get drunk and all the time he was drunk he would come home late in the evening and start shouting at his wife while still in the street near his home. As soon as he entered the homestead, one would hear the wife screaming. He would be beating her.

I never understood and I would be so horrified, feeling sorry for the wife, but there was nothing anyone could do as adults kept quiet. The worst thing was that he would beat her even when she was pregnant, and she was ever pregnant. She had so many children that the husband was unable to take care of them. Like many women in the rural areas, she was a housewife and depended entirely on him. His children would walk around wearing tatters or torn clothes and first thing in the morning they would be coming to our house so that when we ate breakfast we should dish up for them. They would stay and play in the yard until lunch time and we had to dish up for them again. My mother would send them home for supper because she never wanted children out after sunset.

Coming to Johannesburg and staying in Soweto, I was shocked to hear people talking about how men beating their wives was regarded as something normal. For example, most of the young women I associated with told me about how their fathers abused their mothers and no one could do anything about it because even the families of these men rallied around them. Meanwhile, the families of the women would encourage them to endure the hardships.

Growing up in a traditional setting, I came to a realisation that a patriarchal system is more entrenched and worsened by the migrant labour system that created a situation of total dependency by women on their working husbands. This perpetuated the worst women oppression, which is also exacerbated by the normalisation of GBV. GBV is now a huge challenge in South Africa, but, if it had been addressed a long time ago, at least after 1994, this country would not be reeling from the combined onslaught of brutal violence against women and children.

The first start would have been to tackle patriarchy head on, as GBV results from it through socialisation and culture. Indeed, patriarchy is a hotbed for GBV. I would like to further pinpoint that women will continue to be oppressed for as long as patriarchy is still promoted in society. As long as men believe that they have power and dominance over women, and that women should be submissive, this country will never rid itself of gender-based violence.

It is a fallacy to believe the narratives that female inferiority and male superiority were created by God. These are the flaws that women themselves should fight and eradicate by challenging cultural conditioning and social stereotypes. It is a culture of silence that is not unique to this time, but which has defined the experiences of women throughout the generations.

Quiet endurance has, through the ages, been synonymous with femininity. Hence, societies and women have accepted the notion that, if your husband whips or beats you to punish you, it is okay. This is to an extent that many families hide marital rape and violence, as well as physical abuse committed by their husbands, uncles or any close male family members because of shame and stigma. Hence, the escalation of violent crimes that the country is experiencing like never before. They persist long after apartheid structures have been dismantled because patriarchy has not been dealt with.

In South Africa, during the liberation struggle women assisted men to fight racism because it was hurting the men. But because sexism suits them, they ignore the fact that sexism also hurts women. Thus, it is for women to fight and free themselves from the patriarchal yoke of oppression. Here, I am addressing all women – black, white, Indian and coloured – to say that they should not be apologetic in their quest to own and control their lives. Lots of talk been made over the decades: there is no need for frank discussion on this. It does not need dialogue either, only action. It needs a conversation in the form of action, as the time for talking is long past and this is now time for change. If this does not happen earnestly, women will forever be trapped in the vicious cycle of poverty. Women have been stuck in a memorialised site where they experienced so much oppression and pain.

The time has come that women should refrain from entertaining the flimsiest of reasons for tolerating domestic violence and abuse and normalising this kind of violence.

Sexism and racism are two sides of the same coin and they both thrive on power and control. Thus, in South Africa violence has two siblings: patriarchy in the form of sexism; and racism in the form of apartheid. They both privilege mainly men. This explains the reasons why thirty years after the first democratic elections, South Africa is still laced with a dollop of unadulterated sexism and racism, The country is still reeling from the legacy of institutionalised sexism and racism in the form of patriarchy and apartheid. These are the two monstrous systems that have yet to be tamed.

But what is patriarchy? Nkiru Igbelina-Igbokwe (2013) defines patriarchy as a deeply-rooted, institutionalised social system that justifies men's domination of women and their hold on economic, religious, social and political power. This social system is deeply rooted, so much so that it is given cultural glory. To argue against it is seen not as fighting against male privilege, but as attempting to destroy African tradition. To challenge patriarchy is to dispute the idea that it is men who should be the dominant figures in the family and society. Hence, gender-based violence is entrenched in the strong patriarchal ideologies of control, subversion and subordination of women and girls, thus, scaling femicide which is fuelled by patriarchal social norms.

Efforts to resist this has mostly been undertaken at individual levels. As a result, patriarchy continues to thrive. Kati Dijane's article in 2023 is right to question whether women are the cheerleaders of patriarchy. The reason is that women have even accepted and enculturated it in the form of teaching their daughters to behave in a way that makes sure that they stand a chance of getting married. This is the extent of how poisonous the system is. Many of us witnessed this indoctrination by our mothers, especially when it comes to preparing a girl for being a future wife and marriage material.

So, patriarchy starts at home and then rears its ugly head in society, where women struggle to get an equal education or salaries, a voice, or the respect and dignity that men enjoy. Women who are strong-willed and vocal are frowned upon as being loud and disrespectful. Those who choose to identify themselves outside of marriage or children are looked down on as lonely and abnormal. Whether we like it or not, as women we are defined within the frames of patriarchy and men find it difficult to respect our bodies as they belong to them.

This reminds me of the incidents that my sister and I experienced while staying with our father in Houghton. We would take a walk on Sunday afternoons. Along Munro Drive we would be confronted by rich white men, mainly coming from the Lower Houghton direction. They drove luxury cars such as a Jaguar. While walking on the pavement, they would drive close to us with their car windows lowered. My sister, because she'd stayed there longer, would ask me not to look at them, but the first day I saw this man who behaved suspiciously I became curious and looked. I realised that he was showing us his private parts.

I was shocked and puzzled, and I asked my sister what he was doing. She started rebuking him. It happened all the time. We would rebuke them. Apparently, they mistook us for prostitutes or sex workers, although we dressed decently, or perhaps they were just being silly. Some would drive past as soon as we indicated that we were not interested, but some would insist, and we just ignored them and took another street. That was weird and indecent.

I realised later that prostitution is a serious business in Yeoville, Berea, Bellevue and Hillbrow. Hence, whenever white men saw black girls in the street, they assumed that they must be prostitutes. Again, women in general are always regarded by men as sexual objects.

One time, as we were taking our afternoon stroll, there was this black man who always sat on the street pavement where we passed. He must have spotted us. He would start provoking us by advancing on my sister forcefully. We told our father. He gave me a stick one Sunday afternoon and told me to carry it with me, and said that, when the man started, I must hit him. As usual, he did that one day and did not realise that I was carrying a weapon hidden behind my back. I started charging at him. He ran away and we never saw him again. Our problems were solved.

I knew why my father gave me that responsibility. In his mind I was his boy in a girl's body, and he knew that I would stand up to the task. How funny. What I am trying to illustrate here is that patriarchy preached male superiority and female inferiority over the years, such that when men see women all that they think about is to conquer them because they are entitled to women's bodies. I reiterate that this is something that must be stopped by women themselves.

Chapter Six

IN THE QUEST FOR A BETTER LIFE, EDUCATION IS THE KEY

As the title of the book says, like dust I kept on rising. Nothing was to deter me from getting a good education to better my life. I was always pushing myself to the point of being hard on myself to achieve my goals – and I have, with flying colours. I wanted to have a better life, not an easy life, and there is a difference there. At my age I am still full of adventuring because there are myriad possibilities out there. Hence, I am not afraid of aging nor mortality because I have lived a purpose-driven life. I am grateful that God gave me the opportunity to share my story that hard work, determination and endurance do pay you. You do not need to wait for free handouts, nor steal. There is no short cut in life and the world owes you nothing, so there are no easy things. As they say, easy come, easy go, and that is a fact.

Every time I went to a new environment, the first thing I did was to try to find places where I could study for my Matric. While I was in Venda, doing nursing, I found out from nurses who came before me about night adult school. One of the nurses had already registered at one of the high schools nearby offering night adult school. She promised to take me there, but only in January the following year because it was already mid-year. Unfortunately, I'd had to leave the hospital at the end of the year because I was pregnant.

After having my child, while at home struggling to find a nursing job I decided to go to a Roman Mission School commonly known by locals as Romeng. It was nearby two famous sister boarding schools called Our Ladies, a girl mission high school close to Pax, a mission high school for boys. In the mission complex is a hospital, which was where I delivered my child. I was told that they offered adult education and they had an examination centre for adult matriculants.

I borrowed books from a girl who I was with while at secondary school. She'd had the opportunity to continue her studies to matric level and had completed it. I did not have money to buy books, so I therefore borrowed her books for Afrikaans, English and biology. I registered immediately. At the end of the year, I sat for examinations and managed to pass two subjects – Afrikaans and biology – but with very low marks. I was not happy. I could not continue with my studies there because my father recommended that I come along with him to Johannesburg to find a job.

My father's employer would give him his Sunday newspaper after reading it. One afternoon, after my father had finished reading it, I started paging through it and came across an advertisement by Damelin Correspondence College. They had a programme for those who wanted to do their matric. I asked my sister to give me some money. I went to the address reflected on the paper to enquire. When I got there, I was told that full time classes were only offered to white children. However, I could still buy textbooks or prescribed books for students and study part time.

After buying my books, I realised that I still had enough money, so I decided to buy some textbooks for my sister, with the view to encouraging her to further her studies as she too did not have matric. She was good at commercial subjects. The idea of encouraging my sister to study did not work. After some time I realised that she was not studying; she only liked reading magazines. I asked her why she did not register and start studying, and she said she would start the following year.

One day while in my father's room, cleaning, I'd just finished ironing the washing load I'd washed in the morning. I then decided to pack my father's ironed shirts in a suitcase. Upon opening it, I found the books I had bought her still wrapped in the same Damelin plastic bag. It was the second year since I'd bought the books. I was disappointed because I knew she was brainy, but I opted to keep quiet. After all, it was her life. To date, I am the only child with a matric certificate let alone degrees. I accept that not everyone is academic material. And I must say that she became an entrepreneur of note. She had a successful day care centre (crèche) business for over 30 years. It was rated the best in her area. She worked very hard and created a life of her own and I am proud of her.

Nonetheless, at Damelin, the Indian gentleman called Mr Khan who assisted with the buying of books told me about the UNISA library downtown, where they allowed black students studying through UNISA to use the facility. He gave me the address and I went there to enquire. UNISA is a distance learning institution, so students were studying through correspondence. They also allowed those who were studying for matric to use the facilities. They were also assisted by volunteers, only for those who would be writing exams for a matric senior certificate.

One morning I visited the venue with the aim of starting with my studies. There I met someone who was also studying matric through correspondence. The girl's name was Nobuhle, and she became my friend. I was attracted to her by her dreadlocks. I had never seen anyone wearing such beautiful, dignified hair before. I walked over to her and greeted her; she greeted me back. I told her my name and she did the same in return. She had long dreadlocks and a very beautiful face. She also told me that I could still sit for my examination at the centre called Tony Factors Downtown, where the UNISA library was housed. The centre was where Edgar's shop was situated in the Johannesburg CBD.

As we met every day in the library where we used to study, she happened to tell me about Rastafarians. She was a converted and devoted Rastafarian. I was moved by what I learned about the religion and its place in Africa, and how it ties in with what it means to be an African. I also loved reggae music: Bob Marley and the Wailers, Peter Tosh, Jimmy Cliff, and Toots and Maytals. I still love it. It does something to me. It really moves me.

Particularly, I love Bob Marley. One of the things that drew me to Rastafarians was and still is Bob Marley and the Wailers' music. I adored Bob Marley because he made profound life-affirming music. His music is still my favourite. It makes sense and more, so it kept the revolutionary spirit going in me. It was such a consolation and affirmation that South Africa, like the rest of Africa, will be liberated one day. The music is real and invigorating, and it soothes my soul. It truly inspired me during apartheid's trying and difficult times. For me, Marley remains my favourite cultural icon by far.

Going back to my search for a better life through education. While I was working in Greenside I saw in a local newspaper a certain lady advertising an adult school she was running for domestic servants and at the centre they were also providing adult matric school. I saw the advert while I was at the library in Emmarentia, a suburb across the main street called Barry Hertzog, dividing Greenside and Emmarentia. In the library I found several elderly white women reading books. Everyone turned in my direction when I started going through the books. I was an unwelcome visitor, as the library was meant for whites only. The only black people there were employees.

I had come across the library when I one day went to the local shopping centre to buy groceries. It was the only shopping centre close by. I told myself that I would come back next time and use it for studying when I was off. While there, one elderly woman murmured that I was not allowed to be there. The librarian came over and told me politely that the facility was for whites only, but she could allow me to borrow books. I did just that. Under the intimidating eyes of those whites in the library, watching my every movement, I started looking for the books I wanted. I managed to get a few. I went back to the librarian's desk. She recorded them and issued me with a card that recorded the books I had taken and when to return them. Every time I returned them, I would request some more. I wanted to improve my English vocabulary as much as I could, so I took English books.

This reminds me of an Afrikaans newspaper headline that read: "*Die dag toe die duiwel in die dorp gekom het*", I think it was Beeld Koerant (newspaper). This referred to a mass protest march organised by Cyril Ramaphosa while he was still COSATU secretary and Jay Naidoo. I had been in Johannesburg only a few years, and I had never seen so many people wearing red chanting and singing: the whole Transvaal came to a standstill.

Arriving at my employer's house, I asked her for permission to use her telephone. She agreed and I called the number I had taken from the newspaper and explained to the lady that I was interested in attending evening lessons she offered at the adult centre. She agreed that I could come to see her in her house in Emmarentia and gave me a street address and directions. She was such a kind white woman. I went to see her before starting with my night duty. When I got to her house, she really welcomed me warmly and allowed me to sit on her sofa. I could sense that her husband and his teenage children were not comfortable with me.

She explained to me what was offered there, and she was impressed by the fact that I was doing matric because her students were all domestic workers who were keen to learn how to read and write. The centre was doing what is called today adult education. She volunteered to give me a lift to the centre, as it was quite far away and the lessons were in the night and, worse, I was to pass through a public park called Rooseveldt Park.

The centre was in Northcliff, I forget the street, but what I remember is that it divides Linden and Northcliff. She would pick me up every time I was off on Thursdays and take me to the adult centre. There were about five ladies who were taking matric lessons. I enrolled for English and history and sat an examination at the end of the year.

There were times that I would study whilst on night duty, especially when Mrs Grollman was sleeping, and her sister went to bed too. Her son insisted that I called her and her sister madam, his daughter little madam and him master. I refused and called him Mr Aubrey, the mother Mrs Hilda, her sister Ms Ann, and his daughter just by her name, Pepper.

They did not switch the light off in the passage while sleeping, so I would lie down on the carpet and study.

One night I read about the Second World War, Hitler's war. I was shocked at how he'd killed the Jews mercilessly (what is referred to as the holocaust).

The Story of a Rural Girl Who Kept Rising and Rising

While I was still working for the above employer, night duty was a very good opportunity for me, because I was working mostly in the night and I could use my free time during the day to attend to my studies. However, as a black child I was not allowed to write examinations in town but had to do so in a township, and the nearest township for me was Alexandra. I was to register there to be permitted to write examinations towards the end of the year.

My nearest examination centre was Alexandra Adult Centre. I went and looked for the venue and I was registered. However, I happened to learn later that there was a venue in Braamfontein where I could write. I worked in Greenside; the venue would be more convenient for me compared to going to Alexandra. So, I went to Alexandra Centre to inform them that I would prefer to write at the nearest centre I heard about. They did not have any problem, but I'd thought it was proper to let them know. The examination centre was at Wits West Campus' Sports Hall. The place next to where the Rand Showground was before it moved to Nasrec Expo Centre.

My employer's sister was called Ann. One morning, as she pulled out of the garage going to work, she saw me leaving the house carrying books. She asked me where I was going, and I told her that I was going to Braamfontein. She offered me a lift because she passed there to work. While inside the car she asked me what was that I was going to do there. I said that I was going to Wits University to write my examination. She was not impressed and wanted to know why I wanted to be educated. I said that I wanted to better my education so that I could get a good job. In her mind, that implied that I was not happy with the one they offered me. She kept quiet and dropped me there. She must have told her sister and brother, but I did not care, No one was to hold my life at ransom, not even the apartheid system.

I passed both my subjects. I got symbol D for history and E for English, but I was so pleased because I could finally see the light. I meant to use their inferior education to my advantage. I was not going to be a victim but the victor that I am today. I left no stone unturned. I was on a mission.

Talking about turning stones, while I was still living with my father and trying to find employment, I'd registered for a course in first aid and had attended classes in the evening. I'd graduated and received my certificate. Shortly after that I was employed as the assistant nurse. Then I was still keen on pursuing nursing, and I thought the course would give weight to my nursing applications.

Before I was fired from my first job in Johannesburg, my friend back home got married and requested that I be her best lady or maid. At her wedding I met her uncle and two of his white friends. They were studying together at Wits University for a postgraduate degree. As we were chatting, I told them that I would like to acquire my matric certificate so that I could be able to find myself a better job. I was told of a black student programme held at Wits by white students and started after 1976 riots. It was called an alternative education.

The educational crisis for black schooling had deepened considerably during that period. Some leaders in black communities organised alternative education for black children because it was their central role to ensure that education played an important role in the struggle for democracy in South Africa. The 1976 riots mainly affected black communities, particularly Africans, because under apartheid different laws had been passed to provide separate education for the different ethnic or population registration groups. So, the Bantu Education Act of 1953 had begun the era of apartheid education. In 1959, universities were segregated. The Coloured Persons Education Act of 1963, and the Indian Education Act of 1965 were passed. In 1967, the so-called National Education Policy Act was passed, which laid down the guiding principles for white education.

White liberal students volunteered to teach black children between their lectures. The university offered them a venue in the Social Science Block to hold classes there. It was situated at the Wits' East Campus. I went and enquired, found the place and registered. This was a very good opportunity for me, because I was working mostly in the night, and I could use my free time during the day to attend my studies. I enrolled for three more subjects and decided to improve my English symbols, so I enrolled for that. Unfortunately, the programme was terminated mid-year and we could not attend classes there. The university wanted to use the venue.

Some of the students decided to continue to offer voluntary teaching to black children. They managed to secure a venue at the Race Relations offices situated at Auden House, Jorrisen Street, in Braamfontein, not far from the university. The classes were held on Saturdays only. The following year, towards the end of the year, we were informed that the institution would no longer accommodate students for Saturday lessons.

However, it was at Race Relations that I joined student politics because I happened to meet very revolutionary black students, most of them victims of the 1976 riots. After we'd finished with our lessons, we would remain behind and start talking about politics. I was conscientious and became very interested and ultimately became revolutionary, although not quite as militant as other students, especially those from the then Vaal Triangle, now Sedibeng. They were very militant, typical products of 1976. Simon Tseko Nkoli was one of those militant students.

The first time I saw him, I was still at Wits. He was always loitering on the campus. I never saw him in one of our classrooms. I could see that he was well known because he was an activist, although then I was not much into politics. He used to make advances on me and I did not quite like him. I thought he was too forward and loud. When we met again at Auden House, he was surprised to see me amongst comrades. He came to me and said, "I did not know you were also a comrade," and he laughed. He was very revolutionary; it was not surprising that he was amongst the Delmas Treason Trialists.

What impressed me about them, however, was their dedication to education. In the process I developed such a deep hatred for whites, irrespective of the fact that Caroline remained my only best friend and I loved her dearly. For me, it was not about whites *per se,* but about the system. Unfortunately, like patriarchy, apartheid privileged whites, while patriarchy privileges men in general. It is therefore very difficult to separate one from another. As students, we would sit there and strategise as to how as youth in the country we could bring the apartheid government down. I heard of people skipping the country to go and train as freedom fighters. I thought that that was an option and if I had had the connections, I would have left.

It was not long before the police were tipped off about our meetings. They raided us as soon as we converged, and they would beat us. Some were arrested, but luckily I managed to escape each time, with the aid of a friend of mine by the name David Mahloko. He was a very revolutionary and experienced *seyainyova*. He could not talk about anything other than politics or how we needed to fight until we were all free. He also had a friend by the name Mahlodi, from East Rand. She was very revolutionary and I liked her thinking. We just clicked.

Talking about revolutionary friends, joining the matric student at Wits University and later at Auden House opened my eyes to the political situation in the country. I began to be aware of political issues from those students coming from the townships. I became very political and a revolutionary, but not yet militant. I started practising my newly-acquired revolutionary knowledge on my employers.

What I hated most about my white employer's son was that he never wanted black people to look him in the eyes when speaking. One day, his mother complained about something and he wanted to establish facts with all of us. When he approached me, I looked straight into his eyes while talking to him, and he reprimanded me that I should not do that. An argument ensued. I told him that I would not look down when I was talking to him because it did not make sense to me. He got very angry and threatened to fire me. He told his mother and she promised me that she would talk him out of the idea of firing me.

During a day shift, when I was working a double shift, my employer and I had some kind of disagreement and I told her that she was as cruel as Hitler. I forgot that the family were of Jewish origin. She was very angry, especially since she hated Hitler. When the son visited her the next day in the afternoon, she told him of what I said. The day nurse came to relieve me that evening, and the son said nothing to me. The following day, when I reported for my night duty, the son was there. I was surprised because he never stayed that late. He called me and told me that I was fired, and I had to leave their premises with immediate effect because I had likened his mother to Hitler. It was only then that I remembered that they were Jewish. I asked for their telephone to call my father and informed him of what had happened and asked that he should come to fetch me. He had a small Volkswagen car. I went and stayed with my father but continued with my studies.

Mahlodi and I became good friends. She one day invited me to join a meeting in Soweto at a place called Intokozweni in Tladi township. I agreed, although I had never been to Soweto and I did not know what it looked like. I was keen on attending the meeting because she'd already told me that most of the women there had been in the struggle for a long time. Some of their husbands had gone underground or were exiled. I asked my boyfriend (now husband) to take me there. He knew Soweto because he was already teaching in Orlando West (Phefeni High School). He agreed and we met in town and took a taxi to Soweto.

Indeed, it was true, because some of the speakers were Sister Bertina Ncube, Albertina Sisulu, Matilda Gxowa, Emma Mashinini and a lady by the name of Amanda Kwadi. We went in and I sat there listening attentively. It was the first time I'd attended such a meeting, and I was fired up. I was more than ever determined to join the struggle. The next time we met, Mahlodi gave me Amanda Kwadi's telephone number to contact. I telephoned her and arranged that we meet. She was working in Johannesburg CBD as a trade unionist

After some time, Amanda Kwadi called me to confirm our meeting. I agreed, and we met at St Johns College during lunch time. She introduced herself and told me about her background. Most of the introduction and the rest of the conversation was around how we should further the struggle by mobilising workers from a trade unionist point of view. She encouraged me to try to mobilise workers at St Johns College, to conscientious them about their rights as articulated by the likes of Karl Marx.

I agreed and started talking to other workers about our political situation and how we should free ourselves from oppression and exploitation. I did not know much about Karl Marx's philosophy, so I started reading his books from the library to acquaint myself. The library had a collection of his books and other useful literature.

I was attracted to his popular slogan, "Workers of the World Unite". I grew to like Karl Marx and his thinking, and I became more knowledgeable. This empowered me because, in my first year history lessons, terms such as dialectical materialism, bourgeoisies and proletariats fascinated me. The more I read his books and some African literature, the more I started to realise that a lot had to change in the country for us to realise real liberation or emancipation. I also started collecting books and biographies of leaders such as Mahatma Ghandi, Fidel Castro and Muamar Gadhafi, as well as African literature writers such as Chinua Achebe and Wole Soyinka (Akinwande Oluwole Babatunde) and many others. I have a vast collection of that, as well as those that are written about the revolution in African countries and Latin America.

In the meeting I had with Amanda Kwadi, I told her about the poor conditions African labourers worked under at the school. She was prepared to come and address them if I happened to organise a meeting. Fortunately, they were afraid and never agreed to my meetings. I am saying fortunately because, if they had agreed, the information could have leaked to management and they would have fired me. I was not ready for that.

Cynthia Hugo was never to hear of the plan; she was going to be disappointed. It was not so long after I knew Amanda that the white trade unionists Neil Agget, also Amanda's friend, was assassinated by the police force for taking part in the liberation struggle. I was so shocked by the news and I realised how dangerous the apartheid system was. My hatred and anger towards the unjust system kept on growing and I knew that I could not just sit back and watch, doing nothing.

Henceforth, politics became part of my life. I used to accompany Amanda to Khotso House, were political activities used to take place and most of Neil Agget's commemoration took place there.

My parents were very apolitical. I tried to engage them about these issues, but they just discouraged me, as did my sister. The activities mentioned above took place in the night, that is, from 8 o'clock to 4 o'clock in the morning. I enjoyed listening to speaker after speaker as they emphasised the need to continue with the struggle (the armed struggle for liberation). Everyone would be singing revolutionary songs and there was no sleeping. A lady by the name of Gcina Mhlophe was the main entertainer. She mesmerised me with her revolutionary poems. She is a well-known poet and storyteller, excellent.

I always lied to my father about my whereabouts because I knew he would not allow me to go. Most of those meetings would be interrupted by the police raiding and what scared me most was to be arrested. I would not be able to explain that to my father, but with God's Grace I was never caught.

Later, Amanda Kwadi invited me to attend a meeting in town where she was a speaker. The theme of that meeting was Women Forward! Issues that they discussed were around: leading women fighting for independence; women in detention; women in the UDF; women fighting racism and sexism; Women resisting triple oppression; Women's duty to build the nation; We thank the women; and Guide for educators. They would be chanting and singing revolution songs and shouting a slogan: "Women forward!"

She later invited me to a meeting, also held at Khotso House, at which I had the opportunity to listen to Emma Mashinini addressing the audience. Emma Mashinini was a famous black woman trade unionist. When I moved to stay in Soweto we both stayed in Orlando West, and I remember when her house was once petrol bombed by the apartheid police force

Talking about Emma Mashinini, I am reminded of Jay Naidoo's article in City Press, dated 16 July 2017, when he described her succinctly:

> The last time I spoke to Ma Emma was a few months ago at the launch of my book in Johannesburg. She looked as graceful and as elegant as ever. She radiated warmth and empathy. Her spirit shone brightly through a body slowed down by age and reliant on a firm stick. We hugged. Her smile was serene, but her eyes were troubled. I spent a long time wondering about the sadness I saw in her. That I saw in Ahmed Kathrada. That I see in the mirror of my soul. It is the sadness deep in the heart of Andrew Mlangeni, Denis Goldberg and so many others who have given so much of their lives to the cause of justice.
>
> I thought back to the first time I met Ma Emma. I heard her before I saw her. It was at Khotso House in Johannesburg, home to the SA Council of Churches. She was surrounded by a crowd of workers. I was a new kid on the block in this big city of Egoli, nearly four decades

ago. I was intrigued. I pierced the gathering, attracted by the magnetism of a small, powerful woman holding the floor. Her wisdom permeated the crowds around her, embracing all in the courageous wonder of what is possible in life. Radiating integrity, discipline, a good head and a pure heart, her voice rose and fell like the tides of change, with the silky passion that knocks on the door of conscience. I knew then that she would be my lifelong teacher.

Ma Emma was a gentle giant who masked the dynamism of her fierce commitment to justice. I never knew someone so small make such a big difference in the lives of others. She guided us on the art of living with kindness and solidarity. But one never underestimated the rock that lay within. Many did, and to their amazement, they learnt to respect and admire how she lived her life.

As I sat with Ma Emma that last time, I knew that she was sharing her last testament with me. It has been a magnificent and inspiring journey. We saw our Mother Earth as our teacher. She led us to see ourselves as beings of love, light, compassion, and generosity. We saw ourselves as servants of a higher purpose. We knew right from wrong, good from evil and justice from injustice. Our work was driven by our shared commitment to unity, to building a nation that truly served our people and delivered on the covenant of a "better life" that we had promised in 1994. Much has happened since then, some good, like having her in our lives, and some bad.

We should take the lessons from those disappointments and use the growing anger that is engulfing the country to reset our moral compass towards the inspiring dreams and hopes that we embraced at the beginning of our democracy. We understood that changing the system, and even entrenching freedom in the permanence of a constitutional democracy, was insufficient to defend and advance the rights of our people. We understood that our most urgent task was to change the human being.

Sharing food, caring for infants, and building social networks helped our ancestors. So, we needed to ask ourselves these questions: What does it mean to be human? How do I live with humanity in life, in our politics, in our economy and in our community? I know Ma Emma knew of this need. Decent, humble, dedicated, and sincere, she was a mother who believed in the inherent goodness of every human being. She had a profound love for ordinary people, the underclass, and the working people. I know she has gone to a better place. And she still showers us with love. My heart is full of gratitude for how she has lived her life because she has made a difference in so many other lives. I learnt so much from her as she opened her arms to me and so many activists in those difficult times. Today much is grey. We have lost time. Our leaders failed to imbibe the life lessons of our past. We have become drunk on power. But we know that the cycle will change. Each generation must find its voice, its struggle and its destiny.

That time is now upon us. We often talked about the challenges that we had left to young people. We spoke about creating safe and sacred places for an intergenerational conversation about solutions to the challenges we face, both local and global. We understood that the world had changed much since we built the trade union movement in the 1980s. Those changes are terrifying for our youth. We are leaving them an ecological emergency and a world of growing joblessness, poverty, and inequality. The youth have a legitimate right to be angry with us. Our conversations about change are old, our ideologies, institutions, and ways of working, archaic. We saw the need to co-create the new narratives and social networks that empower the next generation to deal with our volatile present.

Naidoo recounted that

> Emma lived a life on Earth where she regarded everything that sustained us as sacred. She learnt to tread softly. She left no scars of bitterness, sorrow and want. With you, Ma Emma, we learnt to be patient guides and to understand that listening with empathy is the wisest way to learn life lessons. Our people know that we cannot solve all the problems we have now. But they want to know, to participate in and to discuss how we can solve the challenges of our country together. Above all, they want humble, honest, and ethical leaders. Ma Emma, I thank you from the bottom of my heart for all you have done for our country, our people and humanity. Never did I hear a word of complaint or regret. You are the matriarch I was always happy to call my mother. I must say, these women truly nourished my political hunger, I was never to look back.

I became involved in the liberation struggle politics, and they just consumed my life. I remember one time, while walking along

Louis Botha Avenue coming from a Rastafarian concert in town, I saw a pamphlet inviting people to attend Solomon Mahlangu's Commemoration in Alexandra. Mahlangu had been hanged in 1979 for his involvement in the armed struggle. The occasion was happening on the afternoon that I saw the pamphlet. I went home, ate something and went back to Louis Botha Avenue to catch a Putco Bus to Alexandra. I did not know the place that well. I looked for the venue and found it. I went in and sat down.

The meeting was addressed by Paul Mashatile. I listened to the speeches and revolutionary songs such as *Gorrila wee ilanga le shonile seyo lala phe*, all the time punctuated by a slogan, *Viva Comrade:* Mandela, Sisulu Oliver Tambo, Chris Hani etcetera. In closing, we were reminded of the last words Solomon said before he was hanged: "My blood will nourish the tree that will bear the fruits of freedom. Tell my people that I love them. They must continue the struggle." I could feel a lump in my throat, it was the first time I'd heard that, although when he was hanged I was at the Wits campus, attending matric classes. The mood had been sombre and one could sense tension in the air. The campus was abuzz with students raising their fists and saying Black Power. My life was not to be the same again, especially since I am Mahlangu as mentioned earlier, but then I did not grasp the extent of our oppression and what Mahlangu stood for. I kept on asking myself, what is it that I was doing there.

A militant student I spoke about earlier had connections with other University students from traditionally black institutions, especially Turfloop. My friends Mahlodi Nkadimeng and David Mahloko requested that I join them in a secret meeting at a place called Wilgerspruit, where we would be addressed by Turfloop student leaders. Transport was arranged and we went late in the evening. The meetings were held in a community centre.

The place was very scary and remote, away from residential areas and towns. It was literally not visible from the main road because of thick forest and slopes around it. Arriving there, I started to have a very bad feeling about the whole thing, and I kept on thinking about my father.

At that point, the students from universities arrived. The transports that brought them dropped them off far away, to disguise our vicinity. Once in the venue, we were not allowed to switch on lights, to avoid been traced by the police force. It was just darkness all around. I remember them talking about how we should acquire guns and ammunitions. The idea was to shoot whites and render the country ungovernable.

Though I bought into the idea, I started to panic. They told us that when we got these weapons, we should target buildings such as the Carlton Centre and blow it up, so that the government would realise how serious we were. It was not long before we started hearing gunshots in the distance. Even though it was not the first time I had gone there, it was the first time I'd come face to face with the police. Some of the students knew that we had been sold out and that the police were after us. They told us not to panic, but the gunshot sound did not stop for most of the evening. They could not trace us, and eventually the sound died out and they left.

I felt that the revolution must be waged for several reasons. Coming from the rural areas, walking in the street was dangerous during apartheid government. The danger was ever lurking around, not so much of being kidnapped, raped or murdered as a woman – those incidents were not as common as it is nowadays. One was afraid of being attacked by whites just for the mere fact that one was black, or arrested by police for not having legal documents.

I remember one incident in which my cousin was walking in the street of Yeoville on a Sunday afternoon. He was wearing his best clothes, coming to visit us. As he walked past a block of flats, a group of white children threw eggs at him. To them it was a joke, but the idea was to humiliate a black person in a suit.

For a person like me it was even more difficult because I did not have legal documents qualifying me to reside in Johannesburg. These papers were called a *dompas*. This was like an internal passport that black people had to carry. It indicted where a person was allowed to work and live. I always had to run from the police. It was a daily routine for police then, to drive around all day hunting, chasing and collecting suspects, loading them in a police van and only returning to the police station when the van was full of illegals in their own country.

This was to be my fate too, as one day young police caught up with me, asking for the *dompas* I did not have. To save myself, I decided to run as fast as I could and escaped. But my luck ran out when one afternoon I was walking in the streets of Braamfontein, to attend my evening classes at Wits. The only means of transport to Braamfontein from Houghton was either boarding a Putco bus from Alexandra via Louis Botha Avenue and to get off in Hillbrow and walk to Braamfontein, or to take a metrobus from Yeoville and get off in Hillbrow as well. There was no connecting means of transport from Hillbrow to Braamfontein. One had to walk across Civic Centre, today known as Johannesburg Metropolitan Council.

As I walked down Jorrisen street from Hillbrow, I was approached by a police van that stopped next to me. There were about five policemen in the back of the van. Their job was to hunt blacks without a *dompas*. They were mostly from Bantustans such as Lebowa because then it was very easy to find work in the police force. Blacks from urban areas never wanted to be policemen. I do not know why.

The policemen came and scattered everywhere, chasing anyone looking for *dompas*. One tall Tsonga-speaking policeman came for me. I tried to run but he was faster than I was so, as I got around the corner of Jorissen Street, he caught up with me. He wanted a passbook. He grabbed me and tried to force me into the van. I tried to fight back, but he was too strong for me. I pleaded with him to let me go as I was attending classes and writing a test that evening, and he agreed.

I felt so scared, angry, humiliated and downtrodden. I hated this country more than ever. All that went through my head was to find a way of skipping the country; I did not care how. I became consumed by hatred and the desire to avenge that grew by the day.

I told my father one day that I felt so vindictive that I wished I could just take garden lawn shears, go into the streets, and start cutting white children's heads off to make a statement. The rage just consumed me, and I am thankful to God that I never got to do anything so evil. Then I did not know about Nat Turner's slave rebellion. It wasn't strange that my thinking was like that of Nat's, because he was sick and tired of the treatment African Americans endured from white people. The treatment was similar to that of black people during apartheid, very sickening. This told me that most of my fellow blacks, particularly Africans, felt that way as the wrath of segregation, oppression and subjugation engulfed our daily lives. I salute Nat Turner. He died a proud person, executed in public by hanging or not. He did not only talk about it: he actioned it.

My father looked at me and for the first time he was not angry but afraid, and he spoke to me politely to say that, even if I did cut off children's heads, nothing would change. He said, with sadness in his voice, "They would just charge you for murder and hang you, just like Solomon Mahlangu. I am Mahlangu too. Gwangwa is my great-great-grandfather's name, and his surname was Mahlangu. Because of family feuds, my great-grandfather and his brother fought, and they separated. He changed my great-great-grandfather's name to become his surname, Gwangwa."

I did not care. All that I wanted was to be treated like a human being. I knew I deserved that. The desire to leave grew much stronger, especially after I learnt that my cousin had left with his wife to go and train as freedom fighters.

As for my sister, she was caught and apprehended so many times. Once arrested, she would remain at the police station until my father went to bail her out. At dusk, after charges were confirmed, she would be taken to the women's prison, where the Constitutional Court is now located. It became some sort of a hobby, considering the number of trips he made to the notorious Number Four Police Station in Hillbrow to bail her out.

These policemen would drive around with her in a Khwela Khwela (branded police vans used to be called a kumpa kumpa, later hippo or yello mello, now nyala). Sometimes, my father and I would go together to the police station to negotiate a trespass fine, and she would be freed. Fortunately, she never spent a night in prison, having to endure the ablution bucket, clanging door, cell reeking of dirt, dust, sweat and urine that my fellow Africans endured when under arrest. I was so disheartened when she narrated to me how she would be thrown into the police van, just like a common criminal.

The idea of leaving the country became a powerful feature in my mind, in that skipping was the only perfect option. One of the things that made me feel strongly about leaving the country was the lack of freedom due to constant threat of arrest by police for not having a pass to be there.

There was a cousin of mine who used to work at Wits Business School in Parktown as a labourer. He also worked as a part time gardener for a certain white family. He was only working for a room to stay in, because he needed accommodation. He was using the room as a disguise. I happened to learn about his activities from my other cousin, who did not know that I intended to leave the country. He confided to me that he did not like what this other cousin of mine was doing. He told me that he was hiding children who had been recruited to go underground for military training in his room. He also told me that he was the one who had arranged for my other cousin and his wife to leave the country. I sensed from his voice that he was angry with what he did. I said nothing, but then and there I was encouraged that I'd finally found someone to help me.

I went to Parktown to meet him. I did not beat about the bushes. I told him frankly that I wanted to leave the country. He was shocked, I could see that from his reaction. He never asked me how I happened to know what he was doing. He paused for a while and responded, "You cannot go. How am I going to look at your father?" He said to me, "Do you know how your parents struggled to have children?" In my mind I just said, "They struggled to have me, but I am here trying to do something for my country." I kept quiet and left. Every time I met him, I would ask him about helping me, and he eventually promised me that he would arrange for me to go with the next load. He never wanted me to know where he was living nor to ask my father either, as he knew where he was staying. I waited until I realised that he did not want to assist me. However, I was not about to give up.

I told my then boyfriend (now husband), trying to convince him to leave with me. Initially, he agreed. But he changed his mind and convinced me otherwise. I felt betrayed and upset, though I understood his standpoint. My husband and I come from the same social, political and economic background; we share a lot in common. We both came from the rural areas and were brought up by migrant labourer fathers (working class). His mother was a housewife, the same as my mine. The reason for not wanting to skip the country was that he'd just started teaching and he was not going to leave just like that. He was more politically mature than I was, and he managed to convince me.

We talked a lot about how we felt, our aspirations and tribulations under adversities. Sekhukhuneland was hard hit by political strife. It started when the previous government introduced the trust land system. The Pedi people from ga-Sekhukhune resisted, and many of them were arrested including the chiefs. They also resisted the introduction of Christianity.

There are many people from there who skipped the country. These are the unsung heroes, as no one ever says anything about their contribution to the struggle. I could recall one of their closest family who served about twenty-seven years for treason and recruited all his boy children to join the struggle, and they went underground to train as Umkhonto Wesizwe combatants. He did not only recruit his sons but his sister's son, who never came back. It was a huge sacrifice indeed. My husband and I went to see him after political prisoners were released from Robben Island in the early 1990s. His name is Mahwidi Phala.

Although I was fascinated to see him, I also had a sense of guilt for having remained behind.

Talking about Sekhukhuland's resistance to white apartheid rule, I personally read about the Sekhukhune people's resilience. For example, the "Pedi strife history" is very interesting. According to South African History Online (SAHO), it started in 1952, and was called a Defiance Campaign. Later, in 1954, a migrant worker-based movement called Sebatakgomo was formed. The movement played a leading role in the 1958 Sekhukhuneland Revolt.

One horrifying example of the extent to which people then resisted Christianity is found in a story of Mantshe (che) Masemola. According to Wikipedia:

> Manche Masemola **was born in** 1913 and died in 1928. She was only 15 years old. Masemola was born in Marishane, a small village near Jane Furse, in South Africa. She lived with her parents, two older brothers, a sister, and a cousin. German and then English missionaries had worked in the Transvaal Colony for several decades and by the early twentieth century there was a small Christian community among the Pedi people, which was widely viewed with distrust by the remainder of the tribe, who still practised the traditional religion.

> Martyrdom: By 1919, an Anglican *Community of the Resurrection* mission was established by Father

Augustine Moeka in Marishane. Masemola attended classes in preparation for baptism with her cousin Lucia, against the wishes of her parents. Her parents took her to a *sangoma* (African traditional healer), claiming that she had been bewitched. She was prescribed a traditional remedy, which her parents made her consume by beating her. Relations worsened, and the mother hid the girl's clothes so she could not attend Christian instructional classes. On 4 February 1928, her parents led the teenager to a lonely place, where they killed her, burying her by a granite rock on a remote hillside. Manche had said that she would be baptised in her own blood. She died without having been baptised. Manche's mother converted to Christianity and was baptised forty years later, in 1969. Manche was declared a martyr by the Church of the Province of Southern Africa in less than ten years.

Reverting to how I was entangled in the politics and the extent to which reggae music became my solace. Besides the fact that reggae music invigorated and inspired me, I must say that the music kept me sane and gave me hope that Africa would one day liberate South Africa. Marley music still holds some power over me; it has a grip on my soul and it still moves me. "I am certain that there is not one person in the whole world, particularly Africa, whose music is so influential and famous to the point of succeeding in creating a revolution that used music as a more powerful tool than bullets and bombs," writes Bill Oxley.

Ironically, Oxley is the very same man who confessed to having assassinated Marley by tainting the nail in his shoes with cancer viruses and bacteria. The nail pierced his skin and that was it. The reason for killing Marley was because, he was "placing the goals of the CIA he was working for in jeopardy and threatening the existence of the United States". I am still shocked. Marley had such a deep love for Africa. I cannot stop thinking that if it is true that people who died become ancestors and they can see us, what he must be feeling about what Africa, as well as South Africa, has degenerated into. All that we witness is nothing but a mess, because of corruption and greed. He must be turning in his grave.

I was so keen on knowing more about Rastafarian that I researched a lot about it. Fortunately, while working in St Johns library I came across two books written about Marcus Garvey and Haile Selassie. They both gave me more perspective and insight into what I am. As far as Rastafarian music, that is, reggae, particularly Bob Marley, I knew about Marley through my friend Caroline. She told me about him coming to Zimbabwe to perform at its independence celebrations.

Zimbabwe: When Bob Marley and Robert Mugabe celebrated its independence.

Caroline told me that she and her friends were planning to go to see him performing live and invited me to come along. She told me not to worry about money as they would assist me with funds for the trip. What I had to do was to apply for a passport. I was keen to go, very excited. I immediately went to Pietersburg (Polokwane) Home Affairs Department to apply for my passport. They did not give me any problem with my application. However, because things were difficult for blacks then, I could not go as my passport was only ready two years (in 1982) after the concert and his subsequent death on 11 May 1981.

I was shattered by his death. I loved his music very much and I still do. But then I did not understand much about his association with Rastafarians, other than that he was singing Reggae music.

Caroline was very sad that I could not come to the concert. She was truly thrilled by his performance, when he sang revolutionary songs such as: *Redemption song, Babylon system, Rumours of War, Zimbabwe, Them tummy full (but we hungry), Buffalo soldier, Who the cap fit, Time will tell, The harder they come, Survival, Small axe; I shot the sheriff*, etcetera. But my favourite of his love songs is, Lively up yourself, So much things to say, Stir it up and Turn your lights down low. I told my family that at my funeral, when the hearse leaves my house they must play *Stir It Up*, followed by *Time Will Tell*. When the coffin goes down into the grave they must play Toots and The Maytals' *Six and Seven Books of Moses*, followed by Jimmy Cliff, *The Harder They Come*.

Quoting Caroline's exact words, she said: Marley gave his audience a "goose-bumps inducing performance". I still get goosebumps playing them today. I also love songs by Toots and The Maytals: *Peace Perfect Peace, Never You Change*; Peter Tosh: *Pick Myself Up* and Jimmy Cliff: *Many Rivers To Cross*. Here at home, Lucky Dube: *Different Colours/One People* and many more.

Let me elaborate more on my encounter with reggae and the Rastafarian religion. The only time I was introduced to the Rastafarian religion, or its philosophy, was when I met Nobuhle at the UNISA library in Johannesburg, mentioned above. I was never converted. I still like it, though. It has a rich history, and what impressed me about it is that they believe in God and have great respect for African culture and above all respect for humankind, particularly women. But, regarding women I took that with a pinch of salt due to their belief in the Old Testament, which promotes patriarchy and the oppression of women. Hence, the Old Testament is used by twisted men to abuse women. But I personally witnessed how they respected women as I used to attend their concerts held at Joubert Park in Johannesburg. I never came across any unbecoming behaviours, especially in an environment where women and men mingled.

I respect Rastafarians because they always commit themselves to everything they do, something that I can relate to. Thus, I believe in the notion that people are not stupid, educated or not. If you do your job with commitment, people can see it and they respond. Thus, I do not understand the attitude of people employed in senior positions in government who do not want to serve the citizens of this country who are paying their salaries. That was my difficulty when working in public service.

In further illustrating Rastafarian religion, I would like to share with readers the article below, just to dismiss the myth and stigma it is shrouded in. One day I was reading the Sunday Times when I came across an article written by Tina Weavind, dated 22 January 2012, and titled: *What Rastafarian Philosophy Meant to Me, Rastafarians rule as professionals.*

The first image that comes to mind when the word Rasta is mentioned is, well, not a doctor or a lawyer. Most people are more likely to picture a musician in a colourful knitted beanie playing reggae in a cloud of aromatic smoke. This is an image a group of professional men, devoted Rastafarians, are hoping to change about their religion, writes Tina Weavind.

The Rastafari movement began in the Jamaican slums in the 1920s and was officially founded on 2 November 1930, when Ras Tafari Makonnen was crowned emperor of Ethiopia. At his coronation he took the name Haile Selassie, meaning "Might of the Trinity". The movement has its roots in the philosophies of Marcus Garvey, a Jamaican who created a "back to Africa" movement in the US. The movement does not have a cohesive structure and there is little formal organisation, with some Rastafarians seeing it as more a way of life than a religion. According to religion facts.com, some of the unifying beliefs are "the belief in the divinity and/or messiahship of Emperor Haile Selassie I, resistance of oppression, and pride in African heritage".

Concurring with the above sentiment, Mathole Motshekga wrote in his April 2004 article, titled *African churches played a huge role*:

> ... Marcus Garvey is renowned for his Africa for Africans campaign... Apart from his political influence, Garvey made an impact in the religious sphere. He believed in the universality of God but argued that Africans should worship God through Ethopian (that is, indigenous

African) eyes. To give effect to his Ethopian (that is black African) theology, Garvey established the African Orthodox Church. The Go of Garvey called Jah (or Iao) taught African humanism (Ubuntu or Botho), which was embodied in the maxim "I and I", which means "I am because we are". The full name of Garvey's God was Jah (or IAO) Abaraka (Greek Abraxas). This was an ancient African (both Ethopian and Egyptian) God, symbolised by the sphinxes of both Ethiopia and Egypt. The name Jah or IOA is the original African concept of the Alpha and Omega from which Moses coined the word Jehovah, which was also spelt Hahu or IHVH in the African mysteries. The God Jehovah was, therefore, originally an African God symbolised by the sphinxes of Egypt and Ethiopia. He further stated that the Garveyan God Jah was the (Aba) of the Divine Light (Kara/Raka) which manifested itself as the ether (or quintessence) and four elements symbolised by the sphinxes of Ethiopia and Egypt.

The Rasta way of life involves the use of marijuana – also known as ganja or holy herb – for religious purposes, and abstinence from alcohol and meat. Rastafaris reject the term "Rastafarianism" because of the "isms and schisms" that they believe characterise "oppressive and corrupt white society", according to religionfacts.com. They believe in Jah, a Judeo-Christian god. In general, Rastafari beliefs are based on the Old Testament. Meaning is also found in the "Holy Piby", a version of the bible compiled by Robert Athlyi Rogers, which removes "the deliberate distortions made by white leaders" during translation into English.

> Jah is believed to have taken on an earthly form as both Jesus, who Rastafarians say was a black man, and Emperor Haile Selassie. Rastafarians also honour Old Testament prophets like Moses and Elijah. Rastas do not believe in the afterlife – they think Africa (called Zion) is heaven on earth. True Rastas are believed to be "ever living" or immortal, both physically and spiritually. They try to avoid any influence from "Babylon", which they define as "the white power structure of the West". Tina Weavind.

The article went on to illustrate that Rastafarianism is not a religion for uneducated, poor, ganja smoking people, thus the title: Rastafarians rule as professionals. She alluded to the fact that there are very educated individuals who are converted Rastafari.

*

Caroline and I kept good contact after our initial meeting at the wedding. After some time, she contacted me and requested that we arrange that I meet her at the Wits East Campus and she directed me to a place where I could find her, at the African Literature Building. She became the only bosom friend I'd ever had to date; I'd never had such a friend before. We just clicked. Then I still had difficulties in constructing English sentences. I never spoke the language with anyone other than my employers, and a few words here and there with my father.

Where I came from, English was taught in North Sotho. Fortunately for me, my father had a very good command of English. As I mentioned earlier, he had been brought up by a missionary priest called Father Gilbert. He never had an

Ndebele name and he was known only as Father Gilbert, named after a Roman Catholic monk who'd brought him up. It was his wish that his children spoke English like English people, that is, taking it through the nostrils (*re ntshe sekgowa ka dinko*).

This reminded me of one day when my employer telephoned me when I had the day off. My father happened to answer his boss' land line. He waited there while I was talking. After I'd finished, he said to me, "Please learn to speak English like English people".

Being myself, I protested, asking him, "How I do I do that?"

He said I must practice. He quickly said I must learn from my sister, who'd mastered it. He was so obsessed with us speaking English properly that one day, while he was listening to the then Radio Bophuthatswana (Bop Radio), he heard this black girl talking English like English people. For the whole day he told us about this girl. Out of curiosity I one day tuned in to the Radio Bop station rather than my usual station, Radio Lebowa. The woman talking there was Felicia Mabuza before marrying Suttle.

Nonetheless, my conversations with Caroline Mackensky were very difficult at the beginning. I found it difficult to construct English sentences, I came from a schooling system were English was taught in North Sotho (Sepedi), but I learnt very quickly. The first time we spent a lot of time together was when she was to take her car for service. I did not know Johannesburg then, but I think it was around the Booysens area. There were lots of scrap yards. We went and, while the car was being fixed, we sat underneath the tree and chatted about lots of things. My background and hers, my dreams and aspirations, and her studies. She was the same age as me but had already completed her first degree, She was doing her honours degree. I really envied her, and vowed to myself that I would one day acquire that level of education, although the chances were almost zero. Caroline and I depicted the South African scenario of two worlds, the first and third. Despite, my dire background, I just believed! I never stop dreaming.

She told me of a student friend of hers, Joanne Yawitch, who was doing a research project about forced removals or re-settlement in rural Limpopo. She was researching on "Betterment". Betterment was a government-introduced project, meant to teach rural people about share cropping in their new settlements. Joanne wanted someone to assist her with translations. I told her that I would like to take the opportunity. Most of the people in the rural areas were illiterate, especially older people. They could only speak Northern Sotho.

During that time, the government was forcefully removing people from fertile land to barren land. The policy that was called Resettlement. There was a lot of resistance and resentment throughout the country. We travelled the breadth and length of rural Limpopo, up to a very deep remote rural area of ga-Malebogo, Bochum, Uitkyk in the northwest, Modjadji in the northeast and Sekhukhuneland in the south of what was called Lebowa Bantustan. It was not voluntary: she paid me very well, far better than my first job. The money came in handy because I did not have any source of income after losing my job. I also gained vast experience and knowledge of what was going on around me.

It was then that I understood that the Bantustan system was a bad government policy and that the National Party was doing more harm to black people than good. From one area to another we stayed at Church Mission Schools such as Fatima Mission in Bochum, Sobiako Mission in Botlokwa and St Cyprian Mission at ga-Mothapo We would stay overnight at the nearest mission. Our last stop was Polokwane, then known as Pietersburg. We slept in a Lutheran Church Mission. I was surprised to see someone who had been a priest at Arkona Parish at ga-Masemola, many years ago when I was little. He was known as *Moruti* (Priest) Val. I told him that I knew him. He was very delighted as I told him about my mother and other people, and he knew them very well. When he left ga-Masemola *Moruti* Mamogobo took over as the first black priest. I think that staying in Church Missions was pre-arranged, judging from the reception we received.

Most of these mission schools were church-based and run by white priests called "Fathers". However, at some places I was not allowed to sleep in the same place as Joanne Yawitch because of me being a black person. That is how the apartheid system of separate development was so deep rooted and entrenched.

It was almost the end of the year when the project came to an end, and she was to prepare for a research report for her studies. I used the money she paid me to buy more books at Damelin for my matric lessons and some I sent home to my mother.

Meanwhile, my sister's friend was a labourer at St John College: that is, doing manual work. Upon realising that I was studying, he became interested. He told me that he too had acquired only a Form 3 certificate. He wanted to further his studies. He recommended that I approach a certain librarian lady at the College. She might allow me to use their library for studying. He knew that I was staying with my sister and my father in a small workers' cottage and studying under those conditions might be difficult.

Indeed, it was. I could only study in the night when my father and sister went to sleep. That was a huge inconvenience as we had only one room and I could not have the light on while they were sleeping. I would alternatively use my father's employer's garages: he had two. I would sit between two Rolls Royces in the garage at night because the light was always switched on. The night watchman allowed me to do that. I must admit that spreading a cardboard box to sit on a cement floor was almost unbearable, especially in winter, but I was determined, and nothing was to stop me.

I heeded Phillip's advice and went to approach the lady named Cynthia Hugo. She was very impressed and respected me for wanting to better my life through education. She grew to love me for my courage and willingness to change my life. She immediately spoke to the head of the school, and they agreed that I could use one of the small rooms above the library for my studies during the day. She spoke to the English teacher to assist me. He agreed, and he would help me with prescribed books such as Shakespeare. She allowed me to use all the books in the library for reference. I went crazy at seeing so many books. I had never seen anything like that before.

Photos taken in St Johns library

She also requested from the school headmaster that they offer me a job to assist in the library: tidying, filing books after students had finished reading them, mending those that were torn and sorting out new books and putting them on the shelves, as well as stocktaking. The headmaster agreed, and I was offered a salary of R70 a month. The money was very little but came in handy, I was just too grateful for their compassion. Already I was comparing it with the salary of R95 I used to receive while working as an assistant nurse. When I told my boyfriend about how much I was earning, he told me that when he'd started teaching, he had earned that much. My father and my sister thought it was a lot of money.

Cynthia Hugo and her colleague taught me everything about librarianship. Having an opportunity to work at St Johns library was breathtaking. I had never seen so many books at high school other than in the public library I used to go to while working in Greenside. I was fascinated by the sea of books. I made a point that during lunch break I would read something.

Fortunately, Mrs Hugo arranged with school management that I could accompany her and the rest of the white staff teachers to the dining hall for lunch. I'd never tasted such delicious meals before. The meal that left my eyes dropping out was a full stuffed chicken for each person. What a treat. There was so much food, I was beyond myself. The meal was so delicious and I was amazed. The cherry on top was a dessert of ice cream. I found myself very lucky. I was treated the same as every other staff member working in the library,

including having tea with them during tea times. She became very fond of me, and really encouraged me in every possible way.

The only thing that always made me sad and somehow guilty was the fact that black workers were not allowed to eat with white staff. They had their own lunch at the compound adjacent to their rooms. They were provided with domestic worker meals like the ones my father's employer provided his workers, with porridge (*pap*) and meat.

At more or less the same time that I secured employment at St Johns College, and not long after the project I was doing with Joanne Yawitch came to an end, Caroline came to see me. She wanted me to accompany them on weekends to Limpopo. She explained to me what it was that they were doing there. I agreed and informed my father. He too agreed that I could join them.

Caroline and other white students from Wits were involved with a voluntary project. It was called the South African Voluntary Service (SAVS), sponsored by the university. Students were given funds to start community projects in the rural areas. They were building community clinics and teaching local people gardening and the like. The project they were busy with was at ga-Molepo, one of the villages in Limpopo. It was a village neighbouring the one in which I met them for the first time at my friend's wedding (ga-Mothapo). My friend's uncle came from ga-Molepo. He must have recommended that they come and start the project in his home village, as he was studying with them.

For two years, I travelled with them to ga-Molepo and surrounding areas doing community work. During that time, they were building a community clinic in the said village. While still constructing the building, before the roof went up, they used to sleep at my place in my parents' house, about 45 minutes from the place via Pietersburg (Polokwane) town. They did not mind sleeping on the floor, nor using dishes for bathing. They ate whatever we were eating.

Once the roof went up, we all slept in the building, at the beginning without windows or doors. Little did I know that this would one day earn me a tertiary full scholarship. I joined them and they taught me how to do bricklaying and plastering. We slept in sleeping bags and did not wash for the three days of being there. We cooked dried vegetables and beans they bought from a shop in Johannesburg, near Westgate station. We had lots of consultation meetings with community members and progress reporting sessions. I assisted them with translation when necessary. I was very impressed by the dedication of the community members; their participation truly inspired me. I was very keen on translating during discussions in those meetings. Because almost all of them had gone up to Standard 6, they were able to read and speak Northern Sotho.

One could read poverty on their faces and, because I had to sit next to them, the smell of distillery harassed my nostrils. I was familiar with that smell: the smell of poverty and destitution referring to a person who does not wash her/his clothes or body because they cannot afford soap. For them, buying soap was a luxury. There were other more important things to be prioritised, such as a bag of mielie meal. I call that the smell of poverty and destitution. Poverty smell is one smell I will never forget.

Those trips came in handy for me as they gave me the opportunity to see my mother and my daughter often. When the building was almost finished and habitable, there were times when I would take my daughter along with me. I remember one day when they were fitting accessories such as scales for weighing children. I just happened to go somewhere. In my absence, they tried to put my daughter on one of scales to make sure that it was stable. She got such a fright that I heard her crying from a distance. It was so funny.

Ga-Molepo is one of the areas in Limpopo with a high level of poverty and destitution, and a high rate of alcoholism and unemployment. Most of the men who came to seek employment in Johannesburg never returned home to their families, hence the high level of female-headed households and poverty. The people could not plough as the area is also prone to soil erosion and drought, very barren.

There was a great need for such a facility. The nearest hospital was about 45 minutes away, in a neighbouring village called Ga-Mothapo. It was a mission hospital. There I witnessed children with Marasmus (acute malnutrition) for the first time. A very bad sight indeed. They were just skeletons with big, protruding tummies and thin legs. One could literally count their ribs. And they also had big heads. This disease is caused by malnutrition and starvation. It starts with kwashiorkor. If not treated immediately then it turns into Marasmus. I was devastated and felt a great desire to do something to change the lives of the people in these communities. All that people needed was food aid or security and employment.

About a decade later, I witnessed starving children in Africa. One day, while watching Morning Live News on SABC Television, broadcast by Vuyo Mbuli, among other things he reported about the situation in Sudan. An image of what appeared to be a little girl, fallen to the ground from hunger, while a vulture lurked on the ground nearby, appeared on the screen. I do not know what came over me. I cried loudly; I was hysterical. All the memories of starving children in Limpopo Mission Hospital came flushing back and played in my head for a long time. Then later I saw a newspaper report on the above subject. The headline read: *How the Vulture and the Little Girl Ultimately led to the Death of Kevin Carter, Denis Lesak* – 17 December 2015

But what captured my mind is in this is Archbishop Tutu's comments.

I'm really, really sorry. The pain of life overrides the joy to the point that joy does not exist. …depressed … without phone … money for rent … money for child support … money for debts … money!!! … I am haunted by the vivid memories of killings & corpses & anger & pain … of starving or wounded children, of trigger-happy madmen, often police, of killer executioners … I have gone to join Ken if I am that lucky.

The final line is a reference to his recently deceased colleague Ken Osterbrock.

Desmond Tutu, Archbishop Emeritus of Cape Town, South Africa, wrote of Carter, "And we know a little about the cost of being traumatised that drove some to suicide, that yes, these people were human beings operating under the most demanding of conditions."

It is sad that in South Africa, being a democratic country and very rich, little has changed. Instead, we see countless black, white, coloured and Indian people becoming poorer. The ruling party continues to ignore issues facing black people, particularly Africans: their poverty and destitution. Their slogan, "a better life for all" has been replaced by a better life for politicians. These are the majority who are brainwashed and exploited as they are fed with misinformation and falsehoods.

Every five years there is always a rush to gain votes, diverting attention from the urgent need for genuine social and economic progress for the black majority. The quest for votes has become synonymous with access to the country's valuable resources and the proverbial "pot of gold". The problem stems from excessive political manoeuvring and vote gathering, rather than focusing on the emancipation of the black majority. South Africa is in a mess, with so many poor people starving to death daily. My question is: Are those in power feeling any guilt, let alone depression?

Nonetheless, I truly enjoyed taking those trips because I learnt a lot, and I had the opportunity to visit home every Sunday, before coming back to Johannesburg. If we did not have meetings with members of the community on Saturday afternoon or Sunday morning, we would go to places such as Magoebaskloof in

Tzaneen. Magoebaskloof is one of the most beautiful areas in Limpopo, a tourist attraction. Besides being mountainous, it has one of the most beautiful kloofs in the country. It has huge fruit plantations, nurseries and tea plantations, as well as farming areas. There is a beautiful waterfall and other tourist attraction areas.

Unfortunately, this was during the apartheid era, during which white people were not to be seen with blacks, unless they were their employees. We would go to town to buy fast food for lunch on our way. Black people were not allowed to buy anything inside the shop. I had to buy through the window. Caroline and others would insist that I come with them into the shop, but the shop owners would get very angry and threaten to beat us. They would throw me out, calling me a kaffir. It was very scary. The others were then forced to purchase takeaways so that we could go and sit under the tree in a convenient spot, just to accommodate me, and they would leave us alone.

One afternoon we did the same. We went to a different place in the same town, but young Afrikaner boys followed us. They started swearing and causing such a fuss and threatened to shoot us. We had to drive away to save our lives.

One Sunday afternoon we decided to visit Mpumalanga (Graskop), via Strydom Tunnel on our way back to Johannesburg. We visited tourist attraction areas such as Blyde Rivier (River), running along the mysterious Drie (Three) Rondavels mountains. I have never seen such natural beauty in my entire life. Those are the best tourist attraction areas in Mpumalanga. I was so lucky to be able to visit those areas; very few black people had such an opportunity.

What hurt me most was that we passed fruit plantations that  had initially belonged to black people but which had been taken from them and were now owned by white people. Most blacks there are very poor and destitute in a land of plenty. They are instead employed as farm workers.

We visited the place called God's Window, also in Mpumalanga. It is such a mysterious spot. Standing on that spot one can see as far as what was called Lourenco Marques (now Maputo) in Mozambique. I was told that on some days it becomes so misty that one cannot see a thing. I was so fortunate that on that day the window was very  clear: amazing. It is called God's Window because it is the only spot from which one can see that far; not any other spot. It is still a mystery to me as to who discovered it, and how it happened.

From there, we decided to drive to Nelspruit town for lunch. We got there and bought our lunch. Whites there were as conservative and racists as those in Tzaneen. Of course Nelspruit is an Afrikaner dorpie (small town) now called Mbombela. Some of us went to the toilet, but there were toilets marked "Whites Only" and "Blacks and Asians". I went to the toilet. On coming back there was these young, unruly Afrikaner boys, who started swearing at us and threatening violence. They approached our car, armed with all sort of things. Luckily, they were not in possession of guns. We all ran to the Combi, climbed in, locked the doors and fled the area. They chased us on foot. I was so traumatised. I prayed silently because I knew that if they caught up with us, they might kill me or all of us. They could not catch up with us and turned back.

This was the day that I realised how bad living in South Africa was, and I just wanted out. Caroline and her boyfriend Christopher Russel could not hide their frustration. I guess that these types of incidents were some of the reasons why they wanted to leave the country too.

The project was also supported by the Lebowa government's department of health and the chief. We managed to finish the entire structure of the clinic and built a cement water tank adjacent to the clinic. Merick was a student doctor, so he assisted in equipping the clinic so that the community could start using it, at least for primary health care. The community members were pleased, and we started teaching them about gardening and fruit tree planting for orchards. All unemployed men and women would converge at the clinic and start preparing the soil for planting. Meanwhile, the university provided us with money to equip the clinic so that it would be fully functional.

The Lebowa government agreed to staff it with nurses and doctors. When we were about to complete the finishing up touches and were preparing for the launch, an entourage of representatives from the Department of Health arrived in black Mercedes Benzes and ordered us to stop with the project and never put our feet back there. No explanation was given, other than it was an instruction from government. It was our saddest day. We left. I was only told that it is functioning as a public clinic run by the government but I've never been back there.

The university still had a budget to continue with similar community projects and this was from overseas donor monies.

Where I came from, there was one clinic. Meanwhile, the neighbouring villages had to travel a long distance to the clinic. I then motivated that they do a similar project in some of these villages. I told our chieftainess about my intention, and she agreed. While still at ga-Molepo, the challenge was that we no longer had sleeping accommodation since we had been chased away from Molepo Clinic. I invited them to spend nights at my parents' homestead with, of course, my mother's permission. She already knew them because they had stayed with us at the initial stages of ga-Molepo project.

My mother had introduced them to the chieftainess because it was protocol. No strangers should stay in the village without her knowledge. She'd got used to them. When I approached her with the idea of a project, she was quite keen.

I do not know what really happened, but suddenly her attitude just changed. She no longer wanted the students to stay at my parents' house, saying that our house was too small. In other words, as ordinary people we could not be seen accommodating precious white people. She wanted them to stay at her house.

They started building those clinics in two villages: Christiana and Bergzicht. People there could not pronounce it and simply referred to it as *Bersaga* (Sepanapudi). It was named by white farmers who'd occupied the area earlier. The clinics were completed, and they are still functioning until to date. However, I stopped accompanying them because I realised that the chieftainess was starting to cause trouble for my mother because my mother had told her to tell members of the community that I was the one who'd initiated the idea, for I deserved recognition and some credit. The chieftainess, however, took all the accolades for herself without recognising me. The students insisted on visiting my mother, even though they were no longer staying in my parents' house. I had been hoping that the chieftainess would name one of the clinics after me.

After the SAVS community project came to an end, Caroline and Christopher left for Zimbabwe. While there, she kept in good contact. We communicated, of course through writing letters. She told me about Zimbabwe, especially the education system. She encouraged me to arrange that I send my daughter over so that she could get a better education. I got interested as the situation in South Africa made me very sick. I hated the government system and I wanted out of the country.

I told my parents about Caroline's suggestion, but my mother refused outright, and I gave up. But I still intended to skip the country, via Zimbabwe. Caroline's departure left a great void in my life, I felt very lonely. I want to confess that I used to resist loneliness. Then I was so foolish not to note the difference between being alone and being lonely. My mind was clouded by the desire to become somebody and wanting to be someone irrespective of the system that aimed at turning me into nothingness. In this case I felt alone. This reminded me of the Williams Brothers' song *I Am Just a Nobody*. To me this was meant to be the opposite. I had to be somebody, who could tell everybody about how God can save all of us, but only if you believe.

As Caroline and I exchanged letters, I told her that I intended to leave the country. She then spoke to her friend, who was working as a truck driver delivering fuel (driving a petrol tanker) to neighbouring Southern African states such as Swaziland, Botswana, Mozambique and Zimbabwe. He agreed to smuggle me out. He told me that he was planning to hide me in the cab of the petrol tanker behind the driver's seat, and I was to lie down in there until he reached Zimbabwe. In the meantime, he would arrange with Caroline to pick me up at a strategic place.

The thing with me is that I am very courageous. I would have done it if I had not been convinced otherwise. My mother told me that if I ever went ahead with my plan and skipped the country, she would just die. I believed that, but my boyfriend (now husband) really talked sense into me.

I only knew later in life that one of her relatives, who was close to my mother, had skipped the country after the banning of liberation struggle movements. His parents died broken-hearted because they did not know where he was. He was a Pan African Congress (PAC) member and in the Azanian People's Liberation Army (APLA), PAC's armed wing (known as POQO before). His name was Solomon Moruthane Makunyane Bapela. He wrote his obituary (*tsa bophelo bja gagwe*) in Sepedi (North Sotho) before he died. In this he documented his life while in exile as a member of Pan Africanist Congress (PAC).

Before he died, he visited us one time, but I realised that my mother did not want me to spend time with him alone. I tried to find out where he was because every time we visited his homestead he was never there and no one spoke about him. Even if my mother mentioned his name, it was in passing. It was after reading his obituary that I put the puzzle of why my mother avoided that I spend time with him alone.

When all failed and I could not skip the country, I eventually gave up the idea and focused on my studies. Having thought hard about my plans, and also considering my parents' views and those of my boyfriend, including the complications related to skipping the country, I eventually realised that it would not be possible for me to leave. I became discouraged and I was still very anxious and angry.

Things in Zimbabwe changed for the worse. Whites became targets of vigilante groups and so many left the country as some were killed. In South Africa, things became bad, with the Nationalist Party's policy of "Total Onslaught" (Swart Gevaar) gaining momentum. Cock (1989) wrote: "The Total Onslaught Strategy was defined as involving the coordination with all the means available to the state of the military, economic, psychological, political, sociological, diplomatic, cultural and ideological fields of state activity. It was further argued that South Africa was the target of a total onslaught, and therefore required a total strategy capable of combining effective security measures with reformist policies aimed at removing the grievances the revolutionaries could exploit. Although the notion of total war was the brainchild of the then apartheid Minister of Defence, General Magnus Malan, in 1977 it intensified dramatically with the Soweto uprising and the independence of Angola and Mozambique. But it was only in the 1980s that the then apartheid government deployed members of the South African Defence Force (SADF) in the townships to defend white minority rule against black resistance."

Caroline and Christopher decided to leave Zimbabwe as well. I still remember the day she came to see me at work at St Johns College. As soon as I saw her, I had this feeling that something was wrong. She looked very sad. She walked straight over to me and hugged me in full view of the staff who were working in the library, the students and my boss Cynthia Hugo, who was watching us from her office. She knew of my best white friend, but had never met her. She quickly came to us and greeted her. They spoke for a while, and she asked me to take her to a room that I used for my studies upstairs above the library. We went there and sat down around a small desk.

She started telling me of the reasons she had come to see me during the day. She would normally have come to see me in the evening at my father's place. She told me that Christopher and she had decided to leave the country. She told me that she could not live in a country, her own words, which had "the grand design that brought a government dedicated to the promotion of the exclusive interests of whites and the degradation of Africans". She said that she truly hated racism, and that the idea of watching me being treated the way that I was treated every time she went out with me made her ill.

Caroline continued to encourage me to further my studies and gave me R350. It was a lot of money then, twice my monthly salary. I told her that I would use the money for my studies. She told me that she'd heard of someone who offered matric students science classes in the evening at Wits East Camp, the same place I'd attended classes before. She offered to take me there before they left.

The following week she asked Christopher to come to fetch me from my father's workplace on his motorbike. It was the first time I'd ridden on a bike. When we got to the university he accompanied me to the SS block. Mr Smith, the owner of Star School, offered classes for mathematics and his wife offered physical science. They were both there already. I registered for mathematics and physical science. The lessons were held in the evening.

For the whole week, Caroline transported me to the university in Braamfontein on Christopher's motorbike. Initially, they promised to teach me how to ride a motorbike like they had with driving a car, but we never got a chance. While driving on the motorbike one afternoon, she missed the corner off Rose Road into St Andrews Avenue, before getting into Harrow Road, and the bike fell on its side. Fortunately, Caroline was driving slowly and we were not hurt.

After they left, I went for my lessons on my own. They started at 18h00 and finished at 19h30. The very same day that she gave me the money, I showed it to my father after work. He was impressed and shocked at the same time because he himself had never earned such an amount of money in one month.

I remember how Merick, one of Caroline's friends who'd completed medicine, encouraged me to study medicine once I'd completed my matric. He promised to give some of his books to me. When I was about to complete my matric, that is the Senior Certificate, I decided to apply for Medicine at Wits. I was sent forms to complete, and one of the requirements for black children applying to study at Wits was to have a section in the forms completed by a medical doctor, to determine the status of their health. The forms were also to be certified at a police station. All of this was meant to control the influx of black children into white universities.

Applying to study medicine was a dream stretched to the limit. Nonetheless, I submitted the forms, and my application was rejected, stating my poor results as a reason. I promised myself that I would one day go to university. Little did I know that I would later receive my two degrees and attempt a Doctorate of Philosophy from the same university.

While in Australia, Caroline and Christopher got married and had two children. After one year, Caroline came back to South Africa to show her parents their first-born child. She called me and arranged that we meet, so we met in town at Union Building where Turret College was housed. She was with her mother. I met her for the first time. She too wanted to meet me. Caroline told me that her mother had always wanted us to meet. Caroline knew both my parents, but she'd never wanted me to meet her father because of his racist attitude, she told me.

She went back to Australia after a week. We carried on exchanging letters, but with distance we eventually lost touch.

Chapter Seven

MARRIED LIFE AND MOVING TO STAY IN SOWETO

My boyfriend proposed to me, and we got married. That was one of the best things that could ever have happened to me. I was ecstatic. I surprised myself, as I had never fantasised about marriage. I did not think I even wanted to get married. I guess my mind shifted after I'd had a child because I did not want a fatherless child. Again, my boyfriend, now my husband, became such a good friend and my confidant from the outset. I truly enjoyed his company and valued his companionship. The idea of having him in my life for good somehow erased my fear of bringing my child up without a father as it is never guaranteed that once one has a child with a boyfriend he will ultimately commit.

We had almost everything in common. We both came from the rural areas, raised by migrant labourer fathers and housewife mothers. We valued education and understood South African politics. In addition, having someone who could reason like me also alleviated the pain I carried through my life regarding the bleak future we faced due to living under the most horrible and inhuman government system. The conditions I and my fellow Africans lived in were lonesome, so the idea of having him in my life was a blessing. I just loved the idea. Somehow, it gave me a sense of worth and a reason to live, particularly for my daughter. My daughter always took centre stage in my life, but this was so different.

I still remember so vividly the day that he proposed. He came to see me at my father's workplace in Houghton. It was a routine that he visited me every weekend. He stayed in Soweto. I really enjoyed his company and looked forward to weekends, and he never wanted me to visit him before we got married. Where I came from, it was not allowed that a girl visited a boyfriend or went to stay with him before they got married. I liked the idea because for me it was a sign of someone who was disciplined and principled. Besides, my father was very strict he would not have allowed me to visit a boyfriend, unless I lied to him, something I did not want to do.

My parents, I guess his too, were still very conservative. My boyfriend had to pay *lobola* first and introduce his parents before he could start talking to my father. This was exacerbated by the fact that my father hated townships. He called them *skoonplaas* (I guess due to the fact that townships looked more organised when compared to villages). The other reason that made him loathe townships was because of the perception most people from rural areas had about hooliganism and rampant killings (*tsotsi* lifestyle) in the townships. He was not going to risk my life.

One incident that convinced him that Soweto was indeed dangerous was when the son of one of his relatives was stabbed and died at a very young age; he was from Dube. I am told that he was stabbed with what was commonly known as an okapi; that was the type of a knife *tsotsis* carried with them.

The day my boyfriend proposed was no different from other Saturday afternoons when he came to visit me. Like with all his visits, I walked him to a bus stop in Yeoville to catch a municipal bus to town. Once we parted, and he'd boarded the bus and gone, I ran straight home to tell my father about my boyfriend's intentions. He thought I'd gone mad. For him it was such a silly joke, especially since he never knew I had a boyfriend, as we always met in a park nearby. He must have thought that I'd never heard from him since my daughter had been born. Then, children did not talk about such things with their parents.

It was not much later that my boyfriend arranged that his father and other relatives came to meet my father to kick start the traditional *lobola* negotiations. The date was set, and the meeting was to take place at my father's workplace. I really do not know what happened to my father that day. He knew beforehand and had given my sister and me the money to go to buy food and prepare it for the visitors. He must have got cold feet, for when I woke up in the morning my father was nowhere to be found.

As time went on, I hoped that he would be back before my boyfriend's family arrived. He never came. They arrived, and his father suggested that they hang around for a while as he might have been held up somewhere. My sister prepared breakfast for them because they'd arrived early in the morning; then lunch towards midday and he was still nowhere to be found. They decided to leave in the afternoon.

I was shattered. I cried so much that my boyfriend, who'd waited outside, did not know what to do. My sister and I were very embarrassed, especially since my husband's father had come all the way from Sekhukhuneland, as he was no longer working. He used to work in Pretoria, by he was pensioned off. He'd travelled that far to come and negotiate for his son's *lobola*. He'd come along with his elder son, who stayed in one of the East Rand townships, that is east of Johannesburg in a township called Katlehong. My husband came from a village called Mathibeng in Malegale, not very far from ga-Masemola, where my mother came from. Like ga-Masemola the area has a beautiful, picture-perfect mountainous landscape. The picturesque scene can be seen in the background.

I really felt so sick with disappointment that I almost hated my father. He only came back on the morning of the following day; that is, Sunday. I was already awake, waiting anxiously for him. Before he could sit down, I was on top of him. I needed an explanation, but until today I could not make sense of his explanation. He went to the grave with the truth. My suspicion was that he was not very happy that I was getting married before my elder sister, because even on the day I told him that we intended marrying, he asked me not to tell her, so it was he who told her, and he only did that after some time.

Where I come from, getting married was a serious business. He must have felt pity for my sister. She was always my parents' beloved: the first- and last-born scenario (nonsense). However, nothing was going to stop us from committing to one another. We had come a long way. His father arranged that they come to meet him again, and this time he was not going to disappear. I guarded him like a hog, and the father came with my husband's uncle and the elder brother.

They agreed on the amount for *lobola*, but the ceremony was to take place at home, in Limpopo, with my mother and my closest relatives present. This is one occasion that my people at home take very seriously. There are rituals to be performed and everything is to be negotiated, agreed upon with witnesses present, before it is sealed and blessed. Both our parents agreed and arranged that the occasion should happen while my father was on his annual leave. He only took it in February of every year; it had to coincide with his employer's holiday time. His employer visited overseas once a year during that time. It was also agreed that, because they did not know the place, I should accompany them. The date was set. The only means of transport then was to travel by train.

The unusual or awkward part about the whole arrangement was that I was to take my in-laws – that is father and uncle – to go and carry out a customary marriage for me called *lobola* negotiation. When it happened, I did not think much about it. It is only after some time that when thinking about it, it sounds weird. I feel like someone who was so desperate to get married that I had to drag my father-in-law to go and marry me. I do not think it ever happened to any one before.

Nonetheless, we took that trip from Johannesburg Park Station, and boarded the train to Beitbridge. It left Johannesburg at 8PM, stopped at almost every station, and arrived at the station that we were to get off called Lanseklip on the farm called

Percy Five at 6AM, This is the train station before Pietersburg (Polokwane Park Station), so far the biggest in Limpopo.

I was told that before the Nationalist Party introduced the forced removals policy, my grandparents stayed on this farm and my father and his siblings were born there. I was also told that my grandmother died very young from birth complications and she was buried there. It is a pity that no one could identify her grave site anymore, as it was not marked. I would have loved to visit her.

As the train rolled, rumbled and screamed all the way, I used to look through the window. Along the way I saw many Metrorail workers working along the railway line. Their job was to constantly maintain the railway tracks. Metrorail was one of the government sectors that was the main job creator though cheap labour. Then, there were Metrorail cleaners, that is, those who cleaned the platforms and the trains themselves, and those who were railway police, sold tickets at the railway stations, and checked tickets inside the trains. Then there were train conductors, who signalled the driver that everyone had boarded the train so it could move off. I heard people referring to them as *dikontae*, conductors. In the areas where there were no railway lines, there was buses ferrying people from the cities to the rural areas or used locally. Then it was only white men who were drivers of either trains or buses, and blacks were doing manual labour. Many of them were from the rural areas.

The train travelled the whole night. Black commuters were only allowed to board third class coaches of the mainline trains and whites boarded first and second class coaches. I used to envy them because they looked very comfortable. Their coaches had leather seats, neat toilets and sleeping areas. Most of the third-class coaches were over full and filthy, with some of the passengers standing up along passages between seats for the whole night. The seats were made of hard plastic in an open coach with everyone sitting face to face. Even if one fell asleep, one would just sleep where seated.

My future father-in-law, my husband's uncle and I were lucky to get seats from Johannesburg Park Station. I really felt pity for them having to travel under those conditions at their age. They could have sent someone younger to represent them straight from home; it would have been closer and more convenient. But the old man did not want to take chances. He wanted to marry his son himself. I admired that and felt very honoured. I loved him so much. In fact, I was fortunate that I got married into a very warm and loving family. I got along with my mother-in-law until she died at the age of 91.

There was a bus that transported people from the train station, stopping at almost every village along the main-road from Lanseklip, via ga-Mashashane and all the villages; the same transport I'd used while still at secondary school.

We got home at around 8AM. My husband's father and uncle were received warmly.

When such occasion take place, relatives and neighbours are invited. My closest family were invited to assist my father with negotiations and serve in the role of witnesses, so they were to be there first thing in the morning, including negotiators (*batseta*). My father's sister was there. She had come the night before. She stayed in one of the far distant surrounding villages. My mother's Self-Help Society, joined by women only, was also there to ensure that the traditional beer was ready and to start with the cooking. After negotiations were completed, the feasting started. Now and again women would be ululating, signalling happiness and prosperity. Before anyone could start eating, they dished up for children first.

I went back to Johannesburg but still stayed with my father. After a week, my husband came to see me. He requested my father that, now that we were officially married, I go with him for a weekend, just to know where he stayed in Soweto. I had never been there. I went and spoke to my father, but he refused outright, stating that paying *lobola* in his opinion was not marriage. I went and told my husband. I could read disappointment on his face, but he agreed and left.

After he'd left, the previous incident of my father disappearing on the day of *lobola* negotiations came flashing to my mind. I felt that what he was doing was ridiculous and unfair, especially since my husband truly respected him and, in our culture, *lobola* was a marriage. Although by Western law customary marriage was not recognised, back home this was the only form of marriage for most of the people. After all, very few people would do what is commonly known as a white public wedding, not even Christians.

In Kalkspruit, as compared to ga-Masemola, public or western weddings were never heard of. When a man decided to pay *lobola*, and the date was set, those who were nominated to come and negotiate *lobola* would come before sunrise (dawn) for the occasion. The family of the bridegroom would also select a few girls to come and be with the bride. They too had to be there before dawn. I remember witnessing those personally. Once there, the bride and what is today bridesmaids sat in one house (hut) with their heads covered with shawls. The bridegroom's family, only men, would wait outside the homestead until they were allowed in.

The process was very laborious. Once everything was done, by about midday, and the negotiations were completed, then the bridesmaids and the bride were allowed to take off the shawls that covered their heads and faces. When it was winter it was okay, but in summer it got very hot. But one had to endure it all, in the name of tradition and custom.

Later, food was served. Meat and porridge (pap) would be served on a corrugated iron sheet – those used for roofing – and the men would eat together there. The celebration ensued until late in the night, with people drinking traditional beer and dancing. However, the occasion was not commercialised as it is today. There were no presents for the bride whatsoever, other than the offering of maize or beans brought along by members of the community.

Before sunset, the bride would accompany her future in-laws, and off they'd go. That would be her start of *go kotisa*, meaning staying with her mother-in-law and the rest of the family. That is for better or worse, sort of. The father-in-law and sons would go back to work if they were working as migrant workers in the cities.

Go kotisa is the period that a woman spends at her in-laws to assimilate into that family. The practice is prevalent in African culture. The time spent at the in-law's house is normally characterised by very early mornings, where the new bride handles chores such as sweeping the yard, making breakfast for the entire family, and looking after all the children who live at the home. This assimilation period turns into a period of hard labour. The mother-in-law polices the *makoti* and her girl children join in mistreating and abusing her. As a result, it brings strain to the relationship as well as putting pressure on the *makoti* and her husband.

The Story of a Rural Girl Who Kept Rising and Rising

I thought that my father was really going too far, so I decided to defy him and did the unthinkable. Late in the evening, I decided to look for a car. I found one and packed my things into it. My father was sitting outside, and I went to him and told him that I was leaving to follow my husband. He did not believe his ears and eyes. I already had my suitcase in my hand. He looked at me, but never uttered a word. I said, "Goodbye, Papa," and left. I had already bid farewell to my sister, who was so scared on my behalf, knowing our father.

The thing with me is that I am very courageous. I believe that I am so courageous that I could jump from a moving aeroplane at the height of 17 000 000 kilometres above sea level and survive. This sounds arrogant, but I am so courageous that it sometimes scares me.

The car was already waiting in the street. I had never been to Soweto before but when I explained to the driver regarding where my husband was teaching and that he stayed in the school cottage he knew the place. My husband did not know that I was coming. He was awakened by the knock at the gate and looked very puzzled and confused, but somehow relaxed. He assured me that everything would be okay.

A few days after I eloped, we then decided to go and sign with the Marriage Council at a Home Affairs (people simply called the place *ga commissioner* or *ga Mohle*). We were both over 21 years old, so we were eligible to sign as wife and husband. I guess my husband wanted us to formalise our marriage as soon as possible because of what had happened between my father and me. During the old order (apartheid), everything was divided according to ethnic groupings, so we had Home Affairs Offices for blacks situated between Market and Commissioner

Street, Central Business District of Johannesburg and so forth. We intended to have our public wedding the following year.

Four months before our public wedding, my father, my husband and I were involved in a near fatal car accident. My cousin in Mamelodi had invited us to one of her children's birthday parties. My sister remained behind because she was not well, so the three of us went.

My father owned a second-hand blue Volkswagen Kombi. It came before the third generation of Toyota Hiace minibus taxis called Zola Budd. The term was coined because of the similarities between Zola Budd, a world-renowned long-distance runner, and a taxi that has a lot of mileage and covers many kilometres every day.

Coming back, my father asked me to drive because he had been drinking liquor and he felt bit intoxicated. I'd only acquired my licence about eight months previously, but I agreed, and we drove off. As we were driving along the N12 Freeway approaching Menlo Park, he kept on insisting that I drive faster so that we could get home earlier because my sister was sick, and my husband was to travel to Soweto.

I tried to accelerate a little bit, though I was nervous. All of a sudden – I do not know what happened – I lost control of the car. In panic, instead of pressing the brake, clutch and second gear to slow it down, I pressed the accelerator. The car veered off the road, overturned and landed on the driver's side. Then I think it was the time it flung me on the passenger side, and I was unconscious.

When I regained consciousness, I was lying on the floor of the car. The seat was not there as it had gone through the windscreen. My father, who had been sitting on the passenger seat, was on the driver seat behind the steering wheel, unconscious. I thought he'd died and started screaming and shaking him.

He regained consciousness and I saw his hand bleeding. Fortunately, it was not broken; it was only the skin that was peeled off. My husband told me that the Combi had turned over three times and every time it hit the ground on its side it would stand up and roll again. He witnessed all that because he was conscious all the time. Fortunately, none of us was thrown out, although the windscreen and side windows glass was not there and some of the seats had been thrown out: the one on the passenger side and at the back. My husband's shoe soles came out and my father's wristwatch was missing.

My husband had been sitting at the back and he was not hurt. There were lots of motorists who left their cars on the side of the freeway to come and assist. Some thought that we must have died, and they were shocked that we'd all survived. The car was a write-off, so we had to walk to Menlo Railway Station. Luckily it was nearby and we boarded a train to Johannesburg Park Station. We were covered in dust.

I shudder to think that we almost died four months before our wedding that took place in April. The accident happened in December. I only discovered later that I'd strained my neck when I started feeling discomfort at the back of it, but the doctor confirmed that it was only a strain.

Nonetheless, with God's Grace, the wedding took place. By then I'd already kissed and made up with my father.

My parents wanted a white wedding. My husband and I refused to have a traditional white wedding, though we had public wedding, hence my attire was not like that my mother was wearing when she got married. The typical white dress, black suit, and white shirt with bow tie for my husband similar to the one my father was wearing.

Photo of my parents' wedding. Surrounding my parents are my grandfather's children and my aunt as bridesmaids and groomsmen.

A compromise was reached, and my parents respected our wishes. My husband and I did not marry in church either. That is, we did not go through the tradition of walking down the holy aisle in church to bless our wedding and repeat, "for better, for worse, in sickness and in health," something I call acculturation. What it means is that as a woman you are considered fragile if not handicapped to a point that you could hardly walk to the man you loved and introduced to everyone. Suddenly your father must aid you to him. I find these rituals very demeaning to women, because it must be a man handing you over to another man to control and oppress, disguised as caring and protecting.

What is wrong with a bride walking herself to meet with a groom she chose in the first place?

What is more offensive is that no one accompanies your husband because he is a man. For me, these practices are meant to promote a patriarchal mentality, period! I was glad that I did not go through all this, especially wearing a white wedding dress since that is supposed to mean that "you have never known a man". I already had a child when we married, not that I am proud of that.

I am always puzzled by some prominent women who take pride in the fact that, although they had a fall by having unplanned pregnancies, they were able to dust themselves off and make something out of their lives. That is not a smart thing to say. It is up to those who managed to pick up the broken pieces of their lives to rather mobilise young women and raise awareness to ensure that they do not find themselves in that situation. Prevention is better than cure. However, the biggest challenge this country faces is the sky-rocketing incidents of rape, which contribute to the dire situation that young women and teenagers find themselves in. It fuels the already great problem of unwanted pregnancies that are forever spiralling out of control.

Still on my wedding subject, my mother insisted that the priest be called in. He came to bless us at home . Then, I was one of the few people who had a public or western wedding in the village. My younger sister and my cousin had also had public weddings. Though younger, they'd got married before me. Sadly, they both passed on, relatively young. As far as the blessing of my wedding is concerned, I did it to please my parents, otherwise, for me my wedding was blessed the day we agreed to marry each other.

As one author once wrote: "A marriage is between a woman and a man. Marriage is a covenant between two people, their flesh and soul becoming one, without money coming into it. Love pulled love. Love is the price of love."

For me, the day *lobola*, dowry or bride wealth is paid, is the day the marriage is blessed because both the family meet to seal communal blessings, and the ceremony that goes with that is a true blessing. *Lobola* was seen as a sign of goodwill between two families (reciprocal). Not the distorted notion of buying someone that sick men use to abuse women. Above all, I was humbled by the fact that my wedding ceremony was attended by the whole village: women, men, and children, who I not only knew their faces but knew them by their names. The whole community, the people who raised me, rejoiced together, women ululating a trumpet of pure joy and men dancing and singing opera songs.

One of the two pictures on the next page drew my attention to something of concern: the two young girls of about six or seven years carrying their siblings on their backs supported with a checked shawl like the ones I spoke about earlier. There was this tendency growing up where girls would be given the responsibility of taking care of their young siblings. My mother told me that I hated that because I did not want to be confined to one place because I enjoyed playing, something that signified the need to be free. With a child on your back, one is confined because it would be impossible to play and run around with other children.

Now grown up and thinking about it, I ask myself why it was only girls who had to carry these children? For me it comes across as one of patriarchal socialisation, where girls are to be groomed at a very early age for motherhood. Until today, girls are still prepared for the same gender roles related to domestic chores. Maybe I am wrong. Perhaps it was the only way, as mothers had to do other chores such as fetching firewood, collecting water, cooking, cleaning and taking care of the fields.

Boys were excluded because their roles were that of herding, looking after the livestock. They were taught chores such as hunting, butchering and skinning animals, as well as a midwife role to animals for the instances where they had difficulties in giving birth far away from home. My husband told me that one of his duties as a shepherd was to play the role of a doctor and nurse when they were injured. Boys' duties were also to milk cows and goats. Then there were no tractors, so grown-up able-bodied men and grown-up boys would plough the fields using a plough (*mogoma*) drawn by oxen or donkeys, before planting (*bjala*) seeds in summer season.

My husband and I had first and second attires.

Photo of us wearing our first attire seated around the table with a cake in front of us

Photo of our second attire, bride wearing a suit in different colour and a bride wearing a two piece.

Photo of myself in the middle and my two sisters at my husband's place.

Then the wedding cake was two storeys high and white as snow because it was glazed or wrapped with icing sugar. Inside it was baked with mixed cake fruit, flour and maybe alcohol (brandy) and wrapped in icing sugar, decorated with red artificial flowers. Plastic bridegroom and bride dolls (*bathwana*), wearing Christian traditional wedding clothes, were placed on top of the cake. After all, a wedding without cake is not a Christian wedding at all.

Beside that I also had Ndebele traditional attire at my place and Pedi attire at my husband's place. Our wedding took two days. A day at my place and another day at his place. I never knew the significance of flags at the weddings but both at my place and my husband's our parents' burial society members displayed flags. Before, they used to have flags at the bride's and groom's homestead, and small ones at the homes of close relatives. I wish I'd asked someone with the knowledge. But what I knew was that as soon as the flags went up on top of thatched roof houses or main entrance poles we knew that there is was going to be a wedding.

After the singing and dancing and showing off our wedding attire, my husband and I slowly walked to the reception. We sat there, waiting for food to be served, followed by speeches and the presentation gifts . We were pampered with lots of gifts, crockery, an ironing board, iron, tablecloth etcetera. For instance, my parents' tablecloth and my sister's cutlery, my cousin's coffee set. My parents-in-law bought us pots and my husband's friends and colleagues, as well as mine, bought us dinner sets made from pottery that I still use today.

In our culture or tradition, the wedding would not be complete if your parents did not come to lecture you about the notion of wife material (*go laya*). At my place, my parents, aunts and a representative from the chieftain came to lecture me about the same monotonous saying that as *makoti* you must take care of your husband and the in-laws, and that *lebitla la mosadi ke bogadi* (loosely translated, the grave of a woman is where she is married). This meant that, even if your husband abused you, you must endure, not go back home, and make sure that when you die you are buried there. Even if he himself killed you, he must bury you there as a sign of being wife material.

(far left is my father, followed by his sister, my mother with white beanie and wife of my father's brother (aunt) and lastly a representative from the chieftain (regent) Ntate Jonas Maraba)

This lecture happened even though I had warned my mother that I did not want them to come and say those things to me, because there is no way that I would tolerate abuse by anyone, including my husband, his mother, or his sisters. They did that anyway without my consent because it gave them pride, oblivious to the fact that they were mere cheerleaders of patriarchy. These speeches basically reinforce every patriarchal horror one can imagine. To me, they are outdated. Ironically, at my husband's place nothing of the sort had been mentioned to him. Patriarchy is so evil and all it aims at is to position women as potential wives and mothers

It was during the wedding that as a woman you were told that you must endure the pain that comes with being abused in a marriage or relationship. Often, young women are also instructed not to kill a man's pride by challenging him intellectually, politically or economically. You must be submissive (*o e kokobetse*). In addition, you are taught that a good wife never questions her husband's whereabouts and actions. As a woman you must cook, clean and open your legs whenever your husband wants to have sex. Hence, I always say, women are their own worst enemies, and I am really irritated by senior women in the family for being enablers and custodians of patriarchy.

This is evident in the way they treat their daughters-in-law (*makotis*). It is often the women who tell these brides how they should act, dress and behave so as to be welcomed into the husband's family. It is mothers, aunts and mothers-in-law who tell young, newly married women to bear the harsh treatment received from their partners when they run to them for comfort and advice. If this system is to end, it needs women to genuinely unite and empower each other, instead of subconsciously promoting patriarchy, a system that ends up killing or maiming them.

I never intended to stay with them as a new bride (*makoti*) and do everything for them. I told myself that I would never bring myself to be anyone's slave. Fortunately, my husband shared the same view. Hence, I did everything possible to empower myself by acquiring a good education so that I was self-sufficient. I never stayed with them for even a day. After the wedding we came back to Soweto. We only visited during festive seasons and, because we stayed together that short time, our relationships remained mutually respectful. For me, it would have been difficult to stay with difficult in-laws because, somehow, I hated the idea of family expectations and people's opinions of me. I loved being my own person.

I am grateful that I was never subjected to all the rituals made during the Western weddings, as I learnt later that better and worse and sickness and health refers more to your husband's antics and behaviour than life's tribulations. Often, the last person to benefit from *go kgotlelela* – that is endurance – is the woman who has been conditioned to do so. It is a sign of being *makoti* material, writes Kwanele Ndlovu.

I concur with Kwanele Ndlovu that "Our society is invested so much in the wife material concept, it is reinforced with scriptures and reiterated as the ultimate qualification for any woman to earn the lifelong affection of a man. You must be wife material, or else you are headed for a lonesome life of rejection and loathing. It is prescriptive. It is, above all, precious. Meanwhile, the upkeep of the wife material is quite daunting. Forget the domestic chores and responsibilities of raising children that are inherent to any domestic household. There is added pressure for the woman who is wife material to go an extra mile. That is, till death do us part." However, there is no such thing as a husband material.

Nonetheless, my husband and I were lucky that our parents were still alive to witness our wedding. It was a proud moment for them and they both took pictures with us. Unfortunately, my father in-law died two years after our wedding. I was so devastated. I remember that a year after he died, my mother in-law had to take off her mourning clothes. There were rituals to be performed, including having to remove or cut his children's hair. My elder sister-in-law went ahead and cut mine with scissors. I had not known that I too had to cut mine, meaning that no one had prepared me in advance. It was so abrupt that I was shocked. I cried because I loved my hair, and besides I thought that my hair was my character, my personality and I valued it.

Our wedding's cherry on top was that my white friend Caroline came to my wedding accompanied my her friend Alston. Alston is the guy that Caroline arranged with to smuggle me to Zimbabwe. A white person coming to a rural village for a wedding had never been heard of, especially in the 1980s when apartheid was at its peak. That was and is still the talk of the town, even to date.

The part my husband and I missed was the cake-cutting moment because it can only be cut at the bride's place. So, they returned with it back home, but I remained at my husband's place. I always heard people saying cutting the cake is a wonderful thing. After all, a wedding without a cake is not a Christian wedding at all. There are lots of contradictions in the process because of the clash between tradition and western customs. As a married woman, I was not to return to my place after the wedding, and the cake could only be cut at my place, meaning that we would not get to experience the wonders of cutting our cake: holding a knife together and simultaneously cutting it and feeding each other a piece of cake, as I see newlyweds do, as if people have forgotten how to feed

Photo of my family cutting the cake.

themselves at that moment. This was meant to conclude the wedding ceremony. Instead, the cake was cut in our absence and on our behalf.

The next chapter introduces the readers to my married life in the unfamiliar environment in the townships.

Chapter Eight

MARRIAGE AND LIFE IN SOWETO

The wedding was done and dusted and, as already mentioned, I was already staying with my husband in Orlando West. He was a teacher at Phefeni High School for many years. In fact, it was his first job. Some of the people who became his products are Nepo Kekana, Dada Morero, Thomas "Kolovha" Madigage and many others. He was dedicated and very passionate about teaching. He was also a school choir conductor.

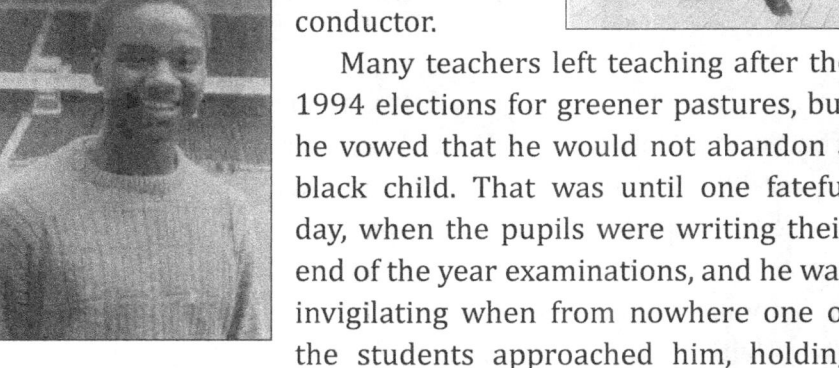

Many teachers left teaching after the 1994 elections for greener pastures, but he vowed that he would not abandon a black child. That was until one fateful day, when the pupils were writing their end of the year examinations, and he was invigilating when from nowhere one of the students approached him, holding an AK 47 pointed in his direction. He said he just froze as there was nowhere he could hide and he did not want to disturb the pupils. The boy stood at the window, looked directly at him and said, "Meneer, is that you? No, you are not the one I am looking for." He turned and walked away, otherwise my husband could have been killed senselessly.

My husband is seated on a chair, surrounded by his girls' choir

I remember that day very well. It was the day I too came back from student protests at Wits. Tokyo Sexwale had visited the university to address students and that day black students marched to Hillbrow police station and then to the then John Vorster Square. I was so excited that when I got home, late in the afternoon, upon entering the house I raised my fist and shouted Viva! Neither my husband nor daughter were impressed. I went to put my bag away and came and sat down. My husband said to me, "I was almost murdered today". I was in such shock. I felt numb, and he explained what happened.

I said, "You really must leave teaching," as for me the township schools were becoming volatile and dangerous. He agreed immediately and started applying for employment outside schools, although he still wanted to be in education. In no time he was offered a job at the Department of Education's Head Office, but was later deployed at District in Braamfontein. That is how he left teaching, sadly under duress.

Since the 1976 riots there had been a lot of problems in the black townships. The problems worsened in the 1980s until the run up to the 1994 elections. There were protests everywhere because the black masses wanted to make the country ungovernable. The government retaliated by introducing curfews and states of emergency. Schools were guarded by soldiers. One could mistake the place for a country at war. I found it very scary,

It was after one year of living in Soweto when the boycott started and we were still staying in Phefeni School Cottage in Orlando West. The house we used to live in was diagonally opposite Mandela's house on Vilakazi street. Zinzi Mandela stayed in her father's house. She used to travel by the train I also boarded. There was a certain guy I saw at the house, because in the morning, when I opened the window of my room, I saw him sitting outside every day. He wore long dreadlocks, and I was told he was Zinzi's boyfriend and the father of one of her children. I envied Zinzi. I wished I had a father like hers, who was willing to fight and die for blacks so as to rid them of the evil apartheid system. There was always a hype of political activities in the Mandela's house.

The police vans and soldiers roamed the streets. The soldiers were sent by government to guard schools, including Phefeni. It was so scary for me to see armed men walking or driving around in their vehicles. One could hear gunshot sounds ringing the whole night, with boys throwing stones at them while at the same time they were trying to restore order and peace.

Township houses did not have inside toilets or running water. It was very unsafe for one to go out after sunset, but one would have to go to the toilet any time of the night when the call of nature demanded.

I was still travelling by train to work, and soldiers would be seen on train station platforms and even on the trains. They used to shoot anyone they suspected of being a troublemaker, especially boys. In the process of running from the police, they would jump fences into other people's houses, putting the occupants of the houses at risk, and a number of people were killed by stray bullets in their houses. Hooligans took advantage of the situation and terrorised communities, as did school children joining boycotts. Everything got out of control and schools were disrupted once more. I guess that black schools were never the same since then.

Crime was and still is a big problem in the townships and the first time I witnessed someone being stabbed in daylight was when I was staying in this house. At the corner of Mandela's house there were always boys hanging out there, playing dice. I was told that most of them belonged to the Mandela Football Club, and they stayed in the house. It was on Sunday, towards midday, when I heard people screaming. When I peeped through the window, I could see that the fight had broken out and I ran to the gate to see what was happening. Two boys were stabbing someone. I could see people standing there and watching.

I was so scared because I'd never witnessed such a thing, especially seeing the amount of blood all over his body. Fortunately, he managed to get loose and run away. I am not sure whether her survived or succumbed to his injuries. However, I heard that it was a common occurrence in the townships for people to be attacked at knife point after dark and robbed.

Some, I learnt, were murdered. Unfortunately, with the advent of a democratic South Africa, guns replaced knives as they are now readily available and people are now dying of gunshot wounds like never before.

When I moved to stay with my husband in Soweto, I was still working with Cynthia Hugo, the senior librarian at St Johns' College. She later established a project called Read Educate and Develop (READ), with the aim of establishing libraries at black

 schools. The project received financial donations from big companies such as Shell, Basil Read, Irene Mennel's Anglo American. St Johns' College  management also supported the initiatives to an extent that one senior librarian employee, Zoe Giddy, assisted Cynthia Hugo  with training. They were training selected teachers on how to establish and manage libraries. Individuals such as Angie Motshekga, who was then a teacher at Orlando High School, Baby Mabalane (Kgositsile), Thandi Macayi, who was a teacher at Selelekela Secondary School in Orlando East, as well as my husband (then my boyfriend) a teacher at Phefeni Secondary School and many others, were selected as school librarians. The project was such a huge success and it still exists to date. She hired me full time. I assisted her  in establishing the project. I worked very hard as a messenger, tea person and administrator: just an all-rounder. She grew fond of me and as her project grew so did her need to employ more staff.

Photo taken during library training. My husband is the one with cream white trousers, squatting in the middle and surrounded by other librarians

One of the ladies who joined us was Sebolelo Mohajane. I knew her already as she was one of the librarians at Thaba Jabula High School in Pimville, were she was a teacher. I happened to know librarians from all the schools, as well as the principals, as I accompanied Cynthia to her workshops. Sometimes they came to our offices if need be.

At the initial stage, I also accompanied her to various meetings when she met with sponsors. For example, I went with her to meet someone at Shell House and the John Orrs manager at Anglo American building. Sebolelo and I were the only two black people employed by READ, so we became close. Management was very pleased with the job I was doing. It really required hard work, considering the number of high schools Soweto had, and I worked alone. Sebolelo Mohajane joined READ when we were still operating at St Johns College in a full-time capacity. I was the one who was entrusted with the responsibility of ensuring that books bought for Soweto school libraries were sorted out and packed nicely before they were dispatched to the schools.

As we were talking, she happened to know that I was studying for matric and that I was registered for mathematics and physical science subjects. She was thrilled to the point of announcing to her pupils that here was a girl who was doing the subjects part time. She truly encouraged and adored me. She was my mentor, despite our age difference and rank. She was employed in the executive, and I was a messenger, tea maker and a storeroom keeper.

We were allocated offices in another block of the school but Cynthia and I still worked in the school library full time. The READ part-time salary she offered me was better than what I earned at St Johns College. I was not happy with being a messenger and tea maker, and I told myself that I must work hard to improve my education.

Sadly, Sebolelo was involved in a horrible car crash and died instantly. At the time, she was no longer with READ but a manager for FUNDA Centre in Soweto, Diepkloof, now called a community college. I still remember arriving home from school. My husband asked me to sit down and he told me that Sebolelo had passed on. I was shattered.

Cynthia later moved her offices to Rosebank, and I went with her. Then I was still not qualified to reside or work in Johannesburg, and that saddened Cynthia. It was at this time that my husband and I decided to get married. Despite all her efforts in trying to register me, this failed. The idea was to help me qualify for a work permit. Unfortunately, to apply for that one had to have a permanent residential address. She also knew that hiring me without papers was a risk for her, as she risked a hefty fine if I got caught working in her offices.

The fact that I was married to someone who qualified to work in Johannesburg did not count in my favour. I went with her to Alexandra Home Affairs Offices to apply for a Section 10 (1) (a) permit, but I was told that I did not qualify because the house that my husband stayed in was not his, but school property, so I remained an illegal foreigner in my own country. I was haunted by the idea that I would never qualify to work in Johannesburg, because I could not obtain a valid working permit due to the circumstances mentioned above. Despite Cynthia's desperate attempts to get me registered – she really went from pillar to post – without a permanent residential address, it was just impossible.

Though risky, as she could had been fined if it was discovered that she was harbouring an employee illegally, Cynthia decided to keep me in her employment. Going to work from Soweto, I used to board a 6 o'clock train from Phefeni station and get off at Westgate Station, walk to the Bree bus rank (two kilometres) and board a bus to Rosebank. Then there were no minibus taxis only meter taxis for whites only. What is now Bree Taxi Rank, used to be a Putco and municipal bus rank, catering only for Africans.

Because of the Separate Development Act, all race groups had their separate amenities. For example, coloureds and Indians had their own bus ranks, also along Bree Street. A bus rank for whites was where the municipal bus rank was. It was called Vanderbijl Park Square and renamed after 1994 as Ghandi Square. It is now named after the renowned Indian leader called Mahtman Ghandi who fought for the Indian freedom from

British Colonisation. He led what was called Passive Resistance. India became independent in 1947.

I travelled by train to home in Limpopo many times, but commuting by train from Soweto was harrowing. They were so many and it was confusing, all worsened by the fact that they were forever full.

My first day of using the train to work from Soweto to Park Station was very traumatic. In the morning it was not much of a problem as I'd heard that the trains coming from Naledi Station via Phefeni Station were going to Park Station. I boarded a 6 o'clock train, very scared. I did not know anyone, and the train was very full of other people hanging on the doors. One had to jump inside quickly, because the train did not stop for too long.

Men would do staff riding, very risky because one could slip and end up underneath the train, decapitated. It happened to many. The one incident I once witnessed at Phefeni Station involved a woman who was to board the train before the one I was to take. When I arrived at the train platform I found people gathered on one spot, staring below the train platform to the train rails. I was told that she'd missed the train entrance step in the process of pushing and shoving around, trying to get in. She had fallen beneath the pavement and her whole lower body was crushed in a sitting position; only her upper body including her head was still intact. She was wearing spectacles. It was such a horrific incident to witness, and it sent shivers down my spine. I always tried to be careful.

If the train were too full, I would let it go. I would rather be late. I got off at Johannesburg Park Station and took a bus to Rosebank from Wanderers street coming from Bree Street. The bus too would be full and some of us had to stand. The transportation system for blacks was very bad. It is still the same, or even worse as all the services have collapsed in this country. Then there were not enough trains for blacks nor buses. We always had to cramp like sardines in a tin while whites would be sitting comfortably.

After work, I boarded a train from Johannesburg Park Station to Naledi Station via Phefeni Station. I was told which train to take from which platform, but I was not told that there were some trains that did not stop at every station. Some were first stops to New Canada or Ikhwesi train stations. Unfortunately, the one that I boarded was first stop Ikhwesi. Everyone got off. I became very confused and asked someone as to how to get to Phefeni Station. I was told to go to the other side of the station and wait for another train going to Park Station.

The train came from Naledi. I boarded the train in the hope that it would stop at Phefeni. The train passed all the stations and stopped at New Canada train station. It was also a first stop. I became frustrated and more scared. I went out and went to the other side to wait for a train going to Naledi. When it approached, someone told me to take it. It was so full that I had to squeeze myself in. It took off and only stopped at Naledi Station another first stop from New Canada train station. I was more traumatised. I started  crying and asked someone to assist me, because it was already getting dark. I had boarded the first train at around 16h15; by this time it was 18h30.

A good Samaritan offered to help me. He told me to wait with him because he was also waiting for an all stations train. It was only then that I managed to get the right train. He told me to memorise the numbers appearing in front of every train. When

I got off at Phefeni, it was already after 19h00. My husband was waiting there, very worried. I had to learn the train numbers as fast as possible, and I never experienced the same problem and got used to travelling by train, although the conditions were very bad, extremely harsh indeed. I am shocked that so many years into democracy nothing had changed as far as transportation is concerned

After four years of working with Cynthia Hugo, both at St Johns College and READ, I took employment with another non-governmental organisation: the Environmental and Development Agency (EDA) in Newtown. When I had been travelling to Limpopo for the South African Voluntary Services (SAVS) project I mentioned before, I happened to meet EDA employees coming back from one of their community projects in Limpopo. They visited our project in one of the villages called ga-Molepo to see what we were doing there. Most of EDA's community projects were in what were called Bantustans such as Lebowa (Limpopo), at a place called Bochum and Tzaneen (Gazankulu) as well as the Transkei (Eastern Cape), in areas such as Matatiele, Herschel and Lusisikisi.

They were assisting local communities with boreholes for water and gardening and pottery (*go dira meeta*). They were sponsored through international donor agencies involved in underdeveloped countries like the World Health Organisation (WHO), OXFAM, Indiana University in Pennsylvania in the United States of America, as well as the University of Reading in the United Kingdom.

EDA needed someone with experience in librarianship. I told them that I had that, and while I was not a qualified librarian I had acquired the experience from where I was working at St Johns College. We exchanged work telephone numbers.

The following week, Corlette Cain (Nidrie) a Human Resource Manager at EDA, called me and told me that they would like to recruit me for the job of resource centre manager and that, as the centre was not in existence, they would need someone who could establish it from the scratch. She asked me to think about it and came back to me few days after. When she did, she told me about the salary offer the organisation was prepared give me. The remuneration package was appealing: twice what I was getting at READ. I accepted the offer.

We agreed to meet so that it could be formalised, and I needed something in writing before I resigned from READ, as well as to serve my notice. I told Cynthia about my decision. I remember how she cried, but there was nothing she could do to counter the offer because EDA remuneration was just too attractive, and she said READ could not afford that.

I'd accepted the offer because they gave me a good remuneration package and that was such a motivating factor. I loved my job at READ and especially the working environment. I might have turned it down but commuting from Soweto to Rosebank, as compared to Newtown where the EDA offices were located, was a challenge, both distance and cost wise. I still had to travel by train from Phefeni Station to Braamfontein Station, a station just before Johannesburg Park Station, which was manageable.

Photos taken at the EDA Head Office. Seated is Bokellaig Khave responsible for administration and bookkeeeping, and I am standing up; and the other photo is of me, seated in the resource centre. As already mentioned, I was responsible for the Resource Centre and Corletee Cain (Nidrie)(no photo) took care of Human Resources.

Some of my colleagues who were doing field work, were Stephen Marais, Grace Ledwaba, Tshepho Khumbane, Jabu Mabaso and Nick Swan. They were all responsible for teaching local communities about how to start vegetable gardens, and maintain them: all issues related to food security. Dan Mogale was a borehole pump technician, who specialised in assisting communities with making boreholes for easy access to water for watering their gardens and for day-to-day necessities, and David Cooper was responsible for fundraising and managing the NGO.

Most of the people who got involved in the projects were women. Hence, one of the main aims was to try to help women in the rural areas to take control of their lives. Apart from farming, they were also taught life skills such as pottery and weaving, which is the craft of forming fabric by interlacing threads. What was quite unique about EDA was that, irrespective of one's level, we all earned the same salary. Hierarchy was blurred in that regard.

Although I enjoyed working for EDA, I was pained by the fact that I still had the challenge of not being registered for permanent work in Johannesburg. The human resource manager Corlette Cain tried to see to it that I got registered, now that I had a permanent residential place and my husband was already qualified to live in Johannesburg under Section (1) (b), and he had already worked for five years in the urban areas, but it was still not easy.

I went with her to the most notorious Home Affairs Immigration Offices in town in Albert Street. The offices specialised in registering people with Section (1)(d) like myself. I made it a point that I brought along all the necessary documentations, such as my passbook (identity document), my husband's, and a letter from him confirming that I lived with him at same address, as well as our marriage certificate.

Corlette and I went there very early in the morning. We stood in a long queue and, when it was our turn to be attended, we were directed to a certain office. In that office was seated a very fat white (Afrikaner) woman who spoke in Afrikaans all the time, offering to assist us. She had a very racist, horrible and belittling attitude. Corlette explained what we were there for and gave her all the documentations. She just glanced at them and said, "*Ag, nee*" – Oh no.

She told us that I did not qualify to work in Johannesburg, even though my husband was working here. In a very rude tone, she said that the house was not my husband's, and he too only had a working permit. I could not believe my ears or my eyes on seeing how she marvelled at that. She even threatened to put a stamp in my *dompas* book, The famous "seventy-two-hour notice". To restrict the so-called immigrants from rural South Africa from coming into the urban areas, those found with illegal documents would have their documents stamped. This made it easy for police to identify a person for arrest and have them banished permanently to the homelands.

In her opinion, I should return to my homeland because I belonged there, and Johannesburg was not my home. She even indicated that she could even ask the police to transport me to the train station by force and wait until I boarded the first train to the rural area, and if I happened to come back I would be arrested and thrown into jail. Corlette pleaded with her not to do that and then the woman instructed her that she must see to it that I returned home.

I was shattered, humiliated and discouraged. I got very angry and before I left I told her that Lebowa was not my home just because I am an African, and being an African I could live anywhere in Africa, because Africa belonged to the Africans. I promised her that I would never return to Lebowa and I would not leave my husband behind. It had happened to my parents, but would not happen to me. She became red in the face. She picked up the telephone with the intention of calling security personnel.

Corlette pulled me away, and we ran to the car and left. I felt very good. I was never registered until in 1985, when the Group Areas Act and other related oppressive laws were relaxed and subsequently abolished in 1991 when the new democratic government was put in place and freed me and I became enfranchised.

The most devastating thing about the laws that governed the apartheid system is that they were purely oppressive and dehumanising: nothing else. Nonetheless, READ and EDA risked employing me without valid documentations. If the place had been raided and it had been found that some of their employees did not qualify to be in Johannesburg, let alone working without permit, they would have been in a big trouble.

However, before the demonic acts were repealed, they were relaxed during the 1980s. For example, several policy adaptations occurred. Particularly after the Riekert Commission Report that the government had accepted, at least in principle. The report recommended that the circumstances of black people in the common areas of South African society must be improved and upgraded.

This was a new agenda for government, since it broke very clearly with the inconsistent and ambiguous stance of the Vorster era. It coincided with the legislation allowing black trade unions in 1980. The government introduced the Black Development Administration Act, and formed various Administration Boards. Most companies bought into this because of the incentives that government offered them. For instance, any company that opted for social responsibility would have tax reductions, or something like that. I've never had the opportunity to read the Commission's report, nor the Act.

Although the notion of reform appeared to be a good idea, is still promoted racial inequalities. Racial inequalities in South Africa have always been dramatic. Until well into the 1970s, it was government policy to neglect or even to depress development for blacks in the industrialised common area of the country in the hope of encouraging them to identify with the separate homelands set aside for them. Lacking in economic infrastructure, these areas could not possibly offer rapidly expanding welfare, and hence the government feared that an increase in the quality of life for black people in the industrialised areas would turn urban black townships into "honey pots", as a senior minister once put it.

However, my situation as a black person, and an African in particular, started to become better after 1982, even though I still did not qualify to reside and work in Johannesburg. In the period 1982 to 1985, the National Party presided over its establishment and worked with P.W. Botha during the pioneering days of reform. This means that there were policy shifts, and the following acts were scrapped: Influx Control, Group Areas Act, Separate Amenities Act and Mixed Marriages Act, etcetera. These laws could not be sustained because there was much resistance to them, as they violated human dignity and rights because of their restrictive and discriminatory nature. The sad story of these laws was that it hampered development. In a nutshell, the apartheid systems were morally wrong and evil.

It was during this period of reform and upgrading of townships that people working for government as professionals could acquire mortgages through the bank of their choice. In 1985, my husband managed to secure a loan from the bank, and we built our first house in a newly developed area called Protea North. Most professionals, such as nurses, teachers, police and similar, bought bonded houses in Protea North and other newly developed areas.

Our daughter came to stay with us. She was still at lower primary school level. Until then, we had been unable to have her live with us because of the difficulties. We had not been able to buy our house in the urban areas and the school cottage we occupied was shared by two other teachers, also from the rural areas. The cottage was a four-roomed house with only two bedrooms, a dining room and kitchen, meaning that the teacher who happened to occupy the house the latest would sleep in the dining room.

According to Nathan (1989), "the government came under fire from progressive critics for pursuing what was termed a black 'urban insider' development strategy at the cost of the marginalised blacks on the other side of the legislative 'fences' of influx control and homeland boundaries. New apartheid was perceived as resting heavily on regional discrimination. The critical view was regularly expressed, and not without validity, until the political wind was taken out of its sails by the Abolition of Influx Control and Restoration of Black Citizenship Acts in 1986.

"Black resistance to white domination in South Africa reached an unprecedented level in the mid-1980s. Entire communities were involved in struggles around their economic conditions and lack of political rights. National political organisations like the United Democratic Front (UDF) mounted the most serious challenge to the apartheid state. The South African Police were unable to handle the situation alone, and at the end of 1984 the SADF was sent to the townships to assist them. As the crisis deepened, the government imposed a series of states of emergency in 1984."

During this period, townships were very volatile, exacerbated by slogans such as "liberation before education", "with a matchstick we shall liberate this country", and calls to make the country ungovernable. In the process, many local government counsellors were killed and some had their properties destroyed. Those suspected of being spies of the Nationalist Party were "necklaced". it was mayhem all around. Gangsters such as Magabazas mushroomed, girl children were kidnapped, raped and killed, as happens in war-torn countries when women become the weapons of war.

Parents panicked and sent their children to attend schools in town. As the calls to reform the country grew louder, some public schools were starting to open to black children. The violence situation in South African townships ran into the early 1990s, with low intensity warfare between ANC and Inkatha Freedom Party (black on black violence) coming into play.

This was followed by the introduction of the Black Local Authorities trend. The limitations and potential of government policies towards the African community are best comprehended by exploring policy reforms at local government level. The crucial change heralded by this legislation was the granting of autonomy to black local authorities. Before this, township local government was characterised by the separation of administrative and political functions. Paradoxically, this major reform step invoked a sustained and violent rejection of the local authorities by various township communities. Black Local Authorities (BLAs), though subjected to severe and often violent rejection by township communities, remained one of the most crucial concessions yet made, marking a significant departure from the past policies affecting urban Africans.

It was at the beginning of 1984 that South Africa was once again engulfed by a major revolt, starting in the Vaal Triangle. This was caused by rent increases implemented by the then newly elected councils in response to government policy that townships generate their own revenue.

The major sources of revenue were rents, profits from liquor sales and service charges. However, profit from liquor was almost eroded as a source of revenue because of attacks on beer halls and bottle stores during 1976 riots. Another factor which fanned the revolt of 1984 to 1986 was the 1984 constitution which created a new tricameral parliament, which drew the Indian and coloured communities into parliament, albeit as junior partners.

The newly introduced local authorities regarded by the Nationalist Party as an alternative to direct representation in parliament caused widespread resentment and contributed in no small measure to the intensity of events during this period.

Reverting to EDA: after two and a half years of been employed there, my job abruptly ended. I had enjoyed working for the organisation. Unfortunately, my conditions of employment were altered. I was office-based and working at the resource centre.

Management felt that the resource centre work was not enough and that I should therefore join everyone in doing field work. This meant that I had to be away for two weeks in every month to go and work at any of their projects in Matatiele, Tzaneen, Bochum or Lusisikisi.

I already had a drivers' licence. I'd obtained it while still working for St Johns College by saving my bonus money. I'd paid R100 for both learners and drivers' licences using my bonus or thirteenth cheque. I had meant to go for a motorbike licence later, because the driving school offered all types of licences. I'd always liked riding a motorbike as well. I did not because the school was closed two years after I got my licence. EDA truly empowered me as far as perfecting my driving goes, especially since I learned in rural areas, where road networks are not complex. They found a driving school to give me practical lessons in driving, especially in the very complex roads of Johannesburg, and they paid for it. To perfect my driving skills, they even allowed me to use one of their vehicles to drive home

I remember how nervous I used to be. One day, I was driving on a freeway called Death Road from Soweto, Orlando West. I was driving at 40 kilometres because I wanted to be extra careful. A traffic officer came up, drove next to my window, and screamed to me, "Drive faster, otherwise I will pull you off the road". I ignored him and just kept on driving. He drove past, and I turned into Booysens Road. On a steep hill, when I was about to join Main Reef Road, there was a traffic jam. I panicked to the point of not been able to control the gears. My car stalled and rolled into the vehicle behind me. I was so frustrated. I thought my employer was going to be furious with me.

I told everyone of what happened when I got to the office, and they just said it was okay, that is how we learn, and took the car for repair, I was so grateful to them.

I was also scared of intersections. I never thought I would get used to them. I remember one day my car stalled in the middle of the intersection between Booysens and Main Reef roads because I panicked. I even forgot how to change gears. Fortunately, I was not driving alone that day and a colleague accompanied me.

My husband and I discussed the proposed work changes and agreed that it was not a good idea. Firstly, we had just got married and there were a lot of things we had to organise, including our lives together. Secondly, as staff we always had meetings late in the afternoon once a week, because most of the staff were doing field work, and I had to attend my afternoon lessons. It was a problem, because I had to be at those meetings. There was one problem after another. Both my education and my marriage were important aspects of my life and I had to ensure that they were balanced successfully. My husband suggested that I resign, and I did that immediately.

I looked for other work for almost a year, until I decided to go and do a secretarial course in town, at a college called Pitmans. It was a one-year certificate course. Although I attended lessons in South Africa, the examination papers were marked in London. I wrote my elementary course and passed all the subjects. Pitmans College was run by SACHED Trust, an institution for adult education, either matriculants or UNISA-registered black students. Once I'd completed my secretarial course, I hoped to secure employment as a secretary, but for almost a year after I'd completed it I could not find any employment. All was not lost, as my typing skills helped me do most of my typing work, such as assignments and research reports while at university. It also came in handy when I was appointed as assistant secretary in the Premier's Office and subsequently as Gauteng Liquor Board Head of Secretariat. In both these work environments, touch typing is critical because one must produce minutes timeously and accurately.

I wanted to do an advanced course in accounting and English. Unfortunately, the college was closed a year after I completed my first course.

I was told of a community organisation in a mission church in Phiri, Soweto, that offered Pitman Training Courses. When I enquired, I realised that it was operating on the same principles as the one I'd attended in town, and it had advanced training as well. It was run by white sisters stationed at the mission. I was allowed to register and continued with my advanced course as planned. I wrote both advanced accounting and English courses and passed them.

While there, I discovered that they were also engaged in community work. I decided to enquire about the projects. The lady whom I met told me that she was also running a community project at a famous church in Soweto called Regina Mundhi Catholic Church. Lots of political activities used to take place in the church during apartheid. Desmond Tutu played a big role in organising the events under trying circumstances and the watchful eyes of apartheid's police. I asked her to allow me to come and do voluntary work and she agreed.

While at Regina Mundhi, I requested that I establish secretarial courses at the church. I got permission from the parish priest at the church, and I was given a two-roomed building in the churchyard. I intended to recruit young mothers (that is, women who'd dropped out of school because of unwanted pregnancies) to the establishment and train them in these skills free of charge.

Over and above that, I yearned to share with them as a way of encouragement not to give up in life and use myself as an example. I knew that most girls who had a fall were, like me, from a disadvantaged background, and the likelihood was that they might not be able to continue with their studies. I hoped that those who came would work hard to change their lives and break the cycle of poverty and destitution as they would be self-sufficient. My goal was to drive the message home that education remains one of the most important tools, and that, in understanding that to transform and empower themselves they must acquire education, inspiration is the key.

I was inspired. Without wasting any time, I went to SACHED College and requested that they donate materials, equipment and other resources used for Pitman's lessons, as the college had closed its doors the previous year. Fortunately, they still had three typewriters and they agreed to donate them to me, as well as all materials. I used my textbooks to teach students. About six students attended, and I had one volunteer teacher who'd also attended secretarial courses at Rockville Roman Catholic Church.

I arranged with Rockville Centre that my students could register with them, and they agreed. All that they requested from them was registration fees. They all wrote examinations with Pitman's International Examination Board and passed. They were awarded with Secretarial Certificates. Although I was proud of myself to have empowered these women, I was saddened by the fact that I could not get any funds to continue with the school. I needed money to sustain it and pay teachers, including myself. I had to give up the initiative.

Still at Regina Mundhi, I one day discovered that there were ladies who were accommodated inside the church to run a curtain-making project. I went to meet them and introduced myself and asked them what they were doing. They showed me their work. I asked them to teach me how to make curtains, as well as to operate an electrical sewing machine. I knew how to operate a hand sewing machine and pedal machine operated by foot, we called it a *trap* (Afrikaans) machine.

They were willing to teach me, so every lunch time or after work I would sit with them and learn how to operate the electrical sewing and an over-locking machine. It did not take me long to master them, since it was not very different from operating the manual sewing machine I used to have in Greenside. The only difference is that the electric one is operated by foot, while a manual one is operated by hand, but the principles are the same.

I later asked my husband to buy me an electric sewing machine. He agreed and bought me machines for both sewing and over-locking. I was keen on starting my own business in curtain making to assist my husband financially. He was the only one working, so he had to pay for house mortgage, rates and taxes, and our daughter school fees, and buy clothes and groceries for all of us. I wanted to do something.

I went to the Oriental Plaza shopping centre one day and purchased curtain materials, and all the accessories needed to make kitchen and bathroom curtains. I saw a gap, in that Protea North was a newly developed area and people wanted curtains for their houses. I initially started by sewing sample kitchen curtains and went into people's houses, marketing myself. People started placing orders and I made it a point that I designed and made unique curtains with sophisticated trimmings. I received lots of orders, and I managed to create an income to alleviate the burden my husband was carrying. The rest is history.

One morning, I went to work as usual. When I got out of the taxi from home, I found people standing outside, facing in the direction of Potchefstroom Road, which is the main road along which the church is situated. Doctor Abu Baker Asvat had been assassinated at his surgery. He was the founding member of the Azanian People's Liberation Organisation (AZAPO). He was assisted by a nurse by the name Albertina Sisulu. Asvat was called a people's doctor. His practice was across Potchefstroom Road, opposite the church. Then the surgery was surrounded by informal settlements. It was indeed a sad day.

While at Pitmans, I learnt of Turret Correspondence College also run by SACHED Trust. It offered lessons for students studying to sit their matric examinations through the Joint Matriculation Board. SACHED was called the people's college because it was an educational organisation that aimed at countering the imbalance created by the apartheid education system. The lessons took place on Saturdays. I considered attending classes because I did not want to have a Bantu Education Senior Certificate, as it was just worthless. I knew that with it, I would never get to university. The results were always very poor, and it did not matter how hard one tried to improve them.

Making tea in Turret College kitchen.

The Story of a Rural Girl Who Kept Rising and Rising

I already mentioned that I'd moved from studying for the Senior Certificate to Joint Matriculation Board examinations while studying with Star School. I first registered for mathematics and physical science and I received very poor symbols. I realised that continuing with science subjects would be a waste of time because the chances that I'd get good marks with them were slim, so I dropped them. I then opted to join Turret Correspondence College. That was a motivating factor and my answer towards fulfilling my dream of obtaining the Joint Matriculation Board Certificate. I decided to enrol for biology, Afrikaans and English. I got average symbols and the following year I registered for accounting, history and biblical studies. Both elementary and advanced accounting courses I had done with Pitmans had given me a good foundation and I mastered accounting so well that I graced through at my matric level.

I passed my subject but my marks still did not qualify me for "M" level (what is referred to today as Bachelor). My aim was to obtain a university entrance with good results, so that I gained acceptance to universities such as Wits. This was very critical for me because I vowed to myself that I would never allow the apartheid system to dictate to me where I should live or study; it could only coerce me, although I knew that the chances of defying it were almost zero if their laws were still in place and in control of state machinery.

Joining Turret Correspondence College was a godsend, because I had been wondering how I was going to obtain good results to allow me to study at one of the good universities. My prayers were answered. While there, I learnt of a college called Khanya. This was a project that was meant to assist black children to obtain university entrance. I went to enquire, and I was given a brochure and other pamphlets including application forms. The college was funded by Indiana University in the United State. Its aim was to assist disadvantaged black children to have an opportunity to enter the so-called "Ivory Tower" universities such as Wits and the University of Cape Town. Only white children had easy access to these universities. Blacks were encouraged to attend universities meant for each ethnic group: for example Turfloop for Sothos, Tsongas and Vendas; Fort Hare in Transkei for Xhosas; and University of Zululand for Zulus. Otherwise, getting admission to white-only universities was cumbersome, especially since Bantu Education always produced very inferior results.

I took the correspondence and showed it to my husband. We discussed it and agreed that I should apply. I applied, and later I was called for an interview.

One thing that made me realise that God is great was when I was called for a second interview and I was told that they had read my Curriculum Vitae (CV) and had been touched by my contribution to the community, especially several voluntary jobs I had done in rural areas. I was accepted. I was over the moon: very thrilled and encouraged. I told myself that from here going forward nothing would stand in the way of my progress. The programme was only one year long.

The following year I registered with the University of the Witwatersrand (Wits) for my first degree.

Chapter Nine

UNIVERSITY LIFE AS A MATURE STUDENT

I was the little girl who like dust rose from humble beginnings and ascended to the upper academic echelons. Khanya College opened the door to my fulfilling my dreams. Now I could see the light. The college's programme was equivalent to what is called an "A Level" in most British colleges such as St John College. It prepared students who did not perform well with their matric results to qualify for university entrance. The only difference was that courses obtained at Khanya College were credited by selected universities. It was a one-year course and students were allowed to register for only two university entrance courses.

I registered for history and sociology. I was very fortunate to be selected for a four-year full-time scholarship programme. Several donor agencies donated money to various scholarship programmes, such as Educational Opportunities Council (EOC) and South African Council of Churches (SACC). These funds were meant to assist black children with the payment of university fees and a certain portion of the money was for a stipend and accommodation once at tertiary institutions.

I was amongst three students who were ear marked for a British Council scholarship. The scholarship paid for everything (fees, books, accommodation and a stipend, including my gym (aerobics) exercise sessions, both for my junior degree (three years) and postgraduate (one year honours degree)). I worked very hard and always performed very well to ensure that I was not going to forfeit it. There were conditions attached to the scholarship and you needed to pass all courses enrolled for each year.

My ambitions were realised. I obtained my first and second degrees in record time from an Ivory Tower university, something that proved that one's IQ is not determined by one's skin colour and that I am not as inferior as some wanted me to believe. I proved to the system that tried to turn me into a sub-human that it was wrong. It was a true blessing from God, and as I went into a secret place with Him (*lekunutung*), I thanked Him for all the blessings and I named them one by one.

I give credit to Khanya College. It laid a solid foundation for me in terms of empowering me to cope with the tertiary level workload. We were not only taught course work in the subjects of our preference, but we were exposed to how to conduct research.

For my history course, I did mostly oral research. The students were allowed to choose a topic to research and were put in a group of three to go out for a week and research the subject. I remember going to Sekhukhune in Jane Furse and surrounding areas to conduct research about "The Pedi Strife". Luckily, my in-laws came from one of the villages (Mathibeng) in Jane Furse, so I stayed with my mother-in-law for a week, commuting from the village to Jane Furse.

With oral research, one interviewed the people who were affected then. That is a sample study. In most cases, it would be old people. As a researcher, you must sit with and detail their stories. It took a lot of writing and recording. At that time there were no mobile (cell) phones, and we used manual battery tape recorders. This method of research is premised on the fact that old people are your library. It was only after one accumulated oral information that one would go to the library archives to get more references.

I remember that, while doing my history course, we were made to watch a movie about the American Slave Trade. Our lecturer showed us a movie called *Roots*, based on a book written by Alex Haley. It was so moving that a friend of mine Tshiidi Leloka and I became hysterical while watching it and we cried loudly and uncontrollably. Especially when they captured a main character by the name Kunta Kante. The most shocking scene was to watch whites amputating his foot with an axe. They never bothered to sedate him, and he cried so much from the pain he endured. I was shocked at the level of cruelty. I just hated whites.

For my sociology subject, I did most of my research interviews with trade unionists because I was learning more about industrial sociology. Although there was a theoretical part – An Introduction to Sociology of Development – there was also course work for both the subjects.

I must say, I was so fortunate because the whole programme was very informative, especially since it was aligned to the spirit of what SACHED Trust stood for: "...its commitment to establishing participatory, non-discriminatory, and non-authoritarian learning process..."

The programme did not only accommodate South African students and there were others from Lesotho, Malawi, Swaziland and Namibia. My friend Tshiidi was from Lesotho. I do not recall anyone who came from Botswana and Mozambique in our group, though. Khanya College, amongst other things, changed the demographic landscape of how both Wits and UCT used to accept black children to their campuses or academia.

After completing my pre-university programme, I was admitted to Wits University as a Khanya College product. The college students were allowed to register only at the universities of Cape Town and Witwatersrand. The following year, I left my husband with my pre-teenage daughter to go and study for my degree and stayed in a student residential area, visiting them only over weekends. I must acknowledge that that was a big sacrifice, and I will always be grateful to my husband for holding our marriage and the family together as he did, while raising a pre-preteen daughter . I must mention that my husband and I complemented each other. He too studied part-time for his three degrees: Junior degree, Honours degree and Master's degree.

We both sacrificed a lot so as to live the life we envisaged, and it paid off.

We are enjoying what the sweat of our hard work and dedication has brought us. He is one of the people who is so supportive, especially to a wife in the hypocritical patriarchal society like ours, where women are looked down upon and oppressed. I consider myself very, very lucky. I am saying lucky because his attitude towards life saved me a headache. I do not think I would have allowed him to control me or prevent me from acquiring the life of my dream. This might have led to fights and possibly divorce

When we got married, I was in the process of acquiring my matric, as already mentioned. To try and encourage me, one day he told me that I should continue working very hard to obtain matric and further my studies. He reminded me that no one owns a life. If he happened to die, I would be forced to look for a man to take care of me if I could not look after myself. He emphasised that a man is not a job, just as marriage is not a ladder to the good life; a good life is what I should create for myself.

We both fanned away prophets of doom from all corners. There were some people who told him that he was risking his marriage by allowing me to go to the university, because I might be tempted to take a lover. Some would tell me that I was risking my marriage by leaving my husband alone. He would be tempted to cheat on me. Some even suggested that it was not a good idea to leave a man with a daughter, worse a pre-teenage girl. Surely, if he wanted to cheat, he would have done that even while I was with him in the house? As would have been the case with sleeping with our daughter.

Listening to that kind of negative talk will never take you anywhere. One cannot dispute that these things do happen – many people have lost their marriages because they took these kinds of risks – but one needs to be principled as well as having a mind of one's own. Taking risks does not always turn out well, but that should not stop visionary individuals from venturing into a life of their dreams, irrespective of the risks.

The fact that I was older than many students, with an age gap of almost 16 years, never bothered me. There were few black students at Wits University then and many of the black students were from Khanya College. I registered for my BA degree, taking subjects such as Political Science I, II, III, Sociology I, II, III, English as Second Language, Education and Anthropology I, II. Fortunately, I had two credit courses from Khanya College, which were History I and Sociology I, so I proceeded with Sociology II and dropped history.

My life at university revolved around studying. I spent most of my time in the libraries if I were not in the lecture rooms. I had to work extra hard so as not to disappoint myself, my family and those who'd pumped a lot of money into my studies, and the college personnel who'd seen potential in me. I would take the student bus from the residence in Hillbrow and later Berea to the University in the evening, after I'd rested and cooked supper, and come back with the last bus at around 22h00. Then I'd take a nap and wake up at around 03h00 to study for a while and sleep until I woke up for my lectures. It depended on what time lectures were scheduled. If it was an 08h00 schedule, I had to wake up earlier. It became a routine and my way of life for a solid uninterrupted four years. I made it a point that I gathered all the information I needed for my tests, assignments and examinations. The workload was never-ending.

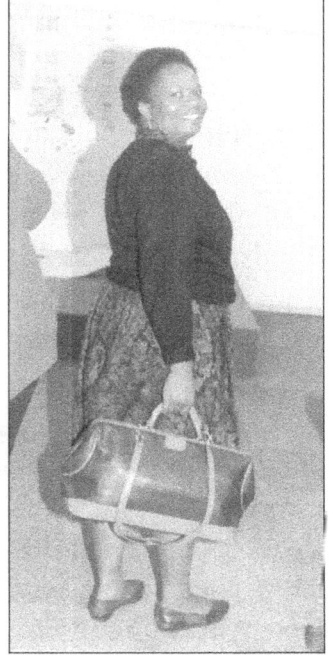

After completing my first degree, I proceeded with my postgraduate studies (honours) with Wits School of Governance under the Faculty of Commerce, Law and Management.

The Story of a Rural Girl Who Kept Rising and Rising

I wanted to specialise in a course that would empower and capacitate me to be able to contribute to the most anticipated dawn of black-led democratic government. I still stayed at student residence, although going to university and leaving my husband with our pre-teen daughter was not easy. I must emphasise that it was a great sacrifice. I lived in one of the university student residential place for mature students in Berea and still went home every weekend. I remember sleeping three hours for all the four years I was at the university. I had to make use of the scholarship. Their policy was that if one failed one was only given on chance to repeat, otherwise one would forfeit it. I was not prepared for that. In addition, I was not prepared to disappoint my husband and make his sacrifices and support in vain. It feels and sounds like yesterday, yet so many things happened and changed. God is great.

While I stayed in Berea in the early 1990s, the wind of change was blowing in the South African political landscape. Robben Island political prisoners had already been released and those in exile were returning home. The student accommodation I resided in was called Rand Lodge. Many returnees were accommodated at a hotel now called Sun 1. It was diagonally opposite my flat on Banket Road. I witnessed their coming back. I saw them being dropped off by minibuses from the airport and we were told that they were people from exile. One could have mistaken them as coming from Limpopo.

Limpopo migrant labourers were known for carrying lots of luggage on their bakkies, and as a result overloading their already *dikorokoro* vehicles; they were referred to as *makuduka* in Zulu. I do not know why those people coming from Limpopo were particularly associated with that, because all homeland states in South Africa had migrant labours. Perhaps it was because of the N1 Freeway, and they were more conspicuous since the route is very open and busy.

I wondered how the returnees managed to carry their luggage in an aeroplane from Lusaka, Nairobi and Cuba to name a few of the places that they were coming from. I used to watch them through the window as they came in. They really looked very destitute, and one could read the suffering and despair on their faces. I really felt guilty that I had remained here at home and had endured the suffering brought upon us Africans by apartheid in at least a familiar environment, while my fellow South Africans had lived in foreign lands under trying circumstances.

My consolation was that we could have not all have left this country and some of us made a difference by staying. We fought standing from our different small platforms. For me, it is not necessary that being out of the country automatically makes one a better hero than those who stayed because we know that not everyone stayed in the refugee camps but instead went to study in universities overseas. In fact, I consider myself as one of those who kept the home fires burning because the ideal of dismantling apartheid remained my goal as a young South African.

Finally, I am free. I was so excited by the fact that South Africa became a democratic country, and I had the opportunity to vote as a citizen of the country for the first time in 1994. I considered myself very blessed and loved by the Holy Mighty God, and I still thank Him for that. The 27th of April 1994, a day before my husband's birthday, became the best day of my life and one that I will cherish for as long as I live. I was free from been hunted like an animal for a mere passbook in my own country. I was free to live where I wanted and walk free in any part of this country, and was no longer a foreigner in my own country. I vowed to myself that I must ensure that I contribute to the building and development of the government of the day in a democratic country. This became an integral part of why I decided to specialise in the Public Policy and Development Administration course for my postgraduate studies.

The course was introduced just after the political prisoners were released and the path for negotiation was taking shape. The course was developed for the purpose of training individuals who wanted to become public servants and assist the new government in developing public policies and manage government administration. I was part of the first group to be trained, so I was among the guinea pigs. I really looked forward to serving this country and making a difference in redressing the legacy of apartheid through efficient and effective service delivery.

I was, however, saddened by the fact that my parents and my father-in-law were not lucky enough to have seen the dawn of democracy. My father died on the eve of that, in January 1994, four months before the elections.

Chapter Ten

WHEN THE UNTHINKABLE HAPPENS

Both my parents died in the space of one year. I was lost. I've already mentioned that I was raised by a staunchly Christian mother and an atheist father. My father did not play a big role in my life by virtue of him being a migrant labourer coming home only at particular times. However, he played a significant role as a provider, and I am grateful for that. My mother saw me through my childhood, youth and the initial stages of my adulthood.

Maybe it was because of her difficult upbringing that she resorted to God. I called her a praying mantis (*mampetlele*); she knew the bible so well that she could quote every verse by heart. Growing up, we were accustomed to a routine of a prayer session every night after eating supper. She would make sure that we all converged in one of the houses for prayer meetings: it was a must. She and her sister were both good singers, and she would read the bible and we would all sing. I am the only one who is not gifted in singing, but I would sing the loudest, although out of tune. Time and again they would reprimand me about my bad singing (*o ya shaetsa*), and I would be so upset and hurt. I could not get used to that. I realised later that I took after my father.

My mother (we called her Mama; children of my age called their mothers mme, mma or mmane, and we were the only one calling our mother Mama. As a result, everyone called her Mama) taught us prayers for the morning, night and other occasions, like when a bad or frightening storm was coming, and thanksgiving prayers.

For instance, the night prayer: *Ke lapile keyo lala mahlo aka a fifala, ntae wa legodimong o mpoloke bosegong* (I am going to sleep because my eyes are tired, so God protect me through the night). Morning prayer: *Mahlo aka aya ntitibologa thoto ya dibe tsaka e tlositse* (My eyes opened, and my sinful load is lifted off). This one confuses me as it does not make sense. When a bad storm is coming: *Bana besu lebellang leru le fihlile, mong wa leru le o teng ore se tshoge ke na le wena* (My fellow brethren, the storm is coming but know that God is in control; therefore do not be afraid as He is with you). I am still praying these prayers.

She taught me to look to God during difficult times and trust Him, to praise and honour Him. I learnt that I must praise Him during bad times and good times. I must confess, I was not fond of those laborious sessions because they became too routine, and it is not nice to be forced to do something. I was interested in playing with other children outside, especially during moonlight. I stayed to avoid a hiding, and I am happy today that she did that. It is only now that I realise how she tried to bring me up according to God's principles. Hence, I looked up to my mother because she is the one who gave me roots and grew me wings and taught me to read the bible because for her it was the "Best book to read".

After moving to stay with my father's family, she lost the momentum; I do not know why. She read the bible and prayed alone during night times, before falling asleep. She no longer, involved any of the children. I was at the pre-teen stage then, and preoccupied by school work and other responsibilities. My sister left for boarding school a year after moving to Kalkspruit. It was only my mother and my younger sister. However, she still forced us to attend church every Sunday morning. I dreaded that as well.

My father never attended church, even when he was home during his leave, Christmas time or Good Friday. He hated that. He almost had a bad influence on me because I would not go to church when he was around. Even when my mother insisted that I go, my father would come to my defence.

As I grew up and understood political issues, I read that the missionaries were the ones who brought slavery in Africa, and undermined the African people's way of life, with the notion of a dark and uncivilised Africa. I started hating church and what it stood for. While at high school and tertiary level, I became very political and read lots of Karl Marx's books. I was fascinated by terms such as dialectic materialism, bourgeoisies and proletariat.

I drifted further from believing in God (I wanted to be an atheist). My father loved that, so he encouraged me. He hated going to church, because of an incident that had happened years before, when one of his closest relatives offended his elder brother and he could not forgive him. The fact that he was a local church leader and what he did was unchristian reflected on all Christians' behaviour. For that reason, except for my mother's funeral, he never put his foot into a church until he died.

I still went to church in his absence because I did not want any trouble with my mother. I had to please her, and offending her was not a good idea. Strangely enough, when I eventually left home and came to stay with my father in Johannesburg, I wanted to belong to a church. Unfortunately, due to the Separate Development Act, blacks were not allowed to church with whites, and the closest place I could go to church to was in Alexandra township. I was not working then, so I could not afford to commute to and from church every Sunday.

But the turning point of my spiritual life started when both my parents died. My mother died first, and I was at home when she died. My elder sister and my cousin, upon receiving a telephone call from my father that my mother was gravely ill, went home to see her. They left on the Friday and came back on Sunday. The day that they returned from home, they informed me that she was in a bad shape, and my mother was indeed gravely sick.

It was during a week when there had been a call by COSATU for a total national shut down and the whole country was to come to a standstill. I knew that I had to go home, no matter what. My mother needed me, and I could not fail her. I spoke to my husband. He was hesitant and worried about the looming national strike. I promised him that I would not experience any problem, and he eventually agreed.

I telephoned my sister and my cousin to let them know that I would be going home the following day. I was told that my mother's elder sister was with my elder cousin. She wanted someone to take her home and requested that I fetch her. I woke up very early, took a taxi to town so that I could connect with a taxi to Pretoria (Tshwane). Fortunately, a few taxis were operating. While walking to Park Station, from where I was supposed to catch a taxi to Pretoria, I came across an Indian chemist (pharmacy) and it was open, although most of the shops were closed because of the strike. I went in.

With my little knowledge of nursing I thought of buying medication suitable for a bed-ridden person. I almost bought the whole chemist until the owner asked me where I was taking the medicines to. I said, "I am buying them for my mother who is struck by a stroke". He asked me how old she was and I told him, and he told me that the likelihood was that she might not survive due to her age. I almost burst out in anger, because I wanted her to live. I had to do something to save her. After all, my mother was not that old. He realised that I was upset and advised me which medicines to buy and which not. I paid him and left.

It was on 5 August 1992, a normal late winter day. The only difference was that the mood was very tense and electric. The country was about to embrace one of the biggest stayaways (shutdowns) and marches to the Union Buildings ever embarked upon since the release of political prisoners and those exiled freed to return home.

When I passed Pretoria (now Tshwane), people were already gathering around and gearing up for a march to the Union Buildings. The whole town was painted red. Union members had put on COSATU T-shirts, caps and socks. I can still recall the sound of the voice of then Sam Shilowa (now Mbhazima) resonating throughout the town, singing "*Tina abakamkhondo sizi emizele kua bulala amapone*" (We, the liberation struggle cadres – *mkhondo* meaning spear – are prepared to kill all the Boers – meaning white Afrikaners) one of the favourite revolutionary slogans. What a powerful voice; he should have done something with it.

I sneaked through and between a massive wall of people lined up in the streets to catch transport to my destination. I was not part of the march, although I would have loved to have been. I found myself moving alone in a different direction, like a reed in the river, preoccupied by the thought of my gravely ill mother, wondering whether I would find her still alive. I kept on praying the same monotonous prayer I'd started praying the night before, after having been told of her deteriorating health situation.

With God's grace, there were a few taxis that were still operating, despite the tension. I managed to get a taxi to Mamelodi East, where my cousin-sister was staying. My aunt was ready and waiting for me. We quickly went to catch a taxi back to Tshwane town, to catch another taxi to Pietersburg. Getting into town, it was full of marchers and it was difficult to walk. I had to hurry my elderly aunt so that we could get out of that place before we were blocked. It seemed as if we were the only ones who were walking in the opposite direction to the others.

I got worried about whether we would be able to get a taxi to Polokwane. I started praying. I prayed so hard that I even forgot my aunt. When I looked back, she was just trying to catch up with me. She could not walk fast. I waited for her and, after a closer look at her, I happened to notice that it was not her age taking a toll on her feet: she was wearing her shoes on the wrong feet. I stopped around the corner and assisted her to put them on properly. I laughed, but she did not notice. It was very funny.

This reminded me of when, one Sunday morning at a church service, I was sitting across from where my mother was seated. I realised that she was wearing her shoes on the wrong feet and I could not contain myself. I laughed out loud, and she looked in my direction with stunned face, ready to rebuke me. I quickly pointed at her shoes, and she looked down and to me again. Then we both laughed. It was funny.

When we got to Bosman train station, I realised that there were only a few taxis, and my heart started to pound fast with worry. I started praying again as we approached the spot where the Polokwane taxis were. God is so great. When I got there, there was a last taxi and it needed two people. Taxis were forbidden to transport people that day as drivers were to join the march. The driver asked us to jump in quickly so that he could get out of town fast.

We arrived in Polokwane just after lunch time. I wanted to get home so quickly that I did not even want to stop for lunch, but I realised that my aunt might be hungry. On our way to the taxi rank, I quickly went into a Greek/Portuguese fish and chips shop and bought a packet of chips and bread, as well as a soft drink for her. She ate quickly, and we went and caught a taxi home to Kalkspruit. Fortunately, they were not so much affected by the countrywide call for a stayaway from work.

Even now, everything is still so vivid that it is like yesterday. It was the worst trip I ever took to home and I will never forget it. This was the day that I saw God in action. I knew that from then onwards my life would never be the same, I was not about to take God's love for granted. I had to change and be like Jesus and grow in my faith, meanwhile allowing Him to fill me with His Holy Spirit. He took control of my situation: truly Amazing Grace!

When I got home and went straight into my parents' bedroom. I was crushed. My mother was in such a bad state that I could not recognise her. She was already in coma. I did not even sit down to rest. I just walked over to her, took out the medications I had bought, and tried to do whatever I could. But first I wanted to bathe her. Her right-hand side was not functioning, and she was paralysed from the waist down. She'd already started turning green at her toes, an indication that there was no flow of oxygen supply through the blood from the brain to her lower parts.

My other cousin-sister, who was staying with them, and my aunt, assisted me to lift her. She was just like a cabbage. I could not believe that she was the mother I knew and respected and feared: the very bold and fearless woman with so much wisdom. I changed her linen, bathed her, and rubbed her back parts with surgical spirits and a baby powder to avoid bed sores. I washed her mouth with surgical glycerine, using a piece of a cotton wool, because she could not brush her teeth. Her tongue was swollen and turning grey, as if it were burnt. There was no blood flow to any part of her body. She could no longer swallow anything, not even liquid.

They could not take her to hospital because while she could still talk she'd instructed them not to. My sisters told me it was a weekend before the Wednesday that she'd slipped into a coma; when she'd told my father not to take her to hospital because she was tired of moving from one hospital to another. You know older people: they always have their perceptions about hospitals. My mother-in-law believed that I should not have taken her to hospital, and she could still be alive if I had not.

It was already late, and we went to bed. I hoped that she would be better the following day.

The following day, I went to check her first thing in the morning and to greet my father. She was just the same. After my father woke up and we'd all eaten breakfast, I decided to bathe her. As I did, she just spoke; I do not know how. She told me that she was dying. I said to her, "You cannot because I am here," and she started throwing her arms around. It was funny because she could not move at all. I saw her tears streaming down her cheeks, and my heart sank in agony and dismay. I was helpless.

The medication I'd bought her could not help. I knew my mother well. She would not just cry if she were not hurting. I jumped on top of her bed and hugged her, trying to comfort her. I remember how I tried to wrestle with God because I could not let go of her. She was not to die on me. I would not let her.

I finished bathing her, dressed her in a clean nightdress my husband had bought for her when she'd come to visit us few years previous. It must have been her special nightdress for special occasions, because it still looked new. After I'd finished bathing her, she thanked me (*ke a leboga*) and slumbered back into her coma, never to speak again. I knew that she was pleased and she must have blessed me because I saw her face brighten up through the pain. I think the sores on her tongue were hurting her more than the stroke itself.

I suggested to my father that we must take her to hospital. He was reluctant because she'd made it clear to him before slipping into a coma that they should not return her to hospital. I guessed she was just tired. She had been too many times to hospitals. But it was unbearable to see her in so much pain. My father agreed and I went to the local clinic to ask nurses there to assist me to call an ambulance to take her to hospital. One of the sisters came home with me, and told me that she was in a really bad state. The clinic could not get an ambulance for me. My father's brother's son arrived; he had a bakkie (we simply call it a van). I asked him to assist us to take my mother to hospital.

My father was still hesitant for the reasons given above. I begged him that we should try once more, for the last time. He agreed and opted to accompany us. We took her to hospital. Our nearest hospital, WF Knobel (Wilhelm Friedrick Knobel), is about a one-hour drive. I sat with her at the back. Fortunately, it was not an open bakkie as it had a canopy that shielded us from sun and dust. She could not sit down, so we made her lie down on a sponge on the floor of the van and I just lay down beside her, hugging her, trying to make her comfortable as the van rolled on a dusty and bumpy gravel road. I hugged her because I wanted her to feel the warmth of my body and my heartbeat. In that way she would know that I loved her. Even if I'd had to carry her on my back, I would have. She was my dearest mother and therefore she could not have been heavy for me.

We arrived at the hospital. When we got there, we had to carry her from the bakkie. She was very heavy and we asked the porters, who were just sitting there watching us, to help. All that they did was to bring us a trolley and then they went back and sat down because they were on lunch. We carried her to the out-patient ward. Nurses tried to resuscitate or revive her from her coma, but she could not respond. They took her to the admission room. Once she'd been admitted, we left, but one of the nurses told us that there was no hope. I refused to believe that. My mother had to come back.

The night that we took her to hospital, something very strange happened. We'd finished eating supper earlier on and I was sitting with my father at their special dining room table. They had their own two-room thatched house, consisting of their bedroom and sitting room. In the sitting room they had a four-chair table.

Photos of my parents' homestead

My father was sitting in his usual armchair that faced the entrance door, and my mother had hers, facing their bedroom door. I was sitting in her chair when suddenly something hit me with so much force on my back (right on my spinal cord) that I jumped. This was followed by the sound of broken glass. It was 8 o'clock, because we were listening to the news on the radio.

Most of their photos hung on the wall and we both rushed to check which glass covering the photo frames had broken. There was no glass on the floor and none of the glass covering the photos was cracked. We sat down and looked at each other but said nothing. We tried to dismiss what had happened and continued with our conversation. We did not want to be superstitious.

The day following her admission, I woke up at about 05h00 because I could not sleep. I wanted to catch the only bus to the hospital. It was still too early. The bus only arrived at 08h00. I went outside and started walking towards our outside pit toilet. I stopped next to their bedroom window and started praying. I said, "Please, Mama, if you cannot get better, could you just go because I do not want you to suffer this much". I said, "God, please give me the strength to deal with this. Mama is gravely ill, and I am helpless." I was talking loudly and crying.

My father woke up and said, "Thabo?" He used to shorten my name Lethabo. He did not say a thing more.

On my way back from the toilet, I decided to wash all her dirty clothes, including her blankets. I went to my father and politely asked him to allow me to remove the sheets and blankets from my mother's bed for washing. I apologised for waking him up so early. At the time, there were no double, king and queen-size beds, only a single and a three-quarter size bed. In most furniture shops, one would find two three-quarter size beds with a matching table that went between them: they came as a set. My parents had that, and hence it was easy for me to remove my mother's bedding without disturbing my father. He agreed, but looked very worried.

I did all the washing, hung it on the washing line and started preparing myself for the journey to the hospital. It was the nearest but still about 52 kilometres by bus. I put into my handbag a small plastic bag holding a washing rag, soap, toothbrush, toothpaste and other necessities for her.

I went to wait for the bus at the bus stop. It arrived at 8 o'clock and I boarded it. I was desperate to reach the hospital so that I could see how she was doing. After what seemed like an eternity, the bus arrived at the hospital gate. It had been one hour of travelling because it had to go round to all the neighbouring villages to pick up other people. After all, it was the only bus for the day.

Strangely enough, as soon as the bus approached the hospital gate, my legs started shaking. I did not know what had come over me. Before it could come to a standstill, I stood up. The bus was full and some passengers were standing. I tried to push my way through, and everyone was swearing at me, but I could not care less. I had to see Mama.

I managed to get out before everyone else and I ran very fast until I reached the hospital's female ward door, where I knew she had been admitted. I started asking nurses about her. One nurse told me that it was not yet time to see patients, as the doctors were still doing rounds. She ordered me to wait outside like all visitors until we were called in.

I insisted and walked straight to the reception area. The nurse who had admitted my mother saw me and called me to a small desk around the corner. I greeted her, and before she could respond I asked her about my mother and how she was doing. She just stared at me. I immediately opened my bag and took out the small plastic bag holding my mother's toiletries. I stretched my hand out and said, "Here are her things". She was still staring at me, not taking them nor saying anything.

I asked her whether there was any problem, and she started talking and said to me, "Your mother was in a very bad health condition when you brought her here yesterday". I said yes. She said, "She did not make it". I froze. I could not cry or anything; I just kept quiet. She asked me whether I'd heard her and I said yes. She said, "It was good of you to bring her to hospital. She died peacefully. It would have been unfair for her to die in so much pain." Most of the nurses had known her because she'd frequented the hospital for treatment.

I put her toiletry bag back into my bag and said quietly and politely to her, "Where is she?"

She said, "At the mortuary".

I asked her, "What time did she die?" She told me that she was certified dead at 10 o'clock.

I asked her if I could be allowed to go and see her, and she replied, "You cannot do that alone. Is it not better for you to go home, let them know and come back with your father?"

I became irritable and responded firmly and said, "No, she is my mother. I must see her."

She agreed, and I was not going to let her stop me. I'd already stood up. She called another nurse to walk me to the mortuary. On our way there, I said a short prayer silently, and asked her to give me strength. She was a very strong person, and I knew that she would transfer her wisdom and strength onto me.

We arrived at the mortuary, and the guy working there asked for my mother's name and opened her tray. She was just lying there, looking very peaceful. I touched her forehead and kissed her. I said to her, "Thank you for everything, Mama. I will always love and honour you. Go well, African Woman." I never shed a tear, but turned around and left. I could hear the man pushing her tray in and closing the door as I walked away. I had a lump sitting in my throat, but I could not cry. I had to be strong for my father and my siblings. She transferred her strength and wisdom to me, through God's help. When my mother died, I was doing my second degree.

I went to the main reception, where there is a public telephone booth, and asked to use the phone. The operator told me that it was not working. I immediately decided to go to town. I asked around to find out where the transport to town was, and they pointed me to the main road, a little distance from the hospital. I walked there and boarded a taxi to Polokwane; it took about one hour to get there. I still remember getting into the taxi and sitting in the front seat, next to the driver.

I greeted them and told the taxi driver that my mother had passed on in the night. He kept quiet for a while and no one in the taxi said anything. It was a sombre moment, very silent. It was only after some time that the driver responded and said it was bad news, and paid condolences in North Sotho (*ke maswabi ka seo*). I responded in Sotho and said *ga di lebogwe* (translating, no one ever thanks bad news such as death).

After that, I never uttered a word until I arrived in town. The driver off loaded us at the taxi rank in Polokwane and I thanked him and walked to the post office to telephone my sister from the public phones. I told her that Mama had passed on. She collapsed. I could hear her falling, followed by the telephone receiver. I walked away. I had to do everything fast, because I did not want my father to be told by anyone else. I had to be the one to announce it to him first.

After that, I walked very fast, straight to the taxi rank and boarded a taxi to home. My aunt from Mamelodi, who had come with me, told me that she saw me approaching from the main road, where the taxi had dropped me off, and had noticed that I was walking so fast that I was almost running. She'd suspected that something was wrong, but had not expected the worst.

My father was outside, trying to support one of his grape vines with additional reinforcement. I greeted him and went straight into the house and sat on the chair that my mother normally sat on around the dining room table. He followed me immediately, hoping for the good news about Mama.

Without hesitation I said to him, "Papa, Mama passed on". He kept quiet, and then asked me how Mama was. I said, "Papa, she passed on". He still could not make sense of what I was saying. I repeated it for the third time, talking very slowly. He then said, "What?" I said that she'd died.

I'd never seen someone flying before, but my father did. He flew from the chair he was sitting on, so high that I thought it was a movie, and came crashing down on his chair again. He said, "Thabi," almost calling her. My mother's name is Thabitha, so he called her Thabi but called her Mama when addressing us. He then asked me whether I knew what that meant. Before I could answer, he said, "I've lost my jewel, everything, the one part of me left".

I informed him that I had seen her already at the mortuary and that she was at peace. I also told him that I'd informed my sister, and she would tell others. He stood up and said he had to go and tell everyone, meaning the Gwangwas. He immediately left, and came back as soon as he could. He thanked me so much it was amazing. He told everyone that if it were not for me being around, he would not have known how to deal with Mama's death and kept on thanking me. It sounded like a broken record.

I told my father that the loud sound of breaking glass we had heard the night that she died was a sign. I told him that Mama had died at 8PM (20h00) reminding him of the time we'd heard the breaking glass sound. I said to him that I knew it for a fact because clinically someone is certified dead after two hours and the hospital records said she died at 10PM (22h00). He said, "She was bidding us farewell". I said, "Yes, but why did she have to hit me so hard on my spinal cord?"

My mother had always been hard on me, to the point where I'd thought she hated me. I was the only child she ever gave a hiding to. I only realised later that she loved me and wanted to prepare me for the hardships of life. My parents somehow expected a lot from me, putting too much pressure on me to do the right things always.

My two sisters were always treated with kid gloves, and I envied them. Maybe it was because of the first-born and last-born syndrome. It is only now that I know that it was meant to happen that way. I do not blame them nor my sisters. For me, it was according to God's plan and His holy will because I had to become the person I am today. I learnt to grow a thick skin over the years. Mine is three centimetres thick and I thank my mother for that. That is my interpretation of life.

The news of my mother's death spread like wildfire, and people in the community started flocking to my home to give support and condolences. I needed just that. When something like this happens, the whole world comes crashing down on you. You do not need money or anything other than people's faces.

My siblings arrived before sunset. I could not wait for them to arrive. Apparently, the presence of my father, aunt and other two sister-cousins could not console me. I'd hoped that if all my siblings arrived I would feel relieved, but it was not to happen.

I felt lost and alone. I needed my mother, period. I never shed a tear, even when everyone else was crying, I just stared at them as we related to them what had really happened.

I wanted to stay strong for my mother and support my father. Strangely enough, the following day, I woke up very early. I could not sleep because I kept on trying to make sense of the fact that Mama had died. I left the room that I shared with my other sisters. They were all still fast asleep. Once outside, walking past my parents' bedroom window, I spontaneously started screaming, calling, "Mama..." without any tears coming out of my eyes.

My father woke up and opened the window and just called my name, Thabo. I kept on walking towards our pit toilet. I needed some fresh air and walking the few metres from the main house did the trick. I went into the toilet and knelt and started praying. All that I needed was my God to give me strength and faith.

The week that we were preparing for her funeral, I was very worried about my father's state of mind. He was putting on a brave face, but I noticed his frustration. I made it a point that when he was not around I checked on him. One evening, I could not see where he had gone. I went around, looking for him everywhere. Then I thought of their bedroom. I opened the door and there he was, sitting in the corner. I realised that he was crying. I walked towards him with the intention of hugging him. I wanted to comfort him.

He stood up and started talking in an angry voice, accusing me of always being too forward. I said, "Papa, I am here for you," but he said that no one could be there for him as his wife was. I said his daughters could be. Just to make things worse, he chased me away and an argument ensued.

My aunt and her daughter from ga-Masemola were already there, and they all came running. I heard my sister telling them to leave us alone because we were always like that. I then knew that my father was hurting, and he was inconsolable. I decided to give him some space to grieve until the funeral, though I was still very worried about him.

After her burial, I had go back to Johannesburg, and that was the most difficult thing to do. Leaving her shattered me. Coming to back to Johannesburg was when my mother's death started to hit me hard, and I had to face the reality. The grief was just unbearable. I could not cope with her illness and, worse, her ultimate death. I failed the module that I wrote at that time. Apart from that, I was a brilliant performer, scoring 80% and the lowest 65%.

I cried almost every day. I remember the first day I went for my classes. I was just a mess, especially when everyone I met paid their condolences. Going back to my residence after my lessons, I was walking across the public park facing Johannesburg hospital in Parktown and in a flash I thought of my mother. I started screaming and calling her: "Mama. Mama." I did not even see the people around me. I kept on walking. I was wearing a black band around my upper arm. Africans and even other nationalities knew what it meant. They must have thought I was losing it, though, and I was indeed losing it. My husband was scared because I could not stop crying. I still miss her deeply. However, I have always tried to remember her in a happy way and, as they say, time heals.

When my mother first took ill, it was in the first year I had gone to the university to do my first degree. Then I was not very worried because I knew she was a strong person. I hoped that she would pull through to see me graduate. She was one of the most important people in my life because she'd always encouraged me to study. She could not come to my graduation and neither could my father. I did not feel the void because my husband was there and my elder sister accompanied us. I sent them photographs of my graduation. My father told me that my mother just stared at them in disbelief but very amused. Due to the effect of the stroke, she could not talk properly.

Graduation for my junior degree.

When she died, I was doing my post-graduate degree. I am the only graduate in the family, so she would have been very proud of me. I needed her. She was my confidante, my pillar of strength and a source of motivation and encouragement. While at home, after my mother died, my father fetched one of my graduation pictures and pointed at the hood, asking me, "What is this?" Meaning, what have you graduated in? I told him and explained to him what that meant. I was hurt. I am told that he made a point of telling everyone in the family that one of his children had graduated with a degree. When I heard of that, he'd already passed on.

Graduation for my Master's degree.

The Story of a Rural Girl Who Kept Rising and Rising

He was always proud of his daughters' achievements. I remember how he used to boast about us having obtained Form 3. My mother too, when I was still at the university, made it a point that those close to her knew about that she was proud. Later, when I obtained my honours degree, my mother had already passed on and when I obtained my master's degree, they'd both passed on.

Graduation for my honours degree.

Nonetheless, she left me with good memories. I still read the bible the way she taught me to, particularly the Psalms. Every time I go through some challenges, I always find something in the scriptures, exactly as she told me I would. Beside the Old Testament, I like reading the New Testament as well, particularly Jesus Christ's parables, how He used to perform miracles, His death and resurrection. I truly get intrigued by His thinking and teaching. But the most striking thing about the New Testament is Jesus Christ's crucifixion. This part evokes something in me that I find difficult to explain or comprehend. How He died brings so much agony, pain and tears to me, over and over. There is this hymn that I love so much that says: "... Lest I forget Gethsemane, Lest I forget Thine agony, lest I forget Thy love for me, Lead me to Calvary..."

Reverting to the theme of this chapter, I am using my mother's death to take the reader through my spiritual journey. I view her death as one of the contributing factors towards my spiritual growth. I gradually started to look unto God for lots of things. I realised that He is the only One Who can be there for me in all trying times or circumstances and He has never failed me. My father's death also became a changing factor of my life and I've never looked back but have walked with God in faith always.

I remember one day when I was sitting with both my parents at home. I was still at secondary school. It was after supper and they were sitting around their dining room table with a paraffin lamp in the middle of the table. I do not know what came over me, but I looked at them and said to them, "Please, Papa and Mama, you should never die". The thought of them dying frightened me. They simultaneously responded by just dismissing me. But my father told us that his wish was that when the time came that they died, they should die at the same time, because he could not live without Mama, but I never took it seriously. He died a year after my mother.

As you know, my mother died first. I went home a month after she died, and my father looked okay. When I went home for the second time, I observed some changes in him. He had lost a lot of weight. I just thought it was as a result of losing his wife and he was still recovering from the grief. But, when I went home a year after my mother died, for the ritual that Africans normally perform, I was disheartened to see my father so emaciated.

This is the envelope he addressed to my husband and me, meaning that it was a last letter we received from him . According to African culture, after someone had passed on and has been buried, family members put on black clothes or black bands around their arms as a sign of mourning (*go roula*). They are only removed after a year, especially when it is a parent, wife or husband.

A year after my mother died, I went home for the ritual gathering and performance leading to the removal of the mourning clothes (*go tlosa goba go ntsha tshila*). This is followed by distributing her clothes by sharing them amongst relatives and the children. I wanted nothing but her hymn book and her bible, but of course they insisted that I take one of her items of clothing. I chose her favourite beautiful black two-piece outfit. I still wear it today. I carefully selected these items because in my mind I wanted to become the keeper of my mother's soul. Taking both her bible and hymn book, I knew that I was holding my real mother. I also knew that, for as long as I lived and was wearing her attire, my mother lived too.

It was during this period that I had the shock of my life: my father was just withering away. I said to my sister that he was not going to last for another year. I narrated to my sister that it was his wish. I did not know he had meant, I told her, what he once had said. Indeed, he died a year and five months after my mother's death, fulfilling his wish. He gave up the will to live. He developed heart problems or complications and he never told us.

One day, he collapsed and fractured his femur. Fortunately, my sister was at home and managed to see to it that he was rushed to hospital. He stayed there for one week and then passed on. When my sister called me to say that she'd received a telephone call from my father's elder brother's son, the one who had taken my mother to hospital, that my father's health situation had taken a turn for the worst, and that we must come home immediately, I knew that he would not make it.

We rushed home. On the way, I was seated in the back seat of my sister's friend car alone. My sister was sitting on the front passenger seat with her friend. I still remember very well that we were passing Warmbaths and Nylstroom, heading towards Naboomspruit, driving on the N1. I was listening to my sister and her friend talking about my father pulling through. I interrupted the conversation by saying he was gone. Papa was no more. He'd died. I just knew that he'd died. My sister's friend tried to talk me out of it and said to me try to be positive, but my sister kept quiet for a long time.

My other sister and cousins had already arrived when we got there, but had not been to the hospital. They were waiting for us at home. We all drove to the hospital together. While still at home, resting a bit and just sitting around, my siblings were talking about him, how he might be doing. I said to them that he'd passed on, we would not find him. All that we needed to do was to hurry up to hospital, before the news of his death started spreading. I said to them that I would regret to have this confirmed by strangers.

There was a dead silence. We were drinking tea. My cousin-brother stood up and said, "Let us go". We all left everything and got into the cars and left. As soon as we entered the ward he had been admitted to, I looked around. I could not see him. I immediately noticed an empty bed and started crying, even before the nurse who attended us had uttered a word. He had indeed died, the nurse confirmed. We all went to the mortuary. Strangely enough, his body was stored in the same tray that my mother's had been. I still remembered the number.

I was at peace with his death because I'd had the opportunity to tell him how much I loved him and that he had to get better soon because I needed him. My father's death did not impact on me the same as my mother's. I somehow reacted in the way in which most of us would when we first hear of the passing away of our loved ones. But it was during his death that I was touched by God in a very special way, and I never looked back.

I was brought up by a religious mother and understood Christianity very well, but I was not a born-again Christian. For many years, I attended a born-again church and loved it, but I was never converted. It was only during my father's night vigil or memorial service that something happened to me. When in a tent during the night vigil, the pastor invited those who wanted to be prayed for to come forward. My uncle stood up and went first, and I followed him. The pastor put his hands on my head and started praying. As he was praying for me, something got hold of me. I started crying, jumping and screaming and during those trances my feet lifted off the ground. The priests got hold of me and continued praying until I calmed down. It was after that that I committed myself to God and started growing spiritually.

The scene reminded me of one of the gospel songs I loved so much by Shirley Caesar: "I remember Mama in a happy way". It talks about the children who were playing church, and their mother reprimanded them and complained that they come home and play church yet they are still disobedient, as they talk back and refuse to wash dishes and so on. As they were playing, the Holy Spirit got hold of one of the siblings and it would not let go. When the other children realised that there was something wrong with her, they called their mother. Having observed her for couple minutes, the mother realised that her daughter was not playing and she said, "She ain't not playing".

I had always listened to it for spiritual upliftment, but when it happened to me I knew what it meant. As from then, I knew that I would never look back because I remember every day what the Lord has done for me. I could count my blessing and name them one by one. I am ever surprised by His mercy and goodness, and I thank Him. The incident helped me to grow faster in my journey with God.

My father-in-law died two years after I'd got married and we had moved into our first house. He was relatively young. When he took ill, we had hoped against hope that he would make it. I was hoping that he would get a chance to see his son's first house and spend some time with us. I was very fond of him, his kindness, warmth and love. I still can see his face and hear his voice. We bonded very well, and he was such a gentleman. His face in his coffin never left me and still I miss him.

My mother-in-law lived longer than all of them. She died in her 90s. I had a wonderful relationship with her. She never made me feel like I was an outsider, a daughter-in-law (*ngwetsi* or *makoti*). I got along fine with everyone: my husband's two sisters and four brothers. The one thing that fascinated me about her was that she was a visionary. Even though she'd never put her foot in a classroom (she was illiterate), she motivated her boy children to go to school. Unfortunately, sexism was then so rife that girl children were not supposed to go to school as they would get married and have children.

There was something about her that drew me towards her, something like another a mother. For example, I remember that after my mother's burial I was so lost that the first thing that I needed was to be with her. I took a taxi the following weekend to go and be with her because I needed a mother. She did not seem surprised because she must have known what it meant.

She was such a fascinating person and she became the only person of her age in the area who received God as her Lord and personal Saviour. As I mentioned earlier, the Sekhukhune people resisted Christianity viciously as the so-called civilisation. But when one time she took ill, the youth who'd converted to Christianity in the village – *bazalwani* in Zulu, which my mother-in-law pronounced in Pedi *batsalwani*, having "Pedified" it – and were born-again Christians came and prayed for her. She was so devoted that no one could stop her, and her husband supported her.

She was healed and decided to convert and attended the church in her old age years without fail. She was so inspiring, especially since she could not read nor write, but understood the scriptures and preaching. What fascinated me about both my mothers was their unwavering faith in God. They both believed in God and feared Him. I admired them for that because it is through them that I understood the meaning of being faithful to God.

I am a spiritual person and so is my husband. In a nutshell, destiny brought us together because we both suffered oppression under the apartheid system. It is so monumental for us that we beat the odds and created a comfortable life for ourselves.

I still have clear memories of them, as if it were yesterday. There is no time lapse between the years I spent with them and today. I can still smell their body perfumes, hear their voices and laughter and see their faces so vividly. So is my memory about their death and those days I witnessed them, one by one, being swallowed by their graves. It is so true that, as Daniel Schacter (2013) writes, "Our memory acts as a laboratory for everyday life, a mine, a reserve. With its help, you can engineer the present and possibly the future. They need to be recorded."

After graduating with my second degree, I found employment as a graduate. The next chapter will focus on that.

Chapter Eleven

FINALLY ENTERING THE WORK ENVIRONMENT AS A UNIVERSITY GRADUATE

A Greek author once said, "All impediments are for the good". The many years of struggling to acquire a matric certificate and going to the university under trying circumstances, are the golden thread running through my career life.

Working for a non-governmental organisation

After completing my honours degree at the Wits School of Governance, the university recommended that I attend a one-year course, a Diploma on Minerals and Energy at Cape Town University (UCT). It was a new programme meant to empower blacks in anticipation that, once a democratic government was in place, there would be a need for blacks with skills to manage relevant departments and entities in this regard. Each selected university was to identify two students for the programme. Wits School of Governance was one of those institutions. I was one of those students identified, along with another student.

However, although tempting and I could see great opportunities in it, I politely turned down the offer, suggesting that they should rather send a younger person with no commitments. I stated my reasons: One, I had been at the university for four years already, and I felt that it was not fair to my husband and daughter to be away from them for another year. Secondly, I wanted to find employment so that I could alleviate the financial load from my husband's shoulders, as he had to pay for mortgage, rates and taxes, child's fees as well as clothes and food.

They agreed and two young students, a female and male were sent. I know that they completed successfully and they were both employed by the Department of Mineral and Energy after the 1994 Democratic Elections.

I was fortunate that Wits School of Governance offered me a job on a contract basis because one of their employees went on sabbatical leave. The contract came to an end after six months, so I started looking for employment and after four months I had not found any. I still had good communication with my former employer Cynthia Hugo, and she told me that there was a section in her organisation that needed a new graduate for their one-year internship programme. She asked me to come over and work with them.

When the internship programme came to an end, I started looking for full-time employment. Three months passed without my finding any, but luckily my husband came across an advertisement in which two institutions required new graduates for employment. It was a recruitment agency for university graduates run by Cybriel Xaba. Fortunately, he was staying at the same place as we were.

My husband approached him and made an appointment. They met at his house, although I was not told anything. When he came back, he told me about their meeting and that they'd agreed that I would meet him at his office in town for an interview. I went for the interview for two posts. One was for OK Bazaars Supermarket and the other was for Educational Opportunities Council (EOC). I succeeded in both the interviews, but I had to choose one for placement. I chose EOC. He recommended me to EOC, and later I was called for an interview session with the management. In the session was Eleanor Molefe and Magang Phologoane. I was appointed the same day. The vacant position was that for a student counsellor for a local scholarship programme because at head office we had staff that was responsible for both overseas and local scholarships.

After the 1994 elections, I was tempted to join government but also felt obliged to pay back to the organisation that had made such a difference in my life. This was one of the reasons I remained at EOC.

EOC administered a scholarship programme for black children from previously disadvantaged communities, including mine. As a non-governmental organisation, it received donations from overseas companies – for example from the United States of America through USAID, Britain through the British Council and Canada through Kellog, based in Ontario, and OZ Engineering, a USA company in Arizona and also based in Ottery, Cape Town – just to mention a few. These funds were to be managed as efficiently as possible, and accountability was emphasised because every cent had to be accounted for.

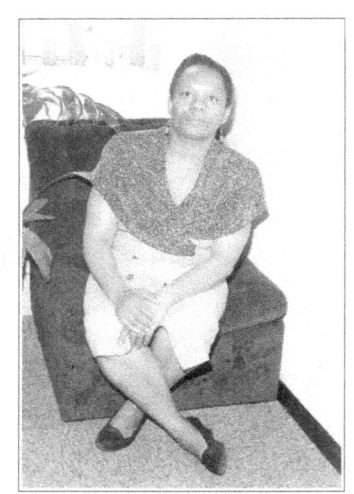

Photo: taken in reception

Hence, it had Trustee Board formed by credible individuals to oversee the overall running of the organisation. It was very interesting to witness how all of us from our different portfolios understood the importance of integrity and ethical behaviour.

It was cascaded down, even to those at a lower level to the tea maker and driver or messenger. The standard was of a high quality: simply the best. Annual reports to each donor agency were to be accurate and done on time, starting from capturing information to compiling the reports. EOC is one environment in which I experienced a high level of professionalism, integrity and ethical conduct or behaviour first hand. It was very empowering as well.

Photo: taken at one of EOC end of the year staff parties. I am the one seated in a white T-shirt, laughing the loudest at Magang Phologoane's jokes. I laughed so much that I even had my arms on my head. He was lying down behind me. Next to me is Lerato, standing in floral leggies. Also standing is Theo with Vincent sitting on a chair. Seated next to me is Jeniffer Koka and Vicky Malele. Those lying down are Seziwe Khoza in a navy blue skirt and white top; next to her is Puleng Zulu wearing a denim suit and Nomusa in a green suit. Across is William Langeveldt in a red cap, seated next to Buti Thlagale, Lentswe Mokgetle, Chris Mokodutlwa, Maggie Mncube, Ursula Mabokela, Lody Zulu, Khadidja and others. Surnames I have not mentioned is because I forgot them.

The EOC scholarship programme was under the leadership of Bishop Buti Thlagale as Chief Executive Officer (CEO) and Eleanor Molefe as his assistant. Some of the senior management at head office were Chris Mokodutlwa, Puleng Zulu, Magang Phologoane and those who joined later were Lulama Chakela, who managed the overseas scholarship programme, Lentswe Mokgatle and William Langeveldt, who both managed a newly established section which was Governance.

My main function, apart from being a student counsellor, was to ensure that once scholarships were advertised I screened all applications, short listed them, prepared for the interview process and oversaw student placements in almost 60 tertiary institutions in South Africa. It was the responsibility for me and two other officials to travel to all these institutions to conduct selection interview processes. At head office there were three student counsellors: Victoria Malele, Jennifer Koka and me. The position was that of middle management and required university qualifications, period. EOC also had regional offices with staff complements like head office.

I remember how I used to criss-cross the country, going for either selection interviews at so-called Bantustan universities or counselling sessions once students were placed. I used to spend a lot of time flying to all these places. My first experience on a flight was when I visited the then Bophuthatswana University, now Northwest. I was sent there alone. I was worried about flying for the first time. Once on the flight I was okay, and suddenly the plane went above the clouds, and I was thrilled. It was only about eight months since my mother had died and I looked out into the sky through that small window, and started wondering, now being above the clouds, how far it was from where my mother's spirit had gone. I stared into the blue sky and started thinking about her earnestly. Ultimately, I found myself crying. Luckily, I was sitting alone. I truly longed for her.

In no time, we arrived at Bophuthatswana airport, and there was someone from the university waiting for me. The interview panel was already waiting for me in the university board room. The reception was very good. We interviewed students for most of the day and completed the interviews. Once finished, I left for my flight back to Jan Smuts Airport, now OR Tambo. Going to the airport and coming back I had to arrange for transport. My husband took me and fetched me as well. I was so proud of myself, and I felt like a very important person (a dignitary).

After that, I spent more time in the air than on land, flying from province to province, either to meetings in provinces where we had offices, or for my routine work. That was such a great honour for me. My second trip was to Turfloop, in Lebowa, now Limpopo. It was not so pleasant because I missed my flight. I was so disappointed and worried about how I was supposed to get to the university, knowing very well that the panel and students were waiting for me, and it was my intention not to disappoint my organisation.

My husband suggested that we go to Noord Taxi Rank in town to catch a taxi to Pietersburg, now Polokwane, in the hope of finding another taxi to the university. I agreed. Fortunately, I did not struggle to find taxis to both Pietersburg and Turfloop and I arrived on time. Coming back, the university arranged transport for me to go and board a flight from Pietersburg airport. It was my most horrible trip. The small plane went through turbulence and we were thrown everywhere. I thought I was going to die. I was the only black person on the flight and that was my consolation because I thought that the pilot would do everything possible to not kill white people. I was so terrified that I found myself standing up and holding the seat and screaming every time it happened. I was relieved when we landed at OR Tambo airport. I truly thought it would crash and I was going to die.

Once students were successfully placed at tertiary institutions, I had to visit all the institutions of learning to ensure that they were properly settled and funded, according to each donor agency. Once they started with their lectures at tertiary institutions, it was my responsibility to visit them for counselling and check on their well-being. EOC had a good relationship with all these institutions. My job was also to coordinate the exchange students programme: that is students who were sent to South Africa from abroad in exchange with students living in South Africa going to those countries to study. The programme was sponsored by Fulbright.

Prior to the democratic elections in 1994, EOC developed a Public Administration (Governance) programme managed by Lentswe Mokgatle and William Langeveldt. The section provided training for politicians from various political organisations such as the African National Congress (ANC), Pan African Congress (PAC), Inkatha Freedom Party (IFP) and United Christian Democratic Movement (UCDM). The idea was to provide them with the relevant knowledge or know-how in preparation for the new democratic government, in anticipation of one of the black liberation organisations winning the election.

The focus was on macroeconomic policy analysis and included topics such as: Macroeconomic Framework, Budgetary Procedures, Fiscal Policy and Growth, Intergovernmental Relations, Policy Simulation, and Interdependence. Some of the people who attended were Amos Masondo, Bob Mabaso, Robert McBride, Paul Mashatile, Trish Hanekom and Jabu Moleketi from ANC, as well as Humphrey Ndlovu from Inkatha and a guy

I only knew as Gerald from ACDP and others. I do not remember anyone from PAC or AZAPO attending.

One of my colleagues, named Khadijha, and I were requested by management to attend so that we could assist with logistical arrangements. Training was done at Eskom Centre in Midrand. While there, we decided to attend the course after all the logistics were done. At the completion of the course in 1995, we too were issued with a certificate of attendance. The course was very informative and very empowering. I was grateful.

I recall when one day EOC held a function at the Parktonian Hotel and important guests were invited. One of the guests was Jonas Mosa Gwangwa. My father always mentioned Jonas' father Wilson, because they had grown up together as brothers. Their fathers were brothers.  Jonas' grandfather was older than ours. I was told that he left home when Jonas was little because of a family feud, but did not know anything else. His grandfather's home is the third house from my home (northern direction). Before I met him, I was told by one of my colleagues, Magang Phologwane, that he had married Jonas Gwanga's daughter while in exile. He introduced me to their children. I met his wife at the certificate presentation for the course attended and later Jonas' son Mojalefa, when he came to visit him at our offices.

My first encounter with Jonas Gwangwa was at the EOC function already mentioned. He was very happy to have met me and he never wanted to leave my side. He went and told his wife, Violet Molebatsi Gwangwa. She called me one day and introduced herself. My father had already passed on, over a year before meeting them. When we made an unveiling of their tombstones – I mean for both my parents – I told Violet, as it was very difficult to get hold of Jonas due to his busy schedule. She promised me that they would come to Kalkspruit, Limpopo, on the day of the unveiling. They came along with all his children. The Gwangwas were pleased to finally meet Jonas. He never looked back, and he decided to buy a house on the same street as mine, the third house to the other direction (south). It was such a pleasant reunion after many years apart, thanks to Magang Pholongwane.

While at EOC, I registered for my master's degree in development studies, which covered Public Administration, with Randse Afrikaans University (RAU), which is today called University of Johannesburg (UJ). I completed it within three years . But, by the time I graduated, I'd already joined government.

South African democratic local government elections were held in 1995. I was still working for EOC. I decided to campaign as a councillor, though I did not know what that entailed. I wanted to campaign for the African National Congress. Then it was the party familiar to most of us blacks. I approached the office. I was told that to be a candidate for ANC I must campaign under SANCO. Somehow, I did not want to campaign under SANCO but a reputable political organisation. Nonetheless, I approached SANCO, but I was told I must be a member first. That bothered me because to my knowledge local government elections are not so much about politics to start with, but about service delivery, and that should attract people who are passionate about that. What bothered and put me off the most was that, as I sat with them and discussed how the campaign would unfold, I was told that I must not worry because the ANC would win the elections anyway. But for me that was immaterial since, as a councillor, one must familiarise oneself with the constituencies. One could only do that by campaigning, including visiting people's homes, just to get to know their challenges. No one was interested in my line of thinking.

However, in the meantime I ran into a pamphlet distributed by the Democratic Patriotic (DP). They wanted black people to be part of their councillors as then the party was made up mainly by whites. Although I was still reluctant to campaign under the banner of any political party, I had never heard of independent candidates as an option. Besides, I did not have the capital to run a successful campaign on my own. I approached them, and they agreed to allow me to campaign under their banner. But the catch was that I had to register as a member. I swallowed my pride and became a member.

I did not trust a white political party, though I was for many years an admirer of Helen Suzman. On second thoughts, I said to myself that maybe this was my only opportunity to make whites pay back for oppressing and denying us blacks the good things they enjoyed. I decided to take advantage of their resources and use them to uplift my people: a payback strategy. I registered and attended their briefing sessions before starting with my campaign. This time I wanted to stand as a councillor with the idea of ensuring that the black communities I would be representing got the service they deserved after many years of oppression and exclusion. Fortunately, the DP shared my sentiment, and I had a lot in common with the party, as far as service delivery and running a clean government is concerned, though I did not agree with their political stands. The other things was that they had been running local elections for many years.

I remember one candidate who tried to campaign for the Pan African Congress (PAC). He could not scratch the surface because of the lack of funding. It was not all about the money, but money played a crucial role, partly because one needs resources to run an effective campaign: printing posters and pamphlets and so on. The ANC relied much on the fact that it was a popular party and the masses were desperate for change, so they would vote for the party, not individual candidates. I did not want that. I wanted people to vote for me, based on what I promised them during the campaign, so that they could hold me accountable.

I did not tell my employers, even when I went to a DP conference in the Cape, because I knew that they were ANC sympathisers, if not supporters. No one knew that I'd started with my campaigns and went into every house in Protea North. I recorded the houses I went to and happened to know my constituency. Most of the residents were happy with my campaigning strategy, but the problem was that they were not happy with the fact that I seemed to be campaigning for our oppressors.

I would explain what local government elections were about, but people were just sceptical, to the point that some would be angry. I remember one time when I was chased out of someone's house. It was then that I realised that many people who had come back from exile had rented or bought houses in Protea North and South. Some asked me why I was not campaigning for the ANC. What disturbed me was that the ANC councillor and a SANCO member was not campaigning. I always found him in the houses that sold liquor, drinking. He was not concerned that I was going house to house, trying to recruit people to join a white party because he knew that people were still anti-white, so few would be swayed otherwise.

I must say, the ANC councillor in the area was very mature and we got along very well. We even remained friends long after the elections because we respected each other. That is the level of political maturity this country needs.

To the contrary, some of my neighbours who were ANC members or sympathisers took it personally and hated me for being a sell-out. I remember an incident that took place during campaigning. The house of a lady who was campaigning for the Nationalist Party was damaged by residents who accused her of being a sell-out. During the last day of campaigning, called *Siya ixoba*, ANC members drove around the streets of Protea North and South and stopped at my house, shouting sell-out or *mpimpi*. My family was scared and we locked the house. I was not afraid of them, though. It was my right to have a freedom of association.

The elections took place, and I came second to the ANC, of course by big margin. I must say I ran a very powerful campaign and I want to believe that some of the developments that took place in Protea North after the elections happened because of my efforts.

My employers only knew about my role in the local government elections when they saw my name in the newspaper. Some of my colleagues were not pleased, but there was one colleague who was impressed and told me that what I had done was brave and a big sacrifice. He said that this was what democracy was all about. Coming from someone who had gone into exile, this was very encouraging. Unfortunately, I could not garner enough votes to become a councillor, but I was pleased with myself, especially when I'd finished campaigning and checked off the list I'd compiled, as well taking stock of my campaigning trail.

The highlight of my campaign was the fact that I did not take my people for granted but took them into confidence that I was willing to work for them and with them, to turn our lives around. This was evident from the records I kept, especially a list of all the houses I had visited in Protea North and South. Then the voting population of both suburbs was 877 people, and what made me proud was that I met all of them face to face, and I documented their stories one by one. I remember several residents telling me that they were so impressed with my campaign that if I had not been campaigning under the DP but for the ANC, they would have voted for me.

I understood because as black people we were never exposed to elections or running any government, so these issues were foreign to us. Hence, it is important to educate citizens about what elections and voting is all about and the importance thereof. It is also important that people should understand why it is necessary to change the electoral system of voting for parties in South Africa, rather than individuals. Nonetheless, I was not a stranger to some of the families. They were familiar with me because I used to sell kitchen curtains house to house, as I mentioned earlier.

After the 1994 democratic elections, it was evident that donor agencies were no longer interested in assisting black students educationally or academically, as it was anticipated that with the dawn of democracy the South African government would be able to fund education for black students. The EOC and its sister organisations, such as the South African Council of Churches, that managed funds for black students, were about to be closed because overseas donor agencies were withdrawing their funding. Hence, I worked for EOC until early 1996 and then joined government. I committed myself to serve my people further. I also wanted to pay back to the EOC for selecting me for a full scholarship programme and to assist other children to realise their dreams. So, I worked very hard for all my stay with the organisation: that is, three and half years. I was very grateful.

It was for the reasons mentioned above that I decided in 1995 that it was time for me to start applying for employment elsewhere. I was very reluctant to join government, because I was very sceptical of African leaders since I'd studied and majored in African Political Science and knew the reasons why Africa is in such a mess. I even cautioned my colleagues to be careful about joining government. However, I realised that the EOC ship was sinking and funds were drying up.

I was encouraged when I saw many government posts advertised in one of the newspapers. They were called "Jobs for Africa". They were advertised just after the local government democratic elections in 1995. The posts were for Gauteng Provincial Government's Department of Development Planning and Local Government. I was not familiar with issues related to Development Planning, but at least I had a theoretical knowledge of local government by virtue of having studied Public Administration. Those jobs that I applied for were all at Assistant Director Level. I could have applied for a higher position but, being myself, I thought that because I did not have any experience of working for government it would be wise for me to start at a certain level so that I matured with time in a new environment such as public service. I was short listed for the three of them and went for interviews and I was recommended for two to choose from.

My life in public service

My first point of entry in the Gauteng Provincial Government was in local government because I became successful in two vacancies I went to interview for. I chose the one for a researcher. I started working as a policy researcher in the Local Government Directorate, with Dan Mashitisho as director. My job was to research various policy-related issues so that a newly-established Department of Local Government ensured that ward councillors received appropriate support in the form of training and development. I was also to research how to have the best systems and procedures for effective service delivery etcetera, and write report proposals for the member of the Executive Council. Then the MEC was Sicelo Shiceka.

Women empowerment is always close to my heart. While still in the department, I motivated to the HOD, Silas Mbenzi, for permission to establish a Women's Forum for those in the lower ranks, such as cleaners. It was meant for women but did not exclude interested men *per se*. Before the notion of outsourcing services such as cleaning and security, all government departments hired their own staff on a permanent basis for manual labour such as cleaning. However, those who were already there had been absorbed from the old government. Hence, there was no talk of tenderpreneurs.

My aim in forming the forum was to try to motivate women in the department to uplift themselves in terms of improving their education. Some could not read and write because of their background. In most societies, women were not encouraged to go to school because of the patriarchal stereotype that it was not necessary, as they would only get married, have children, and look after their husbands.

I also wanted to raise awareness of many important aspects that affected women. I just needed a platform where women, even though on a small scale, could have some fruitful conversations. The meetings would be held during lunch time. Most of these women would consult with me on various issues, extending from job related to personal. The initiatives were supported by management, to an extent that when it was launched the MEC attended and the hall was packed to capacity as the rest of the department staff attended.

Before addressing us, the MEC and HOD called me to the podium. They introduced me to everyone and asked those in the hall to give me a standing ovation. I was truly honoured, especially since it was my first year in government. This gave me hope that things would change for the better, for us blacks in particular.

Unfortunately, I worked in the department for only one and a half years because while there I applied for promotional posts in other departments. I was called for an interview. I was interviewed by both Chief Director Lerato Phalatse and DG Vincent Mtambo. The following day my appointment was confirmed. It was a promotional post to Deputy Director level, also in Gauteng Provincial Government. I was placed in the DG's office, which is in the Office of the Premier. My task was to be an Assistant Secretary to the members of the Executive Council (EXCO). I liked the job because, as an Assistant to the Director General, I had an opportunity to witness policy formulation and decision-making processes. In the Department of Local

Government, as a line department, I had the opportunity to witness the process of policy implementation.

Although the Department of Local Government gave me exposure as far as the policy implementations are concerned, I was keener on knowing how they were formulated. As a graduate in Public Policy and Administration, I had a theoretical background and needed first hand practical experience. When I joined the Premier's Office, Tokyo Sexwale was the Premier. I enjoyed working with him during that short space of time because he was a hands on and down to earth person. I remember how I used to watch him showing the administrative staff how to lay the table, and arrange and present food for EXCO meetings. He was very meticulous about how EXCO meetings were managed. Then I was not sitting in meetings, as I was still going through an orientation process, but I was to ensure that all the logistics were in place before the meetings.

He resigned a few months later and Mathole Motshekga took over. That was when I started sitting in EXCO meetings and, when Premier Motshekga was recalled, Mbhazima Shilowa became Premier.

While still on probation, I was assigned the task of project managing the Public Service Excellence Programme. Although it was spearheaded from the Human Resource Section of the Department, I had to sit on the panel to represent the DG's Office. I felt truly honoured to be part of such an important initiative. When the awards ceremony took place, I was one of the officials present to issue certificate. In the picture is Premier Tokyo Sexwale on the far right Next to him is Dr Dudu Khoza. Next to her is me, and Lerato Phalatse is next to me. DG Vincent Mtambo is on the podium, handing award certificates to the winners.

I was not only sitting in EXCO meetings, but I was also managing and sitting in EXCO sub-committees and Heads of Department (HOD) meetings. My being in these strategic settings afforded me an opportunity to know what all the departments were proposing in terms of policies because all policy memoranda were received and analysed by my section, either for sub-committees or EXCO itself.

I found my work very fulfilling and it inspired me a lot. Being able to strike a balance between EXCO and its sub-committee meetings, where policy decisions were made, and at the same overseeing HOD meetings where the policy implementation was also fulfilled, was what I aspired to gain knowledge in. The Provincial Director General, Advocate Vincent Mtambo, chaired HOD meetings to give a better perspective and directive from EXCO as Head of the Secretariat. There was a director in the office, Judith Mackay, who also sat with me at EXCO from the Director General Unit, but her main responsibility was to manage Executive Decision Support and overall management of the administration of the secretariat section, to which my sub-directorate was attached.

According to hierarchy, in terms of reporting line I reported to her, and she reported to the Chief Director (CD) Lerato Phalatse. But, as far as decisions made from EXCO went, especially those that required urgent attention, I reported directly to the CD. Government is so bureaucratic, and it takes a long time to resolve things. Our other responsibility was to organise EXCO strategic planning meetings called Cabinet Lekgotlas.

Taken at Bakubung Lodge in Northwest where we attended one of the Lekgotlas.

I was, however, the one recording the proceedings and managing all the logistical arrangements for EXCO, sub-committees and HOD meetings. The skills, knowledge and experience I acquired in administration, organisation, coordination and research from my previous work with non-governmental organisations came in very handy. Overall, working in Public Administration's policy-making and implementation environment complemented my academic theoretical background. The linkage between policy decision and policy implementation processes made a perfect flow and gave me valuable understanding and a comprehensive exposure as the right direction for my growth. I worked for the department for five years. I wanted to make the secretariat function my career, especially on issues related to public policies.

I worked with the Director General, who truly inspired me and made me understand the importance of secretariat work to the point that someone from Canada was brought in to train me and the two assistant directors on secretariat work. He was a true technocrat, so working with him directly was such an honour. Over and above motivating and inspiring me, he made me realise my potential, as did the Chief Director. She was impressed by my writing, analytical and managerial skills, as well as my professionalism, and considered me to be the best person ever employed in EXCO. This was credited to the efficient and effective way I administered EXCO, subcommittees and HOD meetings.

We had six subcommittees that were run by assistant directors. I took two of them, including HOD meetings over and above EXCO. Administering and coordinating meetings, as well as minute taking, editing and proofreading my assistants' minutes and agendas, were a big part of our work. There was a stringent turnaround time for producing them. Not only that, but they were also to be accurate and precise. I was lucky because before I joined government I had done a secretarial course, so I was skilled in touch typing. I could type very fast and be accurate at the same time.

After being in government for five years, I realised that I was wrong and right at the same time. I was right in that, after a couple months of being there, I discovered practices or behaviours that did not sit right with me. I realised that some of the personnel had been appointed based on who they were and with whom they associated. When I initially applied for government posts, I decided to apply for a lower managerial position, because I wanted to mature with time in public service.

But, as we mingled and talked, I happened to learn that some people who were hired at middle and top management posts knew beforehand what those posts offered in terms of material things. They knew the type of packages they would receive: for example, cars and other luxurious things. I did not know anything about those things because I was trained that public service jobs revolve around serving the citizens of this country with humility, selflessness and integrity, coupled with a high level of professionalism and ethical behaviour.

The country was only two years into democracy, so the focus was to redress the imbalances of the past government. Already, positions were not filled according to merit but due to entitlement. My commitment became nothing but a fallacy because most of the people appointed at management level where not concerned about service delivery but about the type of cars they were to drive, the luxurious offices they were to occupy and the type of furniture. It was all about material issues. I observed that high positions were not filled through proper procedures, and the process therefore disregarded qualifications and experience required to fill those vacancies. Instead, one had to know someone or lick someone's ass to be recognised and considered for a promotional position.

I was wrong to have believed that South Africa would be different from all other African states lead by corrupt leaders. I was equally very wrong because those who joined the struggle felt a sense of entitlement for rewards. They forgot that everyone joined the struggle on a voluntary basis and that therefore no one owes anyone anything. The majority of them erased their memories of what the liberation struggle stood for. Most did not share the same sentiment that we should all practise selflessness, but for them the idea was to accumulate wealth for themselves, their friends and their families. Someone told me that he was there to enjoy eating broccoli and stocking his bedroom bar or mini fridge with all sorts of beverages that he would drink while watching television in bed and having sex.

My wasted eighteen years of working in public service as a whistleblower and how whistleblowing turned my life into a nightmare

I would like to mention from the outset that this section of my book is not about blame. Hence, I have avoided mentioning the full names of some individuals and have used abbreviations. Instead, it seeks to focus on what happened to me as a whistleblower because it is part of the sum total of my life history and also needs to be told.

How terribly wrong whistleblowing can go. This is something I have never spoken about openly, but I find it necessary to mention it in my autobiography because it is part of my life history. It touched strongly on important principles that I believe in and hold dearly: namely, integrity, professionalism, loyalty and above all the truth. A classic example was when I applied for a director position advertised in my unit. I was overlooked in that I was not even short listed, meaning that I did not qualify for interview so I could not participate fairly with all the other candidates who applied.

The above statement introduces this section of the book in that whistleblowing in government or public service is seen in a negative light rather than being encouraged. Hence, it has doubly dire consequences. It is critical that the protection for whistleblowers be emphasised. Like all whistleblowers, I had good reason for believing that wrongdoing existed. Over and above all, I also had evidence to back up those allegations and I firmly believed that exposing the wrongdoing would accomplish some public good. I was wrong. It was not about to accomplish any good at all, and only caused misery.

After exposing what I knew was wrong, I remember how I was called unpatriotic for exposing someone belonging to the ANC. I was referred to as a sell-out, working for the DA against the ANC government. It was implied that I was a spy. It is this ignorant perception that removes the perpetrator from wrongdoing and focuses on the whistleblower.

I agree with Mark Twain when he said, "Patriotism is supporting your country all the time, and your government when it deserves it". Those who perceive themselves as government and a law unto themselves, must deserve and not just be entitled. On the other hand, John Lewis once said: "Never, ever be afraid to make some noise and get in good trouble, necessary trouble". Whistleblowing is a good and a necessary trouble.

But what is a whistleblower and why is it important? According to Wikipedia, "a whistleblower is an employee who discloses information that the individual reasonably believes is evidence of gross mismanagement; gross waste of funds; an abuse of authority; a substantial and specific danger to public health or safety; or a violation of law, rule or regulation." On the other hand, whistleblowing is when someone raises concerns about wrongdoing, usually within a work context in a public, private or governmental organisation. You may also hear it referred to as "raising the alarm", "making a disclosure" or "speaking up".

Five years down the line, the scepticisms I had before joining government were confirmed. I was right about South Africa becoming like all the African states. After joining government in the public service, all that I saw was naked corruption in the form of nepotism, maladministration and mismanagement. It had become a norm and was something that for me was difficult to turn a blind eye to. When I decided to speak out, I was met with astonishing arrogance and a sense that told me that senior government officials think that they are above everyone, as well as the law. These very same people, because of the way they were put in those positions, do not produce the quality of work or maintain the level of productivity of which they should be capable.

Those who have proper qualifications but are looked down at because of not having proper connections become disgruntled. This is often attributed to the fact that workers will often be restrained from speaking their mind out for fear of reprisal. The predominant cause, however, is likely to be underutilisation of the potential and capabilities of workers by under-qualified and inexperienced management. Hence, employees in government are frequently bored and uninvolved, and this may contribute to their level of productivity falling below their real potential. The issue of employee motivation remains a crucial one in public service.

Reverting back to my whistleblowing saga. One morning, I passed the reception area. A receptionist was sitting there with some officials, and one of them, TM, spoke loudly as I passed that some people who'd applied for a procurement director post in the department were wasting their time. She said the post was hers because she knew which button to press. I did not take note of that and walked away. The following week, I met one of my colleagues in a lift, and he told me that he had been selected onto one of the interview panels for the procurement director post in my unit. I told him that I did not know why I had not been called for an interview. He told me that it was because I had not been short listed, and continued to say that the interview was just a formality as there was someone already earmarked for it. He said, "I came to your floor because they had a briefing with DG on whom to recommend for the post". I asked him who? He said, "It is TM from another unit". he was concerned that she did not even have tertiary education, let alone experience on the job. I immediately remembered what she'd said at reception. She had known that I'd applied, and she was addressing me; in fact, mocking me.

The interview took place and the very same week it was announced that TM had been appointed as a new director in the unit in question. The following day, I lodged a grievance with the HR Chief Director, wanting to know why I had not been short listed, even though I had the required tertiary qualifications and experience.

I guess the Chief Director informed DG that I'd lodged a complainant. Upon hearing that, he confronted me and said, "Ja, you troubled woman, what do you think you are doing? Stop that rubbish of trying to question HR's decision."

I said, "I did nothing wrong other than questioning why I was not short listed".

He pointed a finger at me and repeated, "You must stop if you do not want to get in trouble".

Later, out of curiosity, I asked some of my colleagues, "What does touching the right buttons mean". I was told that it referred to a situation where some women would seduce powerful men, probably sleep with them, in exchange for promotions. This went to an extent that they would blackmail them if they did not comply with what had initially been agreed upon. What is more common is when these powerful men abuse young women by sleeping with them with a promise of higher positions.

To my shock, one day, long after I'd left the Premier's Office and was with the Gauteng Liquor Board, this young woman who'd just joined the department on a contract basis was confiding to some of my colleagues that one of the Chief Directors wanted her to sleep with him. She said that he'd promised her a permanent job, but she said the idea of having sex with him made her feel bilious. One of the permanent staff members told her to sleep with him because it was the only way she would be employed permanently. She further advised her to close her eyes and do as he wanted.

My goose bumps were induced by just the thought, but I opted just to keep quiet, as if I had heard nothing, because the rot in government manifested itself in too many tentacles and it is scary. In fact, one of the reasons I kept quiet was that some of my colleagues believed that I must have slept with some people to get to the level I was.

The plan to write to the Premier about our grievances was already in motion and DG's behaviour was a pushing factor to go ahead, because clearly he, in my view, was not going to stop his glaringly corrupt tendencies.

It all started with the memorandum I wrote to the Gauteng Government Premier, MS. I was not happy with the way the Director General (DG) Reverend LWM was appointing people to vacant positions without following proper procedure, let alone qualifications. It was also about how state resources were abused and some people were favoured over others whenever internal vacant posts were to be filled. I decided to do something about it. I spoke to two of my colleagues, EM and IL. I trusted them and we always confided in one another regarding the frustrations that we endured in the Director General's Office.

Our plan was to make the Premier aware of our concerns. We sat down one day during lunch break and drafted a ten-page-long memorandum. On second thoughts, though, I thought it might be wise to talk with the Premier first and hear what he said. I could not secure an appointment with him for about two weeks, and I realised that time was running out. I suggested to my colleagues that we go ahead with the memorandum. I volunteered to type it.

Once I'd finished typing it, I made copies for each of us to take home, to go through the draft for the purpose of editing before sending it off. The three of us committed to keeping the whole matter confidential. We agreed to meet the following day to finalise the edited version together, before sending it to the Premier's Office, which we did. As they say, Satan or temptation walks with us, and one of our colleagues decided to leak the memorandum the very same evening that I was to correct the final version and send it out the following day.

In the memorandum we complained about, among other things, how one of our colleagues had been promoted to director level without the required qualifications. I was amongst those who'd applied and I was not short listed, even though the post was in my unit and I had experience and qualifications. I had lodged my grievance with our Human Resource Department, but they'd all ignored me. It was not the first time and it had happened much too often since the DG had taken office.

At a deputy director level, it was my task to manage the unit's staff development, performance, filling of posts and procurement. But, more than once, when we had to fill vacant posts, I would advertise with, of course, DG's permission, and follow the normal recruitment policy and procedure with the assistance of Human Resource Unit until the process was completed. Once the process was complete, I would submit recommendations made in the form of a report for DG. Then to follow would be a placement of the successful candidates. But he would override the panel's recommendations and demanded that we appoint the people he had earmarked, even though they did not qualify.

One time, he instructed me to appoint someone who was not even one of the short listed candidates, and she had not been interviewed. In fact, he demanded that I not carry on with the selection interview process as he'd already found someone. The vacant post was for his personal assistant (PA). The vacant post in question was at a higher grade than what was required for a PA. I tried to reason with him, but he insisted that his decision was final, and the person would be starting at the beginning of the month.

He later asked me to procure a government vehicle for a messenger, because we realised that it was very strenuous for our messenger to be walking from one department to another, delivering EXCO memoranda packs. I welcomed that, especially from a security point of view, because EXCO memoranda were treated as strictly confidential. Again, memoranda would come in bulk and were very heavy for the person to carry around. Over and above this, the messenger was not only delivering EXCO packs but other correspondence.

The vehicle was purchased, but to my disappointment it was not used for the intended purposes but for his personal errands. The driver, hired by government, and the government vehicle, were used to transport his children. They were fetched every day from school, dropped at his office so that he travelled home with them after work. I realised that there was a problem, and it was not something that I could turn a blind eye to any longer. All these things were filed because all government trips were recorded on a log sheet. I complained to him about this, but he could not care.

The worst thing was that there was someone who was appointed at a director level to oversee developments and manage his office and my unit. The person was rarely at work and, even if she were at work, she spent most of the time doing things not job related. I also raised that with him several times as a matter of concern, but he would not do anything about it, and I continued doing her work, especially her function during EXCO proceedings.

One fateful afternoon, I wanted DG to sign a memorandum that I had compiled to the HOD for one of the line departments, as it was his responsibility, and it was urgent. I heard him talking in the passage not far from my office. I'd just finished printing the memo and was about to take it to his office for his signature when I heard him talking in the reception area that was between his office and mine. I stood up to take the memo to him, but he was no longer in reception nor in his office.

One of his junior assistants, AS, told me that he was around, and must have gone to the toilet. I waited for a while, and when he did not show up, AS went to look for him, but he was not there. We started looking around and calling for him. I was running out of time and felt frustrated, but we were all surprised because it was not so long ago that he had been walking around. He definitely did not leave our office precinct because my office entrance faced the lifts and I would have seen him going out.

The lady at reception suggested that we open the office next to mine because the last time she'd heard him talking was at that spot. I was reluctant because he should have heard us calling him if he were in that office, even when the door was closed, but she insisted. The door was not locked. DG was hiding behind the door with one of my colleagues who had been seconded to our offices from another unit. They were kissing and we just stood there, puzzled. This was the lady TM I mentioned earlier, regarding the funny remarks she made about pressing the right buttons. I could not believe my eyes. I was shocked; AS too. As if that were not enough, in a few weeks' time TM was appointed as a director.

Talking about touching the right button, the very same lady was heard spreading the rumours that she'd run into DG with a lady colleagues from a different unit in his office in a very compromising situation. The lady was later promoted to a high position. The DG pleaded with her not to tell anyone, and she agreed with one condition: that he promote her. The thing is that in government promotional post do not come by so easily. When they do, they are advertised and people compete for them. Otherwise, one has to create a post and it is a long process, as the public service is highly regulated. As she grew impatient, she started blackmailing him; hence, the secondment to our offices at a higher post from the one she was in before. But, she was not satisfied. She wanted a director-level post.

Talking about promotions, the official who was with me when we found DG in a compromising situation was also promoted from admin officer to assistant director level. She was rewarded for refusing to confess that she was with me when we found DG.

Reverting back to the leaked memorandum meant for the Premier. The morning following the leaked memorandum, everything seemed normal until I was called to DG's office. With him were the Premier's political advisor AM, the Premier's spokesperson TM, and two of my colleagues. DG demanded to know why I had written degrading lies about him. He asked me directly, but I did not know what he was talking about. He threw the memo on the desk right in front of me and I immediately recognised it. I was puzzled as to how he'd got hold of it because it was only the three of us who knew about it, and we'd agreed that we would sign it that day, before it was sent off to the Premier's Office. One of my colleagues had leaked it to TM, the official who had just been promoted to director level, and she'd called DG and arranged that he got it before the following day.

In the said meeting, DG insisted that I explain the content of the memorandum. I looked at it and acknowledged that I had knowledge of it, but mentioned that the draft in my possession was not yet signed nor delivered to the Premier. I told him that I could not comment on the one that he had, as it was not from me. I asked him to direct that question to the person who'd availed it to him. DG tried to threaten me by demanding that I withdraw it. I said that I could not because someone must know about it and had intervened. He became very angry and desperate when I would not budge and told him that I was committed to exposing him. He told me that I would not go far, as he was highly connected.

As mentioned, TM2 and AM were in the meeting. It was TM2 who politely requested I withdraw the memo. I refused. I guess he knew what I was getting myself into and he was worried about me. Nothing could have prepared me for what was to unfold. I said to DG that I was prepared to do what I meant to do as a responsible citizen of this country. He turned grey and shrank. I saw the Premier's advisor AM shaking. Those who met him on the way to his office saw him missing the door to his office and banging his head against the glass. I was told that they had seen him shaking his head and murmuring something, but he never said a word to anyone. I was told that after that meeting he knocked off and went home. He just took off.

When I left the meeting, I felt more courageous and determined. I was not afraid. My colleagues were. I asked them what had happened, and one of them confessed to having leaked it out of fear. Then I still did not have any safety concerns and no threats had been made to my life. I personally had never spoken publicly about the issues. Hence, after the meeting I went straight to my office and carried on with the day's tasks.

This reminded me of one of Maya Angelou's quotes: "One is not necessarily born with courage, but one is born with potential. Without courage, we cannot practise any other virtue with consistency. We cannot be kind, true, merciful, generous, or honest." There is nothing greater than that you can say, "GOD, Thank You, Thank You".

While still in the meeting, DG warned me that I was going to regret what I had done and he adjourned the meeting. Later in the day, the Premier's PA MG issued me with a strongly worded letter of response. The leaking of the letter saved my life, in the sense that I had not known the danger I was putting myself into. All that I'd wanted was to do the right thing. I did not feel vulnerable and under threat and nothing could have prompted me to publicly voice my dismay about DG's behaviour if I had not been certain about it. It was only when the Premier's PA responded to my memo that I felt uncomfortable. If it had not been leaked so that everyone knew about it, my safety as would instantly have been at risk. If I stayed silent and did not report the matter to the Public Protector and other relevant institutions, as well as using the usual channels as I'd intended to do, I was also at risk.

Initially, they tried to make it look as if I were the one who leaked the letter, even though the person who did had confessed straight away. The idea was to try and implicate me, and find a reason to get rid of me. Ironically, when they gave me a charge sheet, the leaking of the document was not part of the content because they could not justify that.

When I realised what was happening, I made a conscious decision that I was not going to retract from the memorandum. In the same breath, I knew that they would not fire me for exposing the truth because my God is for the truth. I lived up to my conviction that I had started it and I must finish it.

I went back to my office and continued working as if everything was normal. I was busy preparing for EXCO minutes to be distributed the following day to MEC offices. Adhering to turnaround times was a task I always took very seriously because in that environment one cannot compromise efficiency. Politicians do not take kindly to inefficiency and there was just no room for mistakes or delays.

The following day, I got to work early to ensure that all logistical arrangements and recording systems were ready. I went to the kitchen to have my breakfast while the MECs came in one by one and helped themselves to breakfast. I was about to go back into the board room, after the Premier had arrived, because it was my responsibility to take him through the Premier's notes, as per matters enrolled on the agenda.

I did not see DG coming behind me, until he poked a finger right between my shoulders and I looked back. He looked very angry and stressed up. He instructed me not to sit in on the EXCO meeting proceedings because as far as he was concerned I was suspended. I refused and I went on to perform my duties.

I did not know whether the MECs where aware of anything. I was not very concerned about DG's threats and intimidation because I knew that even if he suspended me I would fight while at the same time allowing disciplinary processes to take their course.

I left after the meeting, and knocked off. EXCO meetings were strenuous, and I was emotionally tired as well. I needed to go and re-charge. Otherwise, I would have stayed until late to draft minutes before leaving for home. That helped me to remember all the details while still fresh in my mind.

I told my husband about the whole thing. He panicked, and he was very worried. I had to stay strong, for my family.

The next day, I went to work, but since the memo was already leaked I decided to finish perfecting it. I did not want to involve my colleagues because one of them had leaked the draft and the trust was broken into pieces. I knew I was on my own, and it was a fight I would have to fight alone. There was no going back. I also just knew that I had to involve God in the whole matter because I was aware of what happened to people who blew whistles on corruption, especially on high profile public servants.

While still working on it, a colleague and friend of mine from another directorate DK called me, and warned me that people from the Labour Unit, including MJM – I never knew his first name in full as everyone referred to him by surname – and AO had been instructed to investigate me. She further alerted me that they would be coming to ensure that I was served with a suspension letter the very same day and advised me to ensure that the memo reached the Premier immediately. I did exactly that. I personally went and delivered it to his office and found the assistant PA to the Premier, MG. She signed for it. She was one of the officials I got along with very well.

I went back to my office and continued working. In the afternoon, the assistant PA came running to my office, very furious. She had been blamed for being my friend and she was suspected to be the one who gave me information. The other thing was that, when I could not secure an appointment with the Premier, I'd asked her to provide me with the Premier's mobile phone so that I communicate with him directly. She had given it to me but had cautioned me that her senior did not want her to give his telephone number to other people. But I was not other people *per se* – I was serving him – so by right I should have all communication channels to both DG and the Premier.

She was told that she was not supposed to have provided me with the number as I was troublesome. She suspected that I'd told them that I'd got it from her, but I had not. They just speculated correctly. The Premier did not return any of the messages I left on his mobile telephone. I was very puzzled and hurt because I had thought that MG and I got along very well; her outburst took me aback.

Everything happened so fast that I did not have a chance to dispute the allegations. She was not even interested in hearing my side of the story; she just wanted to tell me to get out of her life before I compromised her job. I never spoke to her again until 2007, when she called me requesting that we meet at the coffee shop. She came to apologise. I'd even forgotten about the incident and I assured her that I understood her anger. Of course I did, but things had gone awfully wrong.

I went home and the following day at about 10h00, officials from our Labour Unit came to my office and told me that I was under investigation and served me with a suspension letter. I was to vacate my office immediately. They threw me out of my office like a common criminal and all that I managed to take with was my belongings. Anyway, I did not need anything from them, as I was not going to do my work at home. I was grounded. Blowing the whistle was my only sin, though they argued that it was not about me telling the truth but about how I did it. No one ever substantiated that, other than saying that I'd brought the office into disrepute. That was a buzz word.

Giving me an outright suspension rather than a precautionary warning, where they could have transferred me to another unit, was a blessing in disguise, in that the chances of been trapped and dismissed with the click of a finger were very high. Being at home was safe. Though I was mindful of the fact that my job was hanging by a thread either way, I had the opportunity to clear my head and plan my battle strategy constructively. One thing I knew was that, if I hung on the wings of a prayer in faith and with the knowledge that my Lord is bigger than anything, I could relax.

However, I must mention that on a personal level I worked very well with DG. He was very impressed with my performance and my ability to work under pressure doing what I used to refer to as a dog's job. Even when he suspended me, he made it a point that I was rated for a yearly performance agreement.

The method that government uses to assess employee's performance in Public Service is called the Performance Management and Development System (PMDS). I was rated five, which is the highest rating. It was not for the first time though, because almost every year I received high scores. I was remunerated for my good performance, not that he was doing me any favours. I worked very hard for that recognition, so I deserved my reward. But he could have decided to abuse his power by not approving my high score as a way of punishing me. Managers in some units used that as a punitive measure against employees they were not on good terms with. In essence, PMDS was meant to reward people rather than punish them, and I credited him for that.

One-year suspension on full pay

The following week, after I had been sent home on suspension, I was called to come to the office. I was issued with an acknowledgment letter from the Premier's Office. It was signed by Premier MS himself. I was also to meet with the office's Deputy Director General (DDG) SB, my representative from NEHAWU, ST and two Labour Unit officials. The DDG told me that he had been assigned by the Premier to deal with the matter. He was only to deal with the content of the letter I'd addressed to the Premier and not the leaked document.

They informed me that I would remain officially suspended, and an independent investigator would be appointed to investigate the matter. He also indicated that I would be requested to avail myself whenever they want me to provide them with evidence. I told them that I would prefer to talk to them through my representative from the union, but they still wanted me to come in.

In the meeting I was notified that the allegations I had made were very serious. My union representative asked them why I was to be suspended rather than the person I'd exposed. It became crystal clear that they were not actually dealing with the content of the letter I'd furnished them officially, but with the leaked one. This was evident from how they contradicted themselves in trying to answer my representative's question. For them, I was in the wrong because they felt that I had leaked a memo in which I had made damaging and unfounded

Umnyango ka Ndunankulu
Department of the Premier

Lefapha la Tonakgolo
Departement van die Premier

Ref:	MS 3/8/6
Tel:	(011) 355-6234
Cell:	082 435 4297
Fax:	(011) 355-6230
Date:	03 August 1999

MEMORANDUM

TO : Thea Aboud
Deputy Director: Finance and Administration

FROM : Dulckerine Budricks
Assistant Director: Financial Management and Auxiliary Services

Virement of funds

Please be informed that as there are:

1. not enough funds available on item 1094 [Transport: Air (inland)], standard item B000 [Administrative], and
2. no funds available on item 1041 [Transport: car hire], standard item B000 [Administrative],

the attached payment cannot be processed.

It would be appreciated if you could approve the virement of funds by completing the attached form [Annexe A].

Please note that the as the shifting of funds between standard items are subject to the approval of the Accounting Officer and Treasury approval, it is recommended that funds be shifted within a standard item. This will ensure that payments are processed without delay.

Regards,

Dulckerine Budricks
Assistant Director: Financial Management and Auxiliary Services

This was one of such memoranda written to DG.

The Story of a Rural Girl Who Kept Rising and Rising

allegations about DG, and through that I'd brought the office into disrepute.

The DDG instructed me to provide them with documentation as hard evidence to substantiate my allegations. I could read anger and hatred on DDG and the labour officials' faces, even hear it in the tone of their voices. I agreed to do that. I was told that my colleagues who'd agreed to support me in exposing DG had withdrawn and had done so in writing as well as under oath.

One of my colleagues, IL, whom I'd consulted when writing the letter to the Premier, told me that they were coerced into confessing that they did not agree with the content of the letter. MJM had threatened them and instructed them to do it in writing. However, he said that he refused to lie. He told me that this was the reason why he was never promoted. ESM agreed to do it and she was promoted from administrative clerk to assistant director level, jumping four levels. He made me copies of those letters and I took them home for filing. I stayed at home for about a year before the investigation began.

Before I was thrown out of my office like a common criminal after the leaked memorandum, I'd already started working very hard to collecting valuable and credible information as evidence, so that I could give my case a solid backing. Every time I got hold of information, I would take it home and started compiling files. This was in preparation for when the letter would have been sent to the Premier, because I knew that they would need evidence because "she/he alleges must prove".

The truth is that I could not have pulled the whole thing off if it were not for the assistance I received from some officials in the internal Financial Management and Auxiliary Services Directorate. For example, the deputy director responsible offered to make copies of documents relating to the purchasing of cars, trip authorities and log sheets, but only those that concerned DG.

According to the Deputy Director Thea Aboud, DG had the tendency to force them to release the funds whenever he wanted to purchase something without following proper procedures. Even though they did not agree with such behaviour, their director would often access funds and they were frustrated. The director in question was one of the first officials who jumped ship upon hearing that PP was coming to investigate the office. He did not have the required qualifications for the post.

I am forever grateful to both Thea and her assistant Dulckerine Budricks for having assisted me with copies of the necessary information, otherwise it would have been difficult for me to prove my allegations. It was through their help that I managed to compile six lever-arch files of documentary evidence relating to the unlawful trip authorities, including information on recruitment processes I undertook, etcetera. I was told later that one of the officials informed DG that both Thea and her assistant were helping me with the information. Then, DG transferred Thea immediately to Corporate IT as punishment. She resigned a few years later. When the Office of the Premier was requested to return me to my workstation, after the attempt to dismiss me failed, they instead transferred me to Corporate IT to fill the vacant post left by Thea.

I was called to avail myself to the office time and again. I had an oral interview with DDG and employees from the Labour Unit. They wanted me to verbally give them a detailed account of what I said, that is elaborate on the content of the letter I wrote to the Premier. I repeated myself so many times that it became so monotonous that I almost lost it. I suspect that they hoped that I would contradict myself. My representative informed them that it was better that I elaborate in writing because I'd already provided them with the information they were asking for repeatedly. I wrote them a document in the form of a letter of about 15 pages, substantiating every allegation made.

I also requested some of my colleagues, especially those who had left the office, to support me. Two of them, Mono Mashaba and Phillips, put their testimony in writing about their experiences with the DG and supported everything I said. I am very grateful to them for their loyalty and honesty. They gave weight to my case and made so much difference.

They stated that one of the reasons that they'd left was because of the shoddy way DG ran the office. They were both my assistants and had sat with me in most of the interviews held to fill the vacant posts.

I made copies of all the evidence I collected and filed it neatly for them in six lever-arch files and submitted these to them. I made it a point that the DG's PA signed that she'd received them every time I submitted.

After five months, they called me to meet the team I referred to above. I was informed that they'd found an external investigator who was introduced to me, and I was to come every time the investigator wanted to question me.

My first encounter with him was very unpleasant and intimidating, almost hostile. He twisted every word I said and disregarded my representative from the union. I was never scared. I knew that my God was with me and I just believed. The whole situation frightened everyone in the office in that most colleagues asked me to stop being stubborn and retract. I was told that the officials I was working with were very dangerous. I did not agree with them that I was stubborn in this regard. I would much rather call myself determined, because I never budge on my belief or principles because I am a doer. I set a clear goal of winning the case by carrying it through from start to finish, and it did not matter what pressure was brought to bear. I always thrive under pressure: that is my nature. I knew I was not going to give up. I've never given up on anything I've started, even when life gets hard.

Internal labour investigators started calling me at home and tried to intimidate me. They wanted to come to my house so that they could ask me further questions. I refused and reminded them that I would not speak to any one of them in the absence of my union representative. They stopped calling me, but started writing me letters. I received two registered letters from the Director General's attorney, instructing me to withdraw my allegations about DG, otherwise they would proceed in suing me for defamation of character. In the letter, he even mentioned the amount of R500 000 that I would pay once the court instructed me too.

I was not about to be frightened. Instead, I was more than willing to continue fighting. I realised that they were going to ensure that I was dismissed, and the case dragged on for almost a year.

However, no number of threats and intimidations were going to make me change my mind, no matter how many registered letters I had to collect from post office. I was appalled by their ignorance as they continued on the very same trajectory of using government resources for their own selfishness. For example, the registered letters sent to my address were from Human Resource Chief Directorate. Intimidating letters delivered by their messengers and personnel were sent by the DDG's office through the Security Unit and he was driving a government car and using taxpayers' time. Death threats and telephone calls made by some individuals from the Labour Unit were made from the government land line telephones, using government time and money. In all these things the one thing that I was clear about was that what I had started must be accomplished.

The harassment continued, even though one of the ladies who worked in the Labour Unit wrote a Memorandum to the DG and told him that after reading my letter she believed that I did not deserve to be investigated. Meanwhile, he, as a culprit, was not investigated. She mentioned that what I'd stated in the memo, and the evidence I'd furnished them with in the form of correspondence, she believed. The person to be investigated and suspended was DG, she concluded. She made it a point that I got a copy and I filed it.

DG did not agree with her and still maintained that I must be investigated with possible dismissal. Her point of contention was that as government we encourage people to expose corruption and the Premier had a hotline number in that regard. Ironically, when people do speak out, they are flushed out, especially when it was the most powerful officials who were exposed. I was told that DDG mentioned the content of her memo in one of the meetings he held with staff. The issue was minuted, and one of my colleagues gave me a copy of those minutes. I was told that when the matter was discussed at EXCO level, by virtue of me having been an assistant secretary to it, one MEC shared the same sentiment. He informed them that he agreed with me, but it was only one lone voice in the wilderness. The labour employee was later forced to resign.

It dawned to me that I was going to have a tough time. I could already sense that I was being harassed and intimidated and I said to myself that I had to put up a good fight if I were to survive the whole ordeal. Indeed, I stepped on too many toes, and they were all ganging up against me for their survival.

The first thing I thought of doing was to write a letter to the Public Protector while still on suspension. They responded and acknowledged receipt of my letter, but also mentioned that they had a backlog of cases and that they therefore might not be able to attend to my matter soon, though they were aware of the urgency.

As they say, everyone has an angel. While still on suspension, one of my colleagues, who had also been dismissed for questioning the way in which DG was running the office, contacted me. He was employed in Corporate Services, that is, the unit in which Human Resources, Labour and Persal were located. They all fall under the Premier's Office. He was checking on me after having heard that I had been suspended.

I told him about my situation as well as my whereabouts, and he immediately wanted to assist me. He had a law qualification and understood labour relation issues very well. He told me that if I did not get as much as information as soon as possible before the disciplinary hearing, the likelihood was that they would dismiss me, and I should try to prevent that. He asked me to meet him the following day so that we could discuss it further. We met and he investigated various sections of labour law, especially around disciplinary processes.

Vika then suggested that I personally go the Department of Public Service Commission, Public Protector (PP), Human Rights Commission (HRC) and Gender Commission offices to register with them my grievance, because I was being unfairly treated. Vika accompanied me, and we literally went and knocked at every door in the hope that those relevant institutions would assist me. It was difficult. Vika also emphasised the fact that I should not rely on the representative from my labour union either. He told me how he had been sacrificed. I took his advice and told myself that I had to survive. The only Person I relied on above all was God. I gave it to Him because I knew that the truth is His. I also believed that He was using me to tell the truth. I made a point to pray around it and bind it to Him.

The reason that Vika insisted on me going personally to the relevant offices was that writing letters was not going to work, especially knowing the challenge government has with officials who rarely answer telephones. He also added that I did not have the luxury of time as the hearing date was already decided upon. Before I could digest what he was telling me, he volunteered to transport me as I did not have a car. We planned to spend a day moving from one institution to another. They are all in Tshwane, except for HRC and the Gender Commission, which are in Johannesburg. The Public Protector and HRC showed some interest and wanted to help me. I had meetings with HRC representatives twice, but they retracted after I'd provided them with the information they required to support my case. I never knew the reasons.

The Public Protector Advocate Selby Baqwa secured an appointment to have an interview with me a few days after I went to see them personally. My new-found friend and former colleague volunteered to accompany me to their offices as he had a car. I met the Public Protector himself first and he asked me several questions and informed me how the whole interview process would unfold. I told him that I did not have much time because they had already scheduled a disciplinary hearing in five days to come, on the 26th of July 2000.

I was relieved when PP assured me not to worry about everything; they would take care of it. He later introduced to me two officials, Advocates Millicent Shai and Ms Brenda Monareng, who both worked in his office, and informed me that they would be dealing with me directly. I made it a point that I took everything with me that I deemed necessary, including my six

REPUBLIC OF SOUTH AFRICA

PUBLIC PROTECTOR
MOSIRELETSI WA BATHO • MOŠIRELETŠI WA BATHO
MUSIRHELELI WA VANHU • MUTSIRELEDZI WA VHATHU
OPENBARE BESKERMER • UMKHUSELI WABANTU • UMVIKELI WABANTU

☎ (012) 322 2916 • Fax (012) 322 5093   ✉ Private Bag X677 Pretoria 0001   228 Visagie Street Pretoria

Ref: 7/2-0770/00

26 July 2000

Attention: Mr. S Bolton

The Acting Director-General
Private Bag X61
MARSHALLTOWN
2107

Fax no.: (011) 834 9177

Dear Mr. Bolton

**COMPLAINT: INFORMATION DISCLOSED BY MRS L MALEKA
RE: MEETING WITH THE PUBLIC PROTECTOR**

Our telephone conversation this morning refers.

This is to confirm our agreement that subsequent to the discussion referred to above the disciplinary hearing will not proceed today as you had previously arranged.

I further confirm the agreement to meet on Friday, the 28th of July 2000 at 12h00 at our office in Pretoria, 228 Visagie Street, Sinodale Building – 9th Floor.

Your co-operation will be highly appreciated.

Yours Faithfully

ADV S A M BAQWA, SC
PUBLIC PROTECTOR

lever-arch files, to prove to them that I knew my story and I had evidence to that effect.

The disciplinary interview started at 10h00 in the morning, and I was grilled. There were tapes and microphones everywhere, and it lasted until 20h00 in the night. I did not have transport of my own and if it were not for the godsent angel Vika Ngubane, who then owned a vehicle, I would not have been able to move with the speed that I did. This is the reason I referred to Vika Ngubane as my guardian angel because he came at just the right place and time. I was only assisting him with petrol expenses. He not only helped me with transport, but he also took me through the disciplinary hearing process documentation. He thoroughly educated me on those issues.

The following day, was Thursday and I received a fax letter from a senior advocate in the Public Protector's office. The fax was addressed to the DDG in the Premier's Office, instructing them not to go ahead with the disciplinary hearing. The reason given was that his office would like to do their own investigations. He further told him that my allegations were thoroughly substantiated and genuine, so they warranted thorough investigation. They disputed their investigator's report as biased.

While I was at the Public Protector's office, they told me about many whistleblowers who had been institutionalised at mental or psychiatric hospitals for having done what I did. I remembered DG's utterances when he referred to me as a troubled woman. In other words, they think they own people and are untouchable, so a person who questions or challenges them is considered as being unstable in their head: mad. Hence, they would recommend that such a person go for psychiatric help, knowing that once one is there one would never come back a normal person because they would mess with your brains as the apartheid system did to many. As a Reverend, he should have known better that there is not any mightier than the One above, our Maker. After the interview, I briefed Vika about what had transpired inside the boardroom, as he had not been allowed to accompany me in, and told him how grateful I was for what he had done for me.

A few days after I'd visited their offices, the news of PP coming to investigate the allegations I'd made spread like wildfire. The majority of senior staff members panicked, and all hell broke loose in the office. There was a staff exodus of senior managers. Those who had only Matric or a senior certificate or less, but were holding director and Chief Director posts that required a degree, resigned. In fact, I had not informed my union representative about our plan to seek a second opinion on the issue, because I realised that he was already succumbing to their pressure and the matter was becoming messier and messier. I realised that he was going to compromise me. He was very unhappy with the fact that I had gone to seek assistance whilst he was there. I told him that I had to fight for my career survival and the right to earn an income and, from where I stood, he was not the one to rescue me because he was giving up.

The first thing I did was to thank those colleagues who had stood by me and had supported me in many ways. I threw a small party for them at my house as a way of showing my appreciation and gratitude. I invited Stan Sithole, Mono Mashaba, Isaac Lebina and Peter Ledwaba. Isaac did not come. Maybe he was still afraid to associate with me publicly for fear of reprisals. Vika could not come as he had already left for KwaZulu-Natal (KZN), from where he came.

Lifting of my one-year suspension and subsequent solitary confinement

First Secondment

After one year of being paid for doing nothing, I was told that the Gauteng Legislature's opposition parties wanted to know where I was and what I was doing. The Public Service Commission instructed the Premier's Office to reinstate me, since I could not be dismissed. I was allowed to come to work but not to my workstation. I was told that the Premier's Office could not allow me back because I had brought the Office into disrepute and relationships with the people I'd exposed could not be repaired, so they prevented me from coming back to my workstation.

I was not happy about the lifting of my suspension for various reasons, but was encouraged by the fact that I had been vindicated. I was not excited about it because I knew that I was not off the hook: the war had just began. For example, I was prohibited from returning to my initial workstation. I was instructed to never put my foot there. They even told security that if I did, I must be arrested. I was instead asked to report to another building where Gauteng Corporate Services was housed: 91 Commissioner Street.

Initially, I was asked to join officials who were working on the 11th floor of the building. The lady I was asked to report to was not part of the Premier Office staff. She was there on a contract basis doing some project for DG. There I found officials who had been seconded to the lady from the Human Resource Section, only to find out that these officials had been removed from their workstations because they'd once raised dissatisfaction about their working conditions. Some of them had been investigated and dismissed, but those whom I found there had not been dismissed but were being isolated to punish them. The floor that they were based on was derelict, with filth everywhere. Other offices had pieces of blanket, clothes and other stuff that showed that there were people sleeping there, probably the homeless.

The first time I went to that floor I was very apprehensive and scared, but at least there were people around me. No one came to introduce me to anyone, including the lady I was to report to. She did not know what to do with me, so I just reported to work every day, only to sit there for the whole day, for months in and out. The lady, however, tipped me off that she had been instructed by DG to keep an eye on me and report to them on my every movement.

The leaked letter I had written to the Premier spread to almost all the provincial offices, and people had a copy of it. If it had happened during the time of social media, I would have said it was trending. I remember how some officials managed to trace me and came to see me at the building mentioned with copies of the letters in their hands. In no time, the leaked letter also reached the media, and they too wanted my story.

The leaked letter was so widely publicised that one day someone from the Sunday Times newspaper came to ask for an interview with me. She was accompanied by a photographer to take photos of the area I was placed in before writing my story. They were shocked at the kind of environment I was put in. The one who was taking pictures said that it was solitary confinement and she looked worried. The whole floor was unoccupied and we were the only ones who occupied the one vast room. But I was not afraid. I just kept my faith and believed. She wanted to have my story reported in their newspapers.

It was not in my interests that I appeared in the newspapers. I did not have any problem with the story being been written and published, but without mentioning my name, because I did not want that kind of publicity. When she insisted that she take my photo, I allowed her to. I never heard from them after that. The Sunday Times never followed up on my story. I do not know why.

Just a few weeks after that, someone from the Democratic Party, now the Democratic Alliance, came looking for me. He too wanted my story. I told him the same, that I did not want too much publicity. I informed him, though, that DG was threatening to sue me for defamation of character. He promised to find me a lawyer free of charge, and he did, because the following day he called me and gave me the details of the lawyer and said that he had already spoken to her. He gave me the address so that I could go there and talk to her face to face. She agreed to assist me and kept her promise. I did not have to go to court, nor pay the DG. I am sure the lady on the 11th floor informed the DG about the two visits. She knew what those people were there for because we were all sitting in an open plan office and there was no privacy.

I was quickly moved to some offices in the basement of the same building. I shared the space with rubble that littered everywhere, as well as rats. There was just filth all around me. I was dumped there for almost a year. For that one year at 91 Commissioner Street building, I was not given any task to perform. I was convinced that the idea was to break me and that they were hoping that I would give up and resign, and I was not about to give them that joy.

I had won the first leg and had dashed their hopes of dismissing me outright. So, their desperation grew and became more dangerous. I knew that they might kill me, but I just believed and had faith in God. I was reminded of TD Jakes' words when he said, "Don't expect to be appreciated. Your only expectation should be to get a pay cheque. Do not come to work to have personal relationships. Do not allow what you do to affect who you are. Do your job well but remember your mission. God put you there to be a light. Seek opportunities to change the atmosphere without commenting on the problems. You have a God to talk to. You are on an assignment. Quietness and competence shall be your strength. Do not let your environment get inside of you. You should influence it, not let it influence you. Stop going to work to be fed. You did not come to receive; you came to give. Increase your capacity to work with different personalities. God will often bless you through people you do not even like! Remember, where you are does not define where you are going. This will deliver you from frustration. God has a plan for your life. Keep your eye on the prize. Get the optimum results with minimal confusion. Be effective without making the environment worse. Do not be associated with one group or clique. Labels limit your usefulness. God wants you to work with everybody but be labelled by nobody. Use all your gifts..." (2001)

After a few days of being in the basement, an official from Labour came to tell me to report to one of the officials from the Labour Directorate by the name AO in the same building. I have never come across such a hostile person before or since. The Labour section was located within the Premier's Office, that is, Human Resources, Labour and Personnel and Salary System (PERSAL). This is a central system used for the administration of the public service payroll. The office I mentioned above was among the rubble of broken furniture. The basement was a mess and spooky and very scary. I was told that they had been dumped there when they'd relocated people from the Transvaal

Provincial Administration (TPA) in Pretoria after Gauteng Provincial Government Office was established and based in Johannesburg, during Tokyo Sexwale's premiership.

I was provided with a computer and printer but no task was ever given to me. Whenever Labour personnel came to see me, it was only to check on me to see whether I was reporting to work or to inform me of when my disciplinary hearing would be scheduled. They followed me wherever I went and tried to find something that would implicate me. In fact, they attempted every tactic on earth. Some of the tactics I would have expected from the apartheid police were applied to me, and I was perturbed.

This reminds me of when one afternoon I knocked off and went to wait for my husband outside. It was dangerous for me to drive because, every time I parked my car in the parking lot, I found it had been tampered with. For instance, one time the tyre was flattened, the next time some one scratched it across its body. So, my husband would drop me at work and pick me up after work. We made it a point that he did not wait for me at the same spot because I knew I was being followed. I made it a point that I was alert all the time.

One afternoon, after I got into the car, I looked through the rear mirror of the car and saw MJM on the corner of the street looking in our direction. I said to my husband, "That person standing at the corner is MJM; he was following me," only to find out later that he had taken my husband's car registration number. My husband was driving a work branded car. He phoned my husband's workplace, reporting him and saying that he was giving me a lift in a government car. They told him that there was nothing wrong with that because he'd indicated in a trip authority that he was driving with me. The transport officials informed my husband of the incident the following day. This one frightened me into realising that they were starting to infiltrate my family.

Regarding the office allocated to me on the basement, the worst thing was that I was alone down there, and anyone could have done anything to me without anyone knowing. But I made it a point that I clocked in to work on time and knocked off on time. I knew that they were watching my movements. The case was beginning to take a toll on me and everyone in my house. The more they tried to implicate me, the more I just emerged clear.

I remember one day when I got out of a lift I heard footsteps. Someone was running down the stairs and I thought I heard someone cocking a gun. I walked fast to my office and locked the door. Going to the kitchen to make tea was a mission, and so was answering nature's call to go to the toilet.

I was afraid to go out of my office after I one day discovered that there was someone who occupied the office opposite mine. I saw this young man entering the office and I had never seen him before. I was very curious about that. When I saw him going out of the office, I quickly went to open it. I got the shock of my life to realise that he seemed to have been staying there for a long time. The walls were covered with scary pictures, satanic sort of pictures, and the area was a mess, with clothes and blankets everywhere. He was homeless. I never bothered to tell anyone because I knew that they were not going to do anything. Besides, I was not sure that they did not know that someone was staying there.

Pressure on me intensified when my disciplinary hearing started. The one year of being thrown in the basement was a roller coaster. There my faith was put to the test. It drained the adrenaline out of me and I needed more to help me fight. I remember one morning coming to work at around 07h00. The normal time to start work in the public service was 08h00, but I made a habit of starting one hour earlier. I found that very helpful because it gave me time to prepare on time, especially with EXCO meeting logistics as they are intense and do not allow any room for mistakes, so that became a habit.

Politicians are very difficult people to work with because their work leans more towards protecting their territories.

This reminds me of one morning, when I'd just finished with EXCO preparations. I was very tired and I decided to go and sit on the stairs. The DG came and found me sitting there. He just knew what that meant. He greeted me, and I stood up and what I said was that this was a dog's job. He responded that it was indeed. He was not aware that I'd had to come at 6h00 because my team was on a go slow.

No one was to know, except that one morning of the EXCO sitting, two MECs came early and asked me why I was alone so early. One of the MECs who often came earlier than the rest said, before I could answer, that for the last couple of weeks he'd found me there much earlier and alone. I told them that my team was on a go slow, protesting against the treatment they got from management, particularly around promotional opportunities. Politicians do not want to interfere in administrative work, so they both just kept quiet.

Reverting to my disciplinary hearing, my excitement was short lived. DDG had stopped the disciplinary hearing as per PP instruction, but reinstated it again after two weeks. He decided to defy the Public Protector's instruction. I informed the Office of the Public Protector about that. In the morning, they called me to ascertain whether they were still going ahead with the hearing, and I told them that it was still the case. The morning that was to be my demise, the notorious MJM came to my office to read the charge sheet to me. He had a copy of it in his hand, and read it out loud.

While he was still reading it a fax came through. It was a letter from the Public Protector (Selby Baqwa) himself. He addressed it to me and copied DDG SB, asking him to tell the panel constituted to proceed with my disciplinary hearing to not go ahead. It was the second time that DDG tried to defy the PP. Hence, in the letter he also summoned DDG to come to his office to discuss the matter.

REPUBLIC OF SOUTH AFRICA

PUBLIC PROTECTOR
MOSIRELETSI WA BATHO • MOŠIRELETŠI WA BATHO
MUSIRHELELI WA VANHU • MUTSIRELEDZI WA VHATHU
OPENBARE BESKERMER • UMKHUSELI WABANTU • UMVIKELI WABANTU

☎ (012) 322 2916 • Fax (012) 322 5093   ✉ Private Bag X677 Pretoria 0001   226 Visagie Street Pretoria

Faxed by / Gestuur deur: M.M. Shai.
Date / Datum: _____
Reference / Verwysing: 7/2-770/00.

For Attention / Vir Aandag: Mr. Tsie-

To / Aan: Nehawu
Fax No / Faks Nr: (011) 331 3406

Cover page plus pages / Dekblad plus bladsye: _____

Please contact this office if you have not received all the pages or if parts are unreadable.
Skakel asseblief indien u nie al die bladsye ontvang het nie of indien daar gedeeltes is wat onleesbaar is.

Subject: Complaint: Misplacement of Mrs. Maleka

Message: _____

CONFIDENTIALITY WARNING

The content of this facsimile is confidential by law, intended for a specific individual or purpose. If you are not the intended recipient, be advised that any use, disclosure, copying, distribution, or action taken in reliance on the content of this transmission is strictly prohibited. If you have received this facsimile by mistake, please notify us immediately by telephon to discuss the return of the original.

Sent: _____

LOCATION: 012 3225093   RX TIME 04.09.'00 10:54

REPUBLIC OF SOUTH AFRICA

PUBLIC PROTECTOR
MOSIRELETSI WA BATHO • MOSIRELETŠI WA BATHO
MUSIRHELELI WA VANHU • MUTSIRELEDZI WA VHATHU
OPENBARE BESKERMER • UMKHUSELI WABANTU • UMVIKELI WABANTU

☎ (012) 322 2916 • Fax (012) 322 5093   ✉ Private Bag X677 Pretoria 0001   228 Visagie Street Pretoria

REF. 7/2-0770/00
2000-09-01

Attention: Mrs. Maleka

Department of Premier: Gauteng
Private Bag x61
MARSHALLTOWN
2107

Fax: (011) 355 9372

Dear Mrs. Maleka

COMPLAINT: DISCIPLINARY HEARING

Telephone conversation between you and Ms Monareng and Adv Shai of this office refers.

As already explained, we are through with our preliminary investigation. We have also finalized our report which we have already issued to the Premier, Mr. Mbhazima Shilowa and also copied the Acting Director-General, Mr. Balton.

Our investigation revealed that in addition to the allegations that Mr. Haffegee had established to be well founded, there were also other allegations in which we found that some irregularities had taken place. Although some of these irregularities have not yet been fully established, we found that there was foundation for your allegations. On the above basis we concluded that you could not be treated as the person who is not credible and that the disclosures you made qualify for protection in terms of the Protected Disclosure "Bill".

> The Public Protector recommended that the disciplinary action against you be stopped and a personnel audit of the affected sections be carried out by an independent and competent authority.
>
> At this moment the Public Service Commission is busy with investigation, and they will revert to us once they are through therewith.
>
> Yours Faithfully
>
> ADV M M SHAI
> SENIOR INVESTIGATOR
> 077000_m

I took the letter from the machine, read it, and gave it to MJM. He was angry that I was interrupting him. He always accused me of applying delaying tactics. As soon as he saw the Public Protector letterhead, he became interested and grabbed it from my hand and started reading. What fascinated me was that MJM, arrived in my office to intimidate me, only to arrive at the same time as the arrival of a faxed letter from the Public Protector, stopping the hearing. He was shattered. I could see his face when he read it. Those are the deeds of a Living God.

After reading it, MJM instructed me to follow him. I did, and we headed towards the lift. He pressed seven floor buttons. He was not talking to me, let alone telling me where he was taking me. There was a boardroom next to the lifts. He ushered me in. The Presiding Officer asked me to sit down. There were two other people, one from the Internal Labour Unit and the other was my union representative. The employee from Labour introduced me to everyone and started explaining the procedure to me. He was visibly hostile, and I really got scared for the first time. MJM went out to make a call, I guess to the DDG, because just after that DDG called the Presiding Officer on his mobile phone. MJM came back to give the letter from PP to him, and the meeting was adjourned.

In this, there is something that puzzled me that I would like to share with readers. It was how seriously MJM took his disciplinary hearing job. When he came to my office, he was wearing an orange overall similar to the ones that are worn by prisoners. He would tie it very tight with a belt around his waist. He looked so funny, especially since he was very thin and looked unhealthy – from drinking too much, I am told. I happened to learn later that wearing prisoner's uniform was his strategy to work on his victims psychologically: that is, he was sending a clear message to his victims that he would be sending them to the gallows. This is how he derived joy: in seeing his colleagues dismissed from their jobs for whatever reasons. I was told that he did the same with all the employees he managed to get fired. He had come to my office to work on me psychologically.

I was, however, reminded of one time when the Office of the Premier went for a workshop. We arrived at the venue late in the afternoon, just in time for supper. We were told to meet at the restaurant. We all converged there. While we were all seated and ready to be served, someone arrived and all of a sudden everyone looked restless, and was talking in a hush hush manner. I asked someone next to me what it was all about and he said, "Do you not see who just came in?" I looked around and saw this gentleman sitting down at the table where DG and others were already seated. I was told that it was MSM, and warned that he was notorious for getting people dismissed.

I'd never met him; I just knew his face because I'd seen him several times in the department. I had taken him to be just one of the staff members from another unit, only to find out that he was a feared notorious someone who was working in the Labour Unit. I was shocked when I realised that there were even some of my colleagues who wanted to stand up when he came in: that is, give him a standing ovation. One could have mistaken him for Pablo Escobar (a most feared Columbian gangster and a drug lord). He really knew how to instil fear in people's hearts and minds, and that reminded me of the apartheid police force.

Later, after a few years, when I crossed swords with DG he came onto to me like nothing and I was shocked. I still believe that he was the one who cocked the gun when I got out of the lift one morning, as mentioned above. But I have never made it my business to be afraid of a human being, and there is only one Person I fear: my God.

The same time that the Public Protector started with their investigation, the City Press pursued the story. This time my two angels came in the form of two reporters: Nompumelelo Mkhabela and Dominique Mahlangu. They truly disorganised them as the news of a corrupt Gauteng Provincial Director General appeared on the front page, together with the names of officials implicated.

The article not only carried my story, but they also dug out his wrong doings from previous employment and from his personal life. it was very ugly. My name never appeared, and I never went public. I did not want fame in this but only to tell the truth.

One of the newspaper report cuttings written by Mpumelelo

The matter had already reached the official opposition party, that is the Democratic Party (DP), now the Democratic Alliance (DA). They too wanted my story. It was tabled on the legislature meeting agendas; I did not know why.

My situation became worse and worse by the day, to the point that the idea of being murdered crossed my mind, especially if all their tricks and scheming tactics failed. This was because of the threats I'd received. My family was very scared. I remember my daughter suggesting to me that I resign. I told her that once one started something like this, one did not back off or retract due to pressure, but had to forge ahead and fight vigorously. There is one thing about the truth: you cannot sugar coat it; it remains the truth

Although my family was scared, they were very supportive, particularly my husband. While at the Public Protector's offices, I was told about horrific cases of people who had done what I had done. I was told that those who survived assassination attempts were sent to mental hospitals because no person in their right mind would blow the whistle on corruption in this government. Most high-ranking officials are feared and they are self-declared untouchables.

For example, few months after I went back to the office, while working in her study a certain lady who worked for a national government department was assassinated in her home for blowing the whistle on corruption. I think her surname was Bhengu. Unfortunately, I was unable to follow her story because her death was not widely publicised in the media.

Although this one incident shocked and almost paralysed me, backing off was not an option. I was determined to walk with my God and hold His hand firmly because He was in fact the One Who gave me the courage to tell the truth. I had to have faith. So,

I could not be scared by things like that because if I was, I would be failing the citizens of the country who paid my salary so that I could deliver the service they deserved, rather than having their hard-earned tax monies squandered.

The internal investigation report by IH was concluded and submitted. I was not given a copy or even informed that it had been released. The investigator pronounced that I had indeed brought the office into disrepute because the allegations were unfounded. The office concluded that I should be brought before the disciplinary hearing as soon as possible because the matter had already destabilised and brought discomfort to the office. They were very keen and desperate to have me dismissed. My courage and faith just carried me through, and I was more than determined to soldier on.

My union representative (UR) insisted that I be furnished with the report. It was later brought to me by the investigator and I was requested to respond to the report. UR came to my office, and we went through his findings. The report was not up to standard. Reading it, one could sense a certain level of anger and emotion, driven by hatred towards me. It left lots of loopholes and we took them up on that. We sat down and responded to it, point by point, and in this way we managed to expose all the lies he mentioned in his report. We did not agree with the report and took it on review. The Labour Unit came back with guns blazing, blaming us for trying to apply delaying tactics as usual.

I had already grown suspicious of the investigator because in the meetings I had with DDG and him, before the investigation, I could sense that they knew each other; their body language and facial expressions said a lot. After the investigation, but before the report was released, I decided to do my own investigation.

I managed to get his office telephone number. I called under the pretext that I was from Premier's Office and working on his payment for the investigation he'd conducted. He was working with his wife.

I introduced myself and gave her one of the official's in the Premier's Office's procurement section's name and not mine: in fact, the name of the lady whom I'd found kissing with the DG at midday in her office. She had been appointed as a director of procurement. I requested his tax number, bank details, addresses… almost everything. She gave me all the information without hesitation. I told her that her husband was a wonderful person, and I would like him to represent me one day if needs be. She was impressed. I asked her as to how the Premier's Office happened to find him. She told me that he was a friend to DDG, and both lived in Lenasia. I was so elated. I felt like an FBI agent!

After concluding our response to his report, we sent it to him by fax. Upon reading our response, the investigator got unsettled and afraid because he'd really implicated himself in his report. In our report we pinpointed, amongst other things, the fact that we were aware that he and DDG had known one another long before he was appointed to investigate the matter.

The investigator came to see me as soon as he'd received our written response. He was visibly angry. I was afraid but did not want to show it. He asked me why I'd said the things I'd said in my document. I told him that I could only talk to him through my representative. He started insulting me by telling me that I was trying to project myself as a superhero, as if I was better; hence, I was equally corrupt. He stated that he was told that I did some things that were wrong and tantamount to corruption. He was very furious and tried to intimidate me. It was only the two of us.

I became angry too, and told him that his report was so false and fabricated that it was going to work on his conscience and haunt him for the rest of his life. He told me that I was not going to survive the disciplinary hearing because DDG was determined to flush me out. I asked him whom he was working for and he became angrier. I kept quiet and without saying a further word he left.

The only thing that saw me through was prayer. As Bob Marley once said, "My spirit is my only courage," and this is true. As I grew spiritually stronger, my courage became greater as well. Pema Chodron writes that "Spirituality suggests that everything which manifests itself physically has its root in the spiritual realm. Hence, it is vital to ask, believe and receive. Asking means putting it clearly out there in the universe, believing that a higher power will make it all possible and positioning oneself to receive the blessings when they come."

My mental and emotional turmoil became lighter after I came across Chodron's quote: "Nothing ever goes away until it has taught us what we need to know." This is precisely what whistleblowing taught me.

Reverend WLM was a very ruthless person who enjoyed firing every person deemed to be a stumbling block. He was drunk with power because of his connection to powerful individuals. It explained why all the people I knew and was close to at work turned against me. To some, I became an enemy, but the support I got from my family and particularly my husband, as well as my faith, became the fuel that kept me going. What I am trying to illustrate here is that DG was like what I referred to as a mumpsimus. According to Wikipedia, a mumpsimus is someone "who insists they are right, despite clear evidence that they are not". The idea is to consistently test your patience with the aim to protect their battered legacy: a legacy presented in a way that shapes the narrative to suit them. For a mumpsimus, the only thing that matters is that they stick to their version of events because, as propagandist Joseph Goebbels noted, the more you repeat a lie the more likely it is to be accepted as a fact or truth.

I remember how he tried to trick me into withdrawing my memorandum by promising me a director position. This position was occupied by Judith Hendricks (Mackay). He told me that he was not happy with Judith's performance. Therefore, he wanted to demote her to my position, because he thought I could do a better job in hers, and he was pleased with me. I responded by saying that I could not betray her and asked him why then, because his timing was suspicious. I reminded him that he'd called me a troubled woman when I was trying to establish why I was not short listed for a promotional post. I assured him that if there happened to be a post advertised, I would apply and get it fair and square, if I happened to be given the opportunity.

How could I forget what I was fighting for? I knew him, in that when he decided to demote two directors in the Premier's Office – FM and Dr DK – he used some desperate individuals and, after he'd got what he wanted, he then implicated them and got them fired. One of them came to me and he wanted my advice because his job was on the line. Conniving with evil people in the name of getting high posts does not pay. People must learn to be honest with themselves.

The same happened to EM, the lady who leaked the document. She too was rewarded by DG. He promoted her from administration clerk at level five to assistant director at level nine, without her having any tertiary education or qualifications required for the level. She resigned after few months. IL, one of my colleagues, told me that she'd had a rough time at the office because, firstly, she could not live up to the task; and secondly, some staff members called her a traitor. Knowing Rev WLM to be vindictive, I think he ill-treated her, but I also think that she regretted what she had done to me.

One day, she met me at the entrance of the building I had been transferred to. I think she had come to the Human Resource Unit to hand over her resignation letter. As we approached each other for the first time since she'd stabbed me in the back, she became hysterical and started crying. I said to her that crocodile tears did not impress me, and I left.

Another example of DG's tendency to manipulate people was that of a woman who was a director in the Auditing Unit, also in the Premier's Office. She resigned in a hurry. I met her one day, shortly before I was suspended, and we greeted each other as usual. She was still very young but mature for her age. She looked very stressed and before I could ask her how she was, she said to me, "This place is like hell". We were in a lift and when it opened on her floor she walked out without explaining what she meant.

I found out later that she'd resigned out of pressure because DG had instructed her to not audit some of the information I'd revealed. She'd refused and went ahead. After resigning in such a hurry, she was replaced by her deputy director (DD) who was on level 11. Instead of advertising the post, he appointed DD at Chief Director, level 14, jumping the initial director position that was at level 13. DD jumped one level, because the condition of his promotion was that he should not investigate the allegations I made. He agreed, and was rewarded handsomely.

One afternoon, the very same person who was promoted came to my house, pretending to be checking up on me. He lived not far from me. I had been close to him because we used to attend departmental meetings together and we were both at the same rank, only differing in levels. He was level 11, and I was 12. I did not suspect anything until I realised that he was focusing too much on the status of my case and asking for confidential information. My husband was uncomfortable and told me that this person was fishing for information. He was right, although I only knew later that one of the instructions and a motivation for his promotion was to spy on me. DG was aware of our relationship.

To my surprise, when I came back from my suspension he came to my office. He wanted to see the internal investigation report that had come out recently. I gave it to him and while he was still reading it a friend of mine, Stan Sithole, knocked at the door. I could see that he was uncomfortable. I opened the door. As soon as he saw it was Stan, he tried to hide his face with an A4 sized document and never responded to Stan's greetings.

I could not understand it because the three of us used to hang together, especially since we were at the same rank. As already mentioned, Stan Sithole was one of the colleagues who stood by me throughout, so he had frequented my office ever since I'd come back from suspension. He pulled out a chair and sat down, so this guy did not have a choice but to remove the document and greet Stan, after which he immediately left. Stan and I looked at each, puzzled, and asked each other what that was all about. Stan said, "He was spying on you, and it is one of DG's tricks. It explains the promotion." I told him that my husband also suspected him.

I do not know how the matter reached the Office of the Presidency, but someone working there called one of my colleagues wanting to know about a person who'd crossed swords with the DG, and she wanted to know whether she knew the person. She told her that she indeed knew me very well. The caller told her to advise me to drop the case because I was playing with fire. I was already on suspension when she told me what she'd been told and said that everyone was scared for me. She told me that the lady in question (from the Presidency) had said that she'd overhead a minister in the Presidency (EP) talking to someone from the Premier's office, instructing him to get rid of me, as I was in trouble for challenging DG.

I told her that that was not about to happen as I'd heard those threats too many times. The more that I was reminded of how well connected DG was, and how I would not win, the more determined I was to fight on.

I had so many people spying on me, and some of them I did not suspect. There was this colleague working in the Persal section. He befriended me and frequented my office, pretending to support me. He gave me the impression that he hated those notorious officials from the Labour Unit because according to him they were evil. Another woman colleague warned me not to trust him because he was good at fishing information from people and got them into trouble. He was an assistant director. He also jumped one level and was promoted to director level in another department. He did not have any tertiary qualifications, but it was through DG's recommendation, I am told. He was later fired for sexual harassment.

After some time, the internal investigator came to my office again. He was very apologetic and tried to be polite. Looking at how meek he was, I rejoiced in the knowledge that I'd wiped the smile off his face. My response to the outcome of his investigation humbled and humiliated him. I did not have sympathy for him, nor did I buy into his innocent stand. I asked him to tell one of the Labour officials to stop following me, and that I knew that he was a member of one of the gang syndicates in Soweto and I had all the information. I also told him that I knew that he was working with DG, and that they were used to eliminate people like me. I made it clear to him that I was not afraid of them. He left my office without saying a word. My excitement however did not last long. They always had something up their sleeves.

Strangely enough, just after the Premier's Office internal investigator released his report, a week or so later the Public Service Commission released their report too. The only information I received from them came via the Office of the Premier. It was a letter written to the Public Protector, informing them that the PSC was to conduct their own investigation. I was surprised to hear that the report was already out and in the newspapers. I did not know where they got information from because, since I'd visited their offices to register my grievances, which was done in writing and hand delivered, they'd never acknowledged nor spoken to me. The report was tabled at the Gauteng Legislature. The outcome of their findings was very damning and I was clearly insulted.

Someone I'd once worked with at the Department of Development Planning and Local Government was working at the Legislature then, and he called me on my phone, telling me about the report. I asked him to make me a copy and we agreed to meet. He first warned me that the report was very incriminating.

Once back in the office, I read the report, which cleared the Premier's Office of wrongdoing. I picked up an anomaly immediately. To start with, this was irrelevant because the allegations were levelled against DG and not the Premier's Office. The Public Service Commission report was a blow to me,

Ihovisi lika Ndunankulu
Office of the Premier

Kantoroya Tonakgolo
Kantoor van die Premier

Ref: N Balton
Tel: 355 6200
Fax: 834 9177

Adv S A M Baqwa SC
Public Protector
Pretoria

Your reference: Ray Zungu

Dear Adv Baqwa

INVESTIGATION INTO ALLEGATIONS OF MISMANAGEMENT BY MS LETHABO MALEKA

Your report on the preliminary investigation concerning the above-mentioned matter has reference.

The Public Service Commission informed this Office that sufficient grounds exist for further investigation into this matter in terms of section 196(4)(f)(i) of the Constitution. The Commission designated three officials to investigate this matter. The investigating team composes of the following:

- Ms Nkwanyana Gauteng Regional Office
- Mr Dindi Deputy Director Human Resources Management
- Mr Viviers Deputy Director Employee Grievances

The Commission initially indicated that the investigation would commence on *17 August 2000*, but indications now are that the said investigation only commenced today - *30 August 2000*. The Commission also did not specify the period within which the investigation will be finalized. I will personally address this issue with Professor Sangweni, the Chairman of the Public Service Commission.

All the documents and evidence relating to this matter are in possession of the Commission. After the investigation team has thoroughly investigated this matter and considered all the said documents, they will record their findings and submit a report together with their recommendations on this matter, to this Office.

Chief Director: Management Services
91 Commissioner Street, Johannesburg • Private Bag X074, Marshalltown 2107
Tel: (011) 355-9200

in that it dwelled on one aspect of my grievance, which is the issue of not being short listed for the director post I'd applied for. The National Public Service Commissioner, Professor SS, stated in his report that I was not to be trusted because if I had been offered the post I would not have complained about DG's shenanigans. He referred to me in the report as a disgruntled person.

Although very hurt, I understood that he was protecting DG, as they know each other personally. DG was a former Gauteng Public Service Commissioner and they both came from ANC politics and were home boys from the Eastern Cape. He must have got the information from him, as he'd never bothered to interview me.

When DG first knew of the leaked document, he tried to threaten me: "Do you know who I am?" When I said I did not know nor care, but that the truth must be told for my country's sake, he said he was very connected and untouchable. When they realised that my case was very strong – and that I could not be intimated nor shaken, irrespective of the death threats and horrifying victimisation I endured – he was moved to the National Department of Correctional Services.

As the saying goes: *Monwana wa tlwaela go gorela o dula of kgopane* (loosely translated as: One who is used to stealing will always steal). He stole (misappropriated) R20 000 of petty cash a year after he was deployed to the Department of Correctional Service instead of being expelled. Besides, he had not stood a chance as I pursued him, even there. I was unfazed. I was determined to prove to him who was connected and untouchable.

My personal interpretation was that he was fired because the then Minister of Correctional Services did not come from the ruling party and could not condone that type of behaviour. The worst thing was that it was even revealed that he'd misrepresented his qualifications. The fact that he was not fired based on all those supporting revelations is disheartening. The question is: How many of them are still occupying their positions? Obviously, if one had secured a high post in a very unscrupulous manner, one would not see the importance of merit, and the vicious cycle would just continue until it became some form of a culture or a norm. The Public Service Act and Regulations do not serve any purpose. I know I made a difference as I saved the department a lot of money through unscrupulous appointments in the form of nepotism and fraudulent procurements.

The very same week that the report was released and the content of the report appeared on the newspapers, the Public Protector was in Cape Town for a conference. On the very same day it was reported in the news that a certain lady had reported PP for sexual harassment. This was purported to have taken place in his hotel apartment. What came to my mind was that this was a setup meant to either distract him or retaliate.

This reminded me of this one lady colleague who always called me while I was still on suspension, asking about my well-being and assuring me that she was behind me. She was also very interested in the progress of my case, especially when I told her that the office of the Public Protector would be investigating the matter. She wanted to know about the PP himself, and I told her that I did not know much about him other than that he was keen on following up on my case. She really sounded genuine.

It was not long after the incident I referred to above that she called me to tell me that she and PP were an item; that they were lovers. I put the puzzle together, but maybe it was my imagination running wild. I was upset and not impressed.

I avoided discussing personal things with colleagues and she never called me again. I think that she avoided me even after I had gone back to work.

After a while, I realised that I was going to be in solitary confinement for a long time. My destiny was firmly in my hands and it was up to me to do something about it. As I had ample time and it was not my fault that my employer did not want to allocate any tasks to me, I also thought of taking advantage of a scholarship programme that my workplace offered to staff. I decided to apply for a Doctorate degree (PhD)

Talking about PhD studies,

: **PROTOCOL NUMBER: xxxxxxx**

PUBLIC PARTICIPATION IN POLICY-MAKING AND IMPLEMENTATION WITH SPECIAL REFERENCE TO GAUTENG LIQUOR POLICY
BY: xxxxxxxxxxxxxxxxx
A THESIS SUBMITTED TO THE FACULTY OF COMMERCE, LAW AND MANAGEMENT, UNIVERSITY OF THE WITWATERSRAND, IN FULFILMENT OF THE REQUIREMENTS FOR THE DEGREE OF
DOCTOR OF PHILOSOPHY
SUPERVISOR: xxxxxxxxxxxxxx STUDENT NUMBER: xxxxxxxxx
MAY 2017

and I was given a scholarship to further my studies.

At that point, I was rendered *persona non-grata* and victimised in many ways. What irritated me more is when now and again I was called by our Labour Unit to submit copies of my tertiary qualifications, including my matric certificate. All my degree certificates were already on Human Resource Unit files.

One year after I enrolled for my studies, the victimisation had not stopped. Instead, it was intensified. I had to suspend my studies due to the pressure the investigation was putting on me. I was disappointed because I had overcame the odds to pursue my studies before, and I had succeeded. To recapitulate, I was the first in my family to get matric and I'd never looked back since, moving from being a tea maker *cum* cleaner and a storekeeper to being the first graduate in my family and obtaining three degrees. I obtained my master's degree while juggling work and motherhood. But the case was truly a heavy burden on me, and I had to give up on my attempt at PHD.

Besides my academic achievements, I was the first child to obtain my driver's licence in my family. While working for St Johns' College, I was given a R100 bonus at the end of the year. It came in handy. When the school closed for the December holidays, I decided to go home and register at a driving school. To get a learner's and a driver's licence cost R100. The school was not far from home, so I attended classes and driving lessons every day. I already knew how to drive because my friend Caroline had taught me in her car, which made me the youngest female to drive in my community. I made it a point that I obtained both my learners and licence within

My photo taken next to the car

two weeks. By the time my holidays came to an end after three weeks I already had my licence. Later, my sister went for hers.

My father's car, which was sold, got stolen before the person who bought it could register it officially in his name. When the police found it, it was still in my father's name. They came to inform my father that they had found his car that was stolen and that he should come to Pretoria to claim it. My father asked me to accompany him to the place where recovered stolen car were kept, and we found it. He told them that the car had been sold to someone else.

The official responsible for selling unclaimed vehicles was there. They offered to sell the car in question to him for R40. My father did not have the money with him, but he promised them that once he had secured the amount he would come back to buy the car.

On our way back to Johannesburg, he told me that he did not want it. I indicated to him that I wanted the car, and I would try to save the money. After all, I had the licence. But I had a feeling that he did not want the car anymore. He must have had a good reason for selling it in the first place. The other reason could have been that he did not like the idea that it was a stolen car. So he never wanted to go back. I was disappointed. I had always wanted to own a car one day.

At that time, black people were not allowed to get bank loans so that they could buy new cars from dealers. Thus, my father could only afford to buy second hand, and he bought from white people. I remember how he was always fixing them. He had a mechanic who worked in one of the garages in Hillbrow. He took his vehicles there whenever they gave him problems. I used to accompany him. We walked from Houghton to Hillbrow by foot. The workers in that garage knew me and whenever I passed there they would shout *Ntate* (*Morena* in North Sotho or Mr in English) Mahlangu's daughter. My father introduced himself to people as Mahlangu not Gwangwa.

Back to the story. It did not take long before I was called to appear before the disciplinary hearing session again and I was given an appointment date. I informed the Public Protector and he instructed them not to proceed until he said so. They defied him and insisted that I come. I went but informed the Public Protector of my situation. My representative insisted that I go. When I got there, I was introduced to the presiding officer – who was an external person – the department's legal person, two officials from Labour and my union representative. The presiding officer was very hostile to me, and I immediately smelled a rat. I knew that he was somehow connected to DDG, and I was right. Their investigator and the presiding officer were all friends. This are the type of apartheid tactics that people still use in a democracy.

Minutes before my disciplinary hearing took place, the Public Protector sent an e-mail to the Internal Labour official. He was instructing them to stop the process. He summoned them to his office and warned them not to undermine his authority. The Public Protector officials had started with their investigation.

A few weeks after that, the Public Protector released his report, clearing me. Although the actual report was sent to the Premier's Office, the Office of the Public Protector made a point of seeing that I received my copy.

REPUBLIC OF SOUTH AFRICA

PUBLIC PROTECTOR
MOSIRELETSI WA BATHO • MOŠIRELETŠI WA BATHO
MUSIRHELELI WA VANHU • MUTSIRELEDZI WA VHATHU
OPENBARE BESKERMER • UMKHUSELI WABANTU • UMVIKELI WABANTU

☎ (012) 322 2916 • Fax (012) 322 5093   Private Bag X677 Pretoria 0001   228 Visagie Street Pretoria

Ref: 7/2-0770/00

26 July 2000

Attention: Mr. S Bolton

The Acting Director-General
Private Bag X61
MARSHALLTOWN
2107

Fax no.: (011) 834 9177

Dear Mr. Bolton

COMPLAINT: INFORMATION DISCLOSED BY MRS L MALEKA RE: MEETING WITH THE PUBLIC PROTECTOR

Our telephone conversation this morning refers.

This is to confirm our agreement that subsequent to the discussion referred to above the disciplinary hearing will not proceed today as you had previously arranged.

I further confirm the agreement to meet on Friday, the 28th of July 2000 at 12h00 at our office in Pretoria, 228 Visagie Street, Sinodale Building –9th Floor.

Your co-operation will be highly appreciated.

Yours Faithfully

ADV S A M BAQWA, SC
PUBLIC PROTECTOR

At this moment the Public Service Commission is busy with investigation and they will revert to us once they are through therewith.

Yours Faithfully

ADV M M SHAI
SENIOR INVESTIGATOR

ADV S A M BAQWA, SC
PUBLIC PROTECTOR

irregularities had taken place. Although some of these irregularities have not yet been fully investigated it has been sufficiently established that some regulations have not been complied with. In other words there is some foundation for the complainant's allegations. The complainant cannot therefore be treated as a person who is not credible.

In view of discrepancies in Haffegee's report, some of which have been highlighted above, his recommendation that disciplinary action be considered against Mrs Maleka cannot go unchallenged. In addition to the discrepancies mentioned above Haffegee's report is lacking in the following respects:

- Where he deals with appointments and promotions, he did not establish whether or not they were in compliance with the relevant Public Service regulations.
- Where he deals with restructuring he fails to establish whether or not there was an actual need for restructuring (in order to dispel the allegation that this was done in order to create posts for certain individuals).

The Gauteng Provincial Government has publicly pledged its support for the culture of clean governance. The ideal of clean governance cannot be achieved without cultivating a culture which facilitates the disclosure by employees of information relating to irregular conduct in the workplace.

I appreciate that the Protected Disclosure Bill has not become an operative Act of Parliament but it is my belief that the provisions thereof are in accordance with the constitutional demands for clean governance. It is therefore useful to refer to this Bill for guidance. In that regard it is our submission that Mrs Maleka's disclosures qualify for protection in terms of the Bill. Being subjected to disciplinary action as a result of disclosing information is one of the acts described as " occupational detriment" in the Bill. Such acts are prohibited in terms of Section 3. In that light I am of the view

00/08/21

> that proceeding with disciplinary hearing will be subverting the clean governance effort that the Gauteng Provincial Government stands for.
>
> I therefore recommend that the disciplinary action instituted against Mrs Maleka be stopped and a personnel audit of the affected sections be carried out by an independent and competent authority.
>
> **ADV S A M BAQWA, SC**
> **PUBLIC PROTECTOR**

Copy of PP's investigation report, concluding pages of the 21 pages

Once completed with the investigation, they released their report and cleared me. They also furnished me with a copy of the Protected Disclosure Bill so that I could familiarise myself with my rights. I also researched about it and discovered that world-wide governments are increasingly paying attention to the valuable role of whistleblowers in preventing or disclosing corporate and public service fraud, corruption, scandals and even life-threatening mistakes.

The South African government developed the Protected Disclosures Act 2000 (Act 26 of 2000) because it identified a loophole as far as the protection of whistleblowers is concerned. Its important functions are to encourage and offer people protection in the event that whistleblowers are victimised both in public and private sectors.

The phenomenon of whistleblowing in public administration has come under increasing moral, social and legal scrutiny in recent years. I was under the impression that the South African democratic government recognised that whistleblowers have an important role to play in combating malpractice within an organisation. Time and again there would be communication that employees should expose corruption and hotlines would be provided for people to call. Governments internationally, South Africa included, have established anti-corruption policy agendas, and have incorporated measures aimed at encouraging and protecting whistleblowers. Nonetheless, in my case I was instead the one victimised while the perpetrators were protected. Despite the best rules, regulations and legislation to protect whistleblowers, the reality is that as a whistleblower I was subjected to the full force of retaliation. Fortunately, unlike many less lucky, I am alive to relate my experiences.

I was humbled by how the Public Protector handled my case, especially since I was just an ordinary employee trying to stand up against a high-ranking person. Everyone seemed to be hell bent on protecting him and I was isolated and stigmatised. But Advocate Selby Baqwa did not see it that way. He was indifferent to DG's status. I still feel indebted to him and very honoured. I know how he paid a big price for this.

My travail reminded me of Suna Venter's story. She too was a whistleblower and paid dearly for telling the truth. Believe you me, this is what almost all whistleblowers go through, and there are many stories that were never reported. Venter was one of eight journalists referred to as the SABC 8, suspended by the SABC after they voiced their concern about editorial policies, including refusing to air protest footage. This was subsequently reversed by a new interim board at the broadcaster, following a parliamentary inquiry.

This reminded me of Foeta Krige, also a member of the SABC 8, when he wrote about the loss of a colleague and friend and said: "Her family says her heart condition is believed to have been brought on by trauma and prolonged stress. She died of a condition called cardiomyopathy or Broken Heart Syndrome, resulting from stress."

"After the SABC8 came under fire, Venter was "the victim of continued intimidation, victimisation and death threats", her family said. She received threatening SMSs. Her flat was reportedly broken into on numerous occasions, the brake cables of her car were said to have been cut and her tyres were slashed. Her family said she was abducted and tied to a tree on the Melville Koppies, while the grass around her was set alight. Earlier this year, she was shot in the face with an unknown weapon and had surgery" (from an article in TimesLive, by Claudi Mailovich).

It is common knowledge that many people die of stress-related diseases every year, especially in a country like ours, so what makes this different? For people like Suna, who was amongst the most dedicated, professional and highly competent people in society, and whose ethics and integrity were beyond reproach, being suspended and terrorised for doing her jobs particularly well is analogous to torture by solitary confinement.

I am deliberately comparing this to our past because I personally went through solitary confinement for whistle-blowing. But when this happens at the hands of corporate thugs like the ones we have in our current so-called democratic government, this can be argued as being analogous to the state-sanctioned murder we saw under apartheid, only by more subtle means.

I am deliberately narrating my life stories because for me it is like discipling. Deep down in my heart I know that my story is one of the narratives that must be embraced by everyone who aspires to change their lives for the better. Above all, I realised that what I had done (whistleblowing) was more credible than many things I could have achieved. It required all my energy to be dedicated to it. For me, it was the biggest reward or award in that whistleblowing is a virtue. One thing I know is that my tenacity and resilience in the face of adversity is not only admirable but also inspirational.

How I kept sane through it all

The week that they lifted my suspension, although I still had to go through disciplinary hearings, I was driving with my husband in his car when an angel walked over to our car, waving a pamphlet. My husband lowered his window and took it. He gave it to me, and I read it to him. It was promoting a Wellness International Business Opportunity. I had never heard of it before. We both just dismissed it and threw the pamphlet away. Little did I know that it would one day save my life.

Two weeks later, the same person approached us at the same spot. This time he walked to my window and handed the pamphlet to me. I took it and realised that it was the same pamphlet. My husband said to me, "Maybe you should try it, since you do not know whether you have a job or not. You are in limbo, and you might be dismissed." Faith or no faith, the possibility sunk in. It was true that I had to do something. I could not allow anyone to hold my life to ransom and, as a matter of fact, my life did not revolve around the job.

I started praying around it and committing it to God, because everything goes according to "His plan and His Holy Will". If they dismissed me, it would have been according to His purpose, and I would go where He would take me.

I was very sceptical, despite the fact that I like selling things. I had been in a Wellness business before, and I'd once retailed a product – a different brand – for ten years doing it part-time. Somehow, I had just been attracted to entrepreneurship or marketing. For example, when we moved into our new house in Protea North Soweto (the first house we ever owned) I was not working. The years that I was not working, I used to sew kitchen and bathroom curtains and accessories. I would go into peoples' houses with samples, they placed orders and that is how I augmented my husband's income. I did not know that what I was doing was what is called "direct selling".

Even while I was still at primary school, I used to make woollen hats (beanies) and sell them to people. Then, people's communication channel was through mail, yet most of the shops did not have stamps nor envelopes. My father used to bring home rolls of brown papers that we used for covering our books. I would steal some of it and used the paper glue that they bought for me to cover books with to seal my envelopes on the side, just like the ones we bought in shops. Children bought them from me, and I would give the money to my mother, lying that I'd picked it up in the street when she asked me where I'd got it. Then news about my being the envelope maker reached her ears, and I had to tell the truth. But that did not stop me from continuing with my business until the paper got finished. Direct selling came naturally to me.

Though I was very sceptical about trying the business, the pushing factor was my health situation. I put the pamphlet in one of the drawers of my desk. After some time, I saw it again and decided to telephone this person. He explained how the business worked. We agreed that he would mail some information to me, which he did. I decided to register, although not for business purposes but instead for health and to reduce weight. My case became so stressful for me that I developed lots of stress which became acute, leading to depression. I was always sick. Because of the drugs that I was put on, I could not control my weight.

For starters, the pamphlet saved me health wise. The reality is that, like many whistleblowers, I was on depression medication until the angel introduced me to the Wellness Business Opportunity while still on suspension. I needed something that I could fall back on if I was to be fired. Retailing the product helped take things off my mind and consuming them for my depression worked magic. In no time I was off depression drugs that turned me into a cabbage every time I took them. My family and I still use the products. In addition, I helped lots of unemployed individuals to start their businesses. Some just wanted to do it part time and augment their salaries.

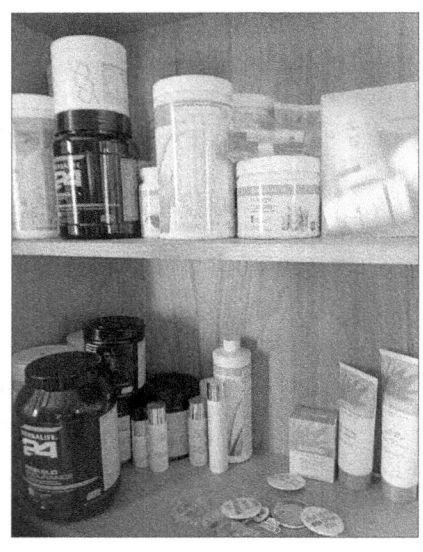

Because I was on tenterhooks, I could not sit on my laurels and I manifested many plans for in case I was to be dismissed. I had Plan A, B, C and so forth, because I knew I had to survive. The notion that "fortune favours the brave" resonates with me.

The thing is that you can only purchase the products when you are a member, because the business used a multilevel marketing strategy through direct selling. I asked myself, "Is this where God wants me to be?" because, truly speaking, this business just found me. I was advised to go to their Success Training Sessions, which took place once a month. My husband and I went. I was blown away. I felt like I belonged there, and loved the idea. The products and business ideas are just perfect, the business is very clean and easy to manage, either part-time or full-time.

The business is called Herbalife, and the couple who recruited me was Dalene and Riaan Swiegers. I am still retailing, and they have been my mentors.

At that time, doing business like this was not easy, as smart phones were in their infancy and one had to distribute pamphlets at shopping malls or street corners. I was still working, so I decided to distribute pamphlets to people's houses during weekends. I would wake up very early and go into the streets to distribute them. I went to most Glenvista homes.

One morning, when I was distributing pamphlets, I found this white man standing in front of his gate. This was on my street. I greeted him but he kept quiet. I stretched my hand towards him with my pamphlet in my hand, but he just stared at me. While I was still puzzled at his attitude, he simply said, "I do not take a pamphlet from a kaffir". I said thank you and threw it into his yard and left.

I was not discouraged by rejections I came across. Instead, I went to every house in the area. I tried to recruit clients and retailed products wherever I was able to, even at work during breaks. I had many people joining and some buying for consumption to address various health issues. I really made a lot of money and enjoyed it.

One of my colleagues reported me to the Labour Unit, complaining that I was selling things at work. The Labour Unit's Mduduzi Zwane called me to come and explain the allegation, which I did. I told him that I only used the products for my health issues, particularly stress, but when other staff members saw me glowing they wanted to know what it was that I was using. I showed them the products and explained how they worked and they placed orders with me. I ordered for them, and they paid for them, and that was all. He believed me and said to me that he did not see anything wrong with what I was doing because it did not interfere with my work.

He became sympathetic to me, particularly since he knew my situation and the level of animosity I endured from my colleagues. He told me that he was impressed by my attitude to life. We became friends and he ensured that I was treated fairly in this matter. However, he advised me to disclose what I was doing. He explained to me how I should go about doing that to protect myself. He was one of my godsent angels in an environment that was hostile.

My challenge was that, being a public servant, the policy is that one is not allowed to receive income additional to what government is paying you. However, one could circumvent that restriction by disclosing. I wrote a letter to the Director General in the Premier's Office, Mogopodi Mokoena, and copied in my Chief Director, motivating that I be granted permission to do the business part-time. I was determined to augment my salary because I knew that I was grounded. With the level of resentment from all quarters, I would never get any promotional posts higher than the one I was at. On the other hand, I'd set standards for my life, and I was not going to allow anyone or anything to stand in the way of the lifestyle I envisaged. I could not let myself and my family down after all the sacrifices.

Both DG and the Chief Director agreed, and DG wrote back to me in response and thanked me for disclosing. I was so humbled and thanked God for his goodness and mercy. That is what I referred to as political maturity. Subsequently, I grew my business as many people joined and became my down lines, taking advantage of buying the products at a cheaper rate because the business uses direct selling as their marketing strategy. Also, as I mentioned above, it works on a multi-level basis.

Besides the direct selling business, I started an interior décor school called Creative Style Interior Décor. It was established and operated from my house over weekends. I am a self-taught interior decorator and designer. My main interest was in furniture upholstery and curtain designing and making. Before I started with lessons, I thought of equipping myself first. I registered for a course in Furniture Upholstering and Photo Framing with Milwaukee International Colleges based in Pretoria. I did my courses through correspondence and completed them. I was issued with diploma certificates. I was about to register for courses in tiling and shoe making (to add to my hobbies) when it closed its doors in South Africa. I never knew what the reasons were. However, for my curtain making and accessory lessons I used interior décor books I'd collected over the years.

The school offered a range of courses, from how to make different types of blinds – Austrian, Festoon, Roman, Fringe and Scalloped-edged roller – to how to make different types of curtains and headings such as swags and tails, as well as bedding

– duvet covers, duvets, fitted and flat sheets, as well types of pillowcases and loose cushion covers. I also love beadwork; beads are like gold for me.

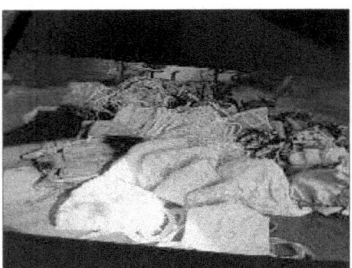

I tried my hand on making clothes. I did not really like it. I hated the pattern cutting part of it, though I sewed many clothes that I still wear. I do lots of knitting as well; the possibilities are endless.

At the time, we did not have smart phones, which would have made my life easier. Today, I can google any craft work and produce the item. During the Covid-19 pandemic, I downloaded all my mask patterns and produced very beautiful items. I could have been referred to as what today is called a hustler, although I do not know what it means.

One of my students was so impressed with the outcomes of my lessons that she recommended a colleague to me. She'd just bought an apartment and was looking for someone to make her Roman roller blinds. I went to see her and took some measurements. She bought the materials, hooks, both female and male Velcro tapes and all that was needed for the project herself. I was only to charge her labour for making them and fitting. Making them was not so much of a problem, but as for fitting them, I really took a chance there as I had never done that before.

I asked my husband to assist me because all one needed was a piece of wood, nails and picture hooks, and a staple gun to attach male Velcro tape to it because the female Velcro tape is to be attached to the material or fabric. He was hesitant but, being a saint-like husband, he agreed, and we went to fit them.

There was just a problem with the walls of the structure. They were not even so the blinds could not fit straight. It was a bit of a mess. She refused to pay me, but I was not going to allow her that as it was not my fault either. I started threatening her and she must have got scared because she paid me my full money. I really felt sorry for my husband as he appeared embarrassed at the shoddy work.

Nonetheless, giving lessons in designing, sewing and making curtains, bedding etcetera was not so expensive because I used samples from pieces of materials or fabric. But upholstering was more expensive as I had to buy machines such as an electric air compressor and big industrial stapler and staples. One can still use simple tools such as nails and a hammer but they are time consuming. I had three sewing machines and two over-locking machines; I still have them.

As mentioned earlier I am a self-taught machinist. I was offering both elementary and advanced courses. All my students completed their courses and were issued with attendance certificates. Unfortunately, I had to discontinue with the project due to lack of funding. All my students were women from disadvantaged communities, so they struggled to pay fees. Some just took advantage because of this entitlement mentality of wanting free things. I could not even raise money to pay my salary as it all went to overheads, so I ran it voluntarily.

I credit my mother for all these life skills; she was very creative and industrious and I took after her. She was a very hard-working and a wise woman. She never stopped trying different things, like being a school governing body member or member of the local community projects. In our district there was a cooperative project, run by government through professional agriculturists (*balemi*). Members of the communities were encouraged to come and trade their crops after harvesting. They would take their grains to the cooperative in exchange for a bag of maize meal. Every year, agriculturists from my place and surrounding areas would have competitions at the cooperatives, where people would showcase their skills in craft work. My mother took part in that and most of the time she would get a first prize. I was proud of her and she was always the talk of the villages. She really encouraged me.

I must mention that I am not only a wellness fanatic, but I am also fitness crazy. For the five years I stayed with my father in Houghton, I used to jog every afternoon after work at St Johns College and every morning on Saturdays, especially before joining the SAVS project. I would run from Rose Road down into Munro Drive, joining Harrow Road and coming back into St Andrew Avenue, the street running along St Johns College. The place is very steep because of the mountain overlooking the park called The Wilds in Upper Houghton. Munro Drive and Harrow Road sandwich the park. I remember how car drivers, upon seeing a black girl jogging in a white suburb, cheered and hooted at me. It was common to see white people jogging in the streets; in fact that is what motivated me. But, while I was jogging I realised that there was a white man following me all the time. It scared me and I told my father. My father would follow me or stand at strategic point where he would see me. The man stopped stalking me.

Later in life, while I was a student at Wits, I joined an aerobics club run by the university. Fortunately, my scholarship programme paid for it. I trained every day at lunch time until I'd completed both my two degrees after four years. I have not slowed down with age; I still do them. I want to mention that people should understand that physical exercise is good for one's health; in fact, it can be a medicine for people struggling with stress. Studying at tertiary level can be very stressful because one works under pressure with limited time. Our instructor encouraged us not to give up on our exercises because they not only alleviated stress but gave one more brain power, in that it pumps blood, along with more oxygen, into the brain and makes one concentrate better and longer. More importantly, it improves one's memory.

Most of the students gave up – they could not cope – but I never did and so I can bear testimony to the benefit of exercising and eating well. When I tell people about healthy living, some tell me that I do not want to get old. That is naïve or ignorant, because one cannot avoid ageing, but how you age is a different story. With us Africans, I initially thought that people were saying it because of lack of exposure. One must age but gracefully. While I was growing up in the rural area, one would rarely come across fat people because of the activities they were doing on the daily basis, such as fetching water far away, looking after cattle, collecting wood many miles away, tilling fields and everything that comes with living in a rural village. So, just merely walking around also plays a vital role to one's health.

Second Secondment: The harder they come

This period of my whistleblowing wilderness reminded me of a favourite song by Jimmy Cliff (James Chambers): The harder they come, the harder they fall... So as sure as the sun will shine, I am gonna get my share now of what is mine and the harder they come the harder they'll fall, one and all..."

I must mention that I was not only seconded and left alone to do what I was instructed to do, it came along with torture. The bullying and victimisation I endured because of my experience as a whistleblower are unimaginable. This lasted for 17 years out of 20 years of employment in government. The more my story became distorted by those who made it their business to do so, the more those who are afraid of whistleblowers (the guilty are afraid) would believe the lies and come down harder than a ton of bricks whenever they got an opportunity. As I was moved to a number of different departments, the whole saga just followed me, and I endured years of hell on earth.

With my second secondment, I was transferred to another Chief Directorate unit, also reporting to the Premier's Office, on the same level. Initially, I intended to fight to be returned to my job, but after what happened to the Public Protector I realised that it was getting nasty, so I agreed to the transfer, with some reservations because I could sense that they would continue victimising me. After being handed a letter of secondment, I was told to go and head Corporate Information Technology's Finance and Administration Sub-Directorate. There, I was allocated a huge office with beautiful expensive furniture and flowers and provided with all the tools of trade such as a laptop and cell phone. I was uncomfortable because I knew that those kinds of offices are allocated to top management. I found out later that the office belonged to the former Chief Director. I did not have any  knowledge about IT, finance and procurement issues or tender procedures. I had a basic knowledge of procurement, though I was self-taught. I was literally thrown into the deep end with the purpose of frustrating me further.

Umnyango ka Ndunankulu
Department of the Premier

Lefapha la Tonakgolo
Departement van die Premier

In the dispute between:

L Maleka
Nehawu

Case number: PSGA 260

Employee party
Representative

And

Office of the Premier
Alwyn Kuger

Employer party
Representative

TEMPORARY SETTLEMENT AGREEMENT

The undersigned parties record the settlement of their dispute in the following terms:

1. The employee will be transferred to Corporate IT temporarily to the post of Deputy Director. As soon as a suitable post is available according to her career path (Policy Decision Secretariat), she will then be permanently transferred there on the same terms and conditions of employment including rank and grade with the same salary and other benefits.

2. The employee will commence duty as Deputy Director: Finance and Procurement Administration with effect from 1 April 2001.

3. An original letter will be placed on the personal file of the Employee to indicate that no charges were or will be brought against her as a result of the disclosure as stipulated in the Public Protector Act 23 of 1994. According to the Act, Mrs Maleka falls within the ambit of "protected disclosure" that no employee shall be subjected to any occupational detriment by his or her employer.

4. Occupational detriment is defined in section1 (vi) of the Act to mean:

   a. being subjected to any disciplinary action;
   b. being dismissed suspended, demoted, harassed or intimidated;
   c. being transferred against his or her will;
   d. being refused transfer or promotion;
   e. being denied otherwise adversely affected in respect of his or her employment, profession or office, including employment opportunities and work security etc.

Labour Relations
91 Commissioner Street, Johannesburg   Private Bag X89, Marshalltown, 2107

Case number PSGA 260

5. In this case, the employee reserves the right to challenge the Employer on her performance appraisal for the period 1 April 2000 to 31 March 2001.

The Parties agree:

- this being a temporary settlement of the said dispute without any further recourse and
- no variation of this agreement will be legally binding unless reduced to writing.

Thus done and signed at *Jatho Tele* on the *23* day of *March 2001*

A Oelofse
Director: HRM

L Maleka

Alwyn Kruger (Representative)

Steven Tsie (Nehawu)

My suspicion that the transfer was not mutual was confirmed. My assistant refused to co-operate and the acting Chief Director never called me to any management meetings. All managers in the unit where very hostile to me. I was always in the dark about what was happening around me, unfortunately. The most junior staff members were more experienced and willing to show me how they performed their tasks, and I tried to learn as fast as I could. The acting Chief Director deliberately elevated my assistant above me and invited her to meetings. Although I was never allocated any task, he allowed me to still manage the staff in my component. They were the ones who taught me lots of things, although of course I tried to consult other people and read.

Someone advised me and pointed to a section in the Public Service Act that says, in the case where an official is placed in an unfamiliar section that is not her/his competency, the department must ensure that the person is empowered to do the job. I always referred to it when I applied for all the courses I attended: finance, human resource, and supply chain courses. When an employee is transferred to another unit and does not have knowledge of the field, they must be sent for training before they can take full responsibility for the tasks.

On hearing about this, I immediately drafted a memo to the IT Chief Director and copied the acting HOD in the Department of Finance and Economic Affairs, as the Corporate IT Chief Directorate Unit was housed in the department. I motivated that I be allowed to go for Diploma Courses on Financial Management, Purchasing Management and Human Resource Management. They agreed to fund me, and I started a Financial Management Course in one of the colleges in Braamfontein called Executive Education Institution; very reputable. I was allowed to attend classes full time. I remember that they even provided me with transport. There was a driver who was supposed to take me in the morning and fetch me in the afternoon and I would take my transport home. Like they say, "when life throws lemons at you, make lemonade out of them".

Stealing from Jimmy Cliff's song "They thought they had the battle won, but they did not know what they had done", I was determined to fight for what I wanted. I knew that the tendency to perpetually ill-treat me was because of fear. I chose to keep my head above water even though they tried to keep me down so as to drive me underwater with the aim of drowning me. But the harder they came, the harder they fell. My suspicions were confirmed and another three years were to pass without my being allocated any job because in their mind I irked them so much that I must be punished.

In the absence of proper work, I always had ample time, so I used it for my betterment. I registered for five diplomas in five years of being in the wilderness and completed them. Amongst them are three that I did part-time with UNISA's Centre for Business Management: Programme in Total Quality Management, Programme in Purchasing and Supply Management and Short Course in Managing the Employment Process.

I also acquired two diplomas with the Executive Education College of Management, situated in Braamfontein: Diploma in Financial Management and Diploma in Personnel Management. My unit dealt with a huge amount of money because they simplified corporate IT functions for all the Gauteng departments. I had to approve payments for purchasing of notebooks and office materials because the provisioning section also fell into my competency. I was to ensure that whatever I approved for payment was accurate. While still at IT and having completed all the courses I needed to empower me do my job, I still did not have any task given to me.

One thing I hate is to be idle. I then stumbled across a short course offered by PSG ONLINE. The course was earmarked for public servants free of charge, and the training was offered on-line. I'd always wanted to understand how the Stock Exchange Market works. All that I wanted was the basics. Being accustomed to turning over every stone I come across, I enrolled for it. After all, I had plenty of time given to me on a silver platter. The course came in handy as it equipped me with knowledge about how to invest in shares and unit trusts. I now understand terminologies such as fundamentals, All Share Index, equities, portfolios, how to interpret world markets performances and so on. It was an eye opener.

Despite the fact that I was the most hated person, something never ceased to boggle my mind. I was always fascinated by the speed that they were willing to approve my applications for a bursary to do the courses mentioned, for all the time that I was doing these courses. Some employees who were interested in furthering their studies would wait for a long time before their applications were approved and funding was released. I never struggled to get any funding as they would make payments promptly as soon as my application was approved. So, I used what was to be a disadvantage to me to my advantage.

All the courses were very expensive but I think that the department reached a point where they did not know what to do with me. I think I was so annoying to them, more like a pest, in that every time I completed a course, I would inform our Human Resource Unit and furnished them with the proof of my completed courses in the form of results and certificates. There was no one time that anyone ever responded in acknowledgement of my achievement.

The downside was that they would not bother to use my acquired knowledge for the benefit of the department or allow me to plough back. I was willing and determined to use all the knowledge I'd acquired to the benefit of government. Unfortunately, I never got that opportunity because the only thing they focused on was to devise some means to frustrate or get rid of me. They were so obsessed with victimising me that it clouded their judgement.

This is what whistleblowers go through. If they happened to decide to allocate me a task to perform, it turned out that there was always an ulterior motive. The idea was an attempt to try to trap me or just frustrate me by not giving me any support. So, it was a vicious cycle. In essence, not utilising me was a punishment but they were actually wasting state resources by paying me for doing nothing. This is one part that frustrated me: getting paid a lot of money for doing nothing, and especially that it happened for all the time of my employment years in public service after blowing the whistle.

Two years and four months after I was with IT, the department called Gauteng Shared Services (GSSC) was established. All transversal functions were to be centralised: for example, IT functions, procurement, human resources and financial matters. There was a huge restructuring and most of the people who were performing those functions were to be transferred to GSSC and those who could not be accommodated, due to duplication of functions, were to be deployed to other units in the line departments.

It was through this process that I realised how bitter and angry some individuals were with me. They took advantage of the process so that when everyone else was placed, I was deliberately left in the IT building alone. It was another attempt to break me so that I would leave. I tried to find out what would happen to me, but no one could provide me with an answer.

The extent to which I'd walked on many toes and had unsettled lots of people with enormous power in government became evident. One day, I decided to call the Human Resource Chief Director for GSSC with the intention of making an appointment to meet with her. I told her who I was and why I wanted to meet her in person. She sounded hesitant but agreed to a meeting. She asked her PA to give me a slot and scheduled a meeting.

On the date agreed upon, I walked to their offices and waited in reception because her PA told me that she was still busy with an urgent matter. I waited for quite a while. While sitting in the reception I could see her through the glass door and she too could see me. She called me in but looked very stressed and irritable. We greeted, and she told me straight in my face that she was aware of my situation, and she had been instructed not to deploy me to GSSC but could not elaborate. She told me that, although she did not condone the way I was treated, she was unable to intervene because my case was messy. She politely said to me, "I am very sorry, I cannot be involved, but to be honest with you I am proud of you. If we could get more people like you, we could fix this place." She said she was tired of been made to do the wrong things. She looked relaxed, as if a heavy load was off her shoulders. I thanked her, we shook hands and I left. She was happy to have met me in person, after she'd heard nasty things about a woman who was trying to take on powerful men. We laughed. It was not long after that I was told she'd resigned.

One afternoon, while walking to go and catch my transport, waiting for my husband at a strategic place, I met one of the heads of department, who placed everything that was going on around me into perspective. "Remember that when one goes through this kind of ordeal, even the closest people distance themselves from you." At that point I was literally on my own. Those who were close to me did not want to greet me, let alone associate with me. Some were turned into spies.

It was rare to come across someone like Stanley Sithole who stood by me all the time, although he was convinced that I would not make it because of what was said in staff meetings about me. He frequently kept me abreast by making copies of minutes for those meetings where I was discussed. He had experience in law, so he saw it from that perspective. But, in my view, discussing my situation in meetings was another way of intimidating staff members.

The HOD I mentioned earlier asked me where I was. I told her. She wanted to know with whom I was working. I asked her what she meant. She told me that there was an instruction from the Premier's Office to all HODs to not allow me to be promoted to any higher level than the one I was on because I was grounded. I said I was not surprised, and that I was content with that because what I had done was worth more than any position and luxuries coming with those positions. I told her that I was content and satisfied because I only responded to what God asked me to do: I listened and actioned, that is all. I'd expected to pay a big price and I knew that He would be there with me. But one thing I knew was that I'd saved this country a lot of money and had served my people well. I said that when someone does something like this, she should get rewarded: instead, I was ostracised.

It was true what she told me. I tried to apply for advertised posts in most government departments. With the type of experience and qualifications I possessed, I should at least have been short listed for interviews, but that happened only once, in one of government's subsidiaries, the National Financial Board. When I went to the interview, the receptionist asked me who I was and her facial expression changed immediately when I told her. I was not the person she was waiting for, her tongue slipped and said. The person she was waiting for was the one for the job. When I was finally called in the interview boardroom, I was met by hostile panel members, except for one white lady who really tried to calm the situation. The Chief Executive Officer and the other three guys just ridiculed and frustrated me. They already knew who I was, and I too knew what it meant, judging from their line of questioning.

The HOD was right in that there was a clear correlation between what she said and the fact that a few weeks before my standoff with DG I'd applied for a Chief Director position (Head of Secretariat) in the Presidency's Office. I was confident that I had what it took to be appointed. I knew secretariat work like I knew myself. The lady from the Canadian government who'd trained me for almost a month had given me the best knowledge ever and I knew I was one of the best placed black people in South Africa to master secretariat work in government.

I had an ambition to become the Kofi Anan of South Africa. I went for an interview for a Chief Director's position as a cabinet secretary in the Presidency. I was interviewed by a panel consisting of Director General (DG) Reverend Chikane, who was in the Presidency then, two Deputy Director Generals (DDGs), Anna Letsebe and I forget the other one's name, and a senior manager from Human Resource. I was the only deputy director short listed for the position. The participants were all directors and Chief Directors who wanted to make a parallel move.

My first interview was very good. I'd prepared thoroughly for it, and once done I could sense that I'd left a lasting impression. I was told that DDG motivated that I be considered straight away, after everyone was interviewed. If I was offered the job I was going to report to her.

It is a pity that in government there are individuals who believe that, due to their political connection, they are entitled for every promotional job. I was taken aback when someone in our offices who was close to the Presidency told me that one of the people who'd also applied for the same post was also called for interview. I knew whom she was talking about because as I left the interview room I'd found her with other candidates who were short listed waiting their turn.

When it was her turn, she went in, but in the process of an interview she confronted the panel, registering her dissatisfaction that I had been short listed. She wanted to know why I was interviewed for the position of Chief Director while I was at a deputy director level. I was told that her behaviour infuriated the National DG, who responded to her that the post was not about who occupied which level but about the requirements. He also told her that they were looking for someone whose qualifications and experience matched the requirement of the advertised post, and I did. For that matter, I was more qualified and had more experience in the field than she did. Maybe her advantage was that she was from exile.

Of all the candidates interviewed with me, only three made it up to the second interviews, but all of them could not make it to the third interview. I was alone; no one could match me. In the third interview I was given a policy topic and asked to compile a cabinet memorandum within 45 minutes. I finished it before that time, and I was spot on. After some time, I met the Human Resource person and he told me that I was recommended for the post.

Strangely enough, after I went for the interview, I had to go to the office of the Premier's advisor. He wanted me to help him with something. While sitting there and talking, he mentioned that he was aware that I'd applied for a Chief Director post in the Presidency. I said yes, and he said that I might be recommended for the post but cautioned me against accepting it because in his view the office was toxic, as some individuals always felt entitled to certain posts. He said to me, "Just know that there dogs eat dogs". I must say, it got me thinking and worried at the same time.

However, on the eve that the appointment was to be confirmed with me, the memo was leaked. A reliable source told me that DG called the National DG and told him about what had transpired. The appointment was stopped and the post was frozen. I saw the announcement in the Sunday Times newspaper. Somehow, I felt very good and proud that there was no second best: I was simply the best. I never received any formal letter stating why the post was not filled and instead was frozen.

The same week that the memo was leaked, I attended a meeting that had been arranged weeks earlier for National and Provincial Secretariat Forum. It was held at the Union Buildings. DDG for Cabinet Secretariat was also in attendance. I'd already seen the article saying that the post was frozen. I said to her it meant that I did not impress. She said, "You did and for that matter you were the right candidate". She looked very upset – her face told all – but I already knew what had happened so I just said to her, "What a pity. I was going to enjoy working with you". I told her that my experience of being with her in the forum had truly inspired me and thanked her for the opportunity. I was, however, saddened by the fact that what happened between me and DG had nothing to do with the post I'd applied for. He just abused his power and connections.

I first met Anna Letsebe in one of our secretariat forum meetings in Mpumalanga, and somehow we just clicked. She respected me a lot because she knew that I was the one who had established the Provincial Forum for all EXCO Secretariats to meet once a year in a rotational schedule. The National Cabinet Secretariat joined later. I formed the forum with the aim of sharing with all the secretariats the knowledge I'd acquired from the training I received from the Canadian government so that we could all develop our own "Best Practices Manual" that would assist us to work in a coordinated and uniform manner.

After that meeting she came to meet with DG, because she was told that of all the provincial secretariats Gauteng performed the best. She actually came to meet me, but she thought it was wise to go through DG. She told DG of her reasons for coming to the office. She told me that before she could ask DG to allow her to talk to me, he immediately asked one of his assistants to call me. When I got there, he introduced me to her and requested that I help her. She said that at that point she knew that she would want me to come and work with her because she already knew that there was a vacant post in her office, that of the Chief Director I applied for, but she did not tip me about the post. It was just a coincidence that I applied. None of the provincial secretaries applied.

Reverting to Corporate Services IT. After my meeting with GSSC's Human Resource Chief Director, the writing was on the wall that if I did not do anything about my situation I was going to fall into the cracks of government corruption. I wrote a letter to the Provincial Director General Mogopodi Mokoena, highlighting my predicament. He is a very pleasant person to be around. I had known him way back, while I was working in the Department of Housing and Local Government but employed in the Local Government section. Our section, that is Local Government, was later merged with Development Planning, and Housing remained on its own. Mokoena was part of the panel that interviewed me for my first job in government. Even though he knew that I campaigned for the Democratic Party in the Local Government Elections of 1995 he did not make me uncomfortable. I knew, because he asked me about it. He commended me for being such a brave person and said that for him it is what democracy is all about.

Getting back to my time in the wilderness, DG instructed the HR office that I be transferred as well, but instead of placing me at GSSC they transferred me to the Department of Finance and Economic Affairs, under the Gauteng Liquor Board Chief Directorate. NP was also transferred there, but moved first and I was moved after some time, regardless of the fact that DG had asked them to finalise my deployment immediately, something that told me that they were defying him.

I was furnished with a letter of secondment before I moved to the department I had been seconded to, and to my shock it was signed by the Director of Human Resource NT and co-signed by NP, instead of acting HOD PM. As acting head of department, he had to sign. I discovered later that NT and NP were very close friends. The letter was confirming my placement as a provisioning administrative clerk level 12.

I realised that the letter was meant to further victimise me by ensuring that I was humiliated. This was the lowest ranked position, which NP himself occupied. The provisioning administrative clerk portfolio is divided into several levels, starting from one to six. It depends on the years of employment. NP was on level 6, half the levels below my actual level of appointment.

I responded and addressed the letter to the Director HR. I thanked them for the offer, but stated my concern around the contradiction between the level of the position and the position itself. I told them that I'd never heard of a clerk being appointed at deputy director level. I could not therefore accept the offer because I could not be paid at level 12 for a level 6 position. I was given a list of funded posts to choose from. I was surprised that Gauteng Liquor Board Head of Secretariat at level 12 was on the list. Nonetheless, I did the formalities and opted for the one I deemed relevant. To correct the above, I was later provided with a letter from the Acting HOD confirming my placement. I did not know on whose instruction.

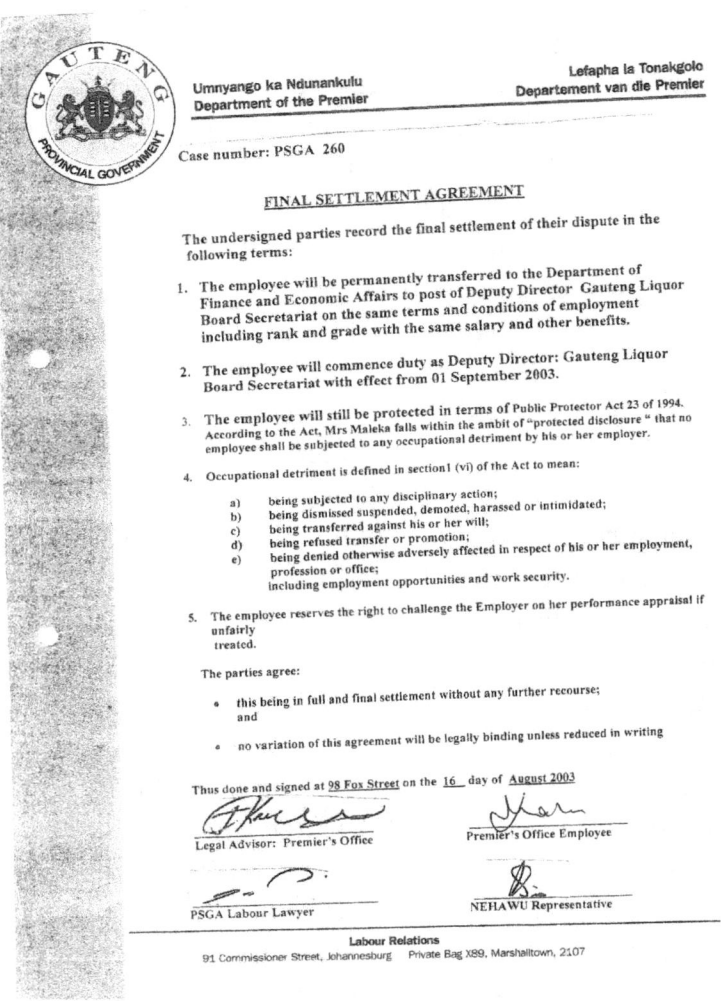

Maleka, Lethabo (GPDPR)

To: Mathanzima, Mlungisi (GPFIN)
Subject: Proposed Placement

[handwritten note: Letter written by Mo Tanki / signed by Mr Ned Pillay on behalf of Mr Maharaj. Hand delivered to me on the 30/07/03 at 78 Fox street, Standard Bank building at 1h15 by a messenger. Lethabo.]

MEMORANDUM

TO : Mathanzima Mlungisi
Dept F& EA (HRM)

FROM : Lethabo Maleka

RE : PROPOSED PLACEMENT

DATE: 30 July 2003

Thank you so much for the offer of the **Post Provisioning Admin Clerk level 12.** I truly appreciate this. However, I will only understand what the post entails once I have an insight since it is not my area of specialisation. I am always willing to learn and I am very teachable.

But since I am given an opportunity to choose from other options presented to me by the department, I will like to indicate that I will be better placed in the following options according to their preferences:

1. **Board Secretariat**. I have a vast knowledge and experience of four years in this function. I know that I will be able to make an integral contribution since I understand it very well.

2. **Regional manager**. My experience in project management, policy formulation, strategic management human resource management and the understanding of government's objectives stand me in better position for the post.

I want to reiterrate that, I do not undermine the position you offered me, but is just that I know that I could perform better in areas that I mentioned above. I cannot reject outright especially that I do not know what it entails. For the last 8 years in government it is the first time that I came across such a position of a Provisioning Admin Clerk at level 12. Only when I can be briefed about that I will say I do understand or not, but if I was without any options, I will be willing to accept it and learn.

Thanks once more for the offer and I hope to hear from you before 31 July 2003 so that I still have the opportunity to confirm.

Yours sincerely

[signature]

My response to the the letter

FINANCE AND ECONOMIC AFFAIRS
FINANSIES EN EKONOMIESE SAKE
TSA DITJHELETE LE IKONOMI
EZEZIMALI NE ZOMNOTHO

Enquiries: Nono Tantsi
Tel: 011 355 8628
Fax: 011 355 8072
E-mail: NonoT@gpg.gov.za

Maleka Lethabo
94 Main Street
Matlotlo House
Marshalltown
2107

RE: PROPOSED PLACEMENT

The above mentioned refers.

DFEA is pleased to offer you **Secretariat** position on job level **12** in the **Liquor Affairs** chief directorate headed by **Moses Moeletsi**.

Attached please also receive a list of DFEA's current vacant funded positions for you to look at, should you have interest in a specific position please contact Human Resources on extension **28454** or room number **237** for information pertaining details in regard to such a position.

Your response to the proposed placement in paragraph one will be appreciated, by close of business on Friday 1st August 2003. Should we not hear from you by then, it will be assumed that our offer is accepted.

We wish you the best in your career with DFEA

Regards

Pradeep Maharaj
Acting HOD: DFEA
31. 7. 2003

Finance and Economic Affairs, 94 Main Street Johannesburg Private Bag X091, Marshalltown 2107
Human Resource Tel: (011) 355-8533 **Fax:** (011) 355-8072

Third Secondment and perpetual secondments within secondments

When I was seconded to another department for the third time, my whistleblowing nightmare reached its climax. According to Cohen (1973) climax is: "The highest and most important point toward which the chain of events in the action has been moving".

What I am about to narrate in this section of the book could be dismissed as normal work environment politics. But, for someone who is a whistleblower it is a different story in that once a whistleblower you become the enemy of every corruption-loving individual in the public service. They will follow you, hunt you, until there is no place to hide and you have to resort to fighting back.

My third secondment was to the post of Head of Secretariat for the Gauteng Liquor Board (GLB). It is located within Gauteng Liquor Licensing (GLL), a Chief Directorate under MM. This was a Chief Directorate within the Gauteng Provincial Government's Department of Finance and Economic Affairs before it was changed to the Department of Economic Affairs. I worked very well with him, despite the fact that he already knew of my whistleblowing history. He had a high regard for me and gave me support, but I cannot say the same for most of the staff members.

The working environment was different from previous settings. The Gauteng Liquor Board was highly regulated and I had to learn the ins and outs of the liquor industry, including the Act and its Regulations. No one wanted to assist me. Everywhere I turned I was met with resentment. So, I had to learn as fast as I could. Having been thrown in the deep end for the second time, I still did not drown. I instead mastered all the swimming strokes required to do the job. It did not take me long before I could interpret the highly regulated liquor law.

Human Resource personnel, despite being embarrassed by me because of the administrative clerk position, did not forgive but tried to humiliate me again. A month after reporting to work, I was called to a meeting with the Director HR and her deputy, plus other union representatives. In that meeting, I was told that my position was out of scope. They explained what that meant. The position that I had been appointed to was of the same rank but a lower salary notch than the one that I was transferred from.

I was surprised, because the list they had given me to choose from reflected the same position and level at the relevant salary level. I was told that I could therefore not qualify for pay progression and I was to remain on the same notch. This meant that I did not even qualify for an annual inflation increment. But when it was sent to GSSC for ratification, the system could not decrease my salary level on Persal. Even though the system rejected their attempt to manipulate it, they insisted that the status quo remained.

I tried to oppose it with all the evidence before me, but they insisted that my level would remain lower than I'd had before. Fortunately, the system kicked that out until they gave up and I was paid my stated salary and received all my benefits as per my conditions of employment. I knew that they would not stop at that and that they would try something else to further their victimisation.

This is how the corruption network gets entangled in government at the expense of taxpayers' money and in the face of poverty, starvation and destitution. I mentioned above that poverty smell, because growing up in the rural areas I could relate to the smell of the distillery. The poverty smell is one smell I will never forget. I will never fathom how my fellow Africans, coming from the same situation as mine, once in a position of power forget that smell to the point of looting resources meant to improve people's lives. Women are at the receiving end of this rampant corruption in our government. Rural women are the hardest hit.

When I was moved for the third time, it was already four years since I had been removed from the Premier's Office for the reasons stated above. I never anticipated that after this long I would still be the most hated person. For me, everything was just a distortion because most people who claimed to have a reason for hating me had left public service and some had died. I could not understand why people still feared and hated me. I was labelled as someone who would always look for corrupt people and those who were corrupt believed this and became very agitated by my presence. More often than not, managers in all the departments I worked in would develop this dislike of me. Initially, it used to surprise and unsettle me until I managed to figure it out. The opinion they formed and acted upon would not go away until I discovered with shock who was behind the whole thing. I had a spy.

When I was transferred to Corporate Information Technology (IT), NP was also transferred to IT from the Premier's office by DDG. He was to report to me. He befriended me and I did not have a problem with that because I did not know him very well. He was placed on a different floor. Somehow, when he was in my office he would always bring the subject of my whistleblowing up, and innocently I would talk to him about it. He was searching for information, probably something that could implicate me. He understood that I did not have expertise in purchasing and supply chain, though I had a bit of knowledge about procurement from my previous job. I learnt later that he used to work for IT as a procurement officer and he was good at it. He somehow undermined me and tried to make me sign incomplete contract forms for IT procurement with huge amounts of money. I became very sceptical of him.

Then later, when they moved everyone to GSSC, they made it a point that he remained behind with me and only moved to another department that I was to be moved into, but not in the same Chief Directorate, but I saw him on my floor very frequently. He was the one who was spreading the lies about me.

As victimisation, intimidation and sheer torture took different turns and twists, I hung onto my prayer song by Yolanda Adams that saw me through the storm. I would play it every morning at 5 o'clock. *The battle is the Lord's*. It goes like this: "There is no pain, Jesus cannot feel. There is no hurt, that He cannot heal. For all things work according to the Master's purpose and His holy will, no matter what you in the balcony are going thru, remember that God only wants a chance to use you..." My response was to say, "Please use me, I am ready". I indeed committed to Him and allowed Him to do just that, no matter how difficult. It did not matter how they tried to twist everything to discredit me, all came down to one thing: that, unlike a lie, the truth is sustainable. I believed in that because the truth belongs to Him.

As soon as I realised what was going on, I told myself not to trust anyone and always work very hard. My strength lies in hard work, and I leaned on that. The job I was placed in was new and no one wanted to help me. I realised that if I did not do anything, I was going to fail, and I was not to play into their hands.

When everyone knocked off for home after work, I stayed behind to catch up. One day, one staff member volunteered to remain behind with me to assist me on how to draw up the agenda according to the Gauteng Liquor Act and Regulations. She even arranged that a government vehicle with a driver be booked to take us (including her) home. They were to drop me off first. I agreed and told myself to be more vigilant and to stay awake. When I got home, I went through the agenda and compared it with the documents and realised that it did not correspond and corrected it.

After a week of doing that I told her that her interpretation of the Act and Regulations was wrong. She said to me, "You are very smart". I only discovered later that it was a setup. The idea was for her to mislead me so that I placed wrong sections of the Acts on the agenda. I was to be humiliated at the board meetings and shown to be incompetent. She immediately stopped assisting me and cancelled the transport arrangement. There was no need any more for me to stay late as I could take my work home.

Fortunately, what I brought along with me was my five-years' experience in the Secretariat for the Gauteng Provincial Government Executive Council (EXCO) or Provincial Cabinet, so tabulating the agenda was a piece of cake. All that I needed to learn was their style of drawing it up. Someone who is not a whistleblower and has never gone through what they go through, will dismiss some of the information I am narrating as insignificant. But, for whistleblowers like me all these nitty gritties are crucial because they do not just happen but are meant to unsettle you.

The Chief Directorates I worked for from 2003 to 2017 had six Chief Directors and board chairpersons. They all knew my story. The more it was distorted, the more they believed it. I was moved from my position so many times that I lost count. I remained a laughing stock, but I would be so resilient and strong that I just frustrated them. Public Service laws are complex, and there was no way that they could fire me. I was determined to exit my job when I wanted to. Because my being there was by my choice and a commitment I'd made to serve my people, I had to satisfy myself. I survived so many traps and setups and disciplinary hearing attempts, as well as humiliations, it is not funny.

Although the spy I mentioned above eventually got tired, the damage had been done. He was, however, rewarded handsomely in that with a Standard 4 he moved so fast on the ladder to become Chief Director. He held cards for them, so it was easy for him to blackmail management for promotions. This is how Public Service Recruitment policies were manipulated to suit twisted individuals like him; something that explains why cadre deployment has survived to date.

But what boggled my mind more was the way those who are supposed to account for government money were (still are) never bothered. More often than not, they would side-line those whom they disliked by making sure that they were rendered redundant if not victimised. Meanwhile, those in their good books, often without proper qualifications, were paid for doing nothing. They are never made to account for anything, although they are promoting fruitless expenditures.

Most staff members loathed me, except two individuals who supported me through out my ordeal, that is, Jabulani Dubula who was in the Administration Unit and Trend Sibuyi who was (is) employed as a liquor inspector under the Inspectorate Unit. I will always be grateful to them. I'd had my share of victimisation emanating from something that happened many years ago, driven by gossip, distortion and malice. When I was transferred to the GLL, I was met with so much hostility it was nerve wracking. I was discriminated against by almost all the units – Human Resources, the transport section, Security, Finance, Information Technology... you name them. They refused to allocate me a parking bay. They would rather allocate bays to their favourite junior staff members who did not even qualify for one. The IT unit refused to allocate a laptop and cellular phone to me. I had to fight before I could be provided with those tools of trade.

I struggled to get an office and furniture when I was moved to the GLL. I had to motivate that I be allowed to go and fetch my furniture from the building I had been in. They agreed but refused to provide me with transport to go and fetch it. The official responsible for government vehicles agreed to fetch the furniture for me, provided I paid him. This even though, according to the transport policy, an official who is transferred from a department to another department must be moved free of charge. My job was piling up because it took weeks before I could have an office. Meanwhile, I was to prepare for board meetings. I was therefore forced to carry my work to the old office, two streets from the department I was moved to, so that I could work, and carry the load of work back.

The ill-treatment was unbearable. I informed the Chief Director of my predicament, and he intervened. He insisted that I be allocated an office and instructed someone responsible for government vehicles to go and fetch my furniture immediately.

When I joined the unit, the board chairperson was an internal person, but from a different unit, that is Consumer Chief Directorate. I was told that he was also one of the officials who earmarked the position of Head of Secretariat. The fact that I was brought in to fill the post unsettled him. I could sense that he did not like me from the manner in which he always ridiculed me, especially when he had to edit my minutes. He would make sure that I corrected them over and over, to the point of rewriting them. As if that were not enough, he would walk around from office to office, showing people those minutes, just to prove that I was so useless that I could not even write minutes, yet he was told that I was very educated.

This was in contradiction to how EXCO members praised me, as did DG, and my immediate Chief Director commended me for being the most diligent compiler of minutes the office had ever produced.

PM was such a serial rumour monger that he managed to influence almost everyone and made them see me in a bad light. He formed so many conspiracy theories about me and almost everyone believed him. Maybe it is true that people gravitate towards conspiracy theories that affirm or validate their personal view. In my case, I thought some officials resorted to conspiracy theories to distract me from my commitment to the truth.

With PT, I was not sure whether his negative attitude towards me was over and above him wanting the post, or if it was also motivated by the circulated rumours about my being a whistleblower. Although all these negativities made me paranoid, I preferred to keep my head up. Rather than wallow in the frustration of being rejected, I deliberately isolated myself and focused on my job. That helped me a lot.

At that point, the old Liquor Act was still in place but was in the process of been amended. The term of the board members came to an end the following year and it was supposed to be replaced by new members. When the process of appointing new board members kick started, as board secretary I was assigned the responsibility of receiving applications for the nominated candidates. I was to also oversee and to coordinate a laborious screening of applications process, short listing and arranging for the interview process. In addition, I was responsible for all the administrative work and logistics, as well as sitting in the interview session with selected members of the panel. After that, I was to carry out the placement and orientation tasks. This was an exciting challenge for me, and I was really looking forward to working for the unit after many years of been sidelined and idling.

This was despite the fact that the job was hectic as they had a massive backlog of liquor applications, and all that was sitting on my shoulders. One of my biggest challenges was to master all the sections of the Act and how to set agendas based on each section as quickly as possible. The most important thing was that I was to reorganise the secretariat unit because it was dysfunctional, as it was not properly constituted and managed.

I worked long hours and very hard. Sometimes I would even take work home. I was pleased with my progress and so was the Chief Director. He was not even aware that the staff members were resistant to assisting me. I chose not to tell him because that would have sounded like I was a crying baby. My mind fixated on the task I was employed for, not to nurse people's egos or entertain their negative attitudes. I saw their behaviour as a mere distraction and I was not prepared to allow that, otherwise I would have lost focus. Hence, I always tell people to grow up and smell the roses. Life does not revolve around anyone person, nor does it owe anyone anything.

Managing the Secretariat Unit effectively was hindered by the fact that there were vacant posts that were never filled in a proper manner. I motivated and fought with management to have the positions filled by relevant staff members, but my requests fell on deaf ears. Instead, it was capacitated by disgruntled individuals who were just thrown in from other units every time I asked for extra staff members. This was GLB Division that is generally known as the cemetery because it was filled with officials who'd fallen out of favour and who were ensconced somewhere in the innards of the Chief Directorate of the entire department.

The above-mentioned Chief Director left the unit a year after I joined. The GLB members were appointed. As part of their orientation, I made a point of organising workshops so that they were properly briefed.

My life became a living hell. Apparently, the new chairperson bought into the negative gossip that did the rounds about me. We had known each other before she became a board chairperson; she was a board member when I joined GLB, with PT as chairperson. I was told that they were good friends. I witnessed that in the first few months that I worked with the old board. Although, I sensed that she did not like me then, she did not show any dislike of me, and being just a mere board member she did not have the power. But things changed when she became the chairperson. She truly derived pleasure from humiliating, belittling and insulting me every time she got an opportunity. Other board members were very frustrated, but afraid of her, as I am told she was once an acting judge. I have never come across someone so notorious and cruel in my entire life. It was especially upsetting since she is a woman, and I am a woman: something I call self-hate.

The other thing that fuelled her hatred towards me was the fact that her friend PT had earmarked the position I was placed in. She'd really wanted him to be appointed, to the point that she'd tried to influence the acting Chief Director. She tried every trick in the book to have me fired. But, because my God is in control everything failed.

The thing is that almost everyone in government seems to love corruption, and the liquor industry is one of the worst working environments prone to corruption. The word prone is an understatement: it is rather infested and littered with sharks. I understood why almost everyone was sceptical of me because for them I was a stumbling block. I had a strong feeling that I was transferred in the Chief Directorate because of its bad reputation, so as to frustrate me.

The acting Chief Cirector appointed was FM, the Chief Director for a sister unit called Consumer Affairs. He acted while they were still looking for someone to fill the post. We got along very well. He was always objective, very humble, and extremely professional with impeccable morals. The new Chief Director was later appointed, CM. He was a spokesperson for the former Department of Finance and Economic Affairs MEC. He too disliked me.

He did not waste any time. He came to my office and told me personally that he did not like me because I thought I was a public relations person in that I went around calling people corrupt. I told him that his source misled him by providing him with a very distorted and fabricated information. I further told him that what I had done is called whistleblowing and had everything to do with being a responsible citizen and an honest public service employee.

He strongly believed that I was Democratic Party member and I therefore did not deserve to work for the ANC-led government. I was taken aback that a Chief Director could confuse the ANC as an organisation and government. We really started off on the wrong footing. I found him very naïve not to remember that our constitution allows for freedom of association, and therefore being a DA member could not be a punishable offence because it is my right.

It was not long before CM and the chairperson ganged up against me. I remember when he called a staff meeting and invited the board members. To my shock, the only item on the agenda was about how I managed the Secretariat Office as well as board meetings. I was bombarded with many accusations and there were some of my colleagues who availed themselves to attest to those false accusations, including someone who was my assistant. Both the chairperson and CM ensured that I was humiliated. Unfortunately, when it was my turn to dispute what was said, I highlighted all the wrong things they'd brought up against me as false, and I disputed all of them with facts and evidence. When they realised that I was about to embarrass them, they adjourned the meeting in haste, never to be repeated.

When everything failed, the next people to be used were those who reported to me. We were a great team but eventually they managed to infiltrate us by hooking up with one of my assistants.

I remember one incident that almost crushed me. My assistant was made, I believe, to find something that would implicate me. She stole a file that was about to be prepared for the board agenda and made it look like I'd lost it. Meanwhile, the file had not reached my office. I knew this for a fact because I always recorded incoming and outgoing files, including those that were set for the board agenda. The Chief Director and the acting Director for Administration sided with her and believed her story and the file was said to have gone missing in my office.

A meeting was called, attended by the Chief Director, acting Director and a Deputy Director managing regional offices where the file had come from and the Director of Human Resources. They told me about the file I was perceived to have lost and warned that losing a file constituted negligence, which warranted investigation and subsequent dismissal if I was found guilty.

I informed them that the file had never reached my office, but no one bought my side of the story. I immediately sensed that something was wrong, as the Chief Director asked the Human Resources Unit to investigate the matter because for him losing a file called for an immediate disciplinary procedure.

I was asked to provide them with a written report detailing what had happened, knowing very well that no one would believe me, including the HR representatives, even though the whole saga pointed to my assistant and the Regional Manager who'd stolen the file. Both my assistant and the regional manager had been long-time friends, I am told, from university.

But, because God cannot forsake His child, the issue about my disciplinary and ultimate dismal was discussed behind my back amongst my colleagues who were prepared to testify against me. A day before the first hearing, one of the caucus group called me and told me what was to happen to me. She must have got cold feet. Before the meeting, I was asked to sign a warning letter admitting that the file got lost while in my possession and that I was negligent. I refused to sign, and asked them to take it further because I was prepared to fight it. I could sense that there were some officials in HR who were in cahoots with the Chief Director.

My assistant became a volunteer witness in my first disciplinary meeting and Human Resource Director was there.

Two of my colleagues were there as witnesses as well. They all agreed that I must own up to the fact that I had been negligent, and agree I should be punished. I asked my assistant to bring evidence that supported her claim that the file was handed to me and that I signed for it. I knew she could not because it did not appear on the list that I'd signed. One of the HR representatives turned down my request, saying it was not necessary. I smelled a rat. I was on my own, and I had to ask my God to take control of the situation immediately.

To frustrate me, they were not only stealing files, for they attempted to steal my laptop several times but failed. Otherwise the information could have got lost and surely I was going to be dismissed. Liquor applications information is very confidential. I know that the idea was to get me fired.

I was surprised when later three of my junior staff members were called in and were asked whether they had a good relationship with me. They were encouraged to say unfounded negative things about me as the Chief Director led them with his questions. Fortunately, they all alluded to the fact that I was a good manager with incredible personal relationship skills, and treated them well even on a personal level and that I was a professional who never took sides.

My assistant interrupted and told them that I was too strict and a disciplinarian. The Chief Director took that as an indication that they were not all that happy with me. They all kept quiet. They in fact did not even know the reason behind them being called to that meeting and that they were supposed to hand me to the hangman. Although they looked disappointed, they still felt that I was a bad person. They were all excused and the initial team remained.

My God intervened during my confusion, humiliation and despair. The conversation I'd had with one of the caucus group members the previous evening flashed straight into my mind. So did the courage and the little voice saying, "Tell them". I started talking and told them everything and the name of the person who'd told me and all the members of the caucus group. Hell broke loose. With my God's help I disorganised them so badly that the Chief Director asked both his chief witnesses, who happened to be in the caucus group, to say something.

PT started talking and telling us what really transpired in that meeting, and he further revealed that the person who'd called me (PM) was the most corrupt official in liquor and she and the regional manager who'd stolen the file were two sides of the same coin as far as corruption is concerned. He qualified it by saying they took lots of bribes from clients and liquor agents.

The Chief Director and the Human Resources officials were tongue tied. Once finished talking, no one was willing to say anything. The Chief Director broke the silence by saying that the lady who'd called me should be investigated, because she might be working with HR officials who are so determined to have me fired, he said she was a danger to the Unit. All the truth came out, but the lady was never followed because they were all birds of the same flock. Their hands were already in the cookie jar and used to receiving brown envelopes (the name given to bribes in GLB).

The case was dropped but that infuriated the chairperson so much that she could not stand me. Her wrath became worse, and I could not tolerate it anymore. I had to do something. She eventually chased me out of board meeting sessions, so that I could not perform my duties. Even though I was no longer sitting in the meetings, she did not stop writing me letters and ridiculing me as well as telephoning me just to scream insults at me. It became obvious that it was personal to the extent that one of my colleagues from the regional offices asked me what it was that I had done to her. She insinuated that I must have stolen her boyfriend, although she was joking.

The situation became worse. Most board members left. The one who was so aggrieved by my treatment passed on later, not because of a broken heart. He had a terminal disease. Before he died of cancer, I went to see him in hospital and he held my hand tightly and said be strong and take care of yourself. Little did I know that he was bidding me goodbye. Unfortunately, the day after visiting him, my cousin's wife died in a car crash and I went to spend few days with them to give support. He died the same week, and none of the staff members bothered to inform me. I only found out when I came back to work.

Coming back to work, I decided to lodge a grievance with the senior managers about my predicament with the chairperson. They did nothing. They never bothered to acknowledge it. The Chief Director in question resigned. The acting Chief Director appointed internally was FM again. He insisted that I go back to the board because it was not allowed that the board should sit without its head of the secretariat. He demanded that if there was something I had done that warranted that I be removed from the board sessions, the chairperson should do it in writing. She refused to do that but insisted that she did not want to work with me and that someone else should be appointed to fill my space.

In the first meeting I attended, the chairperson spoke for about three hours, insulting me instead of doing what she was paid to do, and shamefully she claimed for all those hours. It was such a long speech that everyone got puzzled. I could not take it anymore and told her that I was tired of the ill treatment she meted out to me every time she was at the board meeting, and for such a long time without any provocation.

She approached the acting Chief Director, demanding that I be removed from secretariat duties because I'd disrespected her, forgetting that respect is mutual. He told her that removing me would have serious implications because it would be difficult to identify anyone to replace me, because in his opinion I was doing a good job. She said that she could not work with me; she just did not like me.

He came to see me with the intention of establishing how I felt about the whole situation. I told him that I would rather be recused from sitting at the board meetings because I was tired of nerve wracking confrontations with the chairperson. I also said to him that I was afraid that I would snap and do something I would regret and that was what they wanted. We agreed that for my sake I should avoid her because he could sense that I was already traumatised. I was removed once more. Although I knew that it was a direct contravention of the Public Service and Labour Acts as well as my condition of employment, I wanted peace. At that stage I was willing to allow them to do as they wished because I knew that it was just a continuation of what happened in the Premier's Office.

The situation was very stressful and started to affect my health and my family. Ironically, even though I no longer had any physical contact with her, the chairperson would send my assistant to come and call me whenever there was a crisis during board meetings. She would want me to account for the things that were not even in my competency so that she could find a loophole through which to insult me. She really derived joy in that; it was not funny. Then afterwards she would be so happy and would allow me to leave the boardroom.

I no longer complained to anyone, because the acting Chief Director had told me that I should not go, even when she called me, so I no longer went. She would write me letters or telephone me, accusing me of defying her and following up with insults. Trying to complain by escalating it to the most senior people was a waste of time. I observed that those who had the power to make decisions were afraid to take those decisions because it would compel them to take responsibility. My suspicion is that these positions are filled with people coming from the same inner circles. It is like a relay: the baton is handed over from one to another. It is the question of wrong people in wrong positions. They do not know how to do their jobs because merit in recruiting and appointing people does not apply.

The board's term expired after five years, and a new board was appointed with Advocate SM being the chairperson. I was still not sitting in the board meetings, only running the secretariat office in the background. Then Advocate FM was still the acting Chief Director. I recommended that PT, who was assigned to fill my place in the board, be removed so that I could take my place there. This infuriated new board members because they wanted him, not because he was competent but because he was willing to do the things that he was not supposed to do. They were already informed about my stand. PT was willing to allow them to claim more days than they worked for, my assistant told me, and who knows maybe other illegal things. Claiming for hours they did not work was, as far as I was concerned, tantamount to stealing.

However, FM gave me permission to go back and resume my duties. A day after it was announced that I would be resuming my duties, the new chairperson called me. I thought he wanted to introduce himself to me or just ask for something. I greeted him nicely and he responded very rudely. I was taken aback because I had not even met him. He murmured something and I told him that I had not heard what he'd said. He called me stupid. I knew that I was in trouble once more, and I was right because a similar trend played itself out.

The first day I went to the board meeting, I was received coldly by board members. As for the chairperson, all he did was to ridicule me. I kept my cool. He never stopped tormenting me whenever he got an opportunity.

One time, he came to the board meeting, late as usual. He told me to go and fetch his liquor application pack from his car in another building, a block from where they held the meeting. My assistant was there, but instead he wanted me to leave everything and go there. One thing that came to my mind was to ask why he'd left it there and not brought it along like the other board members, but I decided to obey the instruction. I then asked him which was his parking level and the bay number, as well as his car registration number and model. He answered in an angry tone and said I would find out there where they park, and I was a fool not to know what type of car he drove as it was a Mercedes-Benz E class. My assistant sensed that I was directly provoked, and she insisted that she would go. Before he could answer, she left.

I remember another incident when he happened to lock himself in a toilet, I do not know how. He was screaming that I should come and open for him. I immediately decided to go to the Maintenance Unit so that they could assist me. Someone came along with me. As soon as he came out he screamed at me, calling me a stupid woman, meanwhile blaming me for locking him in the toilet. I was not even near the toilet, which was one floor from the boardroom. I was flabbergasted. As if all the ill-treatment levelled against me were not enough, he refused to engage with me and insisted on referring to PT as head of the secretariat. PT was always there because he was also appointed as an extraordinary member of the board, representing Gauteng Liquor Licensing. Those were the days of my life as whistle-blower.

There was one day when we were filling their claims forms for their monthly remuneration. The chairperson instructed my assistant to add some days when he was not at the board meeting. I was the one who had to check them against their attendance register and sign them for payment. I refused to sign his because the days did not tally, and he could not be paid for the days he did not work. He insulted me and recommended that I be removed from the board.

I wrote him a letter, registering my concern and dissatisfaction about the way he was treating me, especially since he was not the one who'd hired me but the public service. Even if he had hired me, he did not have the right to disrespect me in that manner. I gave it to him at the board meeting. He ran straight to the head of the department KR's office to report me. He was received by one of the senior officials in the office, MM, who then took the matter to the office of the Deputy Director General (DDG) KT and handed the letter to him so that something had to be done to me. FM was on one week's leave, and one of the directors in Liquor, SM, acted as Chief Director.

I recall one incident that left me shattered. That was when MM, who was appointed as acting Chief Director for Gauteng Liquor Licensing Chief Directorate arranged for a workshop at the Gambling Board Offices in Bramley. The meeting was attending by Gauteng Liquor Board officials from deputy director level upward. A senior person from Human Resources, NM, was there. The aim of the meeting was to discuss the new GLB structure. HR officials took us through the new organogram, with names of people reflected on respective portfolios. My name was not there. Upon realising that my name did not appear, I felt a lump in my throat, blocking my airways. I took a deep breath as I immediately realised what was happening. It had happened to me sometimes, but somehow I never got used to the humiliation that went with it.

I asked Max what that was supposed to mean, and he simply said that they would place me somewhere else. I saw some of my colleagues' facial expressions. Some were smiling, others were just as shocked as I was. Obviously, those who smiled had had a preview of what the meeting was all about, and they were happy that I was going to be restructured out. What I observed was that HR personnel in government get very conflicted, because they are not doing what they are trained for, but what senior officials instruct them to do.

Reverting to the issue of myself and the chairperson. The following day, the acting Chief Director SM called me to his office and issued me with a letter to sign. The letter indicated that I was on a precautionary suspension and that I must be transferred to the Human Resource Unit with immediate effect while they did their internal investigation.

I refused to sign it and insisted that I must consult with the Internal Labour Unit representative first. Mduduzi Zwane was a person responsible for disciplinary processes in the department. I took the letter to him. He just glanced at it and went out the office in a hurry without saying anything to me. He left me there in his office and went to the DDG's office to inform him that what he was doing was unprocedural. He only told me when he came back to where he had gone and for what reason. He responded to them in writing on my behalf, disputing the fact that I must be investigated or that precautionary suspension was called for. He nullified their attempt to have me transferred to the Human Resource Unit as well. He mentioned that there was nothing wrong in what I had said in the letter to the chairperson.

The board, influenced by the chairperson, insisted that they did not want to work with me, so I was to be removed for the second time by a different chairperson. I wrote a letter to the HOD for his intervention. He never responded.

Then one of the staff members, PM, who'd hated me from the day I was appointed as head of secretariat, could not hide that she wanted Advocate FM to appoint her in my position. He refused. I went and confronted PM and asked her why she was doing that to me. She cried and went to report me to the acting Chief Director, Adv. FM, and told him that I'd insulted her, which I had not. I was called into a meeting in the presence of other witnesses. There, I lost it. I told her where to get off, that she had been horrible to me since day one and reminded her that she even told me that she was not happy because she or PT were the ones who were entitled to the position. She'd said that she had a problem with someone who claimed to be a corruption buster.

I did not know why PT wanted to be head of secretariat so desperately when he was already head of the secretariat for Consumer Affairs Board on the same level as mine, with only a difference in notch levels: that is he was on notch level 11 and I was on notch 12. I further told her in the meeting that I knew why she wanted the position: it was because she was obsessed with bribes. I also told her that I did not deserve that kind of ill treatment.

DEPARTMENT OF ECONOMIC DEVELOPMENT
GAUTENG PROVINCIAL GOVERNMENT, SOUTH AFRICA

94 Main Street, Matlotlo House, Johannesburg, Tel: +27 11 355-8000   Fax: +27 11 355-8694 | Web: www.ecodev.gpg.gov.za

INTERNAL MEMORANDUM

Enquiries:	Mr. S Mkhulisi
Tel :	(011) 355 8158
Ref. No. :	16617657

Ms. GLM Maleka
Persal No: 16617657

CONSIDERATION OF PRECAUTIONARY TRANSFER: YOURSELF

1. You Ms. GLM Maleka are employed by the Department of Economic Development of the Gauteng Provincial Government, and therefore being an officer of the Public Service of South Africa, are hereby informed that I am considering transferring you with immediate effect as we intend to institute an investigation for alleged misconduct.

2. Further note that, with effect from the 21st March 2011 you have been precautionary transferred to the HR & Logistics unit and you will be reporting to the Acting Director HR & Logistics who will provide you with tasks and activities you have to perform during the period of your transfer.

KANANELO TLEBERE
ACTING HEAD OF DEPARTMENT
DEPARTMENT OF ECOMIC DEVELOPMENT
DATE: 18/03/2011

This is one of many letters issued to me as an attempt to frustrate and humiliate me.

After the meeting, still crying she went to the office of DDG KT and convinced him that she was the suitable person to head the unit. She was temporarily appointed with the click of a finger; the letter was co-signed by another Chief Director, CM, from Black Economic Empowerment (BEE). Their motivation was rejected by the GSSC placement system because it only recognised me. There was nothing they could do with the salary increase because I still occupied the post. She became a glorified head of secretariat without remuneration.

When I heard that she had been appointed, I went to the office of the DDG and found him there. I told him that what he was doing was wrong and that he knew very well how much PM wanted to head the secretariat and that she was very corrupt as she took bribes. He just kept quiet. I remained in my position but not sitting in the board meetings for the fourth time, only managing the office. If you are a whistleblower in government the victimisation follows you unabated.

When the new Chief Director KM was appointed, and reported to work, I was on leave. He had already been told about my problems and predicament with the Board chairperson when I came back. He told me about it. I was not going to tell him anything because I'd already escalated my grievance to the Director General and Head of Department. I reluctantly related my story to him. He then requested that I bring to him some of the supporting correspondence, and the following day I gave him copies. After a couple days, he called me in to say that he'd read the documents and found some of the things I mentioned hard to believe, but did not elaborate. Somehow, I did not ask him to explain. I guess I was just tired and disillusioned.

After that, he never approached me about the matter. Instead, he and the chairperson became friends. After some time, the chairperson complained to him that the people who were assigned the responsibilities of running board meetings were incompetent and he wanted me to come back. KM threatened me that if I did not go back, I would be charged with reneging on my responsibilities and that I was not hired by the board but by the public service administration. He wanted me to go back to the board, even though he knew that the chairperson had chased me away and he had done nothing about it. I did not just walk away. I went back because I knew that he would make it look like I was irresponsible. I did not want to play into his hands because I could see that he'd already developed a similar attitude towards me.

But at the same time I realised that, if I kept quiet, my frustrations would become worse. I made the Labour Unit aware of my situation and registered the whole matter as further victimisation. The Labour Unit intervened by telling him that FM had told them about my situation and the reasons I was no longer sitting at Board meetings. He got scared and allowed me to stay away from meetings. My assistant would record the proceedings and I would do everything in the background. My assistant was transferred to one of the regional offices, and she was replaced by a wonderful, reliable person who could stand up to the chairperson.

The hurtful thing was that the new Chief Director saw my situation as a leeway to put his own people in my position because he had already heard of my story about being a corruption buster. He could not trust me and decided to alienate me under the pretext that the secretariat position required someone with a background in law.

There was one time when the Liquor Licensing Unit was to become an agency. The chief executive officer (CEO) was KK.

The unit was to be restructured into a new model suitable for an agency: that is, to be aligned to the agency organogram. Most of the managers stayed in their positions; it was only me who was shifted from secretariat to head a newly-established unit called Customer Service under the Communication Unit. Other new units had staff components recruited from outside. It was clear that the unit was established with an ulterior motive.

We had a workshop before the agency came into being. It was also the first time we were to meet the new incumbents. Before we started with the agenda of the day, we were asked to introduce ourselves. When it was PM's turn, she simply introduced herself as head of the secretariat. When my turn came, I too introduced myself as the rightful head of the secretariat. I already knew what that was leading to: it had happened so many times.

For instance, in one of the workshops held by the previous Chief Director, CM, PT stood up to introduce himself as head of the secretariat, but CM quickly reprimanded him not to do that and reminded him that I was the head of the secretariat. But when it was my turn, I introduced myself as the neck of the secretariat, just to spite him. During the lunch break, one of my colleagues came to me and told me that I was a witch, and he was not surprised because I came from Limpopo. I was not in the mood for those silly jokes, and I told him that I was not taking that kindly. He responded that it had been a long period over which they had attempted to get rid of me. Apparently, they were failing because I was using witchcraft medicines for protection (*muthi* in Zulu).

Nonetheless, I'd already heard that PM was trying to convince the new management regarding her being a suitable person to be appointed as head of the secretariat permanently. She had been doing that every time a new manager was appointed. When

Gauteng Liquor Agency (GLA) came into being, I had already been in the Liquor Unit for five years. She succeeded, though, but there was always a stumbling block. For example, although she was appointed as head of secretariat, she could not move to a higher salary level. It could not materialise because, according to the government system, one cannot appoint two people on the same rank and salary level. In this instance, although the idea was to turn GLB into an agency, the staff component was still employed under the public service and the system could only recognise me.

I was relieved though to have been moved out of from the secretariat. I was just happy to move away from a highly contested head of secretariat position. After all, I knew why corrupt officials wanted it: it is where most bribery takes place. I decided to make peace with all the changes and focused on my new role in that CEO supported me, and we had a good working relationship. I could say that it was during this time that I felt that someone was finally recognising me, though I could sense that he had been told about me and had opted to be objective. Besides, I performed very well and always delivered on my mandate. It was in my nature that I made it a habit that, when I was assigned with a task, I gave it my all.

The idea of an agency failed, and there were lots of complains from board members that the staff placed in the secretariat were incompetent. They requested that I go back. Even before that, I'd overheard management complaining about PM and that they could not have someone like her in the secretariat. I did not know what had happened. GLA management, that is the CEO and COO, called me and suggested that I return to the secretariat. The idea of going back to the secretariat did not sit well with me. I was not happy because I felt that I was being treated like a yoyo. I did not want to return there, especially since MR was still the chairperson. I negotiated that I be allowed to assume my responsibility for the entire Secretariat Unit but not sit at board meetings to avoid confrontations with her, and it was agreed.

Through one chief director after another and one board chairperson after another, the hatred increased as lies escalated and my story was distorted. After KM was fired, NT was hired as chief director. She continued in the same trajectory. She ill treated me as her predecessors had. Within a month after she was appointed, she decided to alienate me based on the ongoing rumours about me, without verifying them. I was not surprised because she was a long-term friend of MT. I knew that she was feeding her with those lies. MT made me her project in that, when a new senior manager was employed, she would brief them about me. She made it a point that she gathered as much information about what had happened at the Premier's Office, to the point where she kept a copy of the leaked memorandum that she went to source out herself.

Someone from the Premier's Office told me that she frequented one of the official's offices, who was encouraged to dig out more stale information about me. I did not know how she was to benefit from that. Officials like her must have used my situation for their own gain, hoping that they would be promoted to higher positions if they were seen to be against what I had done.

This reminds me of one of the harrowing incidents of intimidation and victimisation I experienced. One day I was in my office. I then heard some noises and commotion in the office next door. I immediately stood up to go and check it out because an official who occupied the office reported to me. As I left my office, I saw some of my colleagues standing in the passage. They ran away when they saw me. At the entrance of the office next door, I met MT. She left before I could ask anything. I was only told later that she was the one who had gone to management to report that in the secretariat there was an office full of liquor application files unaccounted for.

MT gave management the impression that I was the one who'd caused a backlog of liquor applications. She even went to tell some of our colleagues to come and witness, as I would be frogged matched out of the building for misconduct. The same time that the new chief director was appointed, the department had the new member of the Executive Council (MEC) and head of department (HOD). Hence, I am saying that these evil employees always targeted new senior managers as fertile ground to bad mouth me to because they assumed that they might not know anything about the horrific deed I'd committed: that is, blowing the whistle on corrupt practices.

Going back to the commotion in the office next to mine, I went to check what was going on, and in the said office there were some senior managers and HOD. As I came in, one of the managers said to HOD, "Here is the culprit," and I was asked to explain why those files were piled in that office and not been attended to.

Although frustrated at seeing what was happening, I recollected myself. The official responsible tried to explain, but they insisted that I did. Fortunately, I knew the status of every file there, and the official in question was very competent and reliable. I took them through every pile and pointed to the typed list on top of each pile and explained that on each list there was a name, application number and lodgement date, and there was also a summary of the status of the application. Those were in fact shebeen application files that had already been finalised by the board in bulk, and they were only waiting for shebeen permits to be typed and issued. I explained this as HOD interrogated each list.

HOD asked me why the permits were not typed and dispatched. I told him that the secretariat office was poorly staffed as I had only two typists and one administrator who assisted me with board meetings: that is, logistical arrangements. The official who was in the office was in fact on an internship programme.

I continued to report to him that the typists were overloaded because they had to type licences for new applications and other sections, licences for converted applications and shebeen permits. They also had to type refusal letters and letters for those that were postponed. Here I am talking about thousands of each of those mentioned above. I told him that ever since I had come to the secretariat I had made numerous motivations for additional staff with no luck. I had just been ignored. Instead, they would give me interns or those on contract, but that did not alleviate staff shortage as they were not allowed to deal with confidential information. This included functions such as typing licences and dispatching them and sitting at the board meetings to assist with the compilation of minutes and agenda. It is only full-time staff members working in the secretariat who could perform these functions.

HOD listened to me carefully, as if he could not believe what I was revealing to him. He was furious that people had brought him to my office to witness how incompetent I was, only to find the opposite. He pointed at MT who had come back and asked her why she'd misled him and wasted his precious time by lying about the files. He kept on apologising to me and told me that he saw the side of me that was different from what he had been told I was. I just said, "Thank you, sir".

I left and went back to my office. HOD followed me and said, "Mam, I am very sorry". I just kept quiet. He asked me why my office looked so neglected and wanted to know whether cleaners ever came to clean it. I said yes, but it was the general state of neglect that made it look so dirty. He also wanted to know why I had been allocated such a small office for my level. I told him that even this one I'd had to struggle to get. In government, offices and furniture are allocated according to the rank one is at. But, with me my rank did not count because I deserved to be treated differently from everyone because of being a whistleblower. My punishment and humiliation were perpetual and getting worse by the year as the information was distorted.

While he was still in my office, HOD sent for someone to go and call a person responsible for maintenance in HR. She came and he told her that they must ensure that my office was painted, and the filthy carpet removed and replaced by a laminated wooden floor by the end of the week.

When I'd initially seen HOD and his entourage of managers, I'd thought it was the normal walk about routine that they always did, but I was surprised that we had not been informed in advance as was a matter of practice. Once they'd left, I went to find out from an intern what it was all about, and she told me that for the last couple of weeks MT had frequented the office, asking about the files. Somehow, she looked very unsettled and I felt that she was not telling me everything. Not much later, she was taken on a in another unit on a permanent basis and at a higher level than an intern. For me it was strange because when the internship programme came to an end, those who came along were released. If there were vacant posts advertised, they were allowed to apply, but in this instance no post was vacant, so it was created specifically for her.

I was perturbed when, before the end of the week, HOD called an urgent general staff meeting to announce that there would be some changes to be made in GLL's board secretariat. He announced that he would be bringing in some people who were going to take over the secretariat office with immediate effect. The officials he referred to were from the Department of Development Planning and Local Government. I learnt that when the Development Planning section was merged with that at Johannesburg Metropolitan Council, some of the staff members could not be absorbed nor placed anywhere, so they were left there idling for several years. After announcing that, he did not indicate where the current staff, myself included, were going to go or what we were to do. I just said to myself, it does not rain but it pours, though I was not going to try to do anything then, though I felt upset.

As if the embarrassment she'd endured when HOD exposed her in front of staff was not enough, the day after the meeting with HOD, MT came to convey a message to me that she was instructed by the new Chief Director NT that HOD wanted myself and the rest of my team to relocate to another building. I was even told which floor to occupy. This time they were so determined that they even moved me with my furniture. I never bothered to establish with the office of the HOD whether it was true, I just left. The reason for moving me was that the old board's tenure was coming to an end, so they intended to fill the Secretariat Unit with new staff that was going to support the new board.

I was moved to the building a street away without any task to do, so my team and I came to work every day without anything to do for almost two years. I went back to square one: the wilderness. This time the chairperson of the Board was BC. I'd only worked with him briefly as during SM's tenure he was a board member then. The other time was when I was presenting conversion applications to the board. He came across to me as a very kind, loving person. He was later succeeded by LM. I was still in limbo.

I would like to briefly talk about what could be a compelling reason for those who made it their business to ensure that I was flushed from public service by hook or by crook. In government, there are employees who have a huge sense of entitlement; let me tell them, "Entitlement is a curse". So, in the instance where they do not get what they want, they become desperate. As a motivating factor, people like MT, PM and many others targeted me out of their ignorance, in that they thought that once a person becomes a whistleblower they are an enemy to those in power. They never asked themselves why I was not fired in the first instance.

Driven by desperation, they resorted to scheming, back stabbing, ass licking and gossiping. They believed that if they succeeded in making me resign they would be rewarded with higher positions. It became a state of mind, thus they could do it for many years, even if it did not yield any positive result. Maybe, it was because they saw people like NP succeeding because he was moved from administration clerk to deputy director, then to director and to Chief Director in a short space of time. What made their desperation worse was that he had only Standard 6. Of course, many other people benefited from my miseries.

The Chief Directorate I worked for between 2003 to 2017 had six chief directors and board chairpersons and all of them knew my story, albeit in a very distorted form. I was moved from my position so many times that I lost count. I remained a laughing stock, but I would be so resilient and strong that I just frustrated them. Public service laws are complex, and there was no way that they could fire me as I'd done nothing wrong. I was determined to exit my job when I wanted to, because my being there was a choice and a commitment, and I had to satisfy myself. I survived so many traps and setups and disciplinary hearing attempts, as well as humiliation, that it is not funny. Ultimately, I managed to figure out why wherever I went people had this twisted story about me. I had a spy, who eventually got tired, but the damage had been done.

I was told that while I was at the building I mentioned above, the Gauteng Public Service Commission contacted management in a six-monthly routine check up on me, and they wanted to know my whereabouts. I was surprised when we were brought back in a hurry to the departmental building where Liquor Licensing was situated. When we came back, I was told that there was a job for me to do. The job was not that of a board secretary. I was to assist the unit with the conversion applications backlog.

When the Old Liquor Act of 1989 was amended, the new Liquor Act of 2003 was promulgated and came into effect. However, there were thousands and thousands of licences that were issued under the 1989 Act. They were therefore to be converted to the new Act. It was difficult to move with speed in converting them and this disadvantaged the owners of the licences because of the way the grace period was given to convert. After that period, their applications would lapse. This created a huge backlog to a point that it became an embarrassment to the MEC as liquor applicants and consultants alike were up in arms. They wanted their applications finalised so that they could open and trade their businesses. Hence, I was asked to assist.

I knew that it was a trap because that kind of backlog had not been reduced in the two years that I had been in the wilderness, so how could I do it within a very short space of time? More so, I was not setting the agenda and not sitting at the board, and I needed to present them for the purpose of generating minutes and for accountability purposes. This was the question I asked them. It was not a coincidence that they'd thought of me because they knew that I'd never had an applications backlog before.

While I was still sitting at the board meetings, the process of conversion was already in existence. What I did was that I assigned one staff member to deal with them separately. By creating an agenda for them, with recommendations which in turn I could convert into a normal agenda for new applications, and break them down according to their sections, I created a slot for them and presented them in bulk. Board members would have perused the files before coming to the board meeting. All that they had to do was to decide. I did not know what caused the backlog in my absence, though. They were so desperate that they became nice to me and arranged that the board create a slot out of the normal board meeting schedule so that I could come and present the files.

With pleasure, I started working and performed a miracle. In no time the backlog was eradicated, and they had no choice but to praise me, or pretend to. I became the favourite of liquor clients, consultants and applicants alike. NT was later fired and replaced by an acting Chief Director, MM who hated me so much. MM, realising that they might want me back as the head of the secretariat, came up with another backlog project. This time, the project concerned dealing with a backlog of shebeen applications.

The Story of a Rural Girl Who Kept Rising and Rising

Thousands of shebeen outlets were not regulated and the decision had been made that they must also be brought into the mainstream. That was where I came in. In government, if they want to frustrate you, they come up with their buzz word: restructuring. Coming up with a unit to deal specifically with shebeen applications was part of his restructuring process. It happened so many times that I just knew that as soon as a manager came up with a restructuring process in GLB, I would be the one to be restructured.

I used the same method as for conversion applications and it worked wonders. But, when I realised that it was clear that the whole idea was to keep me away from coming back to my position, I decided to fight back.

This time, I decided to pluck up my courage and do something about my situation. I wrote to the Public Service Commission that I was still in limbo. They lied to them and said that I had been brought back to my position. I decided to fight for my job and made so much noise that they could not ignore it, even though they tried to. The Public Service Commission wrote a letter addressed to MM that I be placed accordingly, and I was sent a copy. He defied them. I took it upon myself and informed Deputy Director General MM, asking him to intervene. He instructed those people who'd assumed the role of GLB Secretariat to vacate the offices and I went back to my initial job.

This made things even more miserable for me, as MM could not hide his anger and hatred towards me. However, I must say there are still good people in the Public Service, and MM is one of them.

You must have observed that all the people I've mentioned who treated me well are men. I was shocked when I realised that I could not even recall any woman, especially those who occupied senior positions, who supported me. Most of them remained so hostile to me, in most cases in support of men. This is a stark reminder of the constant threat of self-hate. All that women could do was to ridicule, gossip and body shame each other, rather than uniting and fighting this multi-headed social monster called patriarchy. We cannot forever blame patriarchy. Yes, for many years patriarchy has been preaching the inferiority gospel to women: that patriarchy is created by God. The truth is that it is socially constructed.

Patriarchy has manifested itself in many shapes and forms and it has many tentacles, such as socialisation and culture, sexism, stereotypes, masculinity and the like. Sadly, the said identities are created through performative repetitions, 'over and over", until the lies look like the truth. The idea is to instil and perpetuate this notion via self-hate and low self-esteem amongst women. Hence, it is easy for women in high positions to support men because of the way they got those job positions.

It is commonly perceived in Public Service that women who have ascended to high positions did not get them through merit but that they used their vaginas as a currency in exchange for these positions. Thus, women in these positions are not respected. I once heard one woman middle manager saying, "I would rather remain at this level than sell my body for a position, and further, if I cannot get promotion through proper channels I would rather remain where I am." She said some of these people in these positions cannot comprehend what is discussed in senior management meetings due to their level of education. It is a shame.

Talking about sexual objectification, I personally witnessed this tendency in the event when we would attend work-related workshops or strategic planning sessions where junior and senior management would gather and spend some days out there at a conference centre. There would be these young women who would behave like dogs on heat as they went around sexualising or objectifying their bodies by flaunting them when these powerful men were present with the intention of enticing them. They did (or still do) this in the hope that once they have slept with powerful men they would in turn be recognised for high positions. Unfortunately, they were (or are) oblivious of the fact that the practice of sexualising or objectifying yourself is tantamount to self-hate and it is the biggest contributor to gender-based violence since, in most cases, once these men have slept with them they just discard them like pieces of rotten meat. Some even abuse them physically or emotionally.

I will keep on repeating that the reason why women are victims of male oppression and subjugation is that women themselves give men the impression that their lives revolve around them. Sadly, women have embraced an inferior status, wittingly or unwittingly, and hence patriarchy is still going strong because of our own willingness to be effective transmitters of this evil system. Patriarchy has thrived for so long because we women help it to.

There are three things that have helped it to survive at women's expense: self-hate, lack of self-worth and low self-esteem. Thus, instead of women in high positions supporting and uplifting other women, they subscribe to stereotypes that say that women are men's sexual objects. Hence, I am saying that as women we must educate each other about the detrimental effects of gender stereotypes. We should not only raise awareness, but we must also challenge these harmful attitudes if we are serious about freeing ourselves from patriarchal oppression.

Having said that, however, women could isolate the patriarchal elephant in the room and continue encouraging each other to unite and eradicate patriarchy. It can be dismantled because it is a factor in the subjugation and oppression of women. As Proverbs 27:17 says: "Iron sharpens iron".

Mel Walker illustrated this in four principles. One was the principle of relationship. As women, we must unite and have solidarity with each other to fight patriarchy. Women, let us stop focusing on minor things and focus rather on things that really matter. It also alludes to a principle of accountability that says that we must be frank and sincere by engaging in constructive criticism, not gossip behind each other's back. It also talks to the principle of motivation. As women, we must be mutually beneficial, not talk each other down or kick the ladder away once we have climbed it. Finally, it refers to a principle of willingness. Women are faced with the insurmountable task of defeating patriarchy by doing away with this collective self-hate that renders women invisible and "our own worst enemies". The time is now for women to mentally release themselves from the patriarchal ideology that informs the concept of women as inferior.

Back to the story. The board tenure was coming to an end, and the new board was appointed. The new chairperson was FP. What a technocrat and a professional. I knew that he had been told about me but he chose not to entertain office gossip. He remained objective and only willing to judge me on my performance. This was the first chairperson who ever treated me with respect and integrity. It really alleviated the pressure of office workload and, as back-breaking as my job was, I truly enjoyed doing what I liked doing in the office and board meetings. But I cannot say the same for his deputy chairperson

Dr WM. Initially, she commended me for the good job I was doing. As I recorded decisions and captured minutes, she would ask me to read out loud the decisions made after capturing them, consistently expressing her satisfaction and admiring my accuracy.

Even though I had an assistant to compile minutes, I preferred to also do it myself as a backup. Although no one ever made me do that, I did not have any problem with it. I thought she was too particular, especially by virtue of her being a doctor by profession. I knew the Liquor Act and its Regulations like the back of my hand. It was I who would take them through the process of perusing files and help them to interpret each section individually during the orientation process. But suddenly she changed. She too wanted her preferred official to head the secretariat. She would lash out at me without any provocation.

As head of the secretariat, I would sit at the same boardroom table as them to capture decisions accordingly. It made sense. Even when I was with EXCO, I would sit around the boardroom table, directly opposite to chairperson because she or he would be the one to make the final decisions after deliberations.

One morning, as I came in, she instructed me not to sit with the board. She instructed me not to sit with them and demanded that I should find a small desk and a chair, and sit in a convenient corner. I found one and squeezed myself there. I had my recording system, laptop and everything I needed cramped on a small desk. She instead allowed my assistant to sit with them. I was not going to say nor do anything. All the board members were puzzled but chose to keep quiet because they realised that she had been provocative.

Ever after, my life at the board was to be miserable. It was something I never got used to. Especially that as a self-declared born-again Christian she should have known better. She one day told me that there were other staff members who said bad things about me; in fact, of those she met none seemed to like me. Time and time again they spoke ill of me and for her it could be convincing that they were right. Amongst them she mentioned MT. I told her to let them say what they like, or believe whatever for what it is worth; I could not be bothered.

I'd just got my job back and it was back-breaking and nerve wracking at the same time. My plan was to not allow anything to distract me so I dedicated all my energy to it rather than entertaining toxic office gossip, which is all a mumpsimus does.

When she one day wanted to know what it was that I had done in the Premier's Office that had made people hate me so much, although I tried not to talk about it I decided to tell her in detail what had happened. I am not sure whether that one also added to her change of heart against me or not but that was less of my worry. My concern was her continuous lambasting of me for no apparent reason, simply because she thought she had the upper hand over me. The GLB did not have the power to hire nor fire officials, so I was not hired by them, but I needed to give them as much respect I could.

In instances like this, I always remembered Peter 5:7, which says, "Give all your worries and cares to God, for He cares about you". I tried not to behave like the "professional worriers" among us who takes their worries to God, but having done so take their heavy bag of worries back and carry it further themselves. Others carry this bag all the way because they do not know, recognise or trust God. I avoided falling into one of the above categories because I really wanted to live in total dependence on Him because my never-ending, overwhelming problems made me realise that He constantly provided solutions to all my worries. I tried not to be overwhelmed by worries because for me worries are nothing but a motion of no confidence in God.

The other big problem was back in the office. MM could not stop interfering in my functions and tried to cause trouble for me all time. To all intents and purposes, he was declaring a war. Because not everyone could stomach this kind of evil behaviour without losing it, I thank God that I managed to control my emotions and anger in the face of agony (extreme mental suffering).

I remember how at the official board orientation that I organised outside the office building, he made it a point that he humiliated and ridiculed me in front of everyone, including my team. Everyone was surprised by the treatment, but they could not understand why I was treated like that and they must have thought that I was incompetent. He would ask me to leave the meeting and go and make copies, even though I'd brought staff responsible for logistics because my job was to assist the board with the orientation process, and he was to chair the meeting. Instead, he brought people out of my unit to come and take minutes and write reports so that I was rendered useless.

The other incident that happened within a matter of two days after the board orientation was traumatising. He went to the extent of conniving with one of the consultants to implicate me. This liquor consultant, who was a lawyer by profession, claimed that he responded to the board's request with a motivation about an urgent liquor application matter. The matter was about his applicant who'd appointed him to defend his case in court. He was not satisfied with the board's decision, so he was taking them to court. He had been working with a lady who was appointed as the head of secretariat by the HOD before I went back. They both lied that the said consultant had written a motivation to the board, that it was e-mailed to me, and that I'd failed to inform the board chairperson about it and its urgency. They both claimed that they had copies of the motivation.

They tricked one of the new board members, who was also a lawyer, to assist them to escalate the matter to the board. I managed to prove to the board that I'd never received the motivation. I had all the correspondence on my laptop between myself and him. If I had not and the case had gone to court and they'd won, the department would have incurred the cost, and I would have been in a big trouble. Worse, I could have been fired for negligence.

Consequently, Max and this consultant wrote to the board that I be removed because I was incompetent. The board, especially the chairperson, came to my defence. They had been pestering the board members for quite a while that the staff who had been removed be brought back as they were competent. The consultant was known for corrupting staff members by giving them bribes so that his applications would be given preference on the agenda and would therefore be fast tracked. He knew that I would not agree to do that. When the new board member realised that he had been tricked, he resigned immediately from the board. But it would have cost me my job if I had not had any evidence to the contrary. Their information was just fabricated to suit them.

When MM's acting contract expired, the new Chief Director, NN, was appointed. She too just developed the same attitude as all of them. She interfered in my work so much that I was just frustrated. But I did not want that to derail me. She was later fired, and MM acted again. He continued with his negative attitude towards me. He enjoyed humiliating and belittling me in front of people for no apparent reason. He was just so hostile because he did not want me, because my being there meant that he could not get his hand in the cookie jar.

Everyone in the unit spoke about the brown envelope, meaning bribes from liquor clients. In most cases, the processing of the applications was delayed in the offices, but never at a board meeting. The intention was to frustrate clients so that in the end they would pay bribes in exchange for their applications being fast tracked. That was the strategy.

I witnessed one incident when I went to the reception to fetch something. There I found clients sitting unattended and I asked how they could be helped. They told me that they had been called to come and fetch their licences, but ever since they had not been helped. I asked people in the reception what the problem could be, but they just ignored me. I reached for a pile of licences to be issued and handed them to the poor clients. The idea was to make them so frustrated that they'd ultimately give them bribes in return for them getting their licences.

Now the big question: Why the obsession with the Secretariat Unit? Over and above the Secretariat Unit, the Gauteng Liquor Licensing Chief Directorate has four units at Head Office, Administration and Licensing, Inspectorate, and Client Relations or Communication, and there are four regional offices all reporting to Administration and Licensing.

Applications for liquor licences are made at regional offices. The regional offices have committees structured the same as the board. They too have a secretariat assisting them in generating the agenda, and recording and taking minutes. The committees do not, however, have decision-making powers. Their role is to make recommendation to the board. Once recommended, the applications will be brought to head office. They are recorded accordingly and referred to the secretariat.

There, they are consolidated into one agenda (draft) that will be broken into individual sections. Copies of the files are sent to the board members electronically for perusal three days before the meeting. Before the board meeting, the board must have received their final agendas.

At the actual meeting, the board will deliberate on each file and make recommendations, either grant or reject, unless there is a situation where there are a few documents that are not up to the requirements. Then, the matter will be postponed, allowing the client to submit new documentation.

When I was there, it was at the board secretariat where a consolidated final agenda was made and it was a stage where corruption could take place, in that officials could make applications for some clients jump the queue, if a bribe was paid. These bribes did not come in small monies: they could range between R25 000 to R45 000 per file because most of progressive liquor consultants have money as they represent big liquor outlets and restaurants. The liquor industry is a multi-billion business.

Because of this, I never allowed any of the staff members to generate agendas because in that way I could have compromised myself, and it would have been easy for anyone to trap me.

The other thing was typing licences and issuing them. This function was also done in the secretariat. It would have been easy for officials to issue fraudulent licences to those who were willing to pay handsomely for them. It happened, but it was always easy for the inspectorate to pick this up and confiscate the licence, as well as close serial offenders' businesses or outlets.

Fortunately, my colleagues who typed and issued licences were very reliable, but I also developed my own checks and balances to keep track of records before they were issued. They were recorded, and they had to correspond to those that were on the agenda and granted by the board.

The fact that people could not get their hands on the agenda and licences made them very angry. They would even influence some consultants to try to tempt me. I remember an incident when one of the clients came to my office to check on the status of his application, and deliberately left a brown envelope underneath my documents on the desk. Later, as I went through those documents, I saw the envelope and checked inside it. There was a stack of money there. I put it somewhere safe and kept quiet and he must have thought I'd taken it. Somehow, I just knew it was him.

After a couple of days, he came back to check on the status of his application and I gave the report to him that it was still in the process. He stood there looking at me. I took out the envelope and gave it to him and said, "Is this what you are waiting for?" He left my office without looking back. He knew where to check application status but had insisted on coming to my office.

Officials prone to corruption would be so desperate, to the point of breaking into my office in an attempt to steal my laptop and blank licence papers to try to print fraudulent licences. When it happened several times, I was very frightened because, if they happened to find me there, they would hurt me. What was more horrifying was that even if I reported these incidents, the management simply turned a blind eye.

The most disturbing common perception about whistle-blowers like me is that I was considered unpatriotic and an enemy of the ANC-led government, and accused of thinking that I was a saint. To mind comes an incident when one-time Deputy Director General SN called a general meeting for the

Chief Directorate units he was responsible for: Regulatory Chief Directorates such as Liquor and Consumer Affairs. I happened to be the last person to enter the hall where the meeting was held. I sat in the front sit row and as I sat down I had this official asking the DDG who this troublesome woman in the Liquor Unit was. To my shock the DDG *su-su poned* me with his head: that is, pointed with his head in my direction. I was really perturbed and uncomfortable.

The meeting started and in no time acting HOD BM then entered the boardroom where the meeting was being held and greeted everyone. Without wasting time, she simply said, "PT, as from today you are the Liquor Unit's head of secretariat," and excused herself, allowing DGG to continue with the meeting. Everyone looked at me, expecting some reaction from me. I just stood there stone dead. After all, there was nothing shocking, as it had happened to me too many times. I had learnt not to show frustration because I knew that I was perpetually treated like that with the intention of breaking me. I accepted it, although I did not know that it was the life one had to live as a whistleblower: stigmatised.

The worst thing is that the Liquor Licensing Unit was in itself infested with corruption, and most staff members took bribes. Even those on contract or coming for internship programmes understood the language very quickly: faster than learning the ins and outs of being in a job environment that would give them an opportunity to gain experience. Instead, they focused more on taking bribes. They were also warned about me; one could just sense that from their changed attitude. It is a vicious cycle that would be difficult to eradicate.

Public service, especially GLB, was the work environment in which I met managers with so much arrogance, and where nonchalance became the order of the day. I recalled how one of the chief directors referred to staff members as his subjects. What a shame.

Later, when I started to understand what whistleblowing is about and the consequences thereof, it dawned on me that, despite how public service whistleblowers are ill treated, I was comforted by the realisation that for me whistleblowing is an essential weapon in the fight against corruption. Whistleblowing must be encouraged instead of exposing the whistleblowers to victimisation, prejudice or harm. Protection of whistleblowers would go a long way in encouraging more people to bring allegations of fraud and corruption to the attention of relevant institutions such as the Public Protector. This nowadays is much better because there is an advocacy group called the Whistleblower House Organisation. Life in the workplace for a whistleblower is so lonesome that one could just cry all the time; it is paralysing, I must say.

The reality is that corruption is a lucrative business in government. It is like a vicious tornado that leaves a trail of destruction in the process. Thus, this country is in such turmoil. The evidence is in a visible collapse in service delivery. It explains why this country is in such a mess. Those who are entrusted with the responsibility of serving the people are serving themselves as they scramble for quick riches. The extent of corruption and lack of willingness from those in power to do anything other than protect them renders whistleblowing useless. It is sad that instead of South African rallying around the whistleblowers, they let looters run amok.

"The bottom line is that corruption is a betrayal of our democracy and an assault on the institution that we established together to advance the values of our constitution and the interest or our people," said President Ramaphosa.

But, where I differed with him is when he said: "corruption has become brazen in recent years, going as far as the assassination of whistleblowers", referring to the killing of Babita Deokaran. Many whistleblowers have been murdered (see the dedication part of the book). The Zondo Commission took a myth out of whistleblowing and brought into the open the extent of corruption this government faces, and I feel vindicated. However, what remains a concern is the pace at which Ramaphosa will move. Maybe, just like his predecessors, it will remain just another lip service.

Nonetheless, when my time came to retire, I was worried about the office knowing that in advance because I wanted to leave silently. Everything worked according to my plan. MM was angry that he was not appointed in the chief director post permanently, so he resigned. Once his resignation was announced, I made it a point that he signed my retirement applications. I knew that by the time a new chief director was appointed he would have left.

The new Chief Director, RM, was appointed. I was to experience torrential rain. His attitude towards me in the few days he occupied the office was nerve wracking. I opted not to tell him that I was resigning. I told no one, not even board members, because I knew that it would spread like wildfire. With RM I was baptised with fire. He was so desperate to flush me out that it seemed as though his job depended on it, or he'd been hired to do just that.

For example, it was only a few weeks after he joined GLB that he came to my office, demanding that I made him copies of minutes of board meetings. He handed to me a piece of paper on which he'd listed those that he wanted copies of: that is, with the date on which they were ratified by the board. He insisted that he had to get those copies the same day, even though I was about to knock off, as if it were an emergency. I did not mind, but it was not. I never had any problem working overtime if I had to. Besides, I was already working overtime every day, as I started work one hour earlier every day and I never got to break for tea or lunch; that was on my own accord because it worked for me. I did not expect any remuneration from my employer because I'd decided voluntarily to work those extra hours.

I reached for the minutes filed in stacks of lever-arch files because they were stored in my office for safe keeping. I personally selected those he wanted because they were filed by date, month and year. I went and asked my colleagues responsible for filing, the administrative clerks – to assist me. He said to me that I should carry the task out alone, for accountability purposes. I explained to him that it would faster if I got their help since it was so urgent. Besides, they were the ones who'd collated and filed them, so there was no risk in them helping me. When he became agitated and insisted, I smelt a rat (dead).

Anyway, I conceded to his demand and went to the room where the photocopying machines were stored. He followed me and stood there as I made copies. He called one of my colleagues heading another unit to accompany him while watching me like a hog. He was poking fun at me. It was fun for them as they made a mockery of me and laughed out loud. I was shocked when I realised that some of the minutes were missing. The worst thing was that some of them had the wrong dates printed on them. I realised that I was going into a trap, and I felt devastated and angry, but told myself to try to stay calm and think fast.

All the minutes in those files were originals and I had them stored in my laptop. He started tormenting me and shouting around, wanting to know where the missing minutes were. I just kept quiet and went to my office and printed the missing ones from the computer. I also printed even those with wrong dates, and strangely enough, those in my computer had the correct dates. He refused to accept them, saying that he wanted the original ones signed by the board chairperson. All board minutes signed were also saved on my laptop and my assistant's computer for back up. But no, he wanted the ones in the file because he had an ulterior motive, and he knew already that they had been tampered with.

Later, the board chairperson called me. He sounded very distressed, and he asked me what was happening with the missing minutes. He was obviously embarrassed. I politely told him that something did not add up and I was equally confused. CD had called the chairperson; I did not know what it was that he'd told him. When he called on my mobile telephone, CD was standing in front of me, listening. He must have read the frustration on my face. I promised the chairperson that I would fix it.

In the same breath I asked myself why the chairperson could not recall that minutes for every meeting were captured during the board meeting and perfected the following day, and he always edited them. The board sat on Wednesdays of every week. By Friday of the same week the provisional set of minutes was furnished to board members so that at the next board meeting they would all have read them. Some would even comment on them before the meeting. At the board meeting they were ratified, and the chairperson would move that they be approved, subject to corrections to be made. Before they were sent to the chairperson, I made a point that I edited them, even though I'd already corrected the provisional set. I was just particular about making sure that the records were accurate.

This was critical because minutes were used in instances where the board was taken to court by either liquor applicants or consultants. Otherwise, it would be easy for them to lose court cases and the department would incur huge costs. It was important to avoid such things. The corrected ones would be forwarded to him for his signature and then they were filed. There was never, ever a day when the minutes were not available, and he even checked things like dates. He must have forgotten those processes because everything happened so fast, and I could image how embarrassed he was.

Something surprised me. I realised that he frequently consulted the staff who reported to me in their offices, and sometimes they would come to him. They looked all cosy together. I could smell harassment and victimisation from far away, and I knew that I was being tormented.

I was right. Late in the afternoon, after I'd finished making copies, I went to my office. As I approached the door, someone was standing next to it. I'd never seen him before. He asked whether I was the person he was looking for. I said yes and asked him who he was. I ushered him into my office reluctantly, and we sat down. He told me that he was from the head office's Labour Unit. He said he had been called by RM to come and investigate an incident or case of negligence, referring to the missing minutes. He asked me questions and I responded and showed him the minutes stored in my laptop. I did not only show him signed minutes but I indicated to him that the minutes for the meeting corresponded to the agenda. I pointed him to the draft minutes as well, and they all corresponded.

He was listening attentively. After I'd finished, he said, "Mam, I am not going to do what they have asked me to do: that is, implicate you". He asked whether I could not sense that the whole thing was a setup and said that he would never dismiss someone who had done nothing wrong. He further said that what would be crueller was to do that to someone who was on the verge of retirement. He said for him to do that, someone must have done something very wrong.

The thought that CD wanted to dismiss me, knowing very well that I was about to retire, was an indication of a desperate person, especially since he liked poking fun at my age every time we had a general meeting, which was an indication that he knew how old I was. As if that were an issue for me. I considered myself blessed to have reached that milestone. For him it was something to use to mock someone he did not even know. He must have been confused by the fact that I had not indicated to him that I was leaving soon, although I already secretly had my ducks in a row. In public service one could leave at 60 or 65 years old.

Although I found his behaviour a sign of an idiot, the whole saga threw me into shock, and I was shaking with anger when the labour person told me that it was an inside job, meaning that CD had used some staff members reporting to me who were familiar with the minutes and especially where they were kept. This meant that the files had been interfered with. I had a sense of who that person was, but I did not have any evidence.

The man from Labour then told me that CD desperately wanted to get rid of me and asked me what I had done to him. I told him that I hardly knew him and said he should please ask CD himself. He further said, "When I told my colleagues about your situation, some of them knew you and they said, 'poor woman'. Why have you been witch hunted?"

I asked him whether he ever heard of whistleblowers and he said yes. I asked him whether he'd ever met one, and he said no. I told him, "You have one right in front of you". I said to him that I was a reflection of what whistleblowers go through in these corruption-infested institutions. He asked me whether I was never scared that I would be killed, like many whistleblowers. I said I had been in the whistleblowing wilderness for more than ten years, and in all those years I'd prepared myself for that. It was not that I was not scared but, as a spiritual person, I had faith in God because the truth is His. At this stage he was more sympathetic and polite. At the beginning, he'd sounded arrogant and intimidating.

I was dumbfounded and consumed by rage. I realised that I could not cope anymore. He left and I too left for home. I did not tell anyone at work, but I told my husband. He was helpless, and I was numb. I had been through hell. It had happened so many times while working in that environment and still it was something I could not get used to. It was emotionally challenging and physically as well as spiritually draining at the same time.

The news that there was someone who would finally get rid of me was heard by both my haters and my lovers. Some ululated while others asked me about it with a sense of concern. I had nothing to tell.

The Chief Director RM was not about to stop. Realising that his mission had failed, the following week he called a meeting between myself and two staff members: the one was my assistant, and the other was one of the typists. The meeting was scheduled for late in the afternoon, after working hours. In that meeting I was the agenda. He started ridiculing me and telling me how incompetent I was, and he had a good mind to remove me and replace me with my assistant, who only had Grade 10. How she became my assistant in a non-existent post was a mystery, but nothing was surprising in that environment.

He asked the typist to confirm whether there were licences that were lost or typed wrongly, while I did nothing about it. I do not know what happened to me that day, but I could not take it any longer. I was brutally honest with him. Before the typist could respond, I told him to never make it a habit to call meetings only to ridicule me in front of my juniors. It was like someone was talking for me the way I was factual and pointed to the fact that I was aware that he hated me, and demanded to know why. I assured him that if it was about me being a whistleblower, he must just know that I would not be silent, and no one would silence me.

He was taken aback and said nothing. Instead, he dismissed us, and the meeting was closed. I could sense that he'd briefed the staff before the meeting. When out of his office, I told them to never compromise me like that again. I was still left with few months to my retirement and for me those months were going to be the longest.

Different chief directors had the same attitude towards me, and similar incidents had happened previously. MM had called my unit staff to a meeting and I was the only item on the agenda. He had been sitting there, calling me names and humiliating me. I lost it in that meeting. My father taught me that if someone treated you with contempt in front of an audience, I must do the same there and then in front of the same audience. Otherwise, if I went to confront the person privately, she or he would not feel the pain I felt. It did the trick, I told him the painful truth of what I thought of him in front of staff members. He never did it again. So, the trend of how they treated me was the same, with the same intention. I wondered whether this was what cadres are taught from somewhere: to not tolerate those who stood in their way of eating; that is, looting state coffers.

One day, while at home after a bad day at the office, I remembered my mother's advice that I should read the bible for guidance in life and page it in a particular way. I had done that all my life, casually, until the whistleblowing saga. I intensified my reading because I needed God and most especially answers for my almost daily roller coaster circumstances. But when I came face to face with another hater of whistleblowers named RM, I remembered what my mother had taught me about paging through the bible. Doing this, I found verses that were helpful to me, but I did not know how to consolidate and simplify them so that they became something I could hold on to.

Then, I came across a song sung by Ryan Griffs: I would not be silent. For God promised in Ephesians 6:11 that I will stand by you. In Isaiah 41:13, He promised that: I will help you through when you have done all you can do, and you cannot cope. In Revelation 21:4, He promised that: I will dry your eyes. In Exodus 14:14, He promised that: I will fight your fights and in Deuteronomy 31:6, He promised that: I will hold you tight and will not let go.

I am happy that I did not choose to be silent and that I spoke up, for I knew that He would fulfil all His promises so that I could live to tell my story. I thank Him for that.

At the Premier's Office and at the Gauteng Liquor Board I experienced ravaging corruption first hand. Corruption has been a persistent phenomenon throughout history, which I know, being a student of Political Science and Public Administration. Numerous scholars concur that it has afflicted all forms of government and remains one of the most important challenges to the moral basis of modern states. Corruption in the form of patronage and nepotism is an ethical issue, based in the value system of a nation, and its eradication requires total commitment and concerted efforts by government and civil society to change a polluted moral culture. There is no doubt that political corruption poses a particular danger to newly democratised countries such as South Africa.

I would therefore like to elaborate on what patronage and nepotism are, for readers to understand the reason why the South African public service is riddled with corruption, which is the main contributor to poor performance and service delivery. Also, why corruption is so rife in these institutions and those that benefit are hell-bent on destroying whistleblowers.

Corruption is a composite name for mismanagement, maladministration, patronage and nepotism. Below I will try to define what both patronage and nepotism are.

According to Gibbons and Rowal (1976), "patronage is a process whereby employment in government institutions is awarded by the government based on party political support, or where friends or relatives are employed on a non-merit basis. It entails the assignment of public positions to political supporters and relatives. It is broad in its scope, as the achievements of government depend largely on the number of people who are indebted to government for jobs or contracts. For the political actor, the rewards are power and the retention of office, while the non-political actor might enjoy money in the form of salaries or other benefits".

Scott (1972) suggests that, by employing political affiliates, friends, and family to staff the public service, the political party machine also gains a stable means of maintaining internal discipline and cohesion. For Sylvia (1989), "in terms of a patronage system, government jobs can be a source of long-term stable employment, especially when the party to which the public officials owe loyalty can maintain itself in office. Patronage, however, can result in the selection and appointment of a poor-quality public officials, resulting in the downgrading of the quality of services offered by public institutions. It would lead to maladministration if too much emphasis were placed on political affiliation and family ties when appointments t public office was being considered."

Close to patronage is nepotism. Nepotism, according to Hanekom, (1984), "is derived from the Italian word 'nepoli', meaning nephew, or even more broadly, family. Nepotism is the principle of personnel selection based on subjective criteria and ignoring the merit of the appointment. Preferential treatment is given to an individual who is a member of the family, thereby resulting in discrimination against people who are not family members. Nepotism may be regarded as an irregular and unethical practice and as such can be viewed as a manifestation of corrupt behaviour, because the misuse of authority can lead to unjustifiable benefits accruing to a specific individual relative."

Hillard (1994) argues that in these instances, merit is overlooked while it should be the basic criterion for the appointment and retention of qualified public officials. The idea for poor appointment of the public service is premised on patronage. These employees are unable to separate political work from government work, and they too behave like politicians and are always shielded from accountability by those who appointed them.

As a person who majored in African Political Science, I know why Africa is what it is today. Some of the contributing factors are: greed, corruption, maladministration and nepotism, appointing people without qualifications and experience, who can hardly comprehend issues that are killing the country. If left to escalate, it will one day truly become a very dark for the rest of South Africa. Zimbabwe is a classic example.

For example, in South African public service corruption in the form of patronage and nepotism is matched only by frightening ignorance, a dangerous and toxic combination. These uneducated people occupying high-ranking position think that they are above others, as well as the law, as we now know from the state capture commission. The thing is that government environment attracts individuals without a vision, because of the way they are hired.

We are the last to taste freedom on the African Continent. Surely we should have learnt from other African countries' mistakes, how corruption could become a cancer and consume all of us? It is a pity that nepotism, maladministration, mismanagement and greed cloud people's thinking and are loved. Who cares about redressing the legacy of the enormous damages created by the monstrous apartheid system? All that matters to them is owning a Mercedes Benz, eating and sleeping luxuriously in a mansion, while squandering millions of Rand of taxpayers' money. How they really go to sleep at night is scary. It affects the very same communities that were brutalised in the past, and is incomprehensible. The question is "What now? *Amabenzis* (my Mercedes-Benz), gravy trains or bicycles".

My retirement day finally came on the 28th of April, which was also my husband's birthday. I just exited public service and government for good, without saying goodbye. I remember how I pulled my car from the parking lot I'd allocated to myself after many years of them refusing to allocate me a bay. I did not need their farewell parties nor their flowers. I wanted to go back home and rest. What came to my mind was Hlengiwe Mhlaba's song: "He lifted me up from the deep muddy clay and He planted my feet on the King's highway and that is the reason I sing and I shout, for Jesus came down and He lifted..."

I never thought I would leave my work environment alive. The idea of being killed never left my mind, and I constantly watched my back. I remember how I would never forget to look around every morning when I parked my car, feeling as if someone was about to murder me, and how I checked my car tyres every afternoon when I knocked off. All that I did was to glorify God for having chosen me for the task. As they say, He will never give you something you cannot accomplish. He gave me the best nutritional products in the world to sustain my physical, mental and spiritual health. Some might have survived the assassination attempts, but were left with scars for a lifetime in the form of acute stress that ate their bodies. Some had strokes or a nervous breakdown. Some even lost their families due to unbearable emotional stress. It is bound to affect one's sense of emotional control, and that naturally is transferred to those closest to you because the torture crosses too many boundaries and it does not matter how strong your fighting spirit is.

My whistleblowing story mirrors what we all endure. I am reminded of Kenny Rogers' track, *The Gambler:* "... You have got to know when to hold on, know when to fold 'em, know when to walk away and know when to run..." What it says is that when you are in a compromising situation and faced with your enemies in life, try to assess the situation, stay focused, strategise and act. In this way you will be able to beat them. I, therefore, decided to hold on, even when the situation became ugly. I never walked away, and running was not an option.

In summary I must mention that I feel compelled to say this. Stealing from Foeta Krige's article that documented the Venter story: I am angry at my colleagues who could not look at me in the eye. I am angry at those colleagues who asked me not to make a fuss over corruption. Colleagues who gave me fifteen minutes to leave the premises of the place I loved so dearly: Labour officials AO and MJM, who threw me out like a common criminal. Angry at the informants in the office who fed information to the handlers who passed it on to the intimidators. The spokesperson who used the mighty platform of the newspapers to belittle me and colleagues who made the death threats against me. The Human Resource Directorate that ignored my plight.

I concur with Suna when she said on her Facebook, days before she died: "Some people were for it and said it out loud and clear; some people were against it and made it clearly known; and some people said nothing at all. It is this group I struggle hardest to forgive."

I am also angry at those people: the colleagues who were afraid, who whispered in the lifts, in the smoking rooms and the noisy corners about all the on-going injustices, all while paralysed by fear of my tormentors People who thought I was doing it all for attention; the gossipmongers who spread stories and rumours without facts. I am angry at each and every Premier's Office employee who was part of the silent coup by Reverend LWM. I am angry at every scared Human Resource official who turned a blind eye when looking at documents of illegal and non-procedural appointments and dismissals. I am angry at every administrator working in the legal, internal audit and financial units for not taking responsibility for what was happening at the Premier's Office.

I am angry at people who knew the financial status of the Premier's Office and helped to concoct financial statements and observed wordlessly how the Director General mismanaged and lied to the people he appointed on numerous occasions... I am angry at Premier SM and his MECs who used their power to protect the DG and also angry at the Premier for using his senior administrators such as SB to harass, intimidate and humiliate me, and for SB and his friend investigator and presiding officer to become part and parcel of the web of those who lied about me in senior management and HOD meetings, to defend the man who is responsible for the state that the office was in. All of them had only one objective: to protect their luxurious job so as to continue buying a new Mercedes-Benz every two years and keep their exorbitant packages.

The majority of officials who used to stigmatise and torment me in the worst possible way so as to break me, in the hope that I would succumb under the weight of trauma and leave, were virtual illiterates who occupied positions they did not deserve. For them, the idea of government – which is really supposed to transform and uplift citizens – is that it is a good place to loot. Some of them enjoyed uttering sexist comments about me, saying that if I had slept with powerful men in government to get a high job position, I was going to keep quiet and not try to expose corruption. They were so wrong. In the first place, I was not going to sleep with a man for any position. I am highly educated, and licking the arses of those uneducated and unscrupulous bosses would not have been an option. I would rather "starve in dignity rather than eat in shame".

In the same breath, I was touched by my colleagues who apologised to me. That alone made my ordeal worthwhile. The first person to apologise was Maureen Gugushe. She called me before she retired, when I was already with Gauteng Liquor Board (GLB). She wanted to meet over coffee and then she apologised. I was very impressed, and fully understand why she could only do that when she was about to leave government. This is a woman I knew and respected. She commanded respect, showed integrity and always displayed the level of professionalism that one would not find so often in government environment.

The other person to apologise to me was MG. Matilda and I met again when she joined GLA many years after I'd left Premier's Office. The first day we met, she did not hesitate, and never waited until it was just the two of us. She made a moving apology in the presence of all those who were sitting around the boardroom table. I was touched, knowing the type of person she was. When she said, "I've changed," I believed her, and we got on very well together. As the saying goes, a wise person always somersaults. She used to command a lot of authority as a PA to two Gauteng premiers, TS and MS.

I remember the first EXCO meeting that MS chaired, as it was my responsibility to compile the Premier's notes. The notes were a summary of the agenda of that particular meeting. I was supposed to take him through it so as to keep him abreast of what he was to expect from the agenda. With my notes in hand, I went to their offices fifteen minutes before the meeting. I requested that I see the premier so that I could take him through the notes, but MG rudely told me that I would not do that anymore and I should leave the notes with her; she would do the honours. I was surprised that she did not even ask me to explain what the notes were all about – she was less than interested – but I left.

The meeting was about to start in five minutes, so I went to the boardroom and DG was already sitting there with some of the MECs. I informed him of what had happened, but he simply said leave her to do it. I had a sense that he was afraid of her, otherwise he could have called her to order.

The Premier came in. Before he could sit down and chair the meeting I heard DG asking him whether he had the notes the secretariat had compiled. He did not have them, and no one had briefed him. He sat down to chair the meeting. It would be difficult to do that without the briefing and he was bound to fumble through the agenda. I do not know what happened after that, but for the next meeting I compiled the notes again and took them to MG's office before the meeting. She asked me to take them to the premier's office and pointed me to where his office was. I went and briefed him.

One time, while walking along Fox Street in town, Johannesburg CBD, I met MJM. He greeted me and stood in front of me at the corner of Fox and Simmonds Streets and came closer. He called me a short lady and said, "I am very sorry for all the pains I caused you, knowing the fact that you were right". He said he was only doing his job. I told him that it was water under the bridge and that I understood because even murderers kill people in the name of doing their job. He shook my hand and I said apology accepted.

Though the latter two only apologised to me when we happened to bump into each other, the thought mattered to me. I appreciated it as I felt vindicated further.

There were many whom I met in the streets from the Premier's Office who were still angry with me. Some did not even want to greet me. Bishop Desmond Tutu once said that the most difficult word for people to say is sorry: that is, to apologise.

In this, I would like to also dedicate this book to all the whistleblowers who risked their lives for the love of their country, especially those who lost their lives. They paid a big price. I have found it necessary to attach their faces and names to crime statistics we often read and hear about. When one looks at how violently they died, one is reminded of the violent society we live in. South Africa is very violent. In doing this, I urge all citizens who love this country to never forget them and to continue honouring them. The sacrifices they made to try and rescue South Africa from decaying is their legacy. Whistleblowing is their legacy.

In this I am trying to remind South Africans that in a country as corrupt as ours, this is how far an institution riddled with corrupt individuals will go. They go after whistleblowers in order to cover up. Their murders set back the cries for the strengthening of whistleblower protection.

Also, it shows how again and again they have been left in peril. They are not only killed, but harassed and victimised. Indeed, their deaths are an example of how lack of protection jeopardises the safety of whistleblowers.

This is an attempt to raise awareness that whistleblowers are important fighters of corruption. Above all, they promote transparency as well as clean governance in public and private institutions. Thus, they do not deserve to be killed but to be praised and protected.

January Che Masilela 26 August 2008

Moss Phakoe March 2009

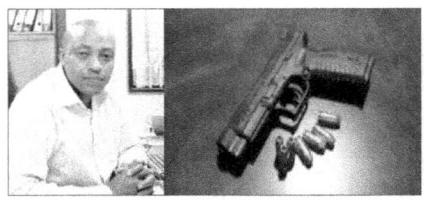
Sammy Mphatlanyane
08 January 2010

Jimmy Mohlala 28 February 2010

James Nkambule 08 October 2010

Andile Matshaya 2012 strangled

Moses Tshake May 2013

Xola Banisi 18 September 2014

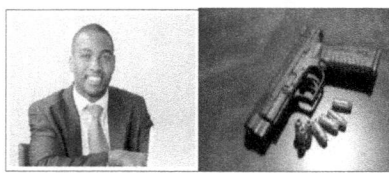
Lawrence Moepi 18 October 2013

Zweli Duma 17 August 2016

Thibello Ignatius Nteso 06 February 2017

Suna Venter 29 June 2017, " broken heart"

Sindiso Magaqa 13 September 2017

Ronald Mani and Timpson Musetsho January and Ralph Kanyane and Valtyn Kekana 22 July 2019

Seipati Lechoano 19 December 2018 "cause of her death not conclusive"; found "stuffed in the boot of her car".

Phillip Madoda Makhanyela 04 August 2020

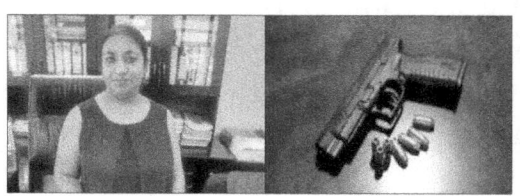

Babita Deokaran 23 August 2021

Chapter Twelve

CONCLUSION: THE PERSON I BECAME

Before concluding this book, I would like to reflect on the contribution that the NGOs I worked for made under trying circumstance: that is, under the Nationalist government's repressive system. This is in comparison with the democratic government ushered in in 1994, with its main objective being to change people's lives for the better. Ironically, it has done the opposite. A corruption resource-eating amoeba became the order of the day. Black people are worse off as poverty and destitution are worsened by the lack of service delivery. Thus, I am saying that it is high time that black people should wake up from their slumber, dreaming of a "better life for all", when it is crystal clear that after thirty years of democracy a better life is only for the few.

For us blacks to allow ourselves to plunge further into poverty should not be an option. As Ngungi wa Thiongo and Ngugi wa Mirii say in the book *I will marry when I want* (1982): "Poverty has no permanent roots. Poverty is a sword for sharpening the diggings sticks..."

This reminds of Tshepo Thobakgale Khumbane's philosophy: "Heal people's minds and work with the resources they have available. Once they have conquered hunger and redeveloped self-respect, respect for others and their environment, they can go on to greater things." When this government awarded her the Order of the Baobab, why was it so difficult to put her philosophy into practice and support people like her financially and otherwise? Are our sticks not sharp enough to dig ourselves out from this poverty hole? That is, on our own, for ourselves. We did that before and got rid of apartheid. We could also get rid of these self-serving politicians. To still hope that the ANC government will take us to greener pastures is self-defeating. Political freedom is nothing without economic freedom, as well as equality.

This government would never come to the rescue of poor black people because their focus is on how to loot. They could have learnt from the poor white poverty alleviation programme implemented in South Africa, rather than doing away with everything that was apartheid without an alternative. The apartheid government copied from other countries on how to address the poor white phenomenon, so there is no need for the ANC government to think that copying from the past government would be stooping too low because of the way they treated blacks. A wise person would also get inspiration from the innovations of the past.

If the ANC think that only they possess all the wisdom and they know how to address the dire situation poor black people are in, they must be cautioned that even a wise person can be taught wisdom. They will not fool people forever with their empty promises, as promises do not mean delivery. There is a saying that: "Clouds may be in the sky, but it does not mean it will rain".

The least they could have done was to rope in individuals who had developmental experience from non-governmental organisations. Instead, they are threatened by them. Tshepo Khumbane was spot on when she said: "Mobilisation for development is not a threat to politicians, it is mobilisation for development, by implication, a better life for all". She further commented that it is her belief that the lack of government support for the work she is doing is twofold: the government of the day is concerned with a "market-based model" of agriculture, that is an attempt to turn rural people into small commercial farmers. People do not have the resources to do this effectively and it makes them ashamed of what they have achieved in the past: culture-based food security. Once the people are food secure the commercial farmers will emerge.

Goldin and Gordon (2010) said that Khumbane in her memoir emphasised the fact that: "The practices of mono-cropping, explicit in this model, do not provide people with a diverse supply of food which they need to ensure a nutritious diet. At the local level, many of the men in positions of local and traditional authority are fearful of the mobilisation element as her philosophy includes the removal of gender inequality and the empowerment of both women and men. But government at all levels is needed to support this if it is to be achieved. Direct financing is not required but an enabling environment must be..."

This explains why all government-funded agricultural projects cannot be sustained. But one must be mindful of the fact that ANC politicians are only interested in squandering money meant to improve the lives of the poor, and for publicity stunts they like short cuts. A classic example is the Estina Farm project in the Free State Province.

Another unsung hero I brushed shoulders with on the journey of changing people's lives for the better is Cynthia Hugo. When Hugo visited Soweto schools and found out that not one of the schools had a functioning library, she single-handedly raised funds to provide core reference libraries in each of the high schools. It was because of concern over lack of reading and library facilities in black communities that, with Cynthia Hugo's dedication and commitment, Read Educate and Develop was born. Over years, the programme expanded throughout the country and trickled down to primary schools.

But, under the democratic government all those facilities have been destroyed. For example, visit the township schools and see if you will find the libraries that READ established. Children are unable to read, why? Go to all the rural areas and see if you will find the development projects EDA's Tshepho Khumbane initiated. Why are people there dying of hunger? Meanwhile, the idea was to cap the cycle of poverty by teaching communities to work the land and produce food (food security) for themselves.

Tshepo Khumbane is right to say that: "The South African government has made numerous attempts to integrate women into the economy using different strategies. Many of these have been unsuccessful and others are unsustainable, requiring continued expenditure." She argues that the strategies are poorly focused. According to her, the various attempts do not consider the mental, social and natural resource damage that resulted from the years under apartheid.

Who could still ask whether women are ready to lead, when it is crystal clear that women have always been great leaders of note and high achievers? Take the sterling work done by scholarship programmes run by NGOs such as Educational Opportunities Council (EOC) and the South African Council of Churches (SACC) in assisting children from disadvantaged communities to acquire tertiary education. Both Eleanor Molefe and

Brigalia Bam respectively contributed to their success immensely. Look at the National Student Financial Aid (NSFA) run by government. It is just in shamble because of corruption. EOC and others like it thrived because they did not squander money. Funds were used for their intended purposes. Ironically, the motivation of these women I have mentioned was born from the necessity to oppose the Nationalist government's system by striving to transform people's lives: be it literacy, food security, education, health or social upliftment in general.

River Thames and London Eye or the Millennium Wheel

Nonetheless, in concluding this book, I would like to reiterate that public servants need not steal to live the life they envisage. I might sound like I am bragging or boasting, but I am not. I am rather expressing my satisfaction with my achievements and my ability to achieve despite adversities, making what seemed impossible possible. I am celebrating life; I just love life.

Singapore's Merlion Park and skyline

So, as a rural girl who like dust just kept on rising, I would like to demonstrate the fact that people do not need to steal, especially not from the poorest of the poor, to acquire the lifestyle they envisaged. I am grateful to my God that I earned my money cleanly. I let my God fight the battle for me. I stayed until my

Petronas twin towers in Kuala Lumpur

Desert Safari in Dubai

Dubai's man-made ocean

retirement. Despite what I went through, I remained resilient, and I came out victorious.

The first thing my husband and I did – being travel enthusiasts and to celebrate everything we'd achieved, especially my still having my life – was to travel. We decided to go on a tour of London. We went to Singapore, and the Malaysian highlights were our visit Kuala Lumpur and the Petronas twin towers.

We took a tour to Dubai. We had the experience of a lifetime on a Desert Safari tour: just a sea of sand and amazing mountains of dunes and a visit to Dubai's man-made ocean. The only downside with Dubai is the blistering heat.

These were not out first overseas tours. We have been to Mauritius. I enjoyed a Catamaran cruise to Saint Gabriel and to one of its exotic islands, Ile Aux serfs by speed boat. Both islands were not habitable then. We visited Thailand's Phuket Islands, such as Pipi, by boat – a true paradise – and took a tour to Big Buddha. Descending the staircases leading to the statue of the Buddha, I stood there, just casting my eyes below. I was blown away, I thought I was losing my mind seeing such beautiful views all

Above photo was taken at one of Pipi Island and Patong below

around. I even screamed with excitement. One could not believe that this country was not so long ago struck by one of the worst natural disasters in 2006, with the Boxing Day Tsunami. Pipi Island and Patong were hard hit, with Patong Island recording most of the fatalities. While there, one could witness some of the devastation, with some hotel buildings still in ruins. However, the rebuilding aftermath was impressive. The area where we stayed was not so hard hit, we were told, although there was massive construction of hotels that were damaged.

I was wondering if anything like that happened to my country, South Africa, would we manage to rebuild it with so much speed, amidst the rampant looting of taxpayers' money like there is no tomorrow? For 30 years very little has been done in terms of bettering the lives of black people. Instead, everything seems to be collapsing at an alarming rate and we seem to be heading towards being another African banana republic.

The Tsunami travelled as far as Mombasa, Kenya. While there, we saw many damaged hotel buildings built along the beaches, it was scary.

We also went on an MSC Cruise to Portuguese Island. What a feat of ingenious engineering: the ship is colossal. Inside, walking in the corridor, one gets a certain feeling knowing that outside is only water.

It looks like a shopping mall with all the facilities one ever needed: a gym, massive restaurant with a la carte menu or buffet, swimming pool and

Water villas and a picture of us taken at one of pools that stretches to the white sandy beach. From afar it looks like it is part of the crystal-clear ocean waters.

jacuzzi or spa, shops selling various items, a cinema and sight viewing on the deck. Bedrooms have everything, such as en-suite bathrooms with toilet and shower. While lying on the bed, one overlooks the ocean during the day.

Our latest travel overseas was to one of the Maldives Islands. This is one of about 1 200 Islands of which 200 are inhabited, grouped in clusters, or atolls. While there, we visited one of the residential islands called Mudhdoo by boat. The place is very hot but the neat streets are spick and span; littering is punishable. The Maldives Islands are heaven on earth.

Photos: taken in a Boat to Mudhoo and while at an Island beach.

Photos:. taken in a Board to sunset cruise.

Photo: Where we standing water receded from the shore and will be covered by water in the afternoon

We truly love touring islands; there is nothing like it.

In Africa, we visited Kenya's Mombasa. Here, we were fascinated by nature's wonders where every morning the water recedes from the ocean shores and comes back in the afternoon the same time, this process is called ebb current. We also enjoyed a cruise in the evening, where we had dinner on a boat in the middle of the ocean and live entertainment. It was the first time I saw a ferry transport service carrying people, goods and vehicles in one space across the ocean. I was told they are the means of transport to and from Tanzania.

Zimbabwe and Zambia's Victoria Falls are one of Africa's natural wonders. Here one tends to see God in Person: just breathtaking. What is more amazing is the rain that pours down on the same spot after intervals (one is drenched by spray at most of the vantage points). One is encouraged to carry an umbrella. From the Zimbabwe side we crossed the border. Of course, there they also check your passport before you can pass into Zambia. We wanted to see the falls from the Zambian side, and we lunched at the Livingston Hotel: magnificent. Zambezi River Sunset Cruise was our highlight. While on the cruise we were lucky to witness elephants crossing.

In Namibia, we drove across the Namib desert by car, cruising across a sea of sand as an adventure. We travelled from Windhoek to Hentjies Bay, a 430-kilometre, about a 5 hour

21 minute, drive. While there, we went to Swakopmund. Driving back in an easterly direction to Windhoek facing the sun, it was so hot that towards midday our skin was so burnt despite using sunburn cream that we suffered blistering sunburn on our arms. They were the only part of our bodies that were exposed to the sun. After a few days, the skin started peeling off. That was part of the adventure.

Photos taken at Swakopmund and Hentjies Bay

The latest trip in Africa was Zanzibar, a Tanzanian Island. There we toured Stone Town Spice farm and went swimming with dolphins.

Here at home, we have gone to Cape Town more than three times, as well as Hermanus; Durban twice, where we could not get enough of those beaches. Northwest has fascinating landscapes; Mpumalanga's Drie Rondavels and God's Window are places to see and Limpopo's Magoebaskloof is one of highlights and a tourist attraction. This is only the beginning as we retired. All that is needed is proper planning and saving money, not stealing. It is important for people not to live beyond their means.

However, the cherry on the top of my journey of life was to see my first granddaughter graduating with a degree. When I started writing the book, that is more than ten years ago, I was in my career wilderness, as explained in the body of the book. In the process of writing it, I decided to enrol for my PhD degree the following year, and I decided to shelve the book as my studies were taking most of my time. I only resumed with it in 2018, after I retired. Then Thakane was 10 years old. Hence I mentioned in my dedication that I wish them to be women of substance and great integrity. Little did I know that 11 years later I would be witnessing Thakane's first graduation.

My grandchildren when they were little

Photo taken at Thakane's graduation. Next to her is her sister Nepo, who is also doing her first-year degree in the same university.

Picture is my husband and me, proud grandparents, and that of her family; very blessed.

The same as Maya Angelou, I am therefore saying: "You Can Write Me Down in History with Hateful, Twisted Lies, You Can Tread Me In This Very Dirt, But Still, Like Dust I Will Rise".

Bibliography

Chandler, T. J.L and Nauright, J. (1996), Making Men: Rugby and Masculinity Identity.

Dijane, K. (2023), City Press Article

Goldin, J. and Gordon, T. (2010), The Journey of Mme Tshepo Khumbane, Republic of South Africa.

Igbelina-Igbokwe, N. (2013), Call to Champion Women 's Empowerment in Africa

Jakes T.D. (2001), Can you stand to be blessed – insights to help you survive the peaks and valleys, destiny image, Publishers, INC, US.

Kaminer, D. and Dixon, J. (1995). Th e Reproduction of Masculinity: A Discourse Analysis of Men's Drinking Talk. South Africa Journal Psychology.

Khumbane, T. (2004), Food security. Tradition knowledge and Permaculture. South African Rural Development Quarterly , Development Bank of South Africa, Volume 2, Midrand.

Ngugi,T. and Ngugi, M. (1980) I will marry when I want. Heinemann Educational Books Ltd, London.

Woolf, V. (1929), A Room of one's own/ Feminism, Women, Literature and Education, Hogarth Press First Edition, United Kingdom.

Wikipedia Online Encyclopaedia.

www.ingramcontent.com/pod-product-compliance
Lightning Source LLC
Chambersburg PA
CBHW060102170426
43198CB00010B/740